Rick

ROME
2006

Rick Steves & Gene Openshaw

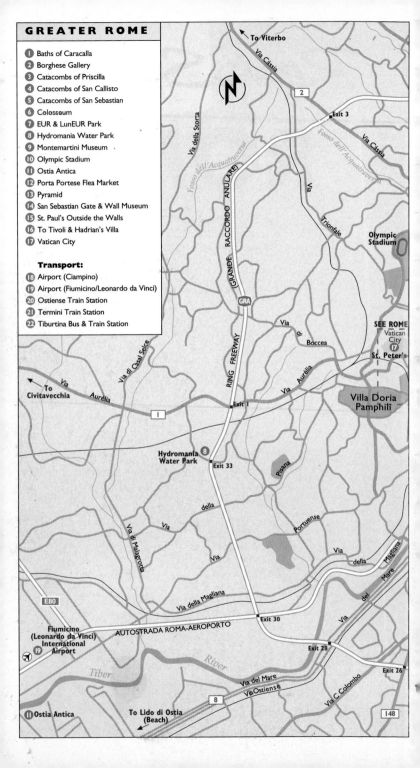

GREATER ROME

1 Baths of Caracalla
2 Borghese Gallery
3 Catacombs of Priscilla
4 Catacombs of San Callisto
5 Catacombs of San Sebastian
6 Colosseum
7 EUR & LunEUR Park
8 Hydromania Water Park
9 Montemartini Museum
10 Olympic Stadium
11 Ostia Antica
12 Porta Portese Flea Market
13 Pyramid
14 San Sebastian Gate & Wall Museum
15 St. Paul's Outside the Walls
16 To Tivoli & Hadrian's Villa
17 Vatican City

Transport:

18 Airport (Ciampino)
19 Airport (Fiumicino/Leonardo da Vinci)
20 Ostiense Train Station
21 Termini Train Station
22 Tiburtina Bus & Train Station

To Viterbo

Via Cassia

2

Exit 3

Via Cassia

Fosso dell'Acquatraversa

Via della Storta

Fosso dell'Acquatraversa

Via

Trionfale

Olympic Stadium

GRANDE RACCORDO ANULARE

GRA

Via di Boccea

SEE ROME
Vatican City 17
St. Peter's

RING FREEWAY

Via Aurelia

Villa Doria Pamphili

To Civitavecchia

Via Aurelia

Via di Casal Selce

Exit 1

1

Hydromania Water Park 8

Exit 33

della

Via

Via

Pisana

Portuense

Via

della

Mare

Magliana

E80

Via di Malagrotta

Via della Magliana

Exit 30

del

Via

Exit 28

Fiumicino (Leonardo da Vinci) International Airport 19

Exit 26

Tiber

River

Via del Mare
Via Ostiense

Via C. Colombo

148

11 Ostia Antica

To Lido di Ostia (Beach)

8

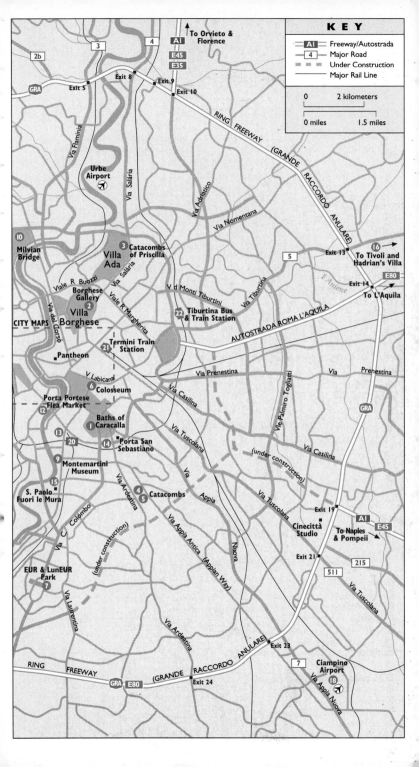

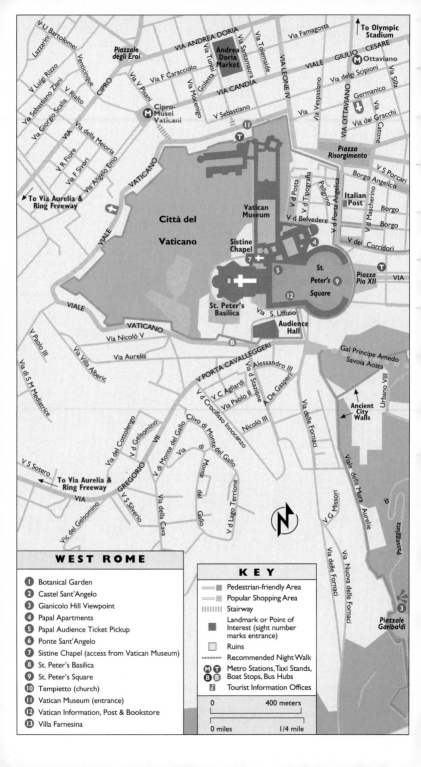

WEST ROME

1 Botanical Garden
2 Castel Sant'Angelo
3 Gianicolo Hill Viewpoint
4 Papal Apartments
5 Papal Audience Ticket Pickup
6 Ponte Sant'Angelo
7 Sistine Chapel (access from Vatican Museum)
8 St. Peter's Basilica
9 St. Peter's Square
10 Tempietto (church)
11 Vatican Museum (entrance)
12 Vatican Information, Post & Bookstore
13 Villa Farnesina

KEY

Pedestrian-friendly Area
Popular Shopping Area
Stairway
Landmark or Point of Interest (sight number marks entrance)
Ruins
Recommended Night Walk
M T B B — Metro Stations, Taxi Stands, Boat Stops, Bus Hubs
i — Tourist Information Offices

0 ————— 400 meters

0 miles ————— 1/4 mile

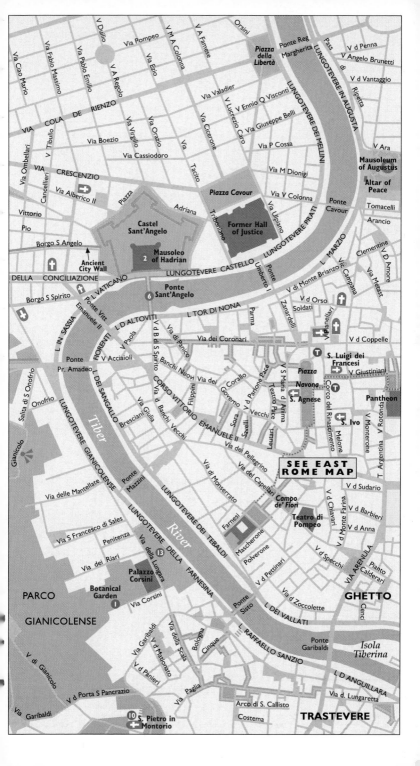

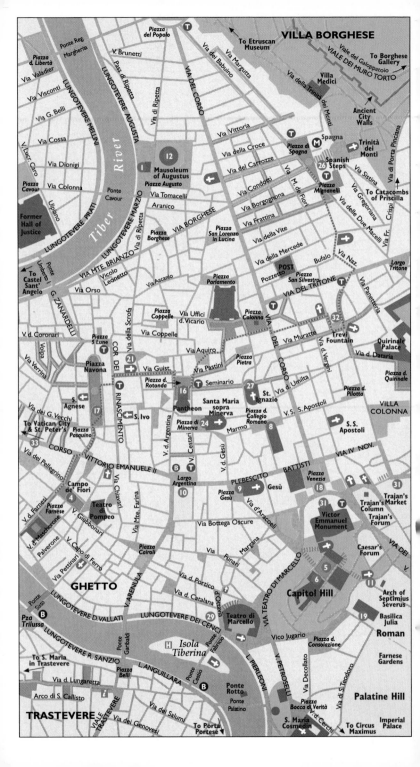

EAST ROME

① Altar of Peace
② Arch of Constantine
③ Baths of Diocletian
④ Campo de' Fiori
⑤ Capitol Hill
⑥ Capitol Hill Museum
⑦ Colosseum
⑧ Galleria Doria Pamphilj
⑨ Gesù Church
⑩ Largo Argentina
⑪ Mamertine Prison
⑫ Mausoleum of Augustus
⑬ National Museum of Rome
⑭ Nero's Golden House
⑮ Palatine Hill
⑯ Pantheon
⑰ Piazza Navona
⑱ Piazza Venezia
⑲ Roman Forum entry points
⑳ San Clemente Church
㉑ San Luigi dei Francesi Church
㉒ Santa Maria della Vittoria Church
㉓ Santa Maria Maggiore Church
㉔ Santa Maria sopra Minerva Church
㉕ Santa Susanna Church
㉖ Spanish Steps (Piazza di Spagna)
㉗ St. Ignazio Church
㉘ St. Peter-in-Chains Church
㉙ Synagogue
㉚ Termini Train Station
㉛ Trajan's Column, Forum, and Market
㉜ Trevi Fountain
㉝ To Vatican City & St. Peter's

VIA VENETO
To U.S. Embassy
VIA Flavia
Cappuccin Crypt
Via di S. Basilio
Via S. Nicola da Tolentino
㉒ Santa Maria della Vittoria
Cernaia
VIA Montebello
VIA Gaeta
VIA Goito
Barberini
VIA BARBERINI
Santa Susanna ㉕
V. ORLANDO
V. Parigi
Piazza Indipendenza
VIA VOLTURNO
Piazza Barberini Ⓜ
Palazzo Barberini
VIA XX SETTEMBRE
V. Torino
Ⓜ Repubblica
Baths of Diocletian ③
V. Einaudi
VIA MARSALA
Via Rasella
V. d. Giardini
VIA DELLE QUATTRO FONTANE
Ministry of Defense
Piazza d. Repubblica
V. d. Terme
Piazza d. Cinquecento
GIARDINI DEL QUIRINALE
San Carlo
San Andrea
Via Modena
Via Firenze
National Museum ⑬
Ⓜ Termini
Ⓑ Ⓣ ㉚ ⓘ Termini Train Station
VIA DEL QUIRINALE
Via Piacenza
Via Napoli
VIA NAZIONALE
VIA GIOVANNI GIOLITTI
Via d. Consulta
Via Genova
VIA D. VIMINALE
VIA A. PRETIS
D'Azeglio
Principe Amedeo
CAVOUR
Via G. Amendola
Cattaneo
POST Ⓣ ⓘ
Milano Palermo
Via
Piazza M. Fanti
V. XXIV MAGGIO
Via Mazzarino
Via d. Serpenti
Via
VIA C. BALBO
Urbana
Piazza del Esquilina
Gioberti
Via Napoleone III
Piazza M. Fanti
Via d. Panisperna
V Cimarra
Santa Maria Maggiore ㉓
Piazza S. Maria Maggiore
VIA C. ALBERTO
Via
Boschetto
V. Quattro Cantoni
V. Olmata
Santa Prassede
VIA
Piazza Vittorio Emanuele II
VIA STATUTO
Forum of Augustus
Via Baccina
Via Madonna
Via
Ⓜ Cavour
VIA GIOV. LANZA
MERULANA
Leonina
Via Cavour
Leopardi
Vittorio Emanuele
FORI IMPERIALI
Vecchia
⑲
Via Sacra
VIA CAVOUR
Via d. Colosseo
Via delle Sette Sale
㉘ St. Peter-in-Chains
Roman Empire Maps
Basilica of Constantine
Via d. Annibaldi
Via Terme di Tito
PARCO OPPIO
Viale del Mte. Oppio
Forum
Colosseo Ⓣ Ⓜ
Arch of Titus
Via Sacra
Nero's Golden House ⑭
Entrance to Palatine ⑮
Arch of Constantine ②
⑲
Viale d. Domus Aurea
VIA LABICANA
VIA DI S. GREGORIO
V. CELIO VIBENNA
Colosseum ⑦
WC
Via di S. Giovanni in Laterano
V. CLAUDIA
V. Ceimontana
㉒ Piazza d. Colosseo
Via dei S.S. Quattro
San Clemente ⑳
To Circus Maximus, Appian Way & Baths of Caracalla
⑮
V. M. Aurelio
Via Capo d'Africa

KEY

Pedestrian-friendly Area
Popular Shopping Area
Stairway
Landmark or Point of Interest (sight number marks entrance)
Ruins
Recommended Night Walk (starts at ④ and ends at ㉖)
Ⓜ Ⓣ Ⓑ Metro Stations, Taxi Stands, Boat Stops, Bus Hubs
ⓘ Tourist Information Offices

0 ——— 400 meters
0 miles ——— 1/4 mile

Rick Steves'

ROME

2006

AVALON
TRAVEL

CONTENTS

Rome

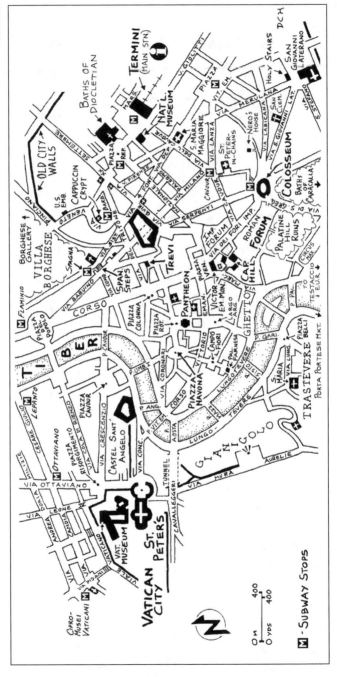

M - Subway Stops

INTRODUCTION

Rome is magnificent and brutal at the same time. Your ears will ring. If you're careless, you'll be run down or pickpocketed. You'll be frustrated by the kind of chaos that only an Italian can understand. You may even come to believe Mussolini was a necessary evil.

But Rome is required, and if your hotel provides a comfortable refuge; if you pace yourself; if you accept and even partake in the siesta plan; if you're well-organized for sightseeing; and if you protect yourself and your valuables with extra caution and discretion, then you'll do fine.

For us, Rome is in a three-way tie with Paris and London as Europe's greatest city. Two thousand years ago, the word "Rome" meant civilization itself. Everything was either civilized (part of the Roman Empire, Latin- or Greek-speaking) or barbarian. Today, Rome is Italy's political capital, the capital of Catholicism, and the center of the ancient world, littered with evocative remains. As you peel through its fascinating and jumbled layers, you'll find Rome's buildings, cats, laundry, traffic, and 2.6 million people endlessly entertaining. And then, of course, there are its magnificent sights.

Tour St. Peter's, the greatest church on earth, and scale Michelangelo's 328-foot-tall dome, the world's largest. Learn something about eternity by touring the huge Vatican Museum. You'll find the story of creation—bright as the day it was painted—in the restored Sistine Chapel. Do the "Caesar Shuffle" through ancient Rome's Forum and Colosseum. Savor Europe's most sumptuous building, the Borghese Gallery, and take an early evening "Dolce Vita Stroll" down the Via del Corso with Rome's beautiful people. Enjoy an after-dark walk from Campo de' Fiori to the Spanish Steps, lacing together Rome's Baroque and bubbly nightspots.

This Information Is Accurate and Up-to-Date

This book is updated every year. Most publishers of guidebooks can afford an update only every two or three years (and even then, it's often by e-mail or fax). Since this book is selective, we can update it in person each summer. The telephone numbers and hours of sights listed in this book are accurate as of mid-2005—but once you pin Rome down, it wiggles. Still, if you're traveling with the current edition of this book, we guarantee you're using the most up-to-date information available in print. For any updates, see www.ricksteves.com/update. Also at our Web site, you'll find a valuable list of reports and experiences—good and bad—from fellow travelers who've used this book (see www.ricksteves.com/feedback).

Use this year's edition. People who try to save a few bucks by traveling with an old book are not smart. They learn the seriousness of their mistake...in Europe. Your trip costs about $10 per waking hour. Your time is valuable. This guidebook saves lots of time.

About This Book

Rick Steves' Rome 2006 is a personal tour guide in your pocket. Better yet, it's actually two tour guides in your pocket: The co-author of this book is Gene Openshaw. Since our first "Europe through the gutter" trip together as high-school buddies almost 30 years ago, Gene and I have been exploring the wonders of the Old World. An inquisitive historian and lover of European culture, Gene wrote most of this book's self-guided museum tours and neighborhood walks. Together, Gene and I will keep this book up-to-date and accurate (though for simplicity, from this point "we" will shed our respective egos and become "I").

The book is organized in this way:

Orientation includes tourist information and public transportation. The "Planning Your Time" section offers a suggested schedule with thoughts on how to best use your limited time.

Sights provides a succinct overview of Rome's most important sights, arranged by neighborhood, with ratings: ▲▲▲—Don't miss; ▲▲—Try hard to see; ▲—Worthwhile if you can make it; No rating—Worth knowing about.

The **Self-Guided Walks** take you through Rome at night, connecting the great monuments and atmospheric squares; land you in Trastevere, the heart of the crusty, colorful neighborhood across the river; and give meaning to the Jewish Ghetto, the city's medieval Jewish quarter.

The **Self-Guided Tours** lead you through ancient Rome, with tours of the Colosseum, Roman Forum, Palatine Hill, Trajan's Column, Pantheon, and Baths of Diocletian. You'll also tour the pilgrimage churches, including the grandest of all—St. Peter's.

And you'll see the great museums: the Vatican Museum, the National Museum of Rome, the Capitol Hill Museum, and the exciting Borghese Gallery.

Sleeping is a guide to my favorite good-value hotels, mainly in several convenient (and for Rome, relatively quiet) neighborhoods near the sights.

Eating suggests restaurants ranging from inexpensive eateries to splurges, with an emphasis on good quality.

Rome with Children, **Shopping**, and **Nightlife** offer my best suggestions on those topics.

Transportation Connections covers connections by train and by plane (with information on Rome's airports), laying the groundwork for your smooth arrival and departure.

Day Trips cover nearby sights: Ostia Antica (includes self-guided tour), Tivoli, Naples, and Pompeii.

Roman History takes you on a whirlwind tour through the ages, covering three millennia from ancient Rome to the city today.

The **appendix** is a traveler's tool kit, with telephone tips, useful Italian phone numbers, a climate chart, and a handy list of Italian survival phrases.

Throughout this book, when you see a ✪ in a listing, it means that the sight is covered in much more detail in one of my tours (a page number will tell you where to look to find more information).

Browse through this book and choose your favorite sights. Then have a great trip! Traveling like a temporary local, you'll get the absolute most out of every mile, minute, and euro.

PLANNING

Trip Costs

Six components make up your trip costs: airfare, surface transportation, room and board, sightseeing/entertainment, shopping/miscellany, and gelato.

Airfare: Don't try to sort through the mess. Find and use a good travel agent. A basic, round-trip United States-to-Rome (or even cheaper, Milan) flight should cost $700 to $1,000, depending on where you fly from and when. Always consider saving time and money in Europe by flying "open jaw" (flying into one city and out of another).

Surface Transportation: For a typical one-week visit, allow $60 to $100 for taxis (which can be shared by up to 4 people); if you opt for buses and the Metro, figure about $20 per person. The cost of round-trip transportation to day-trip destinations ranges from minimal ($6–10 for Tivoli, less than $3 for Ostia Antica) to affordable ($50 for second-class train tickets for a day trip to Naples and Pompeii). For a one-way trip between Rome's main airport and the city center, allow $12 per person by train or about $50 by taxi (can be shared).

Room and Board: You can easily manage in Rome on $100 a day per person for room and board. This allows $10 for lunch, $5 for snacks, $20 for dinner, and $65 for lodging (based on 2 people splitting the cost of a $130 no-frills double room that includes breakfast). If you've got more money, I've listed great ways to spend it. Students and tightwads can enjoy Rome for as little as $50 a day ($25 for a bed, $25 for meals and snacks).

Sightseeing and Entertainment: Figure about $6–12 per major sight (Colosseum, museums), $2 for smaller ones (church treasuries), and $30 for splurge experiences (like concerts). An overall average of $15 per day works for most. Don't skimp here. After all, this category directly powers most of the experiences that all the other expenses are designed to make possible.

Shopping and Miscellany: Figure $2 per postcard, coffee, soft drink, and gelato. Shopping can vary in cost from nearly nothing to a small fortune. Good budget travelers find that this category has little to do with assembling a trip full of lifelong and wonderful memories.

When to Go

Rome's best travel months (also busiest and most expensive) are May, June, September, and October. The most grueling thing about travel in Rome is the summer heat in July and August. Between November and April, you can usually expect pleasant weather and generally none of the sweat and stress of the tourist season. Rome is fine in winter—cold and crisp, with peaceful sights.

In Rome, temperatures hit the high 80s and 90s in summer and drop to the 40s and 50s in winter. Spring and fall can be chilly, and many hotels do not turn on their heat. Air-conditioning, when available, usually only operates from June through September. Most midrange hotels come with air-conditioning—a worthwhile splurge in the summer. (See the climate chart in the appendix.)

Travel Smart

Many people visit Rome and think it's a chaotic mess. They feel any attempt at efficient travel is futile. This is dead wrong—and expensive. Rome, which seems as orderly as spilled spaghetti, actually functions well. Only those who understand this and travel smart can enjoy Rome on a budget.

Buy a phone card and use it for restaurant reservations and double-checking hours of sights. (I've included phone numbers for this purpose.) Enjoy the friendliness of the local people. Ask questions. Most locals are eager to point you in their idea of the right direction. Pack along a pocket-size notebook to organize your thoughts. Those who expect to travel smart, do.

Sundays have the same pros and cons as they do for travelers in the United States: Sightseeing attractions are generally open, while shops and banks are closed. City traffic is light. Rowdy evenings are rare on Sundays. Saturdays are virtually weekdays, with earlier closing hours.

Reserve your hotel room well in advance if you'll be in Rome over a holiday. Hotels get booked up on Easter weekend (in 2006, that's Friday, April 14 through Monday, April 17), April 25 (Liberation Day), May 1 (Labor Day), June 29 (Saints Peter and Paul), November 1 (All Saints' Day), and on Fridays and Saturdays year-round. Religious holidays and train strikes can catch you by surprise anywhere in Italy.

Really, this book can save you lots of time and money. But to have an "A" trip, you need to be an "A" student. Read it all before your trip; note the days when museums are closed and whether reservations are mandatory. For instance, to see the Borghese Gallery, you must reserve ahead. If you go to the Vatican Museum on a Sunday, you'll run smack into closed doors, or—if it's the last Sunday of the month—huge crowds. You can wait an hour to get into the Colosseum, or buy your ticket at a nearby kiosk at Palatine Hill and walk right in. Day-tripping to Ostia Antica on Monday is bad news. A smart trip is a puzzle—a fun, doable, and worthwhile challenge.

RESOURCES

Tourist Offices in the United States

Rome has a number of tourist information offices (abbreviated **TI** in this book); for a list, see page 23.

Before your trip, contact the nearest Italian TI in the United States, and briefly describe your trip and request information. You'll get the general packet and, if you ask for specifics (city map, calendar of festivals, etc.), an impressive amount of help. If you have a specific problem, they're a good source of sympathy.

Contact the office nearest you…

In New York: 630 Fifth Ave. #1565, New York, NY 10111, brochure hotline tel. 212/245-4822, tel. 212/245-5618, fax 212/586-9249, enitny@italiantourism.com.

In Illinois: 500 N. Michigan Ave. #2240, Chicago, IL 60611, tel. 312/644-0996, fax 312/644-3019, enitch@italiantourism.com.

In California: 12400 Wilshire Blvd. #550, Los Angeles, CA 90025, brochure hotline tel. 310/820-0098, tel. 310/820-4498, fax 310/820-6357, enitla@italiantourism.com.

Web Sites on Rome: www.romaturismo.com (music, exhibitions, and events), www.whatsoninrome.com (events and news),

Rome vs. Milan: A Classic Squabble

In Italy, the North and South bicker about each other, hurling barbs, quips, and generalizations. All the classic North/South traits can be applied to Rome (the government capital) and Milan (the business capital). Although the differences have become less pronounced lately, the sniping continues.

The Milanese say the Romans are lazy. Roman government jobs come with short hours—cut even shorter by too many coffee breaks, three-hour lunches, chats with colleagues, and phone calls to friends and relatives. Milanese contend that *Roma ladrona* (Rome the big thief) is a parasite that lives off the taxes of people up North. Until recently, there was a strong Milan-based movement seriously promoting secession from the South.

Romans, meanwhile, dismiss the Milanese as uptight workaholics with nothing else to live for—gray like their foggy city. Romans do admit that in Milan, job opportunities are better and based on merit. And the Milanese grudgingly concede the Romans have a gift for enjoying life.

While Rome is more of a family city, Milan is the place for high-powered singles on the career fast track. Milanese yuppies mix with each other...not the city's long-time residents. Milan is seen as wary of foreigners and inward-looking, and Rome as fun-loving, tolerant, and friendly. In Milan, bureaucracy (like social services) works logically and efficiently, while in Rome, accomplishing even small chores can be exasperating. In Rome, everything—from finding a babysitter to buying a car—is done through friends. In Milan, while people are not as willing to discuss their personal matters, they are generous and active in charity work.

Milanese find Romans vulgar. The Roman dialect is considered one of the coarsest in the country. Much as they try, Milanese just can't say, "Damn your dead relatives" quite as effectively as the Romans. Still, Milanese enjoy Roman comedians and love to imitate the accent.

The Milanese feel that Rome is dirty and Roman driving nerve-wracking. But despite the craziness, Rome maintains a genuine village feel. People share family news with their neighborhood grocer. Milan lacks people-friendly piazzas, and entertainment comes at a high price. But in Rome, *la dolce vita* is as close as the nearest square, and a full moon is enjoyed by all.

www.wantedinrome.com (job openings and real estate, but also festivals and exhibitions), and www.vatican.va (the pope's Web site).

Web Sites on Italy: www.italiantourism.com (Italian Tourist Board in the United States), www.museionline.it (museums in Italy), and www.trenitalia.com (train info and schedules).

Rick Steves' Guidebooks, Public Television Show, and Radio Show

Rick Steves' Europe Through the Back Door 2006 gives you budget-travel skills, such as minimizing jet lag, packing light, planning your itinerary, traveling by car or train, finding rooms, changing money, avoiding rip-offs, buying a mobile phone, hurdling the language barrier, staying healthy, taking great photographs, using a bidet, and much more. The book also includes chapters on 38 of my favorite "Back Doors."

Country Guides: These annually-updated books offer you the latest on the top sights and destinations, with tips on how to make your trip efficient and fun. Here are the titles:

Rick Steves' Best of Europe
Rick Steves' Best of Eastern Europe
Rick Steves' England (new in 2006)
Rick Steves' France
Rick Steves' Germany & Austria

Rick Steves' Great Britain
Rick Steves' Ireland
Rick Steves' Italy
Rick Steves' Portugal
Rick Steves' Scandinavia
Rick Steves' Spain
Rick Steves' Switzerland

City and Regional Guides: Updated every year, these focus on Europe's most compelling destinations. Along with specifics on sights, restaurants, hotels, and nightlife, you'll get self-guided, illustrated tours of the outstanding museums and most characteristic neighborhoods.

Rick Steves' Amsterdam, Bruges & Brussels
Rick Steves' Florence & Tuscany
Rick Steves' London
Rick Steves' Paris

Rick Steves' Prague & the Czech Republic
Rick Steves' Provence & the French Riviera
Rick Steves' Rome
Rick Steves' Venice

Rick Steves' Phrase Books: In Italy, a phrase book is as fun as it is necessary. This practical and budget-oriented series covers Italian, French, German, Portuguese, Spanish, and French/Italian/German. You'll be able to ask the gelato man for a free little taste, chat with your cabbie, and make hotel reservations over the phone.

And More Books: *Rick Steves' Europe 101: History and Art for the Traveler* (with Gene Openshaw) gives you the story of Europe's people, history, and art. It's heavy on Italy's ancient, Renaissance, and modern eras. Written for smart people who were sleeping in their history and art classes before they knew they were going to Europe, *101* helps Europe's sights come alive.

Rick Steves' Easy Access Europe, geared for travelers with limited mobility, covers London, Paris, Bruges, Amsterdam, and the Rhine River.

Rick Steves' Postcards from Europe, my autobiographical book, packs 25 years of travel anecdotes and insights into the ultimate 2,000-mile European adventure (including Rome).

My latest book, *Rick Steves' European Christmas,* covers the joys, traditions, and history of the holiday season in seven European countries.

Public Television Show: My series, *Rick Steves' Europe,* keeps churning out shows. Several of the 95 episodes feature sights covered in this book.

Radio Show: My new weekly radio show, which combines call-in questions (à la *Car Talk*) and interviews with travel experts, airs on public radio stations. For a schedule of upcoming topics, an archive of past programs, and details on how to call in, see www.ricksteves.com/radio.

Other Guidebooks

For most travelers, this book is all you need. But when you consider the improvements they'll make in your $3,000 vacation, $25 or $35 for extra maps and books is money well spent. The tall, green Michelin guide to Rome has solid, encyclopedic coverage of sights, customs, and culture, though very little on room and board (also sold in English in Italy). The well-researched Access and the colorful Eyewitness guides to Rome are popular with travelers. Eyewitness is fun for its great, easy-to-grasp graphics and photos, and it's just right for people who want only factoids. But the Eyewitness books are relatively skimpy on content and they weigh a ton. You can buy them in Rome (no more expensive than in the United States) or simply borrow them for a minute from other travelers at certain sights to make sure that you're aware of that place's highlights. *Let's Go Rome* is youth-oriented, with good coverage of hostels and nightlife. For a list of bookstores in Rome, see page 25.

If you'll be traveling elsewhere in Italy, consider the 2006 editions of *Rick Steves' Italy, Rick Steves' Florence & Tuscany,* and *Rick Steves' Venice.*

Recommended Books and Movies

To get the feel of Rome past and present, consider reading some of these books or seeing these films:

Non-Fiction: *When In Rome* (Robert Hutchinson), *That Fine Italian Hand* and *The Seasons of Rome* (both by Paul Hofmann), *As the Romans Do* (Alan Epstein), *Travelers' Tales: Italy* (Anne Calcagno), *Rome Antics* and *City: A Story of Roman Planning and Construction* (children's books, both by David Macaulay), *The Decline and Fall of the Roman Empire* (Edward Gibbon), *Saints & Sinners: A History of the Popes* (Eamon Duffy), *The Pope's Elephant* (Silvio Bedini), *A Literary Companion to Rome* (John Varriano), *City Secrets: Rome* (Robert Kahn), *City of the Soul: A Walk in Rome* (William Murray), and *Culture Shock!: Rome at Your Door* (Frances Gendlin). Gourmets like *The Marling Menu-Master for Italy.*

Fiction: *The First Man in Rome* (Colleen McCullough), *I, Claudius* (Robert Graves), *Roman Blood* (mystery set in Rome in 80 B.C., first in a series by Steven Saylor), *Silver Pigs* (mystery set in Rome in A.D. 70, first in a series by Lindsey Davis), *Cabal* (mystery set in modern Rome, third in a series by Michael Dibdin), *Open City: Seven Writers in Postwar Rome* (edited by William Weaver), and *Angels and Demons* (by *Da Vinci Code* author Dan Brown).

Flicks: *Gladiator; Spartacus; Ben-Hur; I, Claudius; Quo Vadis; The Agony and the Ecstasy; Open City; The Bicycle Thief; La Dolce Vita;* Fellini's *Roma; Roman Holiday; Three Coins in the Fountain; Arrivederci, Roma; The Roman Spring of Mrs. Stone; Caro Diario;* and *Only You.*

Maps

The maps in this book, designed and drawn by Dave Hoerlein, are concise and simple. Dave is well-traveled in Rome and Italy and has designed the maps to help you orient quickly and get to where you want to go painlessly. In Rome, your hotel or the tourist office have helpful free maps, but the €3 map sold at kiosks listing all the streets is much better. Before you buy any map, look at it to make sure that it has the level of detail you want.

PRACTICALITIES

Red Tape: You need a passport—but no visa or shots—to travel in Italy.

Time: In Rome—and in this book—you'll use the 24-hour clock. It's the same through 12:00 noon, then keep going: 13:00, 14:00, and so on. For anything over 12, subtract 12 and add "p.m." (14:00 is 2:00 p.m.) Italian time is generally six/nine hours ahead of the East/West Coast of the United States.

Business Hours: Traditionally, Italy uses the siesta plan. People usually work from about 8:00 to 13:00 and from 15:30 to 19:00, Monday through Saturday. Nowadays, however, many businesses have adopted the government's recommended 8:00 to 14:00 workday. In tourist areas, shops are open longer.

Shopping: Shoppers interested in pursuing VAT refunds (the tax refunded on large purchases made by non-EU residents) can refer to page 280.

Discounts: Discounts for sights are not listed in this book because they are generally limited to European residents and countries that offer reciprocal deals (the U.S. does not).

Watt's up? If you're bringing electrical gear, you'll need a two-prong adapter plug (sold cheap at travel stores in the United States) and a converter. Travel appliances often have convenient, built-in converters; look for a voltage switch marked 120V (U.S.) and 240V (Europe). If yours doesn't have a built-in converter, you'll have to buy an external one.

News: Americans keep in touch with the *International Herald Tribune* (published almost daily via satellite). Every Tuesday, the European editions of *Time* and *Newsweek* hit the stands with articles of particular interest to European travelers. Sports addicts can get their fix from *USA Today*. Good Web sites include www .europeantimes.com and http://news.bbc.co.uk.

MONEY

Banking

Bring plastic (ATM, credit, or debit cards) along with several hundred dollars in hard cash as an emergency backup. Traveler's checks are a waste of time and money.

To withdraw cash from a bank machine *(bancomat),* you'll need a PIN code (numbers only, no letters on European keypads) and your bank card. Before you go, verify with your bank that your

---

Exchange Rate

1 euro (€) = about $1.20

To convert prices in euros to dollars, add 20 percent: €20 = about $24, €45 = about $54. Just like the dollar, one euro is broken down into 100 cents. You'll find coins ranging from €0.01 to €2, and bills ranging from €5 to €500.

Look carefully at any €2 coin you get in change. Some unscrupulous merchants are giving out similar-looking, gold-rimmed old 500-lire coins (worth $0) instead of €2 coins (worth $2.40). You are now warned!

Damage Control for Lost or Stolen Cards

If you lose your credit, debit, or ATM card, you can stop people from using your card by reporting the loss immediately to the respective global customer-assistance centers. Call these 24-hour U.S. numbers collect: Visa (tel. 410/581-9994), MasterCard (tel. 636/722-7111), and American Express (tel. 336/393-1111).

Have, at a minimum, the following information ready: the name of the financial institution that issued you the card, along with the type of card (classic, platinum, or whatever). Ideally, plan ahead and pack photocopies of your cards—front and back—to expedite their replacement. Providing the following information will allow for a quicker cancellation of your missing card: full card number, whether you are the primary or secondary cardholder, the cardholder's name exactly as printed on the card, billing address, home phone number, circumstances of the loss or theft, and identification verification (your birthdate, your mother's maiden name, or your Social Security number—memorize this, don't carry a copy). If you are the secondary cardholder, you'll also need to provide the primary cardholder's identification verification details. You can generally receive a temporary card within two or three business days in Europe.

If you promptly report your card lost or stolen, you typically won't be responsible for any unauthorized transactions on your account, although many banks charge a liability fee of $50.

card will work and alert them that you'll be making withdrawals in Europe; otherwise, the bank may not approve transactions if it perceives unusual spending patterns. Also ask about fees, whether you'll be using cash machines (can be $5 per transaction) or getting cash advances with your credit card.

It's smart to bring two cards in case one gets demagnetized or eaten by a temperamental machine. If your card doesn't work, try again, and request a smaller amount; some cash machines won't let you take out more than about €150 (don't take it personally). Also be aware that some ATMs will tell you to take your cash within 30 seconds, and if you aren't fast enough, your cash may be sucked back into the machine...and you'll have a hassle trying to get it from the bank.

Visa and MasterCard are more commonly accepted than American Express. Just like at home, credit or debit cards work easily at larger hotels, restaurants, and shops, but smaller businesses prefer payment in local currency (in small bills—break large bills at a bank).

Regular banks have the best rates for changing cash and traveler's checks. For a large exchange, it pays to compare rates and fees. Banks—not exchange offices—have the best rates for cashing traveler's checks. Banking hours are generally 8:30 to 13:30 and 15:30 to 16:30 Monday through Friday, but they can vary wildly. Banks are slow; simple transactions can take 15 to 30 minutes. Post offices and train stations usually change money if you can't get to a bank.

You should use a money belt (a pouch with a strap that you buckle around your waist like a belt and wear under your clothes). Thieves target tourists. A money belt provides peace of mind, allowing you to carry lots of cash safely.

Don't be petty about withdrawing money. You don't need to waste time and money every few days tracking down a cash machine. Change a week's worth of money, get big bills, stuff them in your money belt, and travel!

Tipping

Tipping in Italy isn't as automatic and generous as it is in the United States, but for special service, tips are appreciated, if not expected. As in the United States, the proper amount depends on your resources, tipping philosophy, and the circumstances, but some general guidelines apply.

Restaurants: Check the menu to see if the service is included (*servizio incluso*—generally 15 percent); if not, a tip of 5 to 10 percent is typical (for details, see page 257), though Italians rarely tip.

Taxis: To tip the cabbie, round up. For a typical ride, round up to the next euro on the fare (to pay a €4.50 fare, give €5). If the cabbie hauls your bags and zips you to the airport to help you catch your flight, you might want to toss in a little more. But if you feel like you're being driven in circles or otherwise ripped off, skip the tip.

Special Services: It's thoughtful to tip a couple of euros to someone who shows you a special sight and who is paid in no other way (such as the man who shows you an Etruscan tomb in his backyard). Tour guides at public sites sometimes hold out their hands for tips after they give their spiel; if I've already paid for the tour, I don't tip extra, though some tourists do give a euro or two, particularly for a job well done. I don't tip at hotels, but if you do, give the porter a euro for carrying bags and leave a couple of euros in your room at the end of your stay for the maid if the room was kept clean. In general, if someone in the service industry does a super job for you, a tip of a couple of euros is appropriate...but not required.

When in doubt, ask. If you're not sure whether (or how much) to tip for a service, ask your hotelier or the tourist information office; they'll fill you in on how it's done on their turf.

Begin Your Trip at www.ricksteves.com

At ricksteves.com you'll find a wealth of **free information** on destinations covered in this book, including fresh European travel and tour news every month and helpful "Graffiti Wall" tips from thousands of fellow travelers.

While you're there, the **online Travel Store** is a great place to save money on travel bags and accessories specially designed by Rick Steves to help you travel smarter and lighter, plus a wide selection of guidebooks, planning maps, and *Rick Steves' Europe* DVDs.

Traveling through Europe by rail is a breeze, but choosing the right railpass for your trip—amidst hundreds of options—can drive you nutty. At ricksteves.com, you'll find **Rick Steves' Annual Guide to European Railpasses**—your best way to convert chaos into pure travel energy. Buy your railpass from Rick, and you'll get a bunch of free extras to boot.

Travel agents will tell you about mainstream tours of Europe, but they won't tell you about **Rick Steves' tours.** Rick Steves' Europe Through the Back Door travel company offers more than two dozen itineraries and 300-plus departures reaching the best destinations in this book...and beyond. You'll enjoy the services of a great guide, a fun bunch of travel partners (with group sizes in the mid-20s), and plenty of room to spread out in a big, comfy bus. You'll find tours to fit every vacation size, from weeklong city getaways to longer cross-country and cross-Continent adventures. For details, visit www.ricksteves.com or call 425/771-8303 ext 217.

TRANSPORTATION

Transportation concerns within Rome are limited to the Metro, buses, and taxis, all covered in the Orientation chapter. If you have a car, stow it. You don't want to drive in Rome. Transportation to day-trip destinations is covered in the Day Trips chapters. For specifics on transportation throughout Italy by train or car, see *Rick Steves' Italy 2006*. For advice on travel agencies in Rome, see page 25.

COMMUNICATING

Telephones

Smart travelers learn the phone system and use it daily to reserve or reconfirm rooms, get tourist information, or phone home.

If you have to spell out your name on the phone when making a reservation, you might have trouble with *a* (pronounced "ah" in Italian), *i* (pronounced "ee"), and *e* (pronounced "ay"). Say "*a,*

Ancona," "*e*, Empoli," and "*i*, Italia" to clear up that problem. If you plan to access your voice mail from Italy, be advised that you can't always dial extensions or secret codes once you connect (you're on vacation—relax).

Types of Phones

You'll encounter various kinds of phones in your European travels.

Telecom **pay phones** are everywhere, and take cards only (no coins). About a quarter of the phones are broken. The rest work reluctantly. Dial slowly and deliberately, as if the phone doesn't understand numbers very well. Often a recorded message in Italian will break in, brusquely informing you that the phone number does not exist *(non-esistente),* even if you're dialing your own home phone number. Dial again with an increasing show of confidence, in an attempt to convince the phone of your number's existence. If you fail, try a different phone. Repeat as needed.

Hotel room phones are fairly cheap for local calls, but pricey for international calls, unless you use an international phone card (see below).

American mobile phones work in Europe if they're GSM-enabled, tri-band (or quad-band), and on a calling plan that includes international calls. With a T-Mobile phone, you can roam using your home number, and pay $1–2 per minute for making or receiving calls.

Some travelers buy a **European mobile phone** in Europe. For about $125, you can get a phone that will work in most countries once you pick up the necessary chip (about $30) per country. You may also be able to buy a cheaper, "locked" phone that only works in the country where you purchased it (about $100, includes $20 worth of calls; can be difficult to find in Italy). If you're interested, stop by any European shop that sells mobile phones; you'll see prominent store window displays. You aren't required to (and shouldn't) buy a monthly contract—buy prepaid calling time instead (as you use it up, buy additional minutes at newsstands or mobile-phone shops). If you're on a budget, skip mobile phones and use international phone cards instead.

Paying for Calls

You can spend a fortune making phone calls in Europe...but why? Here's the skinny on different ways to pay, including the best deals.

Italian Phone Cards come in two types: official phone cards that you insert into a pay phone, and international phone cards that can be used from virtually any phone.

Insertable phone cards are used to make calls from pay phones. You can buy these Telecom cards (in denominations of €5, €10, etc.) at tobacco shops, post offices, and machines near phone booths (many phone booths indicate where the nearest phone-card sales outlet is located). Rip off the perforated corner to "activate" the card, then physically insert it into a slot in the pay phone. It displays how much money you have remaining on the card. Then just dial away to anywhere in the world. The price of the call is automatically deducted while you talk. These cards give you your best deal for calls within Italy, and are reasonable for international calls.

International phone cards are an even better deal for overseas calls (as cheap as a nickel per minute to the U.S.). Unlike the official phone cards, an international phone card is not inserted into the phone. Instead, you dial the toll-free number listed on the card, reaching an automated operator. When prompted, you dial in a scratch-to-reveal code number, also written on the card. Then dial your number. You can use the cards to make local and domestic long-distance calls as well. Since they're not insertable, you can use them from any phone—including the one in your hotel room (if your phone is set on pulse, switch it to tone). Generally you'll get more minutes out of a card if you use it from your hotel room, rather than from a pay phone. (For a €5 card, for example, you may get 180 minutes from your hotel room phone, compared to 40 minutes from a pay phone.) Buy cards at small newsstand kiosks and hole-in-the-wall long-distance phone shops. Because there are so many brand names, simply ask for an international phone card (*carta telefonica prepagata internazionale,* KAR-tah teh-leh-FOHN-ee-kah pray-pah-GAH-tah in-ter-naht-zee-oh-NAH-lay). Tell the vendor where you'll be making most calls (*per Stati Uniti*—to America), and he'll select the brand with the best deal. Buy a lower denomination in case the card is a dud. I've had good luck with the Europa card, offering 180 minutes from Italy to the United States for €5. If you have time left on your card when you leave the country (as you likely will), simply give it to another traveler—anyone can use it.

Dialing direct from your hotel room without using an international phone card is usually quite expensive for international calls, but it's convenient. I always ask first how much I'll be charged. Keep in mind that you have to pay for local and occasionally even toll-free calls.

Receiving calls in your hotel room is often the cheapest way to keep in touch with the folks back home—especially if your family has an inexpensive way to call you (either a good deal on their long-distance plan, or a prepaid calling card with good rates to Europe). Give them a list of your hotels' phone numbers before you go. As you travel, send your family an e-mail or make a quick payphone call to set up a time for them to call you, and then wait for the ring.

Soccer: The National Obsession

Winston Churchill said that Italians lose wars like soccer matches and soccer matches like wars. *Calcio* is the national obsession, regardless of age or social class. If you see an animated conversation, it's probably about soccer. Everyone's an expert, quick with opinions on a coach's lousy decision or a referee's unprofessional conduct. Fans routinely insult referees by yelling personal insults, such as *arbitro cornuto* (the referee is a cuckold—his wife sleeps around).

Rome has a special passion for soccer. It has two teams, Roma (representing the city) and Lazio (the region), and the rivalry is fanatic. When Romans are introduced, they ask each other, *"Laziale o romanista?"* The answer can actually compromise a relationship. Both Roma (jersey: yellow and red; symbol: she-wolf) and Lazio (jersey: light blue and white; symbol: imperial eagle) claim to be truly Roman. The Lazio team is older (founded in 1900), but Roma has more supporters. Lazio is supposed to be more upper class, Roma more popular, but the social division is blurred.

The most eagerly awaited sporting event of the year is the derby, when the two teams fight it out at the Olympic Stadium. All of Italy acknowledges that team spirit is most fervent in Rome. Fans prepare months in advance, and on the day of the match they fill the entire stadium with team colors, flags, banners, and smoke candles.

Witty slogans on banners work like dialogues. On one occasion, a Roma banner proclaimed, "Roma—only the sky is higher than you." The Lazio banner replied, "In fact, the sky is blue and white" (like its team colors). The exchange revealed that there had been a Lazio informer on the Roma side, traumatizing Roma fans for weeks. Many tourists go to these matches just for the folklore...to enjoy one of the most Roman of all experiences.

Metered phones are sometimes available in bigger post offices. You can talk all you want, then pay the bill when you leave—but be sure you know the rates before you have a lengthy conversation.

Coin-operated phones, while rare, still exist in some areas. If making a call, have a bunch of coins handy—they go fast.

U.S. calling cards (such as the ones offered by AT&T, MCI, or Sprint) are the worst option. You'll nearly always save a lot of money by paying for your call in any of the other ways I've described above.

How to Dial

Calling from the United States to Italy, or vice versa, is simple—once you break the code. The European calling chart on page 334 will walk you through it. Remember that European time is six/nine hours ahead of the East/West Coast of the United States.

Dialing within Italy: Italy has a direct-dial phone system (no area codes). To call anywhere within Italy, just dial the number. For example, the number of one of my recommended Rome hotels is 06-482-4696. To call it from the Rome train station, dial 06-482-4696. If you call it from Venice, it's the same: 06-482-4696. Italian mobile phone numbers no longer start with zero (these are dialed direct like fixed phone numbers).

Italian phone numbers vary in length; a hotel can have, say, an 8-digit phone number and a 9-digit fax number.

Italy's toll-free numbers start with 800 (like U.S. 800 numbers, though in Italy you don't need to dial a "1" first). In Italy, these 800 numbers—called *freephone* or *numero verde* (green number)—can be dialed free from any phone without using a phone card or coins. Note that you can't call Italy's toll-free numbers from America, nor can you count on reaching America's toll-free numbers from Italy.

Dialing International Calls: When calling internationally, dial the international access code (00 if you're calling from Europe, 011 from the United States or Canada), the country code of the country you're calling (39 for Italy; see appendix for list of other countries), and the local number. Note that in most European countries, you have to drop the zero at the beginning of the number—but in Italy, you dial it. So, to call the Rome hotel from the United States, dial 011 (the U.S. international access code), 39 (Italy's country code), then 06-482-4696. To call my office in Edmonds, Washington, from Italy, you dial 00 (Europe's international access code), 1 (the U.S. country code), 425 (Edmonds' area code), and 771-8303.

E-mail and Mail

E-mail: I've listed several cafés (see page 25), though your hotelier or TI can easily steer you to the nearest Internet access point.

When you see a cluster of orange public phones in a room off a busy street, you might see several computers in the batch. With these, you can use your Italian phone card to access the Internet. You won't be comfortable (no seat), and you'll get cut off if your phone card runs out of time, but this can be a handy, quick way to check your e-mail.

Mail: Mail service in Italy has improved over the last few years, but even so, mail nothing precious from Italy. If you must, use the mail service at the Vatican City (they have two post offices—one next to St. Peter's Basilica, the other within the Vatican Museum). If you need to receive mail while traveling, consider a few pre-reserved hotels along your route. Allow 14 days for U.S.-to-Italy mail delivery, but don't count on it. Federal Express makes pricey two-day deliveries. E-mailing and phoning is so easy that we've completely dispensed with mail stops.

TRAVELING AS A TEMPORARY LOCAL

We travel all the way to Italy to enjoy differences—to become temporary locals. You'll experience frustrations. Certain truths that we find "God-given" or "self-evident," such as cold beer, ice in drinks, bottomless cups of coffee, hot showers, and bigger being better, are suddenly not so true. One of the benefits of travel is the eye-opening realization that there are logical, civil, and even better alternatives. A willingness to go local ensures that you'll enjoy a full dose of Italian hospitality. To connect with a local, ask about soccer, the national obsession (see sidebar).

If there is a negative aspect to Italians' image of Americans (apart from our foreign policy), it's that we are big, loud, aggressive, impolite, rich, and a bit naive. Europeans don't respond well to Americans complaining about being too hot or too cold. To encourage conservation, the Italian government limits when air-conditioning or central heating can be used. Bring a sweater in winter, and in summer, be prepared to sweat a little...like everyone else. Also, Americans tend to be noisy in public places, such as restaurants and trains. Our raised voices can demolish Europe's reserved and elegant ambience. Talk softly.

While Italians, flabbergasted by our Yankee excesses, say in disbelief, *"Mi sono cadute le braccia!"* ("I throw my arms down!"), they nearly always afford us individual travelers all the warmth we deserve.

Judging from all the happy postcards we receive from travelers who have used this book, it's safe to assume you'll enjoy a great, affordable vacation—with the finesse of an independent, experienced traveler.

Thanks, and *buon viaggio!*

BACK DOOR TRAVEL PHILOSOPHY
From *Rick Steves' Europe Through the Back Door*

Travel is intensified living—maximum thrills per minute and one of the last great sources of legal adventure. Travel is freedom. It's recess, and we need it.

Experiencing the real Europe requires catching it by surprise, going casual..."Through the Back Door."

Affording travel is a matter of priorities. (Make do with the old car.) You can travel—simply, safely, and comfortably—anywhere in Europe for $100 a day plus transportation costs. In many ways, spending more money only builds a thicker wall between you and what you came to see. Europe is a cultural carnival and, time after time, you'll find that its best acts are free and the best seats are the cheap ones.

A tight budget forces you to travel close to the ground, meeting and communicating with the people, not relying on service with a purchased smile. Never sacrifice sleep, nutrition, safety, or cleanliness in the name of budget. Simply enjoy the local-style alternatives to expensive hotels and restaurants.

Extroverts have more fun. If your trip is low on magic moments, kick yourself and make things happen. If you don't enjoy a place, maybe you don't know enough about it. Seek the truth. Recognize tourist traps. Give a culture the benefit of your open mind. See things as different but not better or worse. Any culture has much to share.

Of course, travel, like the world, is a series of hills and valleys. Be fanatically positive and militantly optimistic. If something's not to your liking, change your liking. Travel is addicting. It can make you a happier American as well as a citizen of the world. Our Earth is home to six billion equally important people. It's humbling to travel and find that people don't envy Americans. They like us, but with all due respect, they wouldn't trade passports.

Globe-trotting destroys ethnocentricity. It helps you understand and appreciate different cultures. Regrettably, there are forces in our society that want you dumbed down for their convenience. Don't let it happen. Thoughtful travel engages you with the world—more important than ever these days. Travel changes people. It broadens perspectives and teaches new ways to measure quality of life. Many travelers toss aside their hometown blinders. Their prized souvenirs are the strands of different cultures they decide to knit into their own character. The world is a cultural yarn shop, and Back Door travelers are weaving the ultimate tapestry. Come on, join in!

ORIENTATION

Sprawling Rome actually feels manageable once you get to know it. The old core, with most of the tourist sights, sits in a diamond formed by the train station (in the east), the Vatican (west), the Borghese Gardens (north), and the Colosseum (south). The Tiber River runs through the diamond from north to south. It takes about an hour to walk from the train station to the Vatican.

Consider Rome in these layers:

The ancient city had a million people. The best of the classical sights stand in a line from the Colosseum to the Pantheon. (See map on page 37.)

Medieval Rome was little more than a hobo camp of 50,000—thieves, mean dogs, and the pope, whose legitimacy required a Roman address. A colorful tangle of lanes, the medieval city lies between the Pantheon and the river.

Window-shoppers' Rome twinkles with nightlife and ritzy shopping near Rome's main drag, Via del Corso—in the triangle formed by Piazza del Popolo, Piazza Venezia, and the Spanish Steps. (See "Dolce Vita Stroll" map, page 283.)

Vatican City, west of the Tiber, is a compact world of its own, with two great, huge sights: St. Peter's Basilica and the Vatican Museum. (See "Vatican City" map, page 53.)

Trastevere, the seedy, colorful, wrong-side-of-the-river neighborhood, is village Rome. This is the city at its crustiest—and perhaps most "Roman." (See Trastevere Walk, page 77.)

Baroque Rome is an overleaf that embellishes great squares throughout the town with fountains and church facades.

Since no one is allowed to build taller than St. Peter's dome, the city has no modern skyline. The Tiber River is basically ignored—after the last floods (1870), the banks were built up very high, and Rome turned its back on its naughty river.

Greater Rome

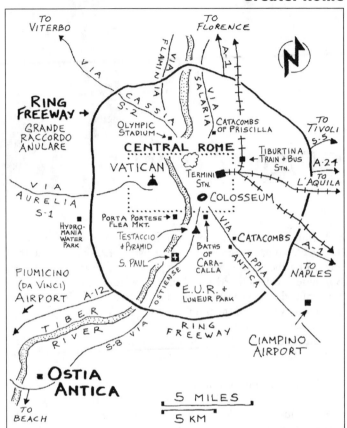

Planning Your Time

After considering Rome's major tourist sights, I've covered just my favorites. You won't be able to see all of these, so don't try—you'll keep coming back to Rome. After several dozen visits, I still have a healthy list of excuses to return.

Rome in a Day

Some people actually try to "do" Rome in a day. Crazy as that sounds, if all you have is a day, it's one of the most exciting days Europe has to offer. See the Vatican City (2 hours in the Vatican Museum and Sistine Chapel, 1 hour in St. Peter's), taxi over the river to the Pantheon (picnic on its steps), then hike over Capitol Hill, through the Forum, and to the Colosseum. Have dinner on Campo de' Fiori and dessert on Piazza Navona.

Rome in Two to Three Days
On the first day, do the "Caesar Shuffle" from the Colosseum to the Forum, then over Capitol Hill to the Pantheon. After a siesta, join the locals strolling from Piazza del Popolo to the Spanish Steps (see my recommended "Dolce Vita Stroll," page 283). On the second day, see the Vatican City (St. Peter's, climb the dome, tour the Vatican Museum). Have dinner on the atmospheric Campo de' Fiori, then walk to the Trevi Fountain and Spanish Steps (see my recommended Night Walk Across Rome, page 69). With a third day, add the Borghese Gallery (reservations required) and the National Museum of Rome.

Rome in Seven Days
Rome is a great one-week getaway. Its sights can keep even the most fidgety traveler well-entertained for a week.

Day 1: City orientation (bus tour), then the National Museum of Rome and the nearby Baths of Diocletian. Afternoon: "Dolce Vita Stroll" (page 283) and shopping.

Day 2: Do the "Caesar Shuffle" from Nero's Golden House (reservation required) to the Colosseum, Forum, Mamertine Prison, Trajan's Forum, Capitol Hill, and Pantheon.

Day 3: Vatican City: St. Peter's Basilica, dome climb, and Vatican Museum. (The museum is less crowded right before it closes, but last admission is early—either 12:15 or 15:15, depending on the day.)

Day 4: Side-trip to Ostia Antica (closed Mon, page 293). Take recommended Night Walk Across Rome (page 69) from Campo de' Fiori to the Spanish Steps.

Day 5: Borghese Gallery (reservation required) and Pilgrims' Rome (the churches Santa Maria Maggiore, San Clemente, and San Giovanni in Laterano).

Day 6: Side-trip to Naples and Pompeii.

Day 7: You choose—Hadrian's Villa, Appian Way with Catacombs, E.U.R., Castel Sant'Angelo, Testaccio sights, Baths of Caracalla, Cappuccin Crypt, shopping, or more time at the Vatican.

OVERVIEW

Tourist Information
While Rome has several tourist information offices (abbreviated **TI** in this book), the dozen or so TI kiosks scattered around the town at major tourist centers are handy and just as helpful. If all you need is a map, forget the TI and get one at your hotel or at a newsstand kiosk.

Daily Reminder

Sunday: These sights are closed: Vatican Museum (except for the last Sunday of the month, when it's free and crowded), VIlla Farnesina, and the Catacombs of San Sebastian. In the morning, the Porta Portese flea market hops, and the old center is delightfully quiet.

Monday: Many sights are closed: National Museum of Rome, Borghese Gallery, Capitol Hill Museum, Catacombs of Priscilla, Octagonal Hall and Museum of the Bath (both at Baths of Diocletian), Castel Sant'Angelo, Montemartini Museum, E.U.R.'s Museum of Roman Civilization, Trajan's Market, Etruscan Museum, Protestant Cemetery in Testaccio, Ostia Antica, and Villa d'Este (at Tivoli). All of the ancient sights (e.g., Colosseum and Forum) and the Vatican Museum, among others, are open. The Baths of Caracalla close early in the afternoon.

Tuesday: All sights are open in Rome, except for Nero's Golden House. This isn't a good day to side-trip to Naples, because its Archaeological Museum is closed.

Wednesday: All sights are open, except for the Catacombs of San Callisto. St. Peter's Basilica may be closed in the morning for a papal audience.

Thursday: All sights are open, except for Galleria Doria Pamphilj and the Cappuccin Crypt.

Friday & Saturday: All sights are open in Rome.

You'll find TIs at the airport (daily 8:00–19:00, tel. 06-6595-6074) and at the Termini train station (daily 8:00–21:00; near track 3, tel. 06-4890-6300, combined with travel agency). These TIs are especially helpful, if they're not too busy.

Smaller TIs (daily 9:00–18:00) include kiosks near the Forum (on Piazza del Tempio della Pace), at Via del Corso (on Largo Goldoni), in Trastevere (on Piazza Sonnino), on Via Nazionale (at Palazzo delle Esposizioni), at Castel Sant'Angelo, and at Santa Maria Maggiore Church. For more information, call 06-3600-4399 (answered daily 9:00–19:00; also see www.romaturismo.it).

At any TI, ask for a city map, a listing of sights and hours (in the free *Museums of Rome* booklet), and *Passepartout*, the free seasonal entertainment guide for evening events and fun. Don't book rooms through a TI; you'll save money by booking direct.

Roma c'è is a cheap little weekly entertainment guide with a useful English section (in the back) on musical events (new edition every Thu, sold at newsstands for €1.20, www.romace.it).

Arrival in Rome

For a rundown of Rome's train station and airports, see Transportation Connections, page 286.

Helpful Hints

Internet Access: If your hotel doesn't offer free or cheap Internet access in their lobby, your hotelier can point you to the nearest Internet café. The city's biggest access point is easyInternet-café, centrally located on Piazza Barberini (cheap and open 24/7, 250 terminals, www.easyinternetcafe.com). A smaller branch is in Trastevere, on Piazza in Piscinula.

Bookstores: These stores (all open daily) sell travel guidebooks—Feltrinelli International (Via Vittorio Emanuele Orlando 84, Metro: Repubblica, tel. 06-482-7878). Almost Corner Bookshop in Trastevere (Via del Moro 45, tel. 06-583-6942), and the Anglo American Bookshop (Via della Vite 102, tel. 06-679-5222).

Laundry: Your hotelier can direct you to the nearest launderette. The Bolle Blu launderette chain comes with Internet access (usually open daily 8:00-22:00, about €7 to wash and dry a 15-pound load, near train station at Via Palestro 59 and at Via Principe Amedeo 116, tel. 06-446-5804).

Travel Agencies: Get train tickets and railpass-related reservations and supplements at travel agencies, rather than dealing with the congested train station. The cost is often the same, though sometimes there's a minimal charge. Your hotel can direct you to the nearest travel agency. Quo Vadis, near the Vatican, is helpful (Via della Conciliazione, 22-24, tel. 06-6880-4941, fax 06-6880-3191, qv.viaggi@tiscalinet.it). Or purchase train tickets from the American Express office near the Spanish Steps (Mon-Fri 9:00-17:30, closed Sat-Sun, Piazza di Spagna 38, tel. 06-67641).

Dealing with (and Avoiding) Problems

Theft Alert: With sweet-talking con artists meeting you at the station, well-dressed pickpockets on buses, and thieving gangs of children at the ancient sites, Rome is a gauntlet of rip-offs. There's no great physical risk, but green or sloppy tourists will be scammed. Thieves strike when you're distracted. Don't trust kind strangers. Keep nothing important in your pockets. Assume you're being stalked. (Then relax and have fun.) Be most on guard while boarding and leaving buses and subways. Thieves crowd the door, then stop and turn while others crowd and push from behind. The sneakiest thieves are well-dressed businessmen (generally with something in their hands); lately many are posing as tourists with fanny packs, cameras, and even Rick Steves guidebooks. Scams abound: Don't give your wallet to self-proclaimed "police" who stop you on the street, warn you about counterfeit (or drug) money, and ask to see your cash. If a bank machine eats your ATM card, see if there's a thin plastic insert with a tongue hanging out that thieves use to extract it.

If you know what to look out for, the gangs of children picking the pockets and handbags of naive tourists are no threat, but an interesting, albeit sad, spectacle. Gangs of city-stained children (just 8–10 years old—too young to be prosecuted, but old enough to rip you off) troll through the tourist crowds around the Colosseum, Forum, Piazza Repubblica, and train and Metro stations. Watch them target tourists who are overloaded with bags or distracted with a video camera. The kids look like beggars and hold up newspapers or cardboard signs to confuse their victims. They scram like stray cats if you're onto them. A fast-fingered mother with a baby is often nearby. The terrace above the bus stop near the Colosseum Metro stop is a fine place to watch the action...and maybe even pick up a few moves of your own.

Reporting Losses: To report lost or stolen passports and documents or to make an insurance claim, you must file a police report (at Termini train station, with Polizia at track 1 or with Carabinieri at track 20; offices are also at Piazza Venezia). To replace a passport, file the police report, then go to your embassy (see below). To report lost or stolen credit cards, see page 11.

Embassies: The U.S. Embassy is at Via Vittorio Veneto 119/A (Mon–Fri 8:30–13:00 & 14:00–17:30, closed Sat–Sun, 24-hour tel. 06-46741, www.usembassy.it), and the Canadian Embassy is at Via Zara 30 (tel. 06-445-981, www.canada.it).

Emergency Numbers: Police—tel. 113. Ambulance—tel. 118.

Hit and Run: Walk with extreme caution. Scooters don't need to stop at red lights, and even cars exercise what drivers call the "logical option" of not stopping if they see no oncoming traffic. As noisy gasoline-powered scooters are replaced by electric ones, they'll be quieter (hooray) but more dangerous for pedestrians. Follow locals like a shadow when you cross a street (or spend a good part of your visit stranded on curbs). When you do cross alone, don't be a deer in the headlights. Find a gap in the traffic and walk with confidence while making eye contact with the approaching driver—they won't hit you if they can tell where you intend to go.

Staying/Getting Healthy: The siesta is a key to survival in summertime Rome. Lie down and contemplate the extraordinary power of gravity in the Eternal City. I drink lots of cold, refreshing water from Rome's many drinking fountains (the

Forum has 3). There's a pharmacy (marked by a green cross) in every neighborhood, including a handy one in the Termini train station (daily 7:30–22:00, located downstairs, at west end), and a 24-hour pharmacy on Piazza dei Cinquecento 51 (next to Termini train station on Via Cavour, tel. 06-488-0019). Embassies can recommend English-speaking doctors. Consider MEDline, a 24-hour home medical service (tel. 06-808-0995, doctors speak English). Anyone is entitled to free emergency treatment at public hospitals. The hospital closest to the Termini train station is Policlinico Umberto 1 (entrance for emergency treatment on Via Lancisi, translators available, Metro: Policlinico). The American Hospital, a private hospital on the edge of town, is accustomed to helping Yankees (tel. 06-225-571).

Getting Around Rome

Sightsee on foot, by city bus, by Metro, or by taxi. I've grouped your sightseeing into walkable neighborhoods. Make it a point to visit sights in a logical order. Needless backtracking wastes precious time.

Public transportation is efficient, cheap, and part of your Roman experience. It starts running at about 5:30 and stops at about 23:30, sometimes earlier. After midnight, there are a few very crowded night buses, and taxis become more expensive and hard to get. Don't try to hail one—go to a taxi stand.

You can use the same ticket on the bus or the Metro (€1, good for 75 min, valid for one Metro ride—including transfers—and unlimited buses); you can also buy an all-day bus/Metro pass (€4, good until midnight) or a one-week transit pass (€16—about the same as 2 taxi rides). You can buy tickets and passes at newsstands, tobacco shops (*tabacchi*, marked by a black-and-white *T* sign), and major Metro stations and bus stops, but not on board. Stamp your ticket before using it (machines are near subway turnstiles and on buses—watch others and imitate). If the validation machine won't work, you can write the date, time, and bus number on the ticket. For more information, visit www.atac.roma.it, or call 800-431-784.

It's smart to either buy an all-day pass or stock up on tickets early on. That way, you don't have to run around searching for an open *tabacchi* when you spot your bus approaching. Metro stations have no human ticket-sellers, and the machines are either broken or require exact change (it helps to put in smallest coin first).

Buses (especially the touristy #64) and the Metro are havens for thieves and pickpockets. Assume any commotion is a thief-created distraction. If one bus is packed, there's likely a second one on its tail with far fewer crowds and thieves. Once you know the bus system, it's easier than searching for a cab.

Rome's Public Transportation

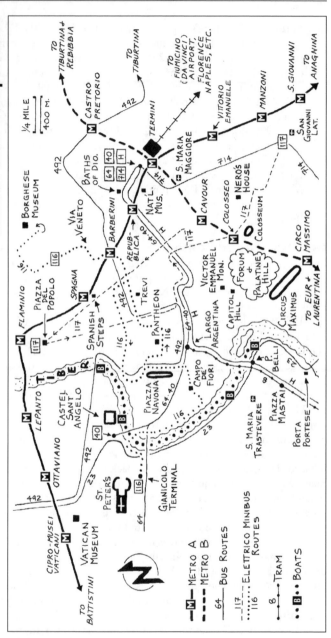

Rome's Metro

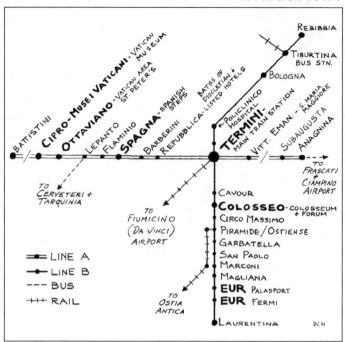

By Metro: The Roman subway system (Metropolitana) is simple, with two clean, cheap, fast lines that intersect at the Termini train station. Note that first and last compartments are generally the least crowded.

While much of Rome is not served by its skimpy subway, these stops are helpful:

Termini—train station, National Museum of Rome, and recommended hotels

Repubblica—Baths of Diocletian/Octagonal Hall, Via Nazionale, and recommended hotels

Barberini—Cappuccin Crypt and Trevi Fountain

Spagna—Spanish Steps, Villa Borghese, and classy shopping area

Flaminio—Piazza del Popolo, start of recommended "Dolce Vita Stroll" down Via del Corso

Ottaviano—St. Peter's and Vatican City

Cipro–Musei Vaticani—Vatican Museum and recommended hotels

Colosseo—Colosseum, Roman Forum, and recommended hotels

E.U.R.—Mussolini's futuristic suburb

By Bus: Bus routes are clearly listed at the stops. Ask the TI for a bus map (bus info: tel. 06-4695-2027). Tickets have a bar code and must be stamped on the bus in the yellow box with the digital readout (be sure to retrieve your ticket). Punch your ticket as you board, or you are cheating. While relatively safe, riding without a stamped ticket on the bus is stressful. Inspectors fine even innocent-looking tourists €52.

Here are a few buses worth knowing about:

#64—Termini (train station), Piazza della Repubblica (sights), Via Nazionale (recommended hotels), Piazza Venezia (near Forum), Largo Argentina (near Pantheon), and St. Peter's Basilica (get off just past the tunnel). Ride it for a city overview and to watch pickpockets in action (can get horribly crowded).

#40—This express bus following the #64 route is especially helpful: fewer stops, crowds, and pickpockets.

#8—This tram connects Largo Argentina with Trastevere (get off at Piazza Belli, just after crossing the Tiber River).

#62—Largo Argentina to St. Peter's Square.

#81—San Giovanni in Laterano, Colosseum, Largo Argentina, and Piazza Risorgimento (Vatican).

#H—Express connecting Termini train station and Trastevere, with a few stops on Via Nazionale (for Trastevere, get off at Piazza Belli, just after crossing the river).

#492—Stazione Tiburtina (bus station), Piazza Barberini, Piazza Venezia, Piazza Cavour (Castel Sant'Angelo), and Piazza Risorgimento (Vatican).

#271—Trastevere (from across Ponte Sisto Bridge) to the Vatican (Piazza Risorgimento).

#571—Express from Via Cavalleggeri (near St. Peter's Square) to the Colosseum.

#714—Termini (train station), Santa Maria Maggiore, San Giovanni in Laterano, and Terme di Caracalla (Baths of Caracalla).

#23—Links Vatican with Trastevere, stopping at Porta Portese (Sunday flea market), Trastevere (Piazza Belli), Castel Sant'Angelo, and Vatican Museum (nearest stop is Via Leone IV).

Rome has cute *elettrico* minibuses that wind through the narrow streets of old and interesting neighborhoods (daily, fewer on Sun). These are handy for sightseeing and fun for simply joyriding:

Elettrico #116—Through the medieval core of Rome: Ponte Vittorio Emanuele II (near Castel Sant'Angelo) to Campo de' Fiori, then to Piazza Barberini via the Pantheon, and finally through the scenic Villa Borghese park.

Elettrico #117—San Giovanni in Laterano, Colosseo, Via dei Serpenti, Trevi Fountain, Piazza di Spagna, and Piazza del Popolo.

By Taxi: I use taxis in Rome more often than in other cities. They're reasonable and useful for efficient sightseeing in this big, hot metropolis. Taxis start at about €2.50, then charge about €1 per kilometer (surcharges: €1 on Sun, €2.75 for nighttime hours of 22:00–7:00, €1 for luggage, €7.25 extra for airport, tip by rounding up to the nearest euro). Sample fares: train station to Vatican–€9; train station to Colosseum–€6; Colosseum to Trastevere–€7. Three or four companions with more money than time should taxi almost everywhere. It's tough to wave down a taxi in Rome. Find the nearest taxi stand by asking a passerby or a clerk in a shop, *"Dov'è una fermata dei taxi?"* (doh-VEH OO-nah fehr-MAH-tah DEHee TAHK-see). Some taxi stands are listed on my maps. To save time and energy, have your hotel or restaurant call a taxi for you; the meter starts when the call is received (generally adding a euro or two to the bill). To call a cab on your own, dial 06-3570, 06-4994, or 06-88177. It's routine for Romans to ask the waiter in a restaurant to call a taxi when they ask for the bill. The waiter will tell you how many minutes you have to enjoy your coffee.

Beware of corrupt taxis. If hailing a cab on the street, be sure the meter is restarted when you get in (should be around €2.50; it may be higher if you called for the taxi). Many meters show both the fare and the time elapsed during the ride—and some tourists pay €8.30 for an eight-and-a-half-minute trip (more than the fair meter rate). When you arrive at the train station or airport, beware of hustlers conning naive visitors into unmarked rip-off "express taxis." Only use official taxis, with a *taxi* sign and phone number marked on the door. By law, they must display a multilingual official price chart. If you have any problems with a taxi, point to the chart and ask the cabbie to explain it to you. Making a show of writing down the taxi number (to file a complaint) can motivate a driver to quickly settle the matter.

By Boat: Tourist-laden boats slowly float their way down the Tiber—trying to re-energize the city's neglected river (single ride–€1, day pass–€2.30, tour–€10, boats depart hourly, daily 8:00–19:30, maybe until 24:00 in summer, tel. 06-678-9361, www.battellidiroma .it). You can access the docks from the following bridges: Ponte Duca d'Aosta, Ponte Risorgimento, Ponte Cavour (Ara Pacis), Ponte Sant'Angelo (Vatican), Ponte Sisto (Trastevere), or Calata Anguillara (Isola Tiburtina).

By Car with Driver: You can hire your own private car with driver through Autoservizi Monti Concezio, run by gentle, capable, and English-speaking Ezio (car–€30/hr, minibus–€35/hr, 3-hr minimum, mobile 335-636-5907 or 349-674-5643, www.montitours .com, concemon@tin.it).

Tips for Tackling My Self-Guided Tours

Sightseeing can be hard work. My self-guided tours are designed to help make your visits to Italy's finest museums meaningful, fun, fast, and painless.

Hours of sights can change without warning. Pick up the latest listing of museum hours at a TI. Don't put off visiting a must-see sight—you never know when a place will close unexpectedly for a holiday, strike, or restoration. Make reservations for the Borghese Gallery (see page 164).

To get the most out of the tours, read the tour the night before your visit. When you arrive at the sight, use the overview map to get the lay of the land and the basic tour route. Expect a few changes—paintings can be on tour, on loan, out sick, or shifted at the whim of the curator. To adapt, pick up any available free floor plans as you enter, ask an information person to glance at this book's maps to confirm they're current, or if you can't find a particular painting, just ask any museum worker. Point to the photograph in this book and ask, *"Dov'è?"* (doh-VEH, meaning "Where?").

I cover the highlights at sights. You might want to supplement with an audioguide (recorded descriptions in English, about €4, usually good), or a guided tour (generally €5 or more). Tours in English are most likely to occur during peak season. The quality of a tour depends on the guide's knowledge, fluency, and enthusiasm.

Museums have their rules; if you're aware of them in advance, they're no big deal. Keep in mind that many sights have "last entry" times 30 to 60 minutes before closing. Guards usher people out before the official closing time.

Cameras are normally allowed, but no flashes or tripods (without special permission). Flashes damage oil paintings and distract others in the room. Even without a flash, a hand-held camera will take a decent picture (or buy postcards or posters at the museum bookstore). Video cameras are usually allowed.

For security reasons, you're often required to check even small bags. Many museums have a free checkroom at the entrance. They're safe. If you have something you can't bear to part with, be prepared to stash it in a pocket or purse.

At the museum bookshop, thumb through the biggest guidebook (or scan its index) to be sure you haven't overlooked something that's of particular interest to you. If there's an on-site cafeteria, it's usually a good place to rest and have a snack or light meal. Museum WCs are free and generally clean.

And finally, every sight or museum offers infinitely more than the few stops I cover. Use these tours as an introduction—not the final word.

TOURS

Rome has many good, highly competitive tour companies. I've listed my favorites here, but without a lot of details on their offerings. Before your trip, spend some time on their Web sites to get to know your options, as each company has a particular teaching and guiding personality. Some are highbrow, and others are less scholarly. It's sometimes required, and always smart, to book a spot in advance (easy on the Web). While it may seem like a splurge to have a local or an American expat show you around, it's a treat that makes brutal Rome suddenly your friend.

Context Rome—Americans Paul Bennett and Lani Bevacqua offer walking tours for travelers with longer-than-average attention

spans. Their orientation walks lace together lesser-known sights from antiquity to the present. Tours vary in length from two to four hours and range in price from €25 to €60. Try to book in advance, since their groups are limited to six and fill up fast (tel. 06-482-0911, U.S. tel. 888-467-1986, www.contextrome .com). They also offer orientation chats in your hotel which can be well worth the price (€50/1 hr).

If you're interested in weeklong classes on Rome, look into the American Institute for Roman Culture—an innovative, educational organization run by Tom Rankin and his colleague, archaeologist Darius Arya (www.romanculture.org).

Through Eternity—This company offers several walking tours, all led by native English speakers who strive to bring the history to life. The tours, limited to groups of 20, include St. Peter's and the Vatican Museum (€40, museum entry not included, 5 hrs, almost daily); the Colosseum and Roman Forum (€25, 2.5 hrs, daily); and Rome at Twilight (€25, nightly). They also offer private tours of Rome, Tivoli, and Pompeii (tel. 06-700-9336, mobile 347-336-5298, 10 percent discount if booked online, www.througheternity .com, info@througheternity.com, Rob Allyn).

Rome Walks—These guides give tours in fluent English to small groups (generally fewer than 10 people). Sample tours include Colosseum/Forum/Palatine Walk (€50, includes admission to Colosseum, 3 hrs), Scandal Tour (€30, 2 hrs to dig up the dirt on Roman emperors, royalty, and popes), Vatican City Walk (€52, includes admission to Vatican Museum, 4 hrs), and a Twilight Rome Evening Walk (€25, all the famous squares that offer lively people scenes, 2 hrs). They also do private tours to more far-flung

Is the Pope Catholic?

Rome's tour guides, who introduce tourists to the city's great art and Christian history, field a lot of interesting questions and comments from their groups. Here are a few of their favorites:

- Was John Paul II the son of John Paul I?
- Who's the guy on the cross?
- Oh, to be here in Rome...where our Lord Jesus walked.
- Is this where Christ fought the lions?
- This guy who made so many nice things, Rene Sance, who is he? (Say it fast, and you'll get the gist.)
- What's the Sistine Chapel worth in U.S. dollars?
- How did Michelangelo get Moses to pose for him?
- What's Michelangelo doing now?

places such as Hadrian's Villa and Villa d'Este (mobile 347-795-5175, www.romewalks.com, info@romewalks.com, Annie).

Roman Odyssey—This expat tour company offers various two- to three-hour, €25 walks led by native English speakers who are also fully licensed local guides (15 percent discount for readers of this book in 2006, tel. 06-580-9902, mobile 328-912-3720, www.romanodyssey.com, Rahul).

Private Guides—Consider a personal tour. Any of the tour compa-nies I list can provide a guide (about €50/hr). I work with Francesca Caruso, a licensed Italian guide who speaks excellent English, loves to teach and share her appreciation of her city, and has contributed generously to this book. She has a broad range of expertise and can tailor a walk to your interests (€100 for 2 hrs or more—she happily stretches the tour to half a day for eager students, individuals, and small groups, chris.fra@mclink.it).

Hop-on, Hop-off Bus Tour—The ATAC city bus #110 tour offers a quick, cheap orientation tour of Rome on big, red, double-decker buses with an open-air upper deck. In less than two hours, you'll have 80 sights pointed out to you (by a live guide in English and up to 3 other languages). While you can hop on and off, the service can be erratic (mobbed midday, not ideal in bad weather). It's best to think of this as an efficient, two-hour quickie orientation with scant information and lots of images. The stops include Via Veneto, Via Tritone, Ara Pacis, Piazza Cavour, St. Peter's Square, Corso Vittorio Emanuele (for Piazza Navona), Piazza Venezia, Colosseum, and Via Nazionale. Bus #110 departs every 30 minutes—at the top and bottom of the hour—from in front of the Termini train sta-tion (runs daily March–Sept 9:00–20:00, Oct–Feb 10:00–18:00, tel. 06-4695-2252). Buy the €13 ticket at the info kiosk marked *i* near platform D.

Archeobus—This hop-on, hop-off bus runs hourly from the Termini train station out to the Appian Way. This is a handy way to see the sights down this ancient Roman road, but it can be frustrating for various reasons (sometimes crowded, service can be sporadic, not ideal for hopping on and off). The trip, in an air-conditioned minibus, includes a basic, uninspired two-hour tour (longer if there's traffic) in Italian and English (€8; tickets sold at platform D in front of train station, hourly departures from station and Piazza Venezia 9:45–16:45, tel. 06-4695-4695).

SIGHTS

I've clustered Rome's sights into walkable neighborhoods, some quite close together. The Colosseum and the Forum are a few minutes' walk from Capitol Hill; a 10-minute walk beyond that is the Pantheon. I like to group these sights into one great day, starting at the Colosseum and ending at the Pantheon.

Don't let the length of my descriptions determine your sightseeing priorities. In this chapter, Rome's most important sights have the shortest listings and are marked with a ✪ (and page number). These sights are covered in much more detail in one of the tours included in this book.

To connect some of the sights by night, try my Night Walk Across Rome (page 69), which includes the Trevi Fountain and Spanish Steps. To join the parade of people strolling down Via del Corso every evening, take my "Dolce Vita Stroll" (see page 284).

Ancient Rome: The Colosseum and Forum Area

The core of the ancient city, where the grandest monuments were built, is between the Colosseum and Capitol Hill.

The following sights are listed in roughly geographical order from the Colosseum area to Capitol Hill. Except for the small St. Peter-in-Chains Church and the Time Elevator Roma, the sights date from ancient Rome.

▲St. Peter-in-Chains Church (San Pietro in Vincoli)—Built in the fifth century to house the chains that held St. Peter, this church is most famous for its Michelangelo statue. Check out the much-venerated chains under the high altar, then focus on mighty Moses (free, daily 7:00–12:30 & 15:30–18:00, modest dress required; the church is a 15-minute, uphill, zigzag walk from the Colosseum, or a shorter, simpler walk from the Cavour Metro stop—exiting the Metro stop, go up steep flight of steps, take a right at the top, and

Ancient Rome

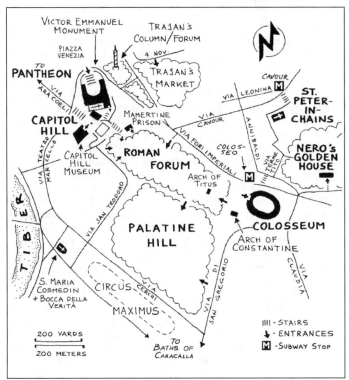

walk a block to church). Note that this isn't the famous St. Peter's Basilica, which is at Vatican City. ✪ See St. Peter-in-Chains Tour on page 222.

▲**Nero's Golden House (Domus Aurea)**—The sparse remains of Emperor Nero's "Golden House" are a faint shadow of their ancient grandeur. Nero (ruled A.D. 54–68) was Rome's most notorious emperor. He killed his own mother, kicked his pregnant wife to death, crucified St. Peter, and—most galling to his subjects—was a bad actor. When Rome burned in A.D. 64, Nero was accused of torching it to clear land for his domestic building needs. Finally, Nero wore out his welcome. The Romans rebelled, the Senate declared him a public enemy, and his only noble option was suicide. With the help of a slave, Nero stabbed himself in the neck, crying, "What an artist dies in me!"

As you consider Nero's house, you'll need to use your imagination. The original entrance to the gold-leaf-encrusted palace was all the way over at the Arch of Titus in the Forum. Nero's massive estate sprawled across the valley (where the Colosseum now

Tips on Sightseeing in Rome

Museums: Plan ahead. The marvelous Borghese Gallery and Nero's Golden House both require reservations (smart to reserve well in advance; for specifics, see Borghese Gallery Tour on page 164 and "Nero's Golden House" listing on page 37).

Many museums have **audioguides**. These small, portable devices give you information in English on what you're seeing. After you dial a number that appears next to a particular work of art, you listen to the spiel (cutting it short if you want). Though the information can be dry, it's usually worthwhile (€4, sometimes 2 sets of headphones are available at an extra cost).

A special combo-ticket called the **Archeologia Card**, which costs €20, covers the National Museum of Rome, Colosseum, Palatine Hill, Baths of Caracalla, Crypt Balbi (medieval art), Museum of the Bath (Roman inscriptions), Palazzo Altemps (so-so sculpture collection), Tomb of Cecilia Metella (on Appian Way), and Villa of the Quintilli (barren Roman villa on the outskirts of Rome). The combo-ticket allows you to see nine sights for the price of three (purchase at participating sights, valid for 7 days). The big plus of this ticket is that you avoid the long lines at the Colosseum (assuming you purchase it somewhere other than the Colosseum).

Hours listed anywhere can vary. Get a current listing of **museum hours** from one of Rome's TIs—ask for the booklet *Museums of Rome*. A few museums—such as the Borghese Gallery and Castel Sant'Angelo—may stay open late in summer, usually on Saturdays. On holidays, expect shorter hours or closures. You can confirm sightseeing plans each morning with a quick phone call, asking, "Are you open today?" (*"Aperto oggi?"*; ah-PER-toh OH-jee) and "What time do you close?" (*"A che ora chiuso?"*; ah kay OH-rah

stands) and up the hill—the part you tour today. Larger even than Bill Gates' place, it was a pain to vacuum. Because Nero compared himself to Apollo, the god of light, his home would have been filled with light. Combine that with a Michael Jackson's Neverland sense of taste. A colossal, 100-foot-tall bronze statue of Nero towered over everything. The estate incorporated an artificial lake and a forest stocked with game. It was decorated with the best multicolored marble and the finest frescoes. No expense was too great for Nero—his mistress soaked daily in the milk of 500 wild asses kept for her bathing pleasure.

When Nero died, the next family—the Flavians—took over. They were of middle-class stock, and wanted to win the hearts of the people by making up for the abuses of Nero. Logically, they built a people's entertainment complex atop the palace—the Colosseum stands where Nero's lake was. The palace was filled kee-OO-zoh). I've included telephone numbers for this purpose.

Rooms can begin closing about 30 to 60 minutes before the overall closing time. If your heart is set on seeing a particular piece of art, don't save it for the finale.

In museums, art is dated with A.C. (for *Avanti Cristo*, or B.C.) and D.C. (for *Dopo Cristo*, or A.D.). OK?

Churches: Churches offer some amazing art (usually free), a cool respite from the heat, and a welcome seat. They generally open early (around 7:00), close for lunch (roughly 12:00–15:00), and close late (about 19:00). Kamikaze tourists maximize their sightseeing hours by visiting churches before 9:00 and seeing the major sights that stay open during the siesta (St. Peter's, Colosseum, Forum, Capitol Hill Museum, and National Museum of Rome), while Romans are taking it cool and easy.

Many churches have "modest dress" requirements, which means no bare shoulders, miniskirts, or shorts—for men, women, or children. However, this dress code is only strictly enforced at St. Peter's and St. Paul's Outside the Walls. Elsewhere, you'll see many tourists in shorts (though not skimpy shorts) touring many churches.

Carry coins. A coin box near a piece of art in a church often illuminates the art for a coin (allowing a better photo). Whenever possible, let there be light. Some churches have coin-operated audio-boxes that describe the art and history.

Miscellaneous Tips: I carry a plastic water bottle that can be refilled at Rome's many public drinking spouts. Because public restrooms are scarce, use toilets when available (Mom always said, "Just try"). Don't leave a museum, restaurant, or bar without considering their facilities.

with dirt during the reign of Trajan to provide a foundation for a sprawling public bath. (This actually helped preserve what's open to the public today.)

Today, while only hints of the splendid, colorful frescoes survive, the towering vaults and the sheer immensity of Nero's palace remain impressive. As you wander through rooms that are now underground, look up at the holes in the ceiling. Ponder how much of old Rome still hides underground...and why the subway is limited to two lines.

Visits, which last 50 minutes, are allowed only with an escort (30 people, about every 30 min) and a mandatory reservation (€5 admission plus €1.50 reservation fee, Wed–Mon 9:00–19:45, last entry at 18:40, closed Tue). Schedule your visit online at www.pierreci.it or by calling 06-3996-7700 during office hours (reserve a few days in advance if you can). Guided tours in English are also offered twice daily for €10; request a tour when you book your reservation. Audioguides cost €2, but listen to the intro before entering or you'll be forever behind. If you show up without a reservation, you could luck out and be allowed in (chances are best on a late afternoon on a weekday). Nero's House is near the Colosseo Metro stop and 200 yards northeast of Colosseum; go through a park gate, up a hill, and it's on the left.

▲▲▲ **Colosseum (Colosseo)**—This 2,000-year-old building is *the* great example of Roman engineering. Used as a venue for entertaining the masses, this colossal, functional stadium is one of Europe's most recognizable landmarks. Whether you're playing gladiator or simply marveling at the remarkable ancient design and construction, the Colosseum gets a unanimous thumbs-up (€10 ticket also includes Palatine Hill and special exhibits, covered by €20 Archeologia Card, daily 9:00–19:00 or until an hour before sunset, Metro: Colosseo, tel. 06-3996-7700). ✪ See Colosseum Tour (including tips on avoiding the long entry lines) on page 94.

▲**Arch of Constantine**—This well-preserved arch, which stands between the Colosseum and the Forum, commemorates a military coup and, more importantly, the acceptance of Christianity in the Roman Empire. When the ambitious Emperor Constantine (who'd had a vision that he'd win under the sign of the cross) defeated his rival Maxentius in A.D. 312, Constantine became sole emperor of the Roman Empire and legalized Christianity. (Free, always open and viewable.) ✪ See Colosseum Tour on page 94.

▲▲▲**Roman Forum (Foro Romano)**—This is ancient Rome's birthplace and civic center, and the common ground between Rome's famous seven hills. Anything important that happened in ancient Rome happened here—it's arguably the most important piece of real estate in Western civilization. While only a few fragments of that glorious past remain, history-seekers find plenty to ignite their imaginations amid the half-broken columns and arches (free, daily 9:00–19:00 or until an hour before sunset, Metro: Colosseo, tel. 06-3996-7700). ✪ See Roman Forum Tour on page 101.

▲▲▲**Palatine Hill (Monte Palatino)**—The hill overlooking the Forum was the home of the emperors, and now contains a museum, scant (but impressive when understood) remains of imperial palaces, and a view of the Circus Maximus (€10 ticket also includes Colosseum—smart to buy ticket at Palatine Hill to avoid long lines at Colosseum; also covered by €20 Archeologia Card, audioguide-€4, daily 9:00–19:00 or until an hour before sunset). ✪ See Palatine Hill Tour on page 114.

▲**Mamertine Prison**—This 2,500-year-old, cistern-like prison, which once held the bodies of Saints Peter and Paul, is worth a look (donation requested, daily 9:00–19:00, at the foot of Capitol

Hill, near Forum's Arch of Septimius Severus). When you step into the room, you'll hit a modern floor. Ignore that and look up at the hole in the ceiling, from which prisoners were lowered. Then take the stairs down to the level of the actual prison floor. Downstairs, you'll see the column to which Peter was chained. It's said that a miraculous fountain sprang up in this room so that Peter could convert and baptize his jailers, who were also subsequently martyred. The upside-down cross commemorates Peter's upside-down crucifixion.

Imagine humans, amid fat rats and rotting corpses, awaiting slow deaths. On the walls near the entry are lists of notable prisoners (Christian and non-Christian) and the ways they were executed: *strangolati, decapitato, morto per fame* (died of hunger). The sign by the Christian names reads, "Here suffered, victorious for the triumph of Christ, these martyr saints."

▲**Trajan's Column, Forum, and Market (Colonna, Foro, e Mercati de Traiano)**—This is the grandest column and best example of "continuous narration" that we have from antiquity (free, always open and viewable, on Piazza Venezia across street from Victor Emmanuel Monument). For a fee, you can go inside Trajan's Market (boring) and part of Trajan's Forum (€6.20, summer Tue–Sun 9:00–18:30, winter Tue–Sun 9:00–16:30, always closed Mon, entrance is uphill from the column on Via IV Novembre, tel. 06-679-0048). ✪ See Trajan's Column, Forum, and Market Tour on page 123.

Time Elevator Roma—The cheesy and overpriced visit is really just for kids (aged 5 and over). It starts with a stand-up Italian-only 15-minute intro, followed by a 30-minute, multi-screen show with seats jolting through the centuries. Equipped with headphones, you get nauseous in a comfortable, air-conditioned theater as the history of Rome unfolds before you—from the founding of the city, through its rise and fall, to its Renaissance rebound, and up to the present (€11, daily 11:00–19:30, shows every 30 min, no kids under 5, Via dei S.S. Apostoli 20, just off Via del Corso, 3-min walk from Piazza Venezia, tel. 06-9774-6243, www.time-elevator.it).

Capitol Hill Area

There are several ways to get to the top of Capitol Hill (also called

"Capitoline Hill"). If you're coming from the north (from Piazza Venezia), take Michelangelo's impressive stairway to the right of the big, white Victor Emmanuel Monument. Coming from the south (the Forum), take either the steep staircase or the winding road, which converge near the top

Rome at a Glance

▲▲▲**Colosseum** Huge stadium where gladiators fought. **Hours:** Daily 9:00–19:00 or until an hour before sunset.

▲▲▲**Roman Forum** Ancient Rome's main square, with ruins and grand arches. **Hours:** Daily 9:00–19:00 or until an hour before sunset.

▲▲▲**Palatine Hill** Ruins of emperors' palaces, Circus Maximus view, and museum. **Hours:** Daily 9:00–19:00 or until an hour before sunset.

▲▲▲**Pantheon** The defining domed temple. **Hours:** Mon–Sat 8:30–19:30, Sun 9:00–18:00, holidays 9:00–13:00.

▲▲▲**National Museum of Rome** Greatest collection of Roman sculpture anywhere. **Hours:** Tue–Sun 9:00–19:45, closed Mon.

▲▲▲**Borghese Gallery** Bernini sculptures and paintings by Caravaggio, Raphael, and Titian in a Baroque palazzo. Reservations mandatory. **Hours:** Tue–Sun 9:00–19:00, closed Mon.

▲▲▲**Vatican Museum** Four miles of the art of Western Civilization, culminating in the Sistine Chapel. **Hours:** March–Oct Mon–Fri 8:45–16:45 and Sat 8:45–13:45; Nov–Feb Mon–Sat 8:45–13:45; closed on numerous religious holidays and Sun, except last Sun of the month.

▲▲▲**St. Peter's Basilica** Most impressive church on earth, with Michelangelo's *Pietà* and dome. **Hours:** Church—daily April–Sept 7:00–19:00, Oct–March 7:00–18:00, often closed Wed mornings; dome—daily April–Sept 8:00–17:45, Oct–March 8:00–16:45.

▲▲**Capitol Hill** Hilltop square designed by Michelangelo with museum, grand stairway, and Forum overlooks. **Hours:** Always open.

▲▲**Capitol Hill Museum** Ancient statues, mosaics, and expansive view of Forum. **Hours:** Tue–Sun 9:00–20:00, closed Mon.

▲▲**Churches near the Pantheon** Four distinctive art-filled houses of worship (San Luigi dei Francesi, Santa Maria sopra Minerva, St. Ignazio, and Gesù) are worth a visit for Pantheon sightseers. **Hours:** Roughly daily 7:00–12:30 & 16:00–19:00.

▲▲**Catacombs** Layers of tunnels with tombs, mainly Christian, outside the city. **Hours:** Open 8:30–12:00 & 14:30–17:30, until 17:00 in winter (San Callisto closed Wed and Feb, San Sebastian closed Sun and Nov, Priscilla closes at 17:00 year-round and all day Mon).

▲**St. Peter-in-Chains** Church with Michelangelo's *Moses*. **Hours:** Daily 7:00–12:30 & 15:30–18:00.

▲**Nero's Golden House** Sparse remains of Emperor Nero's sprawling home. Reservations required. **Hours:** Wed–Mon 9:00–19:45, closed Tue.

▲**Arch of Constantine** Honors the emperor who legalized Christianity. **Hours:** Always viewable.

▲**Mamertine Prison** Prison that held Saints Peter and Paul. **Hours:** Daily 9:00–19:00.

▲**Trajan's Column** Tall column with narrative relief, on Piazza Venezia. **Hours:** Always viewable.

▲**Galleria Doria Pamphilj** Fancy palace packed with art. **Hours:** Fri–Wed 10:00–17:00, closed Thu.

▲**Trevi Fountain** Baroque hotspot—bring coins to ensure a return trip to Rome. **Hours:** Always flowing.

▲**Baths of Diocletian** Once ancient Rome's immense public baths, now a Michelangelo church—Santa Maria degli Angeli—and the Octagonal Hall, a room with minor ancient Roman sculpture. **Hours:** Church—Mon–Sat 7:00–18:30, Sun 8:00–19:30. Octagonal Hall—Tue–Sat 9:00–14:00, Sun 9:00–13:00, closed Mon.

▲**Santa Maria della Vittoria** Church with Bernini's swooning *St. Teresa in Ecstasy*. **Hours:** Daily 7:00–12:00 & 15:30–19:00.

▲**Villa Borghese** Rome's "Central Park," with lake, Borghese Gallery, and Etruscan Museum. **Hours:** Always open.

▲**Cappuccin Crypt** Decorated with the bones of 4,000 monks. **Hours:** Fri–Wed 9:00–12:00 & 15:00–18:00, closed Thu.

▲**Castel Sant'Angelo** Hadrian's Tomb turned castle, prison, papal refuge, now museum. **Hours:** Tue–Sun 9:00–20:00, closed Mon.

of the hill at a great Forum overlook, she-wolf statue, and refreshing water fountain. Block the spout with your fingers, and water spurts up for drinking. Romans, who call this *il nasone* (the big nose), joke that a cheap Roman boy takes his date out for a drink at *il nasone*. Near the *nasone* is a back-door entrance to the Victor Emmanuel Monument (described below).

▲▲**Capitol Hill (Campidoglio) and Museum**—This hill, once the religious and political center of ancient Rome, is still the home of the city's government. The mayoral palace and the twin buildings housing the Capitol Hill Museum (listed below) border Michelangelo's Renaissance square. The square's centerpiece is a copy of the famous equestrian statue of Marcus Aurelius (the original is behind glass in the adjacent museum).

Michelangelo intended that people approach the square from his grand stairway off Piazza Venezia. From the top of the stairway, you see the new Renaissance face of Rome, with its back to the Forum. Michelangelo gave the buildings the "giant order"—huge pilasters make the existing two-story buildings feel one-storied and more harmonious with the new square. Notice how the statues atop these buildings welcome you and then draw you in. The terraces just downhill (past either side of the mayor's palace) offer grand views of the Forum.

The **Capitol Hill Museum** (Musei Capitolini) displays Roman art and statuary. The museum consists of the two buildings (Palazzo dei Conservatori and Palazzo Nuovo) flanking the equestrian statue atop Capitol Hill. The museum's buildings are connected by an underground passage that leads through the vacant Tabularium, with its panoramic overlook of the Forum (€8, €9.90 combo-ticket includes Montemartini Museum—described on page 58, Tue–Sun 9:00–20:00, closed Mon, last entry 1 hr before closing, good €4 audioguide, tel. 06-3996-7800, www.museicapitolini .org). ☉ See Capitol Hill Museum Tour on page 157.

Shortcut from Capitol Hill to Victor Emmanuel Monument: There's a clever little back-door access from the top of Capitol Hill directly to the top of the Victor Emmanuel Monument, saving you lots of uphill stair-climbing. Go up the wide steps in the left corner of the Capitol Hill square (if facing the Forum, the back-door entry is near the drinking fountain and she-wolf statue—follow signs to *terrazze*), pass through the iron gate at the top of the steps, and enter the small unmarked door at #13 on the right. You'll find yourself at the top of the monument with vast views, a café, and the entrance to the Museum of the Risorgimento (see "Victor Emmanuel Monument" listing, below). If you don't take this shortcut, you might decide to...

Descend from Capitol Hill to Piazza Venezia: Leaving Capitol Hill, head down the stairs leading to Piazza Venezia. At the bottom of the stairs, look left several blocks down the street to see a condominium actually built upon surviving ancient pillars and arches of Teatro Marcello.

Still at the bottom of the stairs, look up the long stairway to your right (which pilgrims climb on their knees) at the Santa Maria in Aracoeli church for a good example of the earliest style of Christian churches. While pilgrims find it worth the climb, sight-seers can skip it. The contrast between this climb-on-your-knees ramp to God's house and Michelangelo's grand and elegant stairs leading to Capitol Hill (which you just came down) illustrates the changes Renaissance humanism brought civilization. As you walk toward Piazza Venezia, look down into the ditch on your right to see the ruins of an ancient apartment building from the first century A.D.; part of it was transformed into a tiny church (faded frescoes and bell tower). Rome was built in layers—almost everywhere you go, there's an earlier version beneath your feet.

Piazza Venezia—This vast square is the focal point of modern Rome. The Via del Corso, which starts here, is the city's axis, surrounded by Rome's classiest shopping district. In the 1930s, Benito Mussolini whipped up Italy's nationalistic fervor here from a balcony above the square (to your left with your back to Victor Emmanuel Monument). Fascist masses filled the square scream-ing, "Four more years!"—or something like that. Mussolini lied to his people, mixing fear and patriotism to push his country to the right and embroil the Italians in expensive and regrettable wars. In 1945, they shot and hung Mussolini from a meat hook in Milan.

Victor Emmanuel Monument—This oversized monument to Italy's first king, built to celebrate the 50th anniversary of the country's unification in 1870, was part of Italy's push to overcome the new country's strong regionalism and to create a national identity. Open to the public, it offers a grand view of the Eternal City (free, 242 punishing steps to the top—unless you take the shortcut from Capitol Hill described above).

Romans think of the 200-foot-high, 500-foot-wide monument not as an altar of the fatherland, but as "the wedding cake," "the typewriter," or "the dentures." It wouldn't be so bad if it weren't sitting on a priceless acre of ancient Rome and if they had chosen better marble (this is too in-your-face white and picks up the pollu-tion horribly). Soldiers guard Italy's Tomb of the Unknown Soldier as the eternal flame flickers. At the tomb, stand with your back to the flame and see how Via del Corso bisects Rome.

The Victor Emmanuel Monument houses a little-visited **Museum of the Risorgimento** explaining the movement and war that led to the unification of Italy in 1870 (free, daily 9:30–18:00, café).

Pantheon Area

▲▲▲**Pantheon**—For the greatest look at the splendor of Rome, antiquity's best-preserved interior is a must. Built two millennia ago, this influential domed temple served as the model for Michelangelo's dome of St. Peter's and many others (free, Mon–Sat 8:30–19:30, Sun 9:00–18:00, holidays 9:00–13:00, tel. 06-6830-0230). ✪ See Pantheon Tour on page 127.

▲▲**Churches near the Pantheon**—For more information on the following churches, see page 130. Modest dress is recommended at all churches.

The **Church of San Luigi dei Francesi** has a magnificent chapel painted by Caravaggio (free, Fri–Wed 7:30–12:30 & 15:30–19:00, Thu 7:30–12:30, sightseers should avoid Mass at 7:30 and 19:00). The only Gothic church in Rome is **Santa Maria sopra Minerva**, with a little-known Michelangelo statue, *Christ Bearing the Cross* (free, daily 7:00–12:00 & 15:30–19:00, on a little square behind Pantheon, to the east). The **Church of St. Ignazio**, several blocks east of the Pantheon, is a riot of Baroque illusions with a false dome (free, daily 7:00–12:30 & 16:00–19:00). A few blocks away, across Corso Vittorio Emanuele, is the rich and Baroque **Gesù Church**, headquarters of the Jesuits in Rome (daily 7:00–12:30 & 16:00–19:15).

Walk out the Gesù Church and two blocks down Corso Vittorio Emmanuele to the **Sacred Area** (Largo Argentina), an excavated square facing the boulevard, about four blocks south of the Pantheon. Stroll around this square and look into the excavated pit at some of the oldest ruins in Rome. Julius Caesar was assassinated near here. Today it's a refuge for cats—volunteers care for some 250 of them. You'll see the cats (and their refuge) at the far (west) side of the square.

▲**Galleria Doria Pamphilj**—This gallery, filling a palace on Piazza del Collegio Romano, offers a rare chance to wander through a noble family's lavish rooms with the prince who calls this downtown mansion home. Well, almost. Through an audioguide, the prince lovingly narrates his family's story, including how the Doria Pamphilj (pahm-FEEL-yee) family's cozy relationship with the pope inspired the word "nepotism." Highlights include paintings by Caravaggio, Titian, and Raphael, and portraits of Pope Innocent X by Diego Velázquez (on canvas) and Gian Lorenzo Bernini (in marble). The fancy rooms of the palace are interesting, with a mini-Versailles–like hall of mirrors and paintings lining the walls to the ceiling in the style typical of 18th-century galleries (€8, includes worthwhile audioguide, Fri–Wed 10:00–17:00, closed Thu, from Piazza Venezia

Pantheon Area

walk 2 blocks up Via del Corso and take a left, Piazza del Collegio Romano 2, tel. 06-679-7323, www.doriapamphilj.it).

Piazza di Pietra (Piazza of Stone)—This square was actually a quarry set up to chew away at the abandoned Roman building. You can still see the holes that hungry medieval scavengers chipped into the columns to steal the metal pins that held the slabs together (2 blocks toward Via del Corso from Pantheon).

▲Trevi Fountain—This bubbly Baroque fountain, worth ▲ by day and ▲▲ by night, is a minor sight to art scholars...but a major nighttime gathering spot for teens on he make and tourists tossing coins. ✪ See Night Walk Across Rome on page 69.

East Rome: Near the Train Station

These sights are within a 10-minute walk of the train station. By Metro, use the Termini stop for the National Museum and the Piazza Repubblica stop for the rest.

East Rome

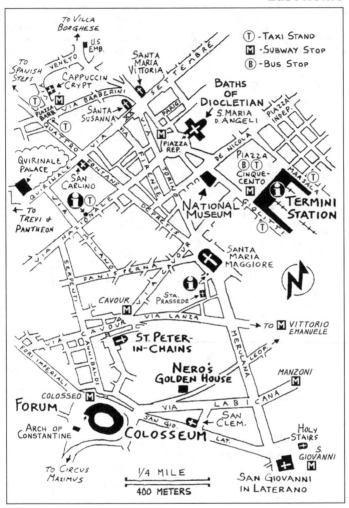

▲▲▲National Museum of Rome (Museo Nazionale Romano Palazzo Massimo alla Terme)—This museum houses the greatest collection of ancient Roman art anywhere, including busts of emperors and a Roman copy of the *Greek Discus Thrower* (€7, covered by €20 Archeologia Card, Tue–Sun 9:00–19:45, closed Mon, last entry 45 min before closing, audioguide-€4, Metro: Termini, tel. 06-481-5576). The museum is about 100 yards from the Termini train station. As you leave the station, it's the sandstone-brick building on your left. Enter at the far end, at Largo di Villa Peretti. ✪ See National Museum of Rome Tour on page 144.

▲**Baths of Diocletian (Terme di Diocleziano)**—Around A.D. 300, Emperor Diocletian built the largest baths in Rome. This sprawling meeting place—with baths and schmoozing spaces to accommodate 3,000 bathers at a time—was a big deal in ancient times. While much of it is still closed, three sections are open: the **Church of Santa Maria degli Angeli**, once the great central hall of the baths (free, Mon–Sat 7:00–18:30, Sun 8:00–19:30, closed to sightseers during Mass, faces Piazza Repubblica); the **Octagonal Hall**, once a gymnasium, now a gallery of Roman bronze and marble statues (free, Tue–Sat 9:00–14:00, Sun 9:00–13:00, closed Mon, faces Piazza Repubblica); and the skippable **Museum of the Bath**, which displays ancient Roman inscriptions on tons of tombs and tablets, but has nothing on the baths despite its name (€5, covered by €20 Archeologia Card, audioguide-€4, Tue–Sun 9:00–19:45, closed Mon, last entry 45 min before closing, Viale E. de Nicola 79, entrance faces Termini train station, tel. 06-4782-6152). ❂ See Baths of Diocletian Tour on page 138.

▲**Santa Maria della Vittoria**—This church houses Bernini's statue of a swooning *St. Teresa in Ecstasy* (free, daily 7:00–12:00 & 15:30–19:00, about 5 blocks northwest of Termini train station on Largo Susanna, Metro: Repubblica).

Once inside the church, you'll find St. Teresa to the left of the altar. Teresa has just been stabbed with God's arrow of fire.

Now, the angel pulls it out and watches her reaction. Teresa swoons, her eyes roll up, her hand goes limp, she parts her lips...and moans. The smiling, cherubic angel understands just how she feels. Teresa, a 16th-century Spanish nun, later talked of the "sweetness" of "this intense pain," describing her oneness with God in ecstatic, even erotic, terms.

Bernini, the master of multimedia, pulls out all the stops to make this mystical vision real. Actual sunlight pours through the alabaster windows; bronze sunbeams shine on a marble angel holding a golden arrow. Teresa leans back on a cloud and her robe ripples from within, charged with her spiritual arousal. Bernini has created a little stage-setting of heaven. And watching from the "theater boxes" on either side are members of the family that commissioned the work.

Santa Susanna Church—The home of the American Catholic Church in Rome, Santa Susanna holds Mass in English daily at 18:00 and on Sunday at 9:00 and 10:30. Their excellent Web site in English, www.santasusanna.org, contains tips for travelers and a long list of convents that rent out rooms. They arrange papal audiences (see page 202) and have an English library that includes my Venice, Florence, and Rome guidebooks (Mon–Fri 9:00–13:00 & 14:00–18:00, closed Sat–Sun, Via XX Settembre 15, near recommended Via Firenze hotels, Metro: Repubblica, tel. 06-4201-4554).

North Rome:
Villa Borghese and nearby Via Veneto

▲Villa Borghese—Rome's scruffy "Central Park" is great for people-watching (plenty of modern-day Romeos and Juliets). Take a rowboat out on the lake or visit the two museums listed below.

▲▲▲ Borghese Gallery (Galleria Borghese)—This plush museum, filling a cardinal's mansion in the park, was recently restored and offers one of Europe's most sumptuous art experiences. You'll enjoy a collection of world-class Baroque sculpture, including Bernini's *David* and his excited statue of Apollo chasing Daphne, as well as paintings by Caravaggio, Raphael, Titian, and Rubens. The museum's slick mandatory reservation system keeps the crowds at a manageable size.

Cost, Hours, Reservations: €8.50, includes €2 reservation fee, Tue–Sun 9:00–19:00, closed Mon. No photos are allowed. Reservations are mandatory and easy to get in English online (www.ticketeria.it) or by phone: call 06-328-101 (if you get an Italian recording, press 2 for English; office hours Mon–Fri 9:00–18:00, Sat 9:00–13:00, closed Sat in Aug and Sun year-round). Reserve a minimum of several days in advance for a weekday visit, at least a week ahead for weekends. ✪ For more on reservations, as well as a self-guided tour, see Borghese Gallery Tour on page 164.

Etruscan Museum (Villa Giulia Museo Nazionale Etrusco)—The Etruscan civilization thrived in this part of Italy around 600 B.C., when Rome was an Etruscan town. The Etruscan civilization is fascinating, but the Villa Giulia Museum is extremely low-tech and in a state of disarray. I don't like it, and fans of the Etruscans will prefer the Vatican Museum's section. Still, the Villa Giulia does have the famous "husband and wife sarcophagus" (a dead couple seeming to enjoy an everlasting banquet from atop their tomb—sixth century B.C. from Cerveteri);  the *Apollo from Veii* statue (of textbook fame); and an impressive room filled with gold sheets of Etruscan printing and temple statuary from the Sanctuary of Pyrgi (€4, Tue–Sun 8:30–19:30, closed Mon, closes earlier off-season, Piazzale di Villa Giulia 9, tel. 06-322-6571).

North Rome

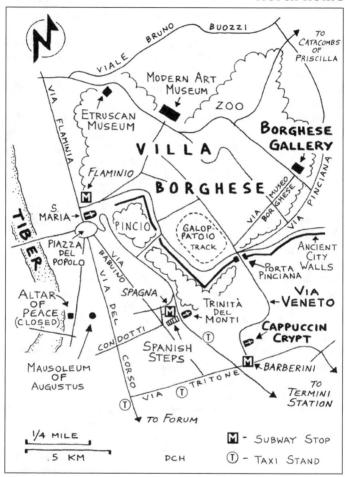

▲**Cappuccin Crypt**—If you want to see artistically arranged bones, this is the place. The crypt is below the church of Santa Maria

della Immacolata Concezione on Via Veneto, just up from Piazza Barberini. The bones of more than 4,000 monks who died between 1528 and 1870 are in the basement, all lined up for the delight—or disgust—of the always-wide-eyed visitor. The soil in the crypt was brought from Jerusalem 400 years ago, and the monastic message on the wall explains that this is more than just a macabre exercise: "We were what you are...you will become what we are now. *Buon giorno.*" Pick up a few of Rome's most interesting postcards (donation, Fri–Wed 9:00–12:00 & 15:00–18:00, closed Thu, Metro: Barberini, tel. 06-487-1185). Just up the street, you'll find the American Embassy, Federal Express, Hard Rock Café, and fancy Via Veneto cafés filled with the poor and envious looking for the rich and famous.

Ara Pacis (Altar of Peace)—Now surrounded by a high fence, this may reopen in 2006 after restoration. In 9 B.C., after victories in Gaul and Spain, Emperor Augustus celebrated the beginning of the Pax Romana (the Roman Empire at peace) by building this altar of peace. Peace is almost worshiped here. The north and south walls show a procession with realistic portraits of the imperial family in Greek Hellenistic style. It's a memorable combination of Roman grandeur and Greek elegance. Even during restoration, the altar can sometimes be seen through the windows (a long block west of Via del Corso on Via di Ara Pacis, on east banks of river near Ponte Cavour, nearest Metro: Spagna).

Catacombs of Priscilla (Catacombe di Priscilla)—For the most intimate catacombs experience, many prefer this smaller, more obscure option to the crowded catacombs on Appian Way (San Callisto and San Sebastian). The Catacombs of Priscilla, which used to be situated under the house of a Roman noble family, were used for some of the most important burials during antiquity. Best of all, because they're on the opposite side of town from the most popular catacombs, you'll have them mostly to yourself. You'll actually be in the care of a nun with a flashlight as you walk through the evocative chambers claimed to show the first depiction of Mary with Jesus (€5, Tue–Sun 8:30–12:00 & 14:30–17:00, closed Mon, beyond Villa Borghese on Piazza Crati at Via Salaria 420, bus #63 from Largo Argentina, or €10 taxi ride, tel. 06-862-06272, www .catacombedipriscilla.com). For more on catacombs, see page 64.

West Rome: Vatican City Neighborhood

Vatican City, a tiny independent country, contains the Vatican Museum (with Michelangelo's Sistine Chapel) and St. Peter's Basilica (with Michelangelo's exquisite *Pietà*). A helpful **TI** is just to the left of St. Peter's Basilica (Mon–Sat 8:30–19:00, closed Sun, tel. 06-6988-1662, Vatican switchboard tel. 06-6982, www.vatican .va). The entrances to St. Peter's and to the Vatican Museum are a 15-minute walk apart (follow the outside of the Vatican wall, which links the 2 sights). The nearest Metro stops still involve a 10-minute walk to either sight: for St. Peter's, the closest stop is Ottaviano; for the Vatican Museum, it's Cipro–Musei Vaticani. For information on Vatican tours, post offices, and the pope's schedule, see page 202.

Vatican City

N

PIAZZA EROI

MARKET

VIA ANDREA DORIA

VIA CIPRO PISAN

VIA. D. MILIZIE

VIA LEONE

CANDIA

OTTAVIANO

CESARE

VIA OTRANTO

V. GIULIO

VIA OTTAVIANO

VIA SCIPIONI

VIA GERMANICO

SEB. VEN.

VIA

"CIPRO-MUSEI VATICANI"

VATICANO WALL

WALL

PIAZZA RISORGI-MENTO

VIA COLA

VIA CRES.

VATICAN MUSEUM

PAPAL APT.

ITAL. POST

BORGO PIO

TO CASTEL SANT' ANGELO

VIALE

GARDENS

SISTINE CHAPEL

PED. ZONE

+ BUS #40→

VIA CORRIDORI

VIA CONCILIAZIONE

RADIO VAT.

ST. PETER'S

OBELISK

AUDIENCE HALL →

WALL

PORTA CAV.

PIAZZA S. PIETRO

BUS #64

VIP

TUNNEL

0 YDS 100 200
0 M 100 200

Ⓣ - TAXI STAND
Ⓜ - SUBWAY STOP
Ⓑ - BUS STOP

❶ Entrance to Vatican Museum
❷ Tourist Info, Post Office, & W.C.

DCH

▲▲▲**Vatican Museum (Musei Vaticani)**—The four miles of displays in this immense museum—from ancient statues to Christian frescoes to modern paintings—culminate in the Raphael Rooms and Michelangelo's glorious Sistine Chapel. Modest dress is required (no short shorts or skirts, no bare shoulders for men, women, or kids).

Cost and Hours: €12, March–Oct Mon–Fri 8:45–16:45, Sat 8:45–13:45; Nov–Feb Mon–Sat 8:45–13:45; closed Sun except last Sun of the month (when it's free, crowded, and open 8:45–13:45). Last entry is about 90 minutes before closing time. Guided two-hour tours in English are offered daily at 10:30, 12:00, and 14:00 for €10 plus museum admission (call 06-6988-4676 to reserve).

Hours are subject to constant change and frequent holidays; check www.vatican.va for current times. ✪ See Vatican Museum Tour on page 174.

▲▲▲**St. Peter's Basilica (Basilica San Pietro)**—There is no doubt: This is the richest and grandest church on earth. To call it vast is like calling God smart. The church strictly enforces its dress code. Dress modestly—a not-too-short dress or long pants, with shoulders covered (men, women, and children).

Hours: Daily April–Sept 7:00–19:00, Oct–March 7:00–18:00. The church often closes on Wednesday mornings during papal audiences. Masses occur throughout the day (see schedule on page 201); my favorite Mass—with compelling music—is in the late afternoon, when the church is less crowded (Mon–Sat at 17:00, Sun at 17:30). The view from the dome is worth the climb (€6 elevator plus 323-step climb, allow an hour to go up and down, daily April–Sept 8:00–17:45, Oct–March 8:00–16:45). Free tours in English are offered weekdays at 14:15 (and often also at 15:00); meet at the TI outside the basilica's entrance. The best time to visit the church is early or late. ✪ See St. Peter's Basilica Tour on page 201.

▲**Castel Sant'Angelo**—Built as a tomb for the emperor; used through the Middle Ages as a castle, prison, and place of last refuge for popes under attack; and today, a museum, this giant pile of ancient bricks is packed with history (€5, Tue–Sun 9:00–20:00, closed Mon, audioguide-€4, near Vatican City, Metro: Lepanto or bus #64, tel. 06-3996-7600).

Ancient Rome allowed no tombs within its walls—not even the emperor's. So Emperor Hadrian grabbed the most commanding position just outside the walls and across the river and built a towering tomb (circa A.D. 139) well within view of the city. His mausoleum was a huge cylinder (210 by 70 feet) topped by a cypress grove and crowned by a huge statue of Hadrian himself riding a chariot. For nearly a hundred years, Roman emperors (from Hadrian to Caracalla, in A.D. 217) were buried here.

In the year 590, the Archangel Michael appeared above the mausoleum to Pope Gregory the Great. Sheathing his sword, the angel signaled the end of a plague. The fortress that was Hadrian's mausoleum eventually became a fortified palace, renamed for the "holy angel."

Castel Sant'Angelo spent centuries of the Dark Ages as a fortress and prison, but was eventually connected to the Vatican via an elevated corridor at the pope's request (1277). Since Rome was repeatedly plundered by invaders, Castel Sant'Angelo was a handy place of last refuge for threatened popes. In anticipation of long sieges, rooms were decorated with papal splendor (you'll see paintings by Carlo Crivelli, Luca Signorelli, and Andrea Mantegna). In 1527, during a sack of Rome by troops of Charles V of Spain, the pope lived inside the castle for months with his entourage of hundreds (an unimaginable ordeal, considering the food service at the top-floor bar).

Touring the place is a stair-stepping workout. After you walk around the entire base of the castle, take the small staircase down to the original Roman floor (following the route of the Hadrian's funeral procession). In the atrium, study the model of the mausoleum as it was in Roman times. Imagine being surrounded by a veneer of marble, and the niche in the wall filled with a towering "welcome to my tomb" statue of Hadrian. From here, a ramp leads to the right, spiraling 400 feet. While some of the fine original brickwork and bits of mosaic survive, the marble veneer is long gone (notice the holes in the wall that held it in place). At the end of the ramp, a bridge crosses over the room where the ashes of the emperors were kept. From here, the stairs continue out of the ancient section and into the medieval structure (built atop the mausoleum) that housed the papal apartments. Don't miss the Sala del Tesoro (Treasury), where the wealth of the Vatican was locked up in a huge chest. (*Do* miss the 58 rooms of the military museum.) From the pope's piggy bank, a narrow flight of stairs leads to the rooftop and perhaps the finest Rome view anywhere (pick out landmarks as you stroll around). From the safety of this dramatic vantage point, the pope surveyed the city in times of siege. Look down at the bend of the Tiber, which for 2,700 years has cradled the Eternal City.

Ponte Sant'Angelo—The bridge leading to Castel Sant'Angelo was built by Hadrian for quick and regal access from downtown to his tomb. The three middle arches are actually Roman originals, and a fine example of the empire's engineering expertise. The statues of angels (each bearing a symbol of the passion of Christ—nail, sponge, shroud, and so on) are Bernini-designed and textbook Baroque. In the Middle Ages, this was the only bridge in the area

that connected St. Peter's and the Vatican with downtown Rome. Nearly all pilgrims passed this bridge to and from the church. Its shoulder-high banisters recall a tragedy: During a Jubilee Year festival in 1450, the crowd got so huge that the mob pushed out the original banisters, causing nearly 200 to fall to their deaths.

Today, as through the ages, pilgrims still cross the bridge, turn left, and set their sights on the Vatican dome. Around the year 1600, they would have also set their sights on a bunch of heads hanging from the crenellations of the castle. Ponte Sant'Angelo was infamous as a place for beheadings (banditry in the countryside was rife). Locals said, "There are more heads at Castel Sant'Angelo than there are melons in the market."

Southwest Rome: Trastevere

Trastevere is the colorful neighborhood across *(tras)* the Tiber *(Tevere)* River. Trastevere (trahs-TAY-veh-ray) offers the best look at medieval-village Rome. The action unwinds to the chime of the church bells. Go there and wander. Wonder. Be a poet. This is Rome's Left Bank. For a self-guided tour, see my Trastevere Walk (page 77).

This proud neighborhood was long a working-class area. Now that it's becoming trendy, high rents are driving out the source of so much color. Still, it's a great people scene, especially at night. Stroll the back streets (for restaurant recommendations, see page 264).

To reach Trastevere by foot from Capitol Hill, cross the Tiber on Ponte Cestio (over Isola Tiberina). You can also take tram #8 from Largo Argentina, or bus #H from Termini train station and Via Nazionale (get off at Piazza Belli). From the Vatican (Piazza Risorgimento), it's bus #23 or #271.

Linking Trastevere with the Night Walk Across Rome: You can walk from Trastevere to Campo de' Fiori to link up with the beginning of the Night Walk Across Rome (page 69): From Trastevere's church square (Piazza di Santa Maria), take Via del Moro to the river and cross at Ponte Sisto, a pedestrian bridge that has a good view of St. Peter's dome. Continue straight ahead for one block. Take the first left, which leads down Via di Capo di Ferro through the scary and narrow darkness to Piazza Farnese, with the imposing Palazzo Farnese. Michelangelo contributed to the facade of this palace, now the French Embassy. The fountains on the square feature huge, one-piece granite hot tubs from the ancient Roman Baths of Caracalla. One block from there (opposite the palace) is the atmospheric square of Campo de' Fiori.

▲**Sta. Maria in Trastevere Church**—One of Rome's oldest churches, this was made a basilica in the fourth century, when Christianity was legalized (free, daily 9:00–17:30). It was the first church dedicated to the Virgin Mary. The portico (covered area just outside the door) is decorated with fascinating ancient fragments filled with early Christian symbolism (for details, see page 65). The church is on Piazza di Santa Maria. While today's fountain is from the 17th century, there has been a fountain here since Roman times.

▲**Villa Farnesina**—This sumptuous 16th-century Renaissance villa, built for a wealthy Sienese banker, is decorated with paintings by Baldassare Peruzzi and a lovesick Raphael (€5, Tue–Fri 9:00–13:00, Mon and Sat 9:00–16:00, closed Sun, Via della Lungara; for more information, see page 84).

Gianicolo Hill Viewpoint—From this park atop a hill, the city views are superb, and the walk to the top holds a treat for architects. Start at Trastevere's Piazza di San Cosimato, and follow Via Luciano Manara to Via Garibaldi, at the base of the hill. Via Garibaldi winds its way up the side of the hill to the church of San Pietro in Montorio. To the right of the church, in a small courtyard, is the **Tempietto** by Donato Bramante. This tiny church, built to commemorate the martyrdom of St. Peter, is considered a jewel of Italian Renaissance architecture.

Continuing up the hill, Via Garibaldi connects to Passeggiata del Gianicolo. From here, you'll find a pleasant park with panoramic city views. Ponder the many Victorian-era statues, including that of baby-carrying, gun-wielding, horse-riding Anita Garibaldi. She was the Brazilian wife of the revolutionary General Giuseppe Garibaldi, who helped forge a united Italy in the late 19th century.

Near Trastevere: Jewish Quarter

From the 16th through the 19th centuries, Rome's Jewish population was forced to live in a cramped ghetto at an often-flooded bend of the Tiber River. While the medieval Jewish ghetto is long gone, this area—just across the river and towards Capitol Hill from Trastevere—is still home to Rome's synagogue and fragments of its Jewish heritage. ❂ For more, see the Jewish Ghetto Walk on page 87.

Synagogue (Sinagoga) and Jewish Museum (Museo Ebraico)— Rome's modern synagogue stands proudly on the spot where the medieval Jewish community lived in squalor for more than 300 years. The site of a historic visit by Pope John Paul II, this synagogue features a fine interior and a simple museum filled with artifacts of Rome's Jewish community (€8 ticket includes synagogue and museum; May–Sept Mon–Thu 9:00–20:00, Fri 9:00–14:00, Sun 9:00–12:30, closed Sat; Oct–April Mon–Thu 9:00–17:00, Fri 9:00–14:00, Sun 9:00–12:30, closed Sat; on the riverbank road called Lungotevere dei Cenci near the bridge crossing Isola Tiberina, tel. 06-6840-0661).

South Rome

▲**St. Paul's Outside the Walls (Basilica San Paolo Fuori le Mura)**—This was the last major construction project of Imperial Rome (c. 380) and the largest church in Christendom until St. Peter's. After a tragic 19th-century fire, St. Paul's was rebuilt in the same general style and size as the original. Step inside and feel as close as you'll get in the 21st century to experiencing a monumental Roman basilica. Marvel at the ceiling, and imagine building it with those massive wood beams in A.D. 380.

It feels sterile, but in a good way—like you're already in heaven.

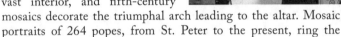

Along with St. Peter's Basilica, San Giovanni in Laterano, and Santa Maria Maggiore, this church is part of the Vatican rather than Italy. St. Paul is supposed to be buried under the altar (without his head, which San Giovanni in Laterano has).

Alabaster windows light the vast interior, and fifth-century mosaics decorate the triumphal arch leading to the altar. Mosaic portraits of 264 popes, from St. Peter to the present, ring the

place—with blank spots ready for future popes (pope #265—Benedict XVI—should show up here any day now). Find John Paul II (to right of the high altar: *Jo Paulus II*) and John Paul I (to his right, with a reign of one month and three days). The church was built upon the grave of the apostle Paul (who was decapitated 2 miles from this spot). Wander the ornate yet peaceful cloister—decorated with fragments from early Christian tombs and sarcophagi of people who wanted to be buried close to Paul (cloister closed 13:00–15:00).

The courtyard leading up to the church is typical of early Christian churches—even the first St. Peter's had this kind of welcoming zone (free, daily 7:00–18:00, modest dress code enforced, Via Ostiense 186, Metro: San Paolo).

▲Montemartini Museum (Musei Capitolini Centrale Monte-martini)—This museum houses a dreamy collection of 400 ancient statues, set evocatively in a classic 1932 electric power plant, among generators and *Metropolis*-type cast-iron machinery. While the art is not as famous as the collections you'll see downtown, the effect is fun and memorable—and you'll encounter absolutely no tourists (€4.20, €9.90 combo-ticket includes Capitol Hill Museum, Tue–Sun 9:30–19:00, closed Mon, Via Ostiense 106, a short walk from Metro: Garbatella, tel. 06-3996-7800, www.museicapitolini.org).

Baths of Caracalla (Terme di Caracalla)—Inaugurated by Emperor Caracalla in A.D. 216, this massive bath complex could accommodate 1,600 visitors at a time. Today it's just a shell—a huge

South Rome

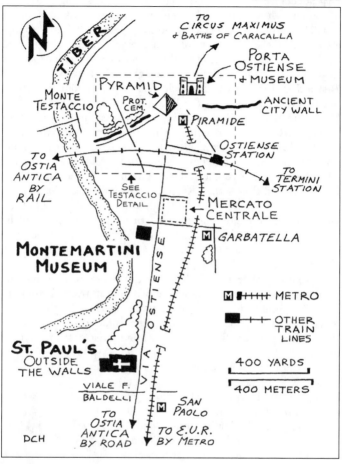

shell—with all of its sculptures and most of its mosaics moved to museums. You'll see a two-story, roofless brick building surrounded by a garden, bordered by ruined walls. The two large rooms at either end of the building were used for exercise. In between the exercise rooms was a pool flanked by two small mosaic-floored dressing rooms. Niches in the walls once held statues.

In its day, this was a remarkable place to hang out. For ancient Romans, bathing was a social experience. The Baths of Caracalla functioned until Goths severed the aqueducts in the sixth century. In modern times, grand operas were performed here from 1938 to 1993. To keep the ruins from becoming more ruined, the performances were discontinued (€5, covered by €20 Archeologia Card, Mon 9:00–14:00, Tue–Sun 9:00–19:30, audioguide-€4, good

€8 guidebook can be read in shaded garden while sitting on a chunk of column, Metro: Circus Maximus, plus a 5-min walk south along Via delle Terme di Caracalla, tel. 06-3996-7700). The baths' statues are displayed elsewhere: several are in Rome's Octagonal Hall, and the immense *Toro Farnese* (a marble sculpture of a bull surrounded by people) snorts in Naples' Archaeological Museum.

Testaccio—In the gritty Testaccio neighborhood, four fascinating but lesser sights cluster at the Piramide Metro stop between the Colosseum and E.U.R. (This is a quick and easy stop as you return from E.U.R. or when changing trains en route to Ostia Antica.)

Working-class since ancient times, the Testaccio neighborhood has recently gone trendy-bohemian. Visitors wander through an awkward mix of yuppie and proletarian worlds, not noticing—but perhaps feeling—the "Keep Testaccio for the Testaccians" graffiti. This has long been the neighborhood of slaughterhouses, and its restaurants are renowned for their ability to cook up the least palatable part of the animals...the fifth quarter. For a meal you won't forget, try **Trattoria "Da Oio" a Casa Mia** (closed Sun, Via Galvani 43, tel. 06-578-2680).

High-end shoe and clothing boutiques are moving into the neighborhood, and this is now one of the best areas in Rome to have shoes custom-made. The Testaccio market (in the center) is hands-down the best, most authentic outdoor food market in Rome. This is where Romans shop while tourists flock to Campo de' Fiori.

Pyramid of Gaius Cestius: The Mark Antony/Cleopatra scandal (c. 30 B.C.) brought exotic Egyptian styles into vogue. A rich Roman magistrate, Gaius Cestius, had this pyramid built as his tomb. Made of brick covered in marble, it was completed in just 330 days (as stated in its Latin inscription) and fell far short of Egyptian pyramid standards. It was later incorporated into the Aurelian Wall, and it now stands as a marker to the entrance of Testaccio (next to the Piramide Metro stop).

Porta Ostiense: This formidable gate (also next to Piramide Metro stop) is from the Aurelian Wall, begun in the third century under Emperor Aurelius. The wall, which encircled the city, was 12 miles long and 26 feet high, with 14 main gates and 380 72-foot-tall towers. Most of what you'll see today is circa A.D. 400, but the barbarians reconstructed the gate later, in the sixth century. If you climb up (enter nearest the pyramid), you can enjoy a free ramble along the ramparts and exhibits and models of Ostia Antica (Rome's ancient port; see page 293) and the Ostian Way.

Testaccio

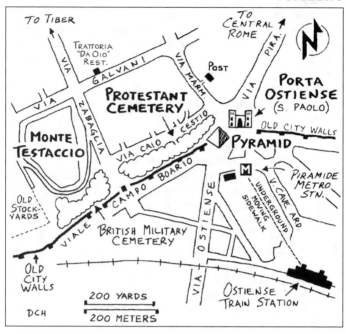

(For more on the wall, visit the Museum of the Walls at Porta San Sebastian; see "Ancient Appian Way," below.)

Protestant Cemetery: The Cemetery for the Burial of Non-Catholic Foreigners (Cimitero Acattolico per gli Stranieri al Testaccio) is a tomb-filled park, running along the wall just beyond the pyramid. The cemetery is also the only English-style landscape (rolling hills, calculated vistas) in Rome, and a favorite spot for quiet picnics and strolls. From the Piramide Metro stop, walk between the pyramid and the Roman gate on Via Persichetti, then go left on Caio Cestio to the gate of the cemetery. Ring the bell to get inside (donation box, Tue–Sat 9:00–18:00, Sun 9:00–14:00, closed Mon; closes an hour earlier in winter).

Originally, none of the Protestant epitaphs were allowed to make any mention of heaven. Signs direct visitors to the graves of notable non-Catholics who died in Rome since 1738. Many of the buried were diplomats. And many, such as the poets Shelley and Keats, were from the Romantic Age. They came on the Grand Tour and—"captivated by the fatal charms of Rome," as Shelley wrote—never left. Head left toward the pyramid to find Keats' tomb, in the far corner. Keats died in his twenties, unrecognized. He wanted to be unnamed on a tomb that read, "Young English Poet, 1821. Here lies one whose name was writ in water." (To see Keats' tomb if the cemetery is closed, look through the tiny peephole on Via Caio Cestio, 10 yards off Via Marmarata.)

From inside the cemetery (nearest the pyramid), look down on Matilde Talli's cat hospice (flier at the gate). Volunteers use donations to care for these "Guardians of the Departed" who "provide loyal companionship to these dead."

Notice the beige travertine post office from 1932 (across the big street from cemetery). This is textbook Mussolini-era fascist architecture. The huge X design on the stairwells celebrates the 10th anniversary of the dictator's reign.

Monte Testaccio: Just behind the Protestant Cemetery (as you leave, turn left and continue 2 blocks down Caio Cestio) is a 115-foot-tall ancient trash mountain. It's made of broken *testae*—earthenware jars used to haul mostly oil 2,000 years ago, when this was a gritty port warehouse district. For 500 years, rancid oil vessels were discarded here. Slowly, Rome's lowly eighth hill was built. Because the caves dug into the hill stay cool, trendy bars, clubs, and restaurants compete with gritty car-repair places for a spot. The neighborhood was once known for a huge slaughterhouse and a Gypsy camp that squatted inside an old military base. Now it's home to the Testaccio Village, a site for concerts and techno-raves. The night scene at Monte Testaccio after 21:00 is youthful and lively with restaurants and clubs (Metro: Piramide).

Ancient Appian Way (Via Appia Antica)

Since the fourth century B.C., this has been Rome's gateway to the East. The wonder of its day, the Appian Way (named after Appius Claudius Caecus, a Roman official) was the largest, widest, fastest road ever, called the "Queen of Roads." Eventually, this most important of Roman roads stretched 430 miles to the port of Brindisi—where boats sailed for Greece and Egypt. Twenty-nine such roads fanned out from Rome. Just as Hitler built the autobahn system in anticipation of empire maintenance, the emperors realized the military and political value of a good road system. A central strip accommodated animal-powered vehicles, and elevated sidewalks served pedestrians. The first section (near Rome) was perfectly straight, and lined with tombs and funerary monuments. Imagine a funeral procession passing under the pines and cypresses and past a long line of pyramids, private mini-temples, altars, and tombs.

Hollywood created the famous image of the Appian Way lined with the crucified bodies of Spartacus and his gang of slave rebels. This image is only partially accurate—Spartacus was killed in battle.

Today the road and the landscape around it are preserved as a cultural park, providing one of the best respites from the city for strolling or biking—especially on Sundays, when its active

Appian Way

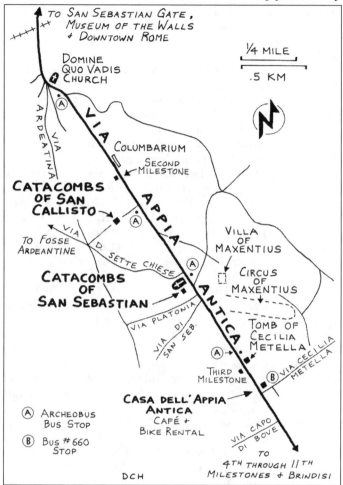

stretch, closest to the city, is closed to traffic and opened to people.

Tourist's Appian Way: The road starts less than two miles south of the Colosseum at the massive San Sebastian Gate. The **Museum of the Walls,** located at the gate, offers an interesting look at Roman defense and a chance to scramble along a stretch of the ramparts (€2.60, Tue–Sat 9:00–19:00, Sun 9:00–14:00, closed Mon, tel. 06-7047-5284). A mile and a half down the road are the two most historic and popular catacombs, those of San Callisto and San Sebastian, described below. (More intimate, less crowded, and at the other end of town—north of the Villa Borghese—are the **Catacombs of Priscilla;** see page 52.)

Besides the two main catacombs described below, the Appian Way offers additional catacombs, ruins, and tombs. As you head north on the Appian Way (from its intersection with Via Cecilia Metella) towards the Catacombs of San Sebastian, you can't miss on the right the massive cylindrical **Tomb of Cecilia Metella**, one of the best preserved of the many tombs of prominent Romans that line the road. Just past the tomb on the right are the ruins of the **Villa and Circus of Maxentius** (the emperor defeated by Constantine in A.D. 312). Farther along the Appian Way, past the Catacombs of San Sebastian and San Callisto, you'll see the **Church of Domine Quo Vadis**, built on the spot where Peter, while fleeing the city to escape Nero's persecution, saw a vision of Christ. It was here that Peter asked Jesus, "Lord, where are you going?" ("Domine quo vadis?" in Latin), to which Christ replied, "I am going to Rome to be crucified again." This miraculous sign gave Peter faith and courage and caused him to return to Rome. And just off the Appian Way on Via delle Sette Chiese is the evocative **Fosse Ardeantine**, a memorial tomb to 335 Italians gunned down by the Nazis as revenge for 32 German soldiers killed in a bomb attack in Rome during World War II.

Getting There: To reach the Appian Way, take the Archeobus from Rome's Termini train station (see "Tours," page 33) or take the Metro to the Colli Albani stop, then catch bus #660 to Via Appia Antica—its last stop and the start of an interesting stretch of the ancient road (the segment between the 3rd and 11th milestones is best). From the bus stop, you can walk to the right (north) for 15 minutes to the Catacombs of San Callisto, or head left (south) onto a stretch of the preserved road that stretches to the horizon. To get around faster, rent a bike.

Café and Bike Rental: At the Via Appia Antica bus stop is Casa dell'Appia Antica, where you can buy a light lunch or rent a bike (bike rental-€3/hr, Tue-Sun 10:00–18:00, closed Mon, at corner of Appian Way and Via Cecilia Metella, just beyond the tomb of Cecilia Metella at Via Appia Antica 175, mobile 338-3465-440). Biking on the Appian Way is a treat (best on Sundays).

▲▲**Catacombs**—The catacombs are burial places for (mostly) Christians who died in ancient Roman times. By law, no one was allowed to be buried within the walls of Rome. While pagan Romans were into cremation, Christians preferred to be buried. But land was expensive, and most Christians were poor. A few wealthy, landowning Christians allowed their property to be used as burial places.

The 40 or so known catacombs circle Rome about three miles from its center. From the first through the fifth centuries, Christians dug an estimated 375 miles of tomb-lined tunnels, with networks of galleries as many as five layers deep. The tufa stone—soft and easy to cut, but which hardened when exposed to air—was perfect for the job. The Christians burrowed many layers deep for two reasons: to get more mileage out of the donated land, and to be near martyrs and saints already buried there. Bodies were wrapped in linen (like Christ's). Since they figured the Second Coming was imminent, there was no interest in embalming the body.

When Emperor Constantine legalized Christianity in A.D. 313, Christians had a new, interesting problem: There would be no more persecuted martyrs to bind them together and inspire them. Instead, the early martyrs and popes assumed more importance, and Christians began making pilgrimages to their burial places in the catacombs.

In the 800s, when barbarian invaders started ransacking the tombs, Christians moved the relics of saints and martyrs to the safety of churches in the city center. For a thousand years, the catacombs were forgotten. Around 1850, they were excavated and became part of the Romantic Age's Grand Tour of Europe.

When abandoned plates and utensils from ritual meals were found, 18th- and 19th-century Romantics guessed that persecuted Christians hid out in these candlelit galleries. This legend grew—even though it was untrue. By the second century, nearly two million people lived in Rome, and the 10,000 early Christians no longer had to camp out in the catacombs. They hid in plain view, melting into obscurity within the city itself.

The underground tunnels, while empty of bones, are rich in early Christian symbolism, which functioned as a secret language. The dove represented the soul. You'll see it quenching its thirst (worshiping), with an olive branch (at rest), or happily perched (in

paradise). Peacocks, known for their "incorruptible flesh," embodied immortality. The shepherd with a lamb on his shoulders was the "good shepherd," the first portrayal of Christ as a kindly leader of his flock. The fish was used because the first letters of these words—"Jesus Christ, Son of God, Savior"—spelled "fish" in Greek. And the anchor is a cross in disguise. A second-century bishop had written on his tomb: "All who understand these things, pray for me." You'll see pictures of people praying with their hands raised up—the custom at the time.

Catacomb tours are essentially the same; which one you take is not important. The **Catacombs of San Callisto** (a.k.a. Callixtus), the official cemetery for the Christians of Rome and the burial place of third-century popes, is the most historic. Sixteen bishops (early popes) were buried here. Buy your €5 ticket and wait for your language to be called. They move lots of people quickly. If one group seems ridiculously large (more than 50 people), wait for the next tour in English (Thu–Tue 8:30–12:00 & 14:30–17:30, closed Wed and Feb, closes at 17:00 in winter, Via Appia Antica 110, tel. 06-5130-1580). Dig this: The catacombs have a Web site—www.catacombe.roma.it—that focuses mainly on San Callisto, featuring photos, site info, and a history.

The **Catacombs of San Sebastian** (Sebastiano) are 300 yards farther south down the road (€5, Mon–Sat 8:30–12:00 & 14:30–17:30, closed Sun and Nov, closes at 17:00 in winter, Via Appia Antica 136, tel. 06-785-0350).

E.U.R.

In the late 1930s, Italy's dictator, Benito Mussolini, planned an international exhibition to show off the wonders of his fascist society. But these wonders brought us World War II, and Il Duce's celebration never happened. The unfinished mega-project was completed in the 1950s, and today it houses government offices and big, obscure museums filled with important, rarely visited relics.

If Hitler and Mussolini won the war, our world might look like E.U.R. (AY-oor). Hike down E.U.R.'s wide, pedestrian-mean boulevards. Patriotic murals, aren't-you-proud-to-be-an-extreme-right-winger pillars, and stern squares decorate the soulless, planned grid and stark office blocks. Boulevards named for Astronomy, Electronics, Social Security, and Beethoven are more exhausting than inspirational. Today, E.U.R. is worth a trip for its Museum of Roman Civilization (described below). Because a few landmark buildings of Italian modernism are located here and there, E.U.R. has become an important destination for architecture buffs.

The Metro skirts E.U.R. with three stops (10 min from the Colosseum). Use E.U.R. Magliana for the "Square Colosseum" and E.U.R. Fermi for the Museum of Roman Civilization (both described below). Consider walking 30 minutes from the palace to the museum through the center of E.U.R.

From the Magliana subway stop, stairs lead uphill to the **Palace of the Civilization of Labor** (Palazzo della Civiltà del Lavoro), the essence of fascist architecture. With its giant, no-questions-asked, patriotic statues and its black-and-white simplicity, this is E.U.R.'s tallest building and key landmark. It's understandably nicknamed

E.U.R.

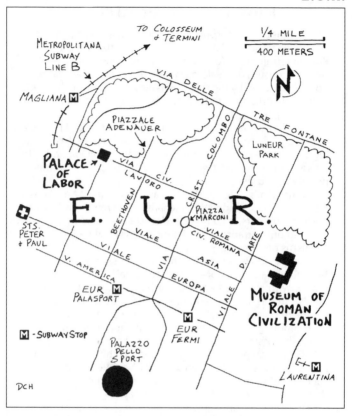

the "Square Colosseum." Around the corner, Café Palombini is still decorated in a 1930s style and is quite popular with young Romans (daily 7:00–24:00, good gelato, pastries, and snacks, Piazzale Adenauer 12, tel. 06-591-1700).

▲**Museum of Roman Civilization (Museo della Civiltà Romana)**—With 59 rooms of plaster casts and models illustrating the greatness of classical Rome, this vast and heavy museum gives a strangely lifeless, close-up look at Rome. Each room has a theme, from military tricks to musical instruments. One long hall is filled with casts of the reliefs of Trajan's Column. The highlight is the 1:250-scale model of Constantine's Rome, circa A.D. 300 (€6.20, Tue–Sun 9:00–14:00, closed Mon; Piazza G. Agnelli; leave the E.U.R. Fermi Metro station on Via America, turn right, and walk past McDonald's, then at T-intersection turn left and go uphill 3 blocks to Via dell'Arte, you'll see its colonnade on the right; tel. 06-592-6041).

Mussolini and Imperial Rome

Benito Mussolini incorporated much from ancient Rome during his dictatorship. His military was organized according to Roman terminology (divided into legions and run by centurions and consuls). The salute with the right arm raised, flat palm down (later used by the Nazis), was also Roman. More hygienic and quicker than a handshake, it fit the dynamic character of fascism.

While the classical values of power and discipline were stressed in the rhythmic march of military parades, convincing the Italians of the need for order was a challenge even to Mussolini. He claimed it wasn't impossible to govern the Italian people...just useless.

Mussolini's title, Il Duce, was from the Latin *dux*—a generic term for leader. When chanted by crowds and carved onto monuments, it likely fueled Mussolini's belief that he was carrying out extraordinary historical missions like Caesar and Augustus before him.

For his fascist symbol, rather than the she-wolf or eagle, Mussolini used the lictor's fasces (an ax belonging to a Roman officer, with rods tied around the handle, carried in front of magistrates as a sign of authority). This was aimed at destroying the popular image of Italy as a joyous, carefree country and for promoting a new image of austerity and order. In ancient times, the ax stood for decapitation, the rods for flogging.

Fascist architecture, like ancient architecture, used a monumental scale, with arches, bold statues, and rhetorical inscriptions—resulting in an austere and impersonal feel that's generally disliked by Romans today.

In spite of his supposed passion for ancient Rome, Mussolini had a dreadful approach to archaeology. He would isolate a major monument and destroy everything around it. Sections of the Imperial Forums were sacrificed to build the wide street, Via dei Fori Imperiali, from Piazza Venezia to the Colosseum. A famous fountain by the Colosseum that had survived almost 2,000 years was torn down without another thought.

Ostia Antica and Tivoli

For details on intriguing sights farther outside of Rome, see the chapters on day trips to Ostia Antica and Tivoli (Villa d'Este and Hadrian's Villa).

NIGHT WALK ACROSS ROME

From Campo de' Fiori to the Spanish Steps

Rome can be grueling. But a fine way to enjoy this historian's rite of passage is an evening walk that laces together Rome's floodlit night spots and fine urban spaces with real-life theater vignettes.

Sitting so close to a Bernini fountain that traffic noises evaporate; jostling with local teenagers to see all the gelato flavors; observing lovers straddling more than the bench; jaywalking past *polizia* in flak-proof vests; and marveling at the ramshackle elegance that softens this brutal city for those who were born here and can imagine living nowhere else—these are the flavors of Rome best tasted after dark.

THE WALK BEGINS

Campo de' Fiori

Start this mile-long walk at the Campo de' Fiori (Field of Flowers), my favorite outdoor dining room after dark (see the Eating chapter, page 256). Note: To lengthen this walk, start in Trastevere; see directions on page 56.

The center of the great, colorful square, Campo de' Fiori, is marked with the statue of Giordano Bruno (see sidebar on page 71), an intellectual heretic who was burned on this spot in 1600. Bruno overlooks a busy produce market in the morning and strollers after sundown. This neighborhood is still known for its free spirit and occasional demonstrations. When the statue of Bruno was erected in 1889, local riots overcame Vatican protests against honoring a heretic. Bruno faces his nemesis, the Vatican Chancellory (the big white building in the corner a bit to his right), while his pedestal reads: "And the flames rose up." Check out the reliefs on the pedestal for scenes from Bruno's trial and execution.

At the east end of the square (behind Bruno), the ramshackle

Night Walk Across Rome

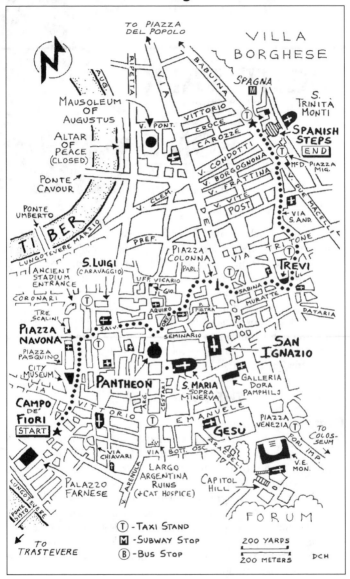

Giordano Bruno
(1548–1600)

Lauded as a martyr to free thought and reviled as an intellectual con-man and heretic, the philosopher/priest Bruno has a legacy only a Roman could love. Details of his life are sketchy, and his writings range from the sublime to the ridiculous.

The young Dominican priest was nonconformist and outspoken from the start. He had to flee Italy to avoid a charge of heresy, and spent most of his adult life wandering Europe's capitals. In Geneva, he joined the Calvinists, until he was driven out for his unorthodox views. In London, he met with Queen Elizabeth, who found him subversive. In Germany, the Lutherans excommunicated him.

In his writings, Bruno claimed to have discovered the "Clavis Magna" (Great Key) to training the human memory. He published satirical plays tweaking Church morals. He advanced the still-heretical (Copernican) notion that the earth revolved around the sun, and speculated about other inhabited planets in the universe. All his works show a vast-ranging mind that was aware of the scientific trends of the day.

In 1593, Bruno was arrested by the Inquisition and sent to Rome, where he languished in prison for six years. (Tortured? Lost in bureaucracy? No one knows.) The exact charge against him remains debated by historians.

Bruno was sentenced to death by fire. He replied: "Perhaps you who pronounce this sentence are more fearful than I who receive it." On February 17, 1600, the civil authorities led him to the stake on Campo de' Fiori. As they lit the fire, he was offered a crucifix to hold. He pushed it away.

apartments are built right into the old outer wall of ancient Rome's mammoth Theater of Pompey. This entertainment complex covered several city blocks, stretching from here to Largo Argentina. Julius Caesar was assassinated in the Theater of Pompey, where the Senate was renting space.

The square is lined with and surrounded by fun eateries. Bruno faces La Carbonara, the only real restaurant on the square. The Forno, next door to the left (7:30–20:00), is a popular place for hot and tasty take-out *pizza bianco* (pizza bread with cheese but no sauce). Step in to at least observe the frenzy as pizza is sold hot out of the oven. Order an *etto* (100 grams) by pointing, then take your snack to the counter to pay.

• *If Bruno did a hop, step, and jump forward, then turned right on Via dei Baullari and marched 200 yards, he'd cross the busy Corso Vittorio Emanuele and find...*

Piazza Navona

Rome's most interesting night scene features street music, artists, fire-eaters, local Casanovas, ice cream, fountains by Bernini, and outdoor cafés (worthy of a splurge if you've got time to sit and enjoy Italy's human river).

This oblong square retains the shape of the original racetrack that was built by the emperor Domitian. (To see the ruins of the original entrance, exit the square at the far—or north—end, then take an immediate left, and look down to the left 25 feet below the current street level.) Since ancient times, the square has been a center of Roman life. In the 1800s, the city would flood the square to cool off the neighborhood.

The **Four Rivers fountain** in the center is the most famous fountain by the man who remade Rome in Baroque style, Gian Lorenzo Bernini. Four burly river gods (representing the four continents that were known in 1650) support an Egyptian obelisk that

once stood on the ancient Appian Way. The water of the world gushes everywhere. The Nile has his head covered, since the headwaters were unknown then. The Ganges holds an oar. The Danube turns to admire the obelisk, which Bernini had moved here from a stadium on the Appian Way. And the Rio de la Plata from Uruguay tumbles backward in shock, wondering how he ever made the top four. Bernini enlivens the fountain with horses plunging through the rocks and exotic flora and fauna from these newly discovered lands. Homesick Texans may want to find the armadillo. (It's the big, weird armor-plated creature behind the Plata river statue.)

The Plata river god is gazing upward at the church of St. Agnes, worked on by Bernini's former student turned rival, Francesco Borromini. Borromini's concave facade helps reveal the dome and epitomizes the curved symmetry of Baroque. Tour guides say that Bernini designed his river god to look horrified at Borromini's work. Or he may be shielding his eyes from St. Agnes' nakedness, as she was stripped before being martyred. However, the fountain was completed two years before Borromini even started work on the church.

At the **Tre Scalini** café (near the fountain), sample some *tartufo* "death by chocolate" ice cream, world-famous among

connoisseurs of ice cream and chocolate alike (€4 to go, €8 at a table, open daily). Seriously admire a painting by a struggling artist. Request "Country Roads" from an Italian guitar player, and don't be surprised when he knows it. Listen to the white noise of gushing water and exuberant café-goers.

• *Leave Piazza Navona directly across from Tre Scalini café, go east past rose peddlers and palm readers, jog left around the guarded building, and follow the brown sign to the Pantheon. The Pantheon is straight down Via del Salvatore (cheap pizza place on left just before the Pantheon, WC at McDonald's).*

The Pantheon

Sit for a while under the floodlit and moonlit Pantheon's portico.

The 40-foot single-piece granite columns of the Pantheon's entrance show the scale the ancient Romans built on. The columns support a triangular, Greek-style roof with an inscription that says "M. Agrippa" built it. In fact, it was built *(fecit)* by Emperor Hadrian (A.D. 120), who gave credit to the builder of an earlier structure. This impressive entranceway gives no clue that the greatest wonder of the building is inside—-a domed room that inspired later domes, including Michelangelo's St. Peter's and Brunelleschi's Duomo (in Florence).

❂ For more information, see Pantheon Tour on page 127.

• *With your back to the Pantheon, veer to the right down Via Orfani.*

From the Pantheon to Piazza Colonna

On the right, you'll see **Tazza d'Oro Casa del Caffè**, one of Rome's top coffee shops, dating back to the days when this area was licensed to roast coffee beans. Locals come here for its fine *granita di caffè con panna* (coffee slush with cream). Look back at the fine view of the Pantheon from here. Then take Via Orfani uphill to Piazza Capranica.

Egyptian Obelisks

Rome has 13 obelisks, more than any other city in the world. In Egypt they were connected with the sun god Ra (like stone sun rays) and the power of the pharaohs. The ancient Romans, keen on exotic novelty and sheer size, brought the obelisks here and set them up in key public places as evidence and celebration of their occupation of Egypt. Starting from the 1580s, Rome's new rulers, the popes, relocated the obelisks, often topping them with Christian crosses so they came to acquire yet another significance that guaranteed their survival: the triumph of Christianity over all other religions.

The tallest (105 feet) and the most ancient (16th century B.C.) is the one by San Giovanni in Laterano. It once stood in the Circus Maximus next to its sister, which now marks the center of Piazza del Popolo.

The obelisks were carved out of single blocks of granite. Imagine the work, with only man- and horsepower, to first quarry them and set them up in Egypt, then—after the Romans came along—to roll them on logs to the river or the coast, sail (or row) them in special barges across the Mediterranean and up the Tiber, and finally hoist them up.

Rome wasn't above cheap imitations. A couple of the obelisks are ancient Roman copies. The one at the top of the Spanish Steps has spelling mistakes in the hieroglyphics.

Piazza Capranica is home to the big, plain, Florentine Renaissance-style Palazzo Capranica. Big shots, like the Capranica family, built stubby towers on their palaces—not for any military use, but just to show off. Leave the piazza to the right of the palace, between the palace and the church. The street Via in Aquiro leads to a sixth-century B.C. **Egyptian obelisk** (taken as a trophy by Augustus after his victory in Egypt over Mark Antony and Cleopatra). The obelisk was set up as a sundial. Walk the zodiac markings to the front door of the guarded parliament building. To your right is Piazza Colonna, where we're heading next—unless you like gelato...

A short detour to the left (past Albergo National) brings you to Rome's most famous *gelateria*. **Giolitti's** is cheap for take-out or elegant and splurge-worthy for a sit among classy locals (open daily until very late, Via Uffici del Vicario 40); get your gelato in a cone *(cono)* or cup *(coppetta)*.

Piazza Colonna features a huge second-century column honoring Marcus Aurelius. The big, important-looking palace houses the headquarters for the deputies (or cabinet) of the prime minister. The **Via del Corso** is named for the Berber horse races—without

riders—that took place here during Carnevale until the 1800s when a horse trampled a man to death in front of a horrified queen. Historically the street was filled with meat shops. When it became Rome's first gaslit street in the 1800s, these butcher shops were banned and replaced by classier boutiques, jewelers, and antique dealers. Nowadays most of Via del Corso is closed to traffic every evening and becomes a wonderful parade of Romans out for a stroll (see "Dolce Vita Stroll" on page 284 in Nightlife chapter).

• *Cross Via del Corso, Rome's noisy main drag, continue through the Y-shaped shopping gallery from 1928, forking to the right, and head down Via dei Sabini to the roar of the water, light, and people of the Trevi Fountain.*

The Trevi Fountain

The Trevi Fountain shows how Rome took full advantage of the abundance of water brought into the city by its great aqueducts. This watery Baroque avalanche was completed in 1762 by Nicola Salvi, hired by a pope who was celebrating the reopening of the ancient aqueduct that powers it. Salvi used the palace behind the fountain as a theatrical backdrop for the figure of "Ocean," who represents water in every form. The statue surfs through his wet

kingdom—with water gushing from 24 spouts and tumbling over 30 different kinds of plants—while Triton blows his conch shell. (From here, the water goes underground, then bubbles up again at Bernini's Four Rivers Fountain in Piazza Navona.)

The magic of the square is enhanced by the fact that no streets directly approach it. You can hear the excitement as you approach, and then—bam—you're there. The scene is always lively, with lucky Romeos clutching dates while unlucky ones clutch beers. Romantics toss a coin over their shoulder, thinking it will give them a wish and assure their return to Rome. That may sound silly, but every year I go through this touristic ritual...and it actually seems to work.

Take some time to people-watch (whisper a few breathy *bellos* or *bellas*) before leaving.

• *Face the fountain, then go past it on the right down Via delle Stamperia to Via del Triton. Cross the busy street and continue to the Spanish Steps (ask, "Dov'è Piazza di Spagna?"—Spagna rhymes with "lasagna"), a few blocks and thousands of dollars of shopping opportunities away.*

Spanish Steps (Piazza di Spagna)

The Piazza di Spagna, with the very popular Spanish Steps, is named for the Spanish Embassy to the Vatican, which has been here for 300 years. It's been the hangout of many Romantics over the years (Keats, Wagner, Openshaw, Goethe, and others). The British poet John Keats pondered his mortality, then died in the pink building on the right side of the steps. Fellow Romantic Lord Byron lived across the square at #66.

The Sinking Boat Fountain at the foot of the steps, built by Bernini or his father, Pietro, is powered by an aqueduct. All of Rome's fountains are aqueduct-powered; their spurts are determined by the water pressure provided by the various aqueducts. This one, for instance, is much weaker than Trevi's gush.

The piazza is a thriving night scene. Window-shop along Via Condotti, which stretches away from the steps. This is where Gucci and other big names cater to the trendsetting jet set. Facing the Spanish Steps, you can walk right about a block to tour one of the world's biggest and most lavish McDonald's (salad bar, WC). There's a taxi stand in the courtyard outside McDonald's; or, if you'd prefer, the Spagna Metro stop (usually open until 23:30) is just to the left of the Spanish Steps, ready to zip you home.

TRASTEVERE WALK

From the Tiber to Villa Farnesina

Trastevere—the colorful neighborhood across the river from downtown—is *the* place to immerse yourself in the crustier side of Rome. This half-mile walk, which at a slow stroll takes 30 minutes, is designed to train your eye to see Rome more intimately. You'll discover a secret, hidden city of heroic young martyrs, lovers kissing on Vespas, party-loving Renaissance bankers, and feisty "Trasteverini"—old-timers who pride themselves on never setting foot on the opposite bank of the Tiber River.

ORIENTATION

Getting There: Trastevere (trahs-TAY-veh-ray) is on the west side of the Tiber River, south of Vatican City and across the river from the Forum and Capitol Hill area. To get there by foot from Capitol Hill, cross the Tiber on Ponte Cestio (which goes over Isola Tiberina). You can also reach it on tram #8 from Largo Argentina or express bus #H from the Termini train station and Via Nazionale; for either of these get off at Piazza Belli, just after crossing the Tiber. From the Vatican (Piazza Risorgimento), take bus #23 or #271.

Church of St. Cecilia: Free, daily 9:30–12:30 & 16:00–18:30; crypt-€2.50; loft with frescoes-€2, Mon–Sat 10:15–12:15, Sun 11:15–12:15, ask the nuns to open the door.

Church of St. Maria in Trastevere: Free, daily 9:00–17:30.

Villa Farnesina: €5, Tue–Fri 9:00–13:00, Mon and Sat 9:00–16:00, closed Sun, tel. 06-6802-7268.

Orto Botanico: Tue–Sat 9:30–18:30, closed Sun–Mon and Aug.

THE WALK BEGINS

• *Start halfway across the Ponte Cestio (Cestius Bridge), the bridge connecting Isola Tiberina (Island in the Tiber) to Trastevere.*

Isola Tiberina and the Tiber River

Rome got its start 3,000 years ago along the Tiber River at this point, which was as far as big boats could sail inland and the first place the river could be crossed by bridge. As a center of river trade, Rome was connected with both the center of the Italian peninsula and the Mediterranean. The area below you would have been bustling in ancient times. Look down and imagine small ports, water mills, ramshackle boats, and platforms for fishing.

The island itself was once the site of a temple dedicated to Aesclepius, the god of medicine. Ancient Romans who were ill spent the night here and left little statues of their healed body parts (feet, livers, hearts...) as thank-you notes. This tradition survives: Today, throughout Italy, Catholic altars are often encrusted with votive offerings, symbolizing gratitude for answered prayers. During plagues and epidemics, the sick were isolated on the island. These days, the island's largest building is the Fatebenefratelli, the public hospital favored by Roman women for childbirth. The island's reputation for medical care lives on.

The high point of the bridge (upon which you're probably leaning) is an ancient stone with a faded inscription dating from about A.D. 370, when this then-400-year-old bridge was rebuilt. Run your fingers over the word "Caesar." It's stapled into the balustrade like a piece of recycled scrap.

This part of the Tiber river flooded frequently, which unfortunately made the land on the north bank the ideal location for the medieval Jewish ghetto (now long gone, but Rome's synagogue remains—see Jewish Ghetto Walk, next chapter).

In the 1870s, the Romans removed the threat of flooding by practically walling off the Tiber, building the tall, anonymous embankments that continue to isolate the river from the city today. There's been no loss. The river's heavy brown sediment makes it a poor trading artery, and these days, there are more modern, faster ways to transport goods.

• *Leave the bridge. If the green riverside Sora Mirella kiosk on the right is open, refresh yourself with the city's most famous grattachecca, crushed ice with fruit-flavored syrup and chopped fruit. Then cross the street and go down the steps into the car-filled piazza.*

Piazza in Piscinula

This square is famous for its church bell tower (the cute little thing directly across from the bridge); dating from 1069, it's the oldest

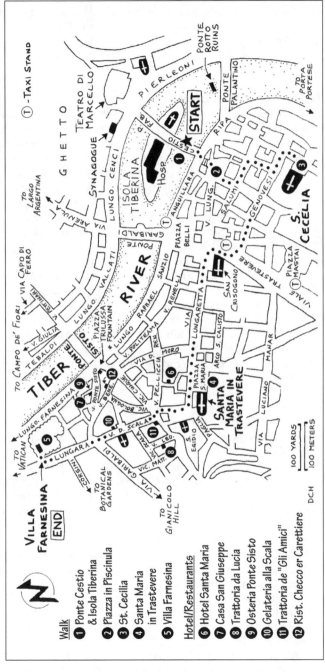

Trastevere Walk

Ⓣ -TAXI STAND

Walk
① Ponte Cestio & Isola Tiberina
② Piazza in Piscinula
③ St. Cecilia
④ Santa Maria in Trastevere
⑤ Villa Farnesina

Hotel/Restaurants
⑥ Hotel Santa Maria
⑦ Casa San Giuseppe
⑧ Trattoria da Lucia
⑨ Osteria Ponte Sisto
⑩ Gelateria alla Scala
⑪ Trattoria de "Gli Amici"
⑫ Rist. Checco er Carettiere

DCH

working one in the city. Study the brown building on the riverside and spot faint traces of Renaissance decoration. Today's earthtone shades of the city echo this original Roman brown.

• *Exit the square from the far corner, opposite where you entered, going uphill on Via dell'Arco dei Tolomei.*

Trastevere Back Lanes

Look up and directly ahead to see the stubby remains of a tower. In medieval times, the city skyline had 300 of these towers (about 50 survive). Each noble family competed for the tallest one until, in about 1250, city authorities got fed up and had them all lopped off. Later—mainly Baroque—construction incorporated most of the remaining "stumps," and you can still see these remnants of medieval Rome all over the old center. Incorporating old structures into new ones was always considered more economical and practical than demolishing and starting again from scratch. In the Middle Ages, Rome had regressed to being a big village; any idea of town planning was lost until the Renaissance.

Notice behind you the terrarium-like roof terrace—the Roman equivalent of a leafy backyard. An *attico con terrazzo* (penthouse with a terrace) is every Roman's dream.

Continue uphill, walking under the low arch. Lots of aristocratic buildings were connected by these elevated passages. Imagine herds of sheep shuffling through here in medieval times while smoke billowed from the windows and doors of poor homes that lacked chimneys.

Turn left and walk along Via dei Salumi (Cold Cuts Street). Because of its vicinity to the river, Trastevere was always a commercial neighborhood, and many of its alleys were named after businesses based here. The streets—rarely paved—were clogged by shop stalls.

The brownish building on your right (pretty ugly unless you're a fascist) is a school from the Mussolini era. The fascist leader believed in the classical motto *"mens sana in corpore sano"* (a healthy mind in a healthy body), and loved being seen fencing, boxing, swimming, and riding. He endowed school buildings with lots of gyms.

At the end of the school, turn right again, heading up Vicolo dell'Atleta. Check out the latest fashions in underwear hanging out to dry. Apartments in Rome tend to be quite small, and electricity is more expensive than in the United States, so few have dryers.

Strolling here, you'll understand why the Italian language has no word for "privacy" (they use our word and roll the r). Reading a letter on the Metro attracts a crowd. Young lovers with no place to go are adept at riding parked *motorini*.

All around, ancient fragments are recycled ingloriously into medieval buildings. Halfway down the alley on the right is a restaurant that, a thousand years ago, was a synagogue. Find the Hebrew faintly inscribed on the base of the columns. A large part of Rome's Jewish community, the most ancient outside of Palestine, lived in Trastevere until the popes moved them into the ghetto on the other side of the river in the 1500s.

• *Continue, turning left on Via dei Genovesi, then right on Via di Santa Cecilia to reach Piazza di Santa Cecilia. Enter the convent courtyard of the church, sit by the fountain, and take a moment to enjoy the peace and quiet.*

Church of St. Cecilia

Trastevere has many early Christian churches like St. Cecilia (daily 9:30–12:30 & 16:00–18:30), because in the second and third centuries, a large community of foreigners lived here, including early Christians from Greece and Judaea, who introduced their cultures and religions to the neighborhood.

Notice the church's eclectic exterior. Its mismatched columns were recycled from pagan temples. The typical medieval bell tower sports an 18th-century facade. This church, dedicated to Cecilia, patron saint of musicians and singers, is popular for weddings. Of Rome's 40 medieval churches, many have two-year waiting lists for weekend weddings. While most young Roman couples favor the more sober elegance of medieval churches over Baroque (usually dismissed as *troppo pesante*— too heavy), the typical wedding gowns here are far from understated.

Inside the church (in the case below the altar), find the statue of St. Cecilia by Stefano Maderno. A Christian convert from a wealthy family in a time of persecution, Cecilia revealed her faith to her pagan husband on their wedding night and told him of her aspiration to remain chaste (uh-oh...). An angel appeared to reason with the frustrated groom. Once converted, he devoted himself to carrying out Christian burials in the catacombs, until he himself was killed. Cecilia was soon condemned as well. The Romans, who tried unsuccessfully for three days to suffocate her with steam in her bath to make it appear accidental, finally lost patience and beheaded her. Cecilia bequeathed her house to the neighborhood community, and this spot has been a place of worship ever since.

In the days when Christianity was illegal, wealthy converts hosted Mass for the local community in their homes. When Christians were finally allowed to build churches, they often did so on the sites of these homes for the sake of continuity. While the Church of St. Cecilia originated in the third century, what we see today was built in the ninth century and extensively restored in the 18th century.

Viewing Maderno's statue of Cecilia, remember that during the Catholic Counter-Reformation, art charged with great emotional impact was used to enhance faith. The new appetite for relics led to a search for Cecilia's remains. When her tomb was opened, Maderno was present and claimed, along with other bystanders, to have seen her body perfectly preserved for an unforgettable instant before it turned to dust. He created this touching statue from his memory of that scene. Cecilia lies with her face turned and hidden, the violence of her death suggested only by the gash in her neck, her fingers indicating the oneness of the Trinity. (Like Italians today, she counted starting with her thumb.)

The canopy above the altar, dating from the 1200s, represents an innovative fusion of Roman and French Gothic architecture and sculpture, showing that the artist (Arnolfo di Cambio) knew his classics and had also been to Paris.

The mosaic in the apse dates from the ninth century. Pope Paschal (on the left), who built the church, holds a little model of it in his hands. His square halo signifies that he was alive when the mosaic was made. His small head suggests he was less important than the others in the scene.

Before leaving, you have two options: downstairs (the ancient remains of Cecilia's house) and upstairs (fancy frescoes). Cecilia's house in the basement is pretty bare, but it does have some early Christian iconography, original mosaic floors, and grain storage bins (follow sign to crypt, €2.50).

In the loft, from where cloistered nuns would view the Mass while hidden behind a screen, are some extraordinary frescoes of angels painted by Pietro Cavallini, a contemporary of Giotto (c. 1300). Scholars debate who influenced whom: Giotto or Cavallini. But there's no debate that the art here shows cutting-edge realism in the expressive faces of angels who sit believably in their chairs (€2, Mon–Sat 10:15–12:15, Sun 11:15–12:15; you'll need to ask the nuns to open the door).

• *Leaving the church, backtrack left, take the first left on Via de Genovesi, and hike straight ahead.*

Piazza Santa Maria in Trastevere

The wide, modern boulevard, Viale Trastevere, bisects Trastevere, which was otherwise spared most of the demolishing and rebuilding suffered by other traditional neighborhoods when Rome become the capital of united Italy in 1870. Crossing Viale Trastevere, you enter the neighborhood's affluent, bustling touristic part. Jog right, cut across the little square (passing under the yellow textbook Baroque facade of the church), and continue down Via dell'Ungaretta, which takes you straight to the next stop. You'll notice the change in atmosphere—the quiet, mystical charm of the first part of your walk has given way to livelier, more colorful surroundings. Look up. Now, along with underwear...you see art. Walk to the big square and sit down on the fountain steps.

You're in the heart of the neighborhood—Piazza Santa Maria in Trastevere, the thumbhole in this urban palette. Here you can easily imagine the Trasteverini of the past preparing for their legendary fights against the inhabitants of other districts (*Gangs of New York*-style).

Piazza Santa Maria is the neighborhood's most important meeting place. During important soccer games, a large screen is set up here so that everybody can share in the tension and excitement. At other times, children gather here with a ball and improvise matches of their own.

• *Dominating the square is...*

The Church of Santa Maria in Trastevere

One of Rome's oldest churches, this was built on the site where early Christians worshipped illegally. It was made a basilica—the first

church dedicated to the Virgin Mary—in the fourth century, when Christianity was legalized (free, daily 9:00–17:30). The portico (covered area just outside the door) is decorated with fascinating ancient fragments filled with early Christian symbolism.

Step inside and grab a pew. Most of what you see dates from around the 12th century, but the granite columns from ancient Roman buildings (notice the mismatched capitals, some with tiny pagan heads of Egyptian gods), and the ancient basilica floor plan (and ambience) survive. The intricate coffered ceiling has an unusual image of Mary painted on copper at the center. The striking 12th-century mosaics behind the altar are notable for their portrayal of Mary—the first to show her at the throne with Jesus in Heaven.

He has his arm around his mother, as if introducing her to us.

Below, the scenes from the life of Mary (mosaics by Cavallini, 1300s) pre-date the Renaissance by a hundred years. (Pop a coin in the box for light.) The first of six panels on the left shows the birth of Mary. A servant in the corner checks the temperature of the water with her hand

before she bathes the baby, introducing an element of tenderness that breaks the abstract rigidity of medieval art. The gold mosaic backgrounds show buildings that are unrealistic, but a good step toward accurate 3-D representation. The incredibly expensive 13th-century floor is a fine example of Cosmati mosaic work—a style of mosaic featuring intricate geometric shapes (in this case, made with marble scavenged from Roman ruins). From here, enjoy simply exploring Rome's most colorful district. Saunter around in the streets that are to the left of the church as you leave.

• *From Piazza Santa Maria in Trastevere, wander through the alleys to Via della Lungara, which leads to...*

Villa Farnesina

Here's a unique opportunity to see a Renaissance villa in Rome. This was built in the early 1500s for the richest man in Renaissance Europe, Sienese banker Agostino Chigi. Architect Baldassare Peruzzi's design—a U-shaped building with wings enfolding what used to be a vast garden—successfully blended architecture and nature in a way that both ancient and Renaissance Romans loved. Orchards and flowerbeds flowed down in terraces from the palace to the river banks. The construction of modern embankments and avenues robbed the garden of its grandeur, leaving it with a more melancholy charm.

Kings and popes of the day knew they wouldn't gain power without generous loans from Agostino Chigi, whose bank had more than 100 branches as far-flung as London and Cairo. This villa was the meeting place of all the aristocrats, artists, beautiful women, and philosophers of his day (€5, Tue–Fri 9:00–13:00, Mon and Sat 9:00–16:00, closed Sun).

In Room 1, the **Loggia of Galatea** features a ceiling painted by Peruzzi, representing the horoscope to show the exact moment of Agostino's birth (21:30, November 29, 1466).

The room's claim to fame is Raphael's painting of the nymph **Galatea** on the wall by the entrance door. She shuns the doting attention of the ungainly giant Polyphemus (not by Raphael) and rides away in the company of her rambunctious entourage on a chariot led by dolphins. Though her chariot speeds her to the right, she turns back and looks up, amused by the cyclops' crude love song (which, I believe, was "I Only Have Eye For You"). The trigger-happy cupids and lusty, entwined fauns and nymphs announce the pagan spirit revived in Renaissance Rome. All the painting's lines of sight (especially the cupids' arrows) point to the center of the work, Galatea's radiant face. Galatea is considered Raphael's vision of female perfection—not a portrait of an individual woman but a composite of his many lovers in an idealized vision.

In Room 2, the **Loggia of Psyche** was painted by Raphael and

his assistants. Imagine this room without the glass windows, as a continuation of the garden outside, where plays were performed to entertain Agostino's guests. Raphael's two frescoes were painted to look like tapestries (complete with ruffled edges), suspended from the ceiling by garlands, making the room appear to be an open bower. The frescoes show episodes in the myth of a lovely mortal woman, Psyche, who caught the eye of the young god Cupid (Eros). In one fresco, the gods of Olympus gather to plan a series of ordeals to test whether Psyche is worthy to marry a god. The other shows the happy ending, as Cupid and Psyche celebrate their wedding feast attended by the pantheon of gods.

The whole setting—the room by the gardens, the subject of the frescoes, the fleshy bodies—has an erotic subtext. At the time, Raphael was having a passionate affair with the celebrated Fornarina (the baker's daughter who lived down the street). Agostino, noticing that his painter was constantly interrupting his workday to be with her, had the girl kidnapped so that Raphael would finally concentrate. But production slowed even more, as Raphael was depressed. Agostino gave up and had the Fornarina move in with Raphael to keep him company as he happily resumed work in this cheery room. The room's imagery abounds with fun both phallic and yonic (the female counterpart of phallic). Next to the ripe and split-open cantaloupe, find the gourd wearing a condom.

The **Room of the Perspectives** (upstairs, accessed from the stairway near the entrance) was another trendsetter, painted by Peruzzi. Walls seem to open onto views and perspectives that actually correspond with what lies outside. The insulting-to-Catholics graffiti on the walls date from 1527, when Protestant mercenaries sent by Charles V sacked the city.

Agostino had his wedding banquet in this room. His parties were the talk of the town. On one occasion, he invited his guests in the (now lost) dining loggia overlooking the Tiber to toss the gold and silver dishes they had just used into the river. (Agostino had nets conveniently placed below the surface.)

The small chamber at the end of the Room of the Perspectives was the **bedroom.** The painting on the wall of the wedding of Alexander the Great and Roxanne was done by Il Sodoma, a devoted fan of Michelangelo and one of the artists who got canned when Raphael took over the decoration of the papal apartments at the Vatican. Had that not happened, the Raphael Rooms at the Vatican would have looked like this.

The bed in the painting actually reproduces the bed made of jewel-encrusted ebony that used to be here. Agostino had famous affairs with the most beautiful courtesans of his day until the pope told him to settle down and get married. Chigi settled down, but his wild-living descendants didn't, and the Chigi family lost its fabulous fortune in the space of a couple of generations.

• *Leaving Villa Farnesina, you have several options: take a cool and breezy break at the peaceful Orto Botanico garden (Tue–Sat 9:30–18:30, closed Sun–Mon and Aug, Largo Cristina di Svezia 24); walk up to Gianicolo Hill for a sweeping view of the city (see page 57); or find your way back to the river and Ponte Sisto, which will lead you to the Campo de' Fiori area (for directions from Ponte Sisto to Campo de' Fiori, see page 56).*

JEWISH GHETTO WALK

Across the River from Trastevere

For centuries, Rome's Jewish ghetto has been the site of both relentless persecution and the undying pride and solidarity of a tightly knit community. Built in the Middle Ages on the banks of a frequently flooded bend of the Tiber River, the ghetto was the forced home of the Roman Jewish population for more than 300 years between the Counter-Reformation (16th century) and Italian unification (19th century). Though most of the old ghetto has been torn down, you can still find a few reminders of the Roman Jews' storied past and lively present. If you want to visit the synagogue and museum, avoid this walk on a Saturday.

ORIENTATION

Getting There: The Jewish ghetto was—and Rome's main synagogue still is—on the east bank of the Tiber. It's located at the north end of the bridge that crosses Isola Tiberina (Island in the Tiber), and it's due west of the Forum and Capitol Hill.

Synagogue and Museum: €8 ticket includes both; May–Sept Mon–Thu 9:00–20:00, Fri 9:00–14:00, Sun 9:00–12:30, closed Sat; Oct–April Mon–Thu 9:00–17:00, Fri 9:00–14:00, Sun 9:00–12:30, closed Sat; on Lungotevere dei Cenci, tel. 06-6840-0661.

Local Guide: Micaela Pavoncello is uniquely equipped to guide visitors through the neighborhood that her family has lived in since ancient Roman times (€110/2 hrs, tel. 328-863-8128, www.jewishroma.com, info@jewishroma.com).

Jewish Ghetto Walk

1. Ponte Fabricio
2. Synagogue & Jewish Museum
3. Largo 16 Ottobre 1943
4. Portico d'Ottavia & Church of Sant'Angelo
5. Via del Portico d'Ottavia
6. Turtle Fountain
7. Jewish Bakery
8. Hotel Arenula

History

Today, of Italy's 35,000 Jews, nearly half call Rome home. Jews here have a uniquely Roman style of worship and even preserve remnants of their own Judaic-Roman dialect. That's because, unlike most of the world's Jewish people, Roman Jews are neither Sephardic (descended from Spain) nor Ashkenazi (descended from Eastern Europe). Italy's Jews came directly from the Holy Land, first arriving in Rome in the second century B.C. as esteemed envoys, and then, after Rome invaded Judea in the first century A.D., as POWs sold into slavery.

Julius Caesar favored the Jews because they were well-networked throughout the empire and they didn't push their religion on others. His successors, such as Titus, suppressed the Jews. As Christianity enveloped Rome and the pope became literally the king of Rome's Jews, the Jews continued to experience discrimination, with laws intended to limit the spread of Judaism (e.g., no proselytizing, new synagogues, or intermarriage). The severity of these laws varied from pope to pope. Through most of the Middle Ages, Rome's Jews prospered and were often held in high esteem as physicians, businessmen, and confidants of popes. The community in Trastevere was even allowed to spill across to the opposite bank of the Tiber.

Starting in the 13th century, anti-Semitism began increasing throughout Europe. Then, in 1492, all of Spain's Jews were either baptized or expelled, with similar decrees following in other European countries. Rome's Jewish population doubled, swelling with refugees. By the 1500s, the Catholic Counter-Reformation—begun to combat rising Protestantism—turned its attention to anything deemed a "heresy," including Judaism. In 1555, Pope Paul IV forcibly moved all of Rome's Jews into a ghetto (across the river from Trastevere) enclosing some 4,000 Jews inside, on a mere seven acres of land. There they lived—in cramped conditions, behind a wall, with a curfew—for three centuries. They could go out by day, but had to return before the gates were locked at night. Jews were forced to wear yellow scarves and caps and were prohibited from owning property or holding good jobs. During Carnivale (Mardi Gras), they were forced to parade down Via del Corso while Christians lined the streets and shouted insults. Through this long stretch of oppression, the synagogue was the only place Jews could feel respected and dignified. It's no wonder such loving attention was given to the Jewish tools of worship.

While Rome's Jews enjoyed a little freedom when Napoleon occupied the city (1805–1814) and after the walls were torn down in 1848, it was only after Italian unification in 1870 that the ghetto's inhabitants were granted full rights and citizenship.

Then came the rise of fascism. Even though Mussolini wasn't

rabidly anti-Semitic, he instituted a slew of anti-Jewish laws as he allied himself more strongly with Hitler. When Mussolini was deposed and the Nazis occupied Rome late in the war, the ghetto community was in even greater danger. Of the 13,000 ghetto-dwellers, 2,000 were sent off to concentration camps.

A measure of healing and reconciliation came with Pope John Paul II, who took a special interest in fostering relations with the Jewish community. It was the late pope who finally acknowledged that the Church should have intervened more forcefully to defend the Jews during the Holocaust. He was also the first pope in history to enter a synagogue (in this very neighborhood—see below). In his last letter, John Paul II thanked Rome's current Rabbi for allowing him to initiate this Catholic–Jewish rapprochement he felt was so long overdue.

THE WALK BEGINS

• *Start at the north end of Ponte Fabricio, which connects the Island in the Tiber and the neighborhood of Trastevere with central Rome (see "Getting There," above).*

Ponte Fabricio

Ponte Fabricio is nicknamed "Ponte Quattro Capi" (Bridge of the Four Heads) for its statues of the four-faced pagan god Janus. In ancient times, it was called "Strangers' Bridge" because foreigners, immigrants, and Jews—who weren't allowed to live in central Rome—would cross this bridge to get into town. Some 30,000 Jews lived in a thriving community in Trastevere. Look down at the river. The embankment was only built in the late 19th century. Before then, this was the worst flood zone of the Roman riverbank—just right for a ghetto.

• *With your back to the river, face the big, yellow...*

Synagogue (Sinagoga) and Jewish Museum (Museo Ebraico)

In the 16th century, when Pope Paul IV forced the Jews to reside within a walled ghetto, the center of its four-square-block area was this synagogue. When Italy became unified in 1870, the ghetto was essentially demolished, replaced with the modern blocks you see today.

The Jews were initially offered better real estate for their synagogue, but chose instead to rebuild here, on the original site. This new "Synagogue of Emancipation" was built in a remarkable three years (completed 1904) with the enthusiastic support of the entire Roman community. This is where Pope John Paul II came in 1986... the first pope in history to enter a synagogue.

In the Ghetto

The word "ghetto" is Italian, first used in Venice in the 1600s to describe the part of town where Jews lived—near the copper foundry ("ghetto" came from *gettare*, "to cast"). Initially the term meant only Jewish neighborhoods, but as the word spread through Europe and beyond, it was used generically to mean any neighborhood where a single ethnic group is segregated.

Follow his Holiness' footsteps and enter the synagogue. (The €8 entry price is steep, but it's the only way to view the interior.) Sit under the impressive dome (square to distinguish it from a Christian church). Ponder the inside of the dome, painted with the colors of the rainbow—symbolic of God's promise to Noah that there would be no more floods. The stars on the ceiling recall God's pledge that Abraham's descendants would flourish and be as many as the stars in the sky. As there were no Jewish architects and no models to study, this church-like synagogue is Art Nouveau with a dash of Tiffany. The sandy color tones are a reminder of the community's desert heritage.

The museum—in a humble room connected to the synagogue—shows off some historic artifacts. You'll see second-century B.C. reliefs with Jewish symbols, finely worked Judaica (religious items), and other relics of Jewish past. Note that Jewish historians don't use "B.C." (Before Christ) or "A.D." (Anno Domini), but rather "B.C.E." (Before the Common Era) and "C.E." (Common Era).

Back outside, notice the yellow church at the head of the Ponte Fabricio, called Santa Maria della Pietà (a.k.a. San Gregorio). When the ghetto was a walled-in town, Catholics built churches at each gate to try and spread their faith to the Jews. Notice the Hebrew script under the crucifix. It quotes the Jewish prophet Isaiah—"All day long, I have stretched out my hands to a disobedient and faithless nation" (Isaiah 65:2) —but misuses it to give it an anti-Semitic twist.

• *Walk behind the synagogue, to the square called...*

Largo 16 Ottobre 1943

This square is named for the day when Nazi trucks parked here and threatened to take the Jews to concentration camps unless the community came up with 110 pounds of gold in 24 hours. Everyone, including non-Jewish Romans, tossed in their precious gold, and the demand was met. The Nazis took the gold. And, shortly thereafter, they took the Jews anyway.

• *Just beyond the square is the...*

Portico d'Ottavia/Church of Sant'Angelo in Pescheria

The big Roman ruins—the Portico d'Ottavia—are the remains of a cultural center...kind of an ancient Rockefeller Center. Later, the columns became incorporated into the Church of Sant'Angelo in Pescheria (8th century). In the Middle Ages, the portico housed a thriving fish market. For centuries, this Christian church was packed every Saturday with Jews—forced by decree to attend Christian sermons.

From here (just before crossing the little bridge), look left down Via del Foro Piscario to contrast the early-20th-century buildings on the left and the last remaining string of 16th-century ghetto houses on the right. Behind you, the huge Roman ruins (now inhabited by a more modern building) is Teatro di Marcello. (Sophia Loren just bought a flat on its top floor.)

• Walk through the gate—as anyone would to enter the ghetto in centuries past—to reach the street called...

Via del Portico d'Ottavia

This main drag—the best preserved of the old streets—is a fine place to get a taste of yesterday's ghetto and today's Rome. This neighborhood has become trendy recently, and apartment prices are now beyond the means of most members of the Jewish community. Ironically, only the poorest Jews couldn't afford to relocate after 1870—and because they had to stay, their descendants have enjoyed healthy real-estate appreciation. Though the Jewish community has long since dispersed all over Rome, most Roman Jews continue to spend time in this neighborhood to enjoy the strong feeling of community that survives. You'll see the old ladies and men—sometimes even bringing their favorite chairs from home—just hanging out together on the corners, shooting the breeze.

Walking down the street, notice kosher restaurants proudly serving *carciofi* (artichokes, which only Jewish grandmothers can cook properly) and shops of fine, locally produced Judaica. The P.L.O. (Palestine Liberation Organization) attacked this area in 1982; you might notice that a police presence still lingers. At  #13, step into a condominium-ized former convent. Imagine the outrage of the Jewish community when the Church built a convent and a Catholic school here in the ghetto to preach to the Jewish children. Notice the gang hanging out and chatting on the corner of the big, modern Jewish school.

Take a right at Via della Reginella. At #28, notice where the six-floor buildings become more elegant and spacious three-floor buildings...marking the end of the ghetto. In the square at the end of the lane is a fun fountain—an old Mannerist work, later embellished with turtles by Bernini. It's said that Bernini cared about the Jews and honored them with the symbol of a turtle—an ancient creature that carries all its belongings on its back.

Back on the main drag, behind the yellow tweety bird, notice the ghetto-era charity box for orphans (still putting donations to good use). On the corner awaits the sweet finale of your ghetto tour: the Jewish bakery. Drop in to check out the cheesecakes, almond-paste-filled macaroons, and "Jewish Pizzas"—like little €2 fruitcakes (Sun–Fri 8:00–19:30, closed Sat).

COLOSSEUM TOUR

(Colosseo)

Rome has many layers—modern, Baroque, Renaissance, Christian. But let's face it: "Rome" is Caesars, gladiators, chariots, centurions, *"Et tu, Brute,"* trumpet fanfares, and thumbs-up or thumbs-down. That's the Rome we'll look at. Our "Caesar Shuffle" begins with the downtown core of ancient Rome, the Colosseum. A logical next stop is the Forum, just next door (and the next chapter), past the Arch of Constantine.

ORIENTATION

Cost: €10 (includes Palatine Hill and special exhibits; ticket valid all day, or—if purchased after 13:00—for 24 hours). The Colosseum is also covered by the €20 Archeologia Card (valid for 7 days, described on page 38).

Hours: Daily 9:00–19:00, or until an hour before sunset.

Getting There: The Colosseo Metro stop is just across the street from the monument.

Avoid Long Lines: The lines in front of the Colosseum are for buying tickets, not for actually entering the sight. (Once you have your ticket, you can muscle through this ticket-buying crowd and go directly to the turnstile, which never has a line.) Instead of waiting in the long Colosseum ticket line (sometimes as long as an hour), consider one of these alternatives:

1. Buy your ticket at either of the two rarely crowded Palatine Hill entrances near the Colosseum—there's one inside the Forum (near the Arch of Titus) and another on Via di San Gregorio (facing Forum entry, with Colosseum at your back, go left on street). This €10 ticket includes entry to both the Colosseum and Palatine Hill.

2. Consider buying the €20 Archeologia Card at a less-crowded sight. The card covers the Colosseum, Palatine Hill, National Museum of Rome, Museum of the Bath, Baths of Caracalla, and more. Buy it at any of the included sights.

3. You can book a tour on the spot. These tours include Colosseum entry, allowing you to skip the line. This will cost you a few extra euros (€15 for the tour, including the €10 Colosseum ticket), but can save time and comes with a brief guided tour. Beware: It can be hard for you to instantly judge the length of the line, because it's tucked into the Colosseum arcade. American students working for the guides might tell you that there's a long line, when sometimes there is none at all. Also note that you may buy a tour ticket, only to get stuck waiting for them to sell enough tickets to assemble a group.

Beware the Goofy Gladiators: For a fee, the incredibly crude modern-day gladiators snuff out their cigarettes and pose for photos. They take easy-to-swindle tourists for too much money. Watch out if you tangle with these guys (they're armed...and accustomed to getting as much as €100 from naive Asian tourists).

Pickpocket Alert: The Colosseum is traditionally a happy hunting-ground for gangs of children pickpockets who distract you with sheets of cardboard (or newspapers or magazines) as they steal your things.

Information: Outside the entrance of the Colosseum, vendors sell handy little *Rome: Past and Present* books with plastic overlays to un-ruin the ruins (marked €11, price soft). Tel. 06-3996-7700.

Tour: A dry but fact-filled audioguide is available at the ticket office (€4 for 2 hrs of use). Guided tours in English depart several times per day and last about one hour (€4).

Length of This Tour: Allow 45 minutes.

Services: A WC is behind the Colosseum (facing ticket entrance, go right; WC is under stairway).

Cuisine Art: For a quick lunch, climb the steps above the WC and cross the busy street to the cafés with expansive views of the Colosseum. However, for a better value (but no views at all), see the recommended restaurants on page 272.

THE TOUR BEGINS

Exterior

• *View the Colosseum from the Forum fence, across the street from the Colosseo subway station.*

Built when the Roman Empire was at its peak in A.D. 80, the Colosseum represents Rome at its grandest. The Flavian Amphitheater (its real name) was an arena for gladiator contests and public spectacles. When killing became a spectator sport, the Romans wanted to share the fun with as many people as possible, so they stuck two theaters together to create a freestanding amphitheater. The outside (where slender cypress trees stand today) was decorated with a 100-foot-tall bronze statue of Nero that gleamed in the sunlight. The final structure was colossal—a "coloss-eum," the wonder of its age. It could accommodate 50,000 roaring fans (100,000 thumbs).

The Romans pioneered the use of concrete and the rounded arch, which enabled them to build on this tremendous scale. The exterior is a skeleton of 3.5 million cubic feet of travertine stone. (Each of the pillars flanking the ground-level arches weighs 5 tons.) It took 200 ox-drawn wagons shuttling back and forth every day for four years just to bring the stone here from Tivoli. They stacked stone blocks (without mortar) into the shape of an arch, supported temporarily by wooden scaffolding. Finally, they wedged a keystone into the top of the arch—it not only kept the arch from falling, it could bear even more weight above. Iron pegs held the larger stones together—notice the small holes that pockmark the sides.

The exterior says a lot about the Romans. They were great engineers, not artists, and the building is more functional than beautiful. While the essential structure is Roman, the four-story facade is decorated with the three types of Greek columns—Doric (ground level), Ionic (second story), Corinthian, and, on the top, half-columns with a mix of all three. Originally, copies of  Greek statues stood in the arches of the middle two stories, giving a veneer of sophistication to this arena of death. If ancient Romans visited the United States today as tourists, they might send home postcards of our greatest works of "art"—freeways.

Only a third of the original Colosseum remains. Earthquakes destroyed some of it, but most was carted off as easy pre-cut stones for other buildings during the Middle Ages and Renaissance.

Colosseum

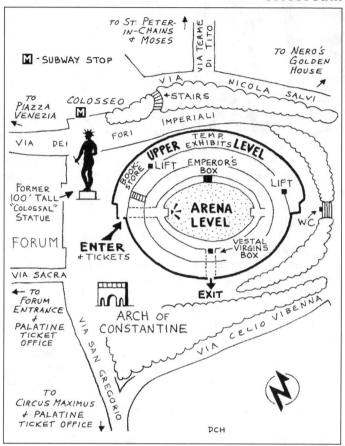

• *To enter, join the ticket line or—if you've already purchased a ticket elsewhere—bypass the line, head left up the passage for groups, and go directly to the turnstile. Once inside, find the Vestal Virgins' Box (see map above).*

Interior

You're at the "50-yard line" on arena level. What you see now are the underground passages beneath the playing surface. The oval-shaped arena (280 by 165 feet) was originally covered with boards, then sprinkled with sand (*arena* in Latin).

Like modern stadiums, the spectators ringed the playing area in bleacher seats that slant up from the arena floor. To build these bleachers, they made a shell of brick, then filled it in with concrete. The brick masses around you supported the first small tier of seats,

and you can see two larger, slanted supports higher up. Originally, the bare brick was faced with marble (lower stories) or plaster (cheap seats). A few marble seats have been restored (at the right end). The whole thing was topped with an enormous canvas awning that could be hoisted across by armies of sailors to provide shade for the spectators—the first domed stadium.

"Hail, Caesar! *(Ave, Cesare!)* We who are about to die salute you!" The gladiators would enter the arena from the left end, parade around to the sound of trumpets, acknowledge the Vestal Virgins (where you're standing), stop at the emperor's box (directly opposite), raise their weapons, shout, and salute—and the fights would begin. The fights pitted men against men, men against beasts, and beasts against beasts.

A walkway stretches across the arena, allowing you to contemplate the games from a gladiator's-eye view, right in the center of the action. Picture 50,000 screaming people around you (did gladiators get stage fright?), and imagine that they hate you and want to see you die. Find the shafts of little elevators near the center that brought you gnarly surprises like wild animals.

The games began with a few warm-up acts—watching dogs bloody themselves attacking porcupines, female gladiators fighting each other, or a dwarf battling a one-legged man. Then came the main event—the gladiators.

Some wielded swords, protected only with a shield and a heavy helmet. Others represented fighting fishermen, with a net to snare opponents and a trident to spear them. The gladiators were usually slaves, criminals, or poor people who got their chance for freedom, wealth, and fame in the ring. They learned to fight in training schools, then battled their way up the ranks. The best were rewarded like our modern sports stars, with fan clubs, great wealth, and, yes, product endorsements.

The animals came from all over the world: lions, tigers, and bears (oh my!), crocodiles, elephants, and hippos (not to mention exotic human "animals" from the "barbarian" lands). They were kept in cages beneath the arena floor, then lifted up in elevators. Released at floor level, the animals would pop

out from behind blinds into the arena—the gladiator didn't know where, when, or by what he'd be attacked. (This brought howls of laughter from the hardened fans in the cheap seats who had a better view of the action.) Nets ringed the arena to protect the crowd. The stadium was inaugurated with a 100-day festival in which 2,000 men and 9,000 animals were killed. Colosseum employees squirted perfumes around the stadium to mask the stench of blood.

If a gladiator fell helpless to the ground, his opponent would approach the emperor's box and ask: Should he live or die? Sometimes the emperor left the decision to the crowd, who would judge based on how valiantly the man had fought. They would make their decision—thumbs-up or thumbs-down. Consider the value of these games in placating and controlling the huge Roman populace. Seeing the king of beasts—a lion—slain by a gladiator reminded the masses of man's triumph of nature. Seeing exotic animals from Africa heralded their conquest of distant lands. And having the thumbs-up or down power over another person's life gave them a real sense of power. Imagine the psychological boost the otherwise downtrodden masses felt when the emperor granted them this thrilling decision.

Did they throw Christians to the lions like in the movies? Christians were definitely thrown to the lions, made to fight gladiators, crucified, and burned alive...but probably not here in this particular stadium. Maybe, but probably not.

Rome was a nation of warriors that built an empire by conquest. The battles fought against Germans, Egyptians, barbarians, and strange animals were played out daily here in the Colosseum for the benefit of city-slicker bureaucrats, who got vicarious thrills by watching brutes battle to the death. The contests were always free, sponsored by politicians to bribe the people's favor or to keep Rome's growing mass of unemployed rabble off the streets.

• *With these scenes in mind, wander around. Climb to the upper deck for a more colossal view. There are stairs near either long end, as well as an elevator in the east corner. On the upper level, there's a bookstore at the west corner and temporary exhibits at the northeast end.*

After you exit, head to the Arch of Constantine (between the Colosseum and Forum, at the west corner of the Colosseum).

Arch of Constantine

If you are a Christian, were raised a Christian, or simply belong to a so-called "Christian nation," ponder this arch. It marks one of the great turning points in history—the military coup that made Christianity mainstream. In A.D. 312, Emperor Constantine defeated his rival Maxentius in the crucial Battle of the Milvian Bridge. The night before, he had seen a vision of a cross in the sky. Constantine—whose mother and sister were Christians—

became sole emperor and legalized Christianity. With this one battle, a once-obscure Jewish sect with a handful of followers was now the state religion of the entire Western world. In A.D. 300, you could be killed for being a Christian; later, you could be killed for not being one. Church enrollment boomed.

This newly restored arch is like an ancient museum. By decorating it with exquisite carvings of high Roman art—works that glorified previous emperors—Constantine put himself in their league. Fourth-century Rome may have been in decline, but Constantine clung to its glorious past.

• *The Roman Forum (Foro Romano) is to the right of the arch, 100 yards away. If you're ready for a visit, see the next chapter.*

ROMAN FORUM TOUR

(Foro Romano)

The Forum was the political, religious, and commercial center of the city. Rome's most important temples and halls of justice were here. This was the place for religious processions, political demonstrations, elections, important speeches, and parades by conquering generals. As Rome's empire expanded, these few acres of land became the center of the civilized world.

ORIENTATION

Cost: Free. (There's a €10 charge to visit Palatine Hill, above the Forum; see next chapter.)

Hours: Daily 9:00–19:00, or an hour before sunset.

Tips: The ancient paving at the Forum is uneven; wear sturdy shoes. I carry a water bottle and refill it at the Forum's public drinking fountains.

Getting There: The closest Metro stop is Colosseo. The Forum's main entrance—where this tour begins—is near the Arch of Constantine and the Colosseum.

Information: Just like at the Colosseum, vendors at the Forum sell small *Rome: Past and Present* books with plastic overlays that restore the ruins (marked €11, offer less). Information office tel. 06-3996-7700.

Tour: A €4 dry but fact-filled audioguide helps decipher the rubble (rent at gift shop at entrance on Via dei Fori Imperiali). Guided tours in English are offered nearly hourly (€4); ask for information at the ticket booth at the Palatine Hill (near Arch of Titus).

Length of This Tour: Allow one hour.

THE TOUR BEGINS

Overview

• *Walk through the entrance nearest the Colosseum, hiking up the ramp marked Via Sacra. Stand next to the triumphal Arch of Titus (Arco di Tito) and look out over the rubble-littered valley called the Forum.*

The hill in the distance with the bell tower is Capitol Hill. Immediately to your left, with all the trees, is Palatine Hill. The valley in between is rectangular, running roughly east (the Colosseum end) to west (Capitol Hill end). The rocky path at your feet is the Via Sacra, which runs through the trees, past the large brick Senate building, and up Capitol Hill.

Picture being here when a conquering general returned to Rome with crates of booty. The valley was full of gleaming white buildings topped with bronze roofs. The Via Sacra—Main Street of the Forum—would be lined with citizens waving branches and carrying torches. The trumpets would sound as the parade began. First came porters, carrying chests full of gold and jewels. Then a parade of exotic animals from the conquered lands—elephants, giraffes, hippopotamuses—for the crowd to "ooh" and "ahh" at. Next came

the prisoners in chains, with the captive king on a wheeled platform so the people could jeer and spit at him. Finally, the conquering hero himself would drive down in his four-horse chariot, with rose petals strewn in his path. The whole procession would run the length of the Forum and up the face of Capitol Hill to the Temple of Saturn (the 8 big columns midway up the hill—#13 on map on page 103), where they'd place the booty in Rome's coffers. They would continue up to the summit to the Temple of Jupiter (no longer exists today) to dedicate the victory to the King of the Gods.

❶ Arch of Titus (Arco di Tito)

The Arch of Titus commemorated the Roman victory over the province of Judaea (Israel) in A.D. 70. The Romans had a reputation as benevolent conquerors who tolerated the local customs and rulers. All they required was allegiance to the empire, shown by worshiping the emperor as a god. No problem for most conquered people, who already had half a dozen gods on their prayer lists anyway. But Israelites' believed in only one god and it wasn't the emperor. Israel revolted. After a short but bitter war, the Romans defeated the rebels, took Jerusalem, sacked their temple, and brought home 50,000 Jewish slaves...who were forced to build this arch (and the Colosseum).

The Forum

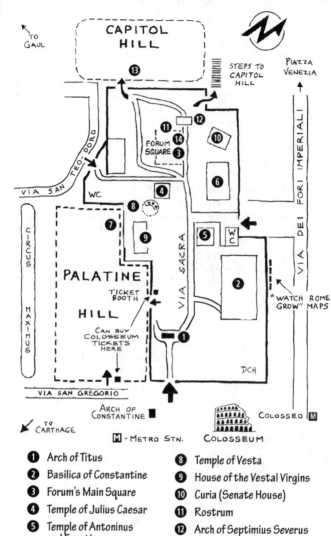

1. Arch of Titus
2. Basilica of Constantine
3. Forum's Main Square
4. Temple of Julius Caesar
5. Temple of Antoninus and Faustina
6. Basilica Aemilia
7. Caligula's Palace
8. Temple of Vesta
9. House of the Vestal Virgins
10. Curia (Senate House)
11. Rostrum
12. Arch of Septimius Severus
13. Temple of Saturn
14. Column of Phocas

Rome—Republic and Empire
(500 B.C.–A.D. 500)

Ancient Rome spanned about a thousand years, from 500 B.C. to A.D. 500. During that time, Rome expanded from a small tribe of barbarians to a vast empire, then dwindled slowly to city size again. For the first 500 years, when Rome's armies made her ruler of the Italian peninsula and beyond, Rome was a republic governed by elected senators. Over the next 500 years, a time of world conquest and eventual decline, Rome was an empire ruled by a military-backed dictator.

Julius Caesar bridged the gap between republic and empire. This ambitious general and politician, popular with the people because of his military victories and charisma, suspended the Roman constitution and assumed dictatorial powers in about 50 B.C., and in a few years was assassinated by a conspiracy of senators. His adopted son, Augustus, succeeded him, and soon "Caesar" was not just a name but a title.

Emperor Augustus ushered in the Pax Romana, or Roman peace (from A.D. 1–200), a time when Rome reached her peak and controlled an empire that stretched even beyond Eurail—from Scotland to Egypt, from Turkey to Morocco.

Roman propaganda decorates the inside of the arch, where a relief shows the emperor Titus in a chariot being crowned by the

goddess Victory. (Thanks to the toll of modern pollution, they both look like they've been through the wars.) The other side shows booty from the sacking of the temple—soldiers carrying a Jewish candelabrum and other plunder. The two (unfinished) plaques on poles were to have listed the conquered cities. Look at the top of the ceiling. Constructed after his death, the relief shows Titus riding an eagle to heaven, where he'll become one of the gods.

The brutal crushing of this rebellion (and another one 60 years later) devastated the nation of Israel. With no temple as a center for their faith, the Jews scattered throughout the world (the Diaspora). There would be no Jewish political entity again for almost two thousand years, until modern Israel was created after World War II.

• Start down the Via Sacra into the Forum. After just a few yards, turn right and follow a path uphill to the three huge arches of the...

THE
ROMAN
EMPIRE AT ITS PEAK:
PAX ROMANA A.D. 100

❷ Basilica of Constantine (a.k.a. Basilica Maxentius)

Yes, these are big arches. But they represent only one third of the original Basilica of Constantine, a mammoth hall of justice. The arches were matched by a similar set along the Via Sacra side (only a few squat brick piers remain). Between them ran the central hall, which was spanned by a roof 130 feet high—about 55 feet higher than the side arches you see. (The stub of brick you see sticking up began an arch that once spanned the central hall.) The hall itself was as long as a football field, lavishly furnished with colorful inlaid marble, a gilded bronze ceiling, fountains, and statues, and filled with strolling Romans. At the far (west) end was an enormous marble statue of Emperor Constantine on a throne. (Pieces

of this statue, including a man-size hand, are on display in Rome's Capitol Hill Museum.)

The basilica was begun by the emperor Maxentius, but after he was trounced in battle (see page 99), the victor—Constantine—completed the massive building. No doubt about it, the Romans built monuments on a more epic scale than any previous Europeans, wowing their "barbarian" neighbors.

• *Now stroll deeper into the Forum, downhill along the Via Sacra, through the trees. Many of the large basalt stones under your feet were walked on by Caesar Augustus 2,000 years ago. Pass by the only original bronze door still swinging on its ancient hinges (green, on right) and continue between ruined buildings until the Via Sacra opens up to a flat, grassy area.*

❸ The Forum's Main Square

The original Forum, or main square, was this flat patch about the size of a football field, stretching to the foot of Capitol Hill. Surrounding it were temples, law courts, government buildings, and triumphal arches.

Rome was born right here. According to legend, twin brothers Romulus (Rome) and Remus were orphaned in infancy and raised by a she-wolf on top of the Palatine. Growing up, they found it hard to get dates. So they and their cohorts attacked the nearby Sabine tribe and kidnapped their women. After they made peace, this marshy valley became the meeting place and then the trading center for the scattered tribes on the surrounding hillsides.

The square was the busiest and most crowded—and often the seediest—section of town. Besides the senators, politicians, and currency exchangers, there were even sleazier types—souvenir hawkers, pickpockets, fortune-tellers, gamblers, slave marketers, drunks, hookers, lawyers, and tour guides.

The Forum is now rubble, no denying it, but imagine it in its prime: blinding white marble buildings with 40-foot-high columns and shining bronze roofs; rows of statues painted in realistic colors; chariots rattling down the Via Sacra. Mentally replace tourists in T-shirts with tribunes in togas. Imagine the buildings towering and the people buzzing around you while an orator gives a rabble-rousing speech from the Rostrum. If things still look like just a pile of rocks, at least tell yourself, "But Julius Caesar once leaned against these rocks."

• *At the near (east) end of the main square (the Colosseum is to the east) are the foundations of a temple now capped with a peaked wood-and-metal roof...*

❹ The Temple of Julius Caesar (Tempio del Divo Giulio, or Ara di Cesare)

Julius Caesar's body was burned on this spot (under the metal roof) after his assassination. Peek behind the wall into the small apse area where a mound of dirt usually has fresh flowers—given to remember the man who, more than any other, personified the greatness of Rome.

Caesar (100–44 B.C.) changed Rome—and the Forum—dramatically. He cleared out many of the wooden market stalls and began to ring the square with even grander buildings. Caesar's house was located behind the temple, near that clump of trees. He walked right by here on the day he was assassinated ("Beware the Ides of March!" warned a street-corner Etruscan preacher).

Though he was popular with the masses, not everyone liked Caesar's urban design or his politics. When he assumed dictatorial powers, he was ambushed and stabbed to death by a conspiracy of senators, including his adopted son, Brutus *("Et tu, Brute?")*.

The funeral was held here, facing the main square. The citizens gathered, and speeches were made. Mark Antony stood up to say (in Shakespeare's words), "Friends, Romans, countrymen, lend me your ears. I come to bury Caesar, not to praise him." When Caesar's body was burned, the citizens who still loved him threw anything at hand on the fire, requiring the fire department to come put it out. Later, Emperor Augustus dedicated this temple in his name, making Caesar the first Roman to become a god.

• *Behind and to the left of the Temple of Julius Caesar are the 10 tall columns of the...*

❺ Temple of Antoninus Pius and Faustina

The respected Emperor Antoninus Pius (A.D. 138–161) built this temple—originally called the Temple of Faustina—in honor of his late beloved wife. After the emperor's death, the temple became a monument to them both.

The 50-foot-tall Corinthian (leafy) columns must have been awe-inspiring to out-of-towners who grew up in thatched huts. Although the temple has been inhabited by a church, you can still see the basic layout—a staircase led to a shaded porch (the columns), which admitted you to the main building (now a church) where the statue of the god sat. Originally, these columns supported a triangular pediment decorated with sculptures.

Picture these columns whitewashed, with gilded capitals, supporting brightly painted statues in the pediment, and the whole building capped with a gleaming bronze roof. The stately gray rubble of today's Forum is a faded black-and-white photograph of a 3-D Technicolor era. (Also picture the Forum covered with dirt as high as the green door—as it was until excavated in the 1800s.)

• *There's a ramp next to the Temple of A. and F. Walk halfway up it and look to the left to view the...*

❻ Basilica Aemilia

A basilica was a Roman hall of justice. In a society that was as legal-minded as America is today, you needed a lot of lawyers—and a big place to put them. Citizens came here to work out matters such as inheritances and building permits, or to sue somebody.

Notice the layout. It was a long, rectangular building. The stubby columns all in a row form one long, central hall flanked by two side aisles. Medieval Christians required a larger meeting hall for their worship services than Roman temples provided, so they used the spacious Roman basilica (hall of justice) as the model for their churches. Cathedrals from France to Spain to England, from Romanesque to Gothic to Renaissance, all have the same basic floor plan as a Roman basilica.

• *Return again to the Temple of Julius Caesar. To the right of the temple are the three tall Corinthian columns of the Temple of Castor and Pollux. Beyond that is Palatine Hill—the corner of which may have been...*

❼ Caligula's Palace (a.k.a. the Palace of Tiberius)

Emperor Caligula (ruled A.D. 37–41) had a huge palace on Palatine Hill overlooking the Forum. It actually sprawled down the hill into the

Religion in Ancient Rome

Religion in ancient Rome was all about the *pax deorum* (peace, or pact with the gods) that guaranteed the prosperity of the incredibly superstitious Romans. To appease the fickle gods, they performed elaborate rituals at lavish temples and shrines. Romans had a god for every moment of their days and each important event in their lives. While the Romans adopted the Greek pantheon, they also embraced the gods from many of the people they came into contact with, sometimes using elaborate ceremonies to persuade these new gods to "move" to Rome. Scholars estimate Romans had about 30,000 gods to keep happy. In this high-maintenance religion, there was Cunina, the goddess who protected cradles; Statulinus, to help children stand up; and Fabulina, for their first words. Fornax was the oven god, Pomona the fruit tree goddess, Sterculinus the manure god, and Venus Cloacina the sewer goddess.

Priests interpreted the will of the gods by studying the internal organs of sacrificed animals, the flight of birds, and prophetic books. A clap of thunder was enough to postpone a battle.

Astrology, magic rites, the cult of deified emperors, house gods, and the near deification of ancestors permeated Roman life. But all these gods didn't quite do it for the Romans—the gods were gradually replaced by the rise of monotheistic religions from the East. In A.D. 312, Emperor Constantine legalized and embraced Christianity. By 390, the Christian God was the only legal god in Rome.

Forum (some supporting arches remain in the hillside), with an entrance from within the Temple of Castor and Pollux.

Caligula was not a nice person. He tortured enemies, stole senators' wives, and parked his chariot in handicap spaces. But Rome's luxury-loving emperors only added to the glory of the Forum, with each one trying to make his mark on history.

• *To the left of the Temple of Castor and Pollux, find the remains of a small white circular temple...*

❽ **The Temple of Vesta**

This was Rome's most sacred spot. Rome considered itself one big family, and this temple represented a circular hut, like the kind that Rome's first families lived in. Inside, a fire burned, just as in a Roman home. And back in the days before lighters and butane, you never wanted your fire to go out. As long as the sacred flame burned, Rome would stand. The flame was tended by priestesses known as Vestal Virgins.

• *Around the back of the Temple of Vesta, you'll find two rectangular brick pools. These stood in the courtyard of...*

❾ The House of the Vestal Virgins

The Vestal Virgins lived in a two-story building surrounding a cen-

tral courtyard with these two pools at one end. Rows of statues to the left and right marked the long sides of the building. This place was the model—both architecturally and sexually—for medieval convents and monasteries.

Chosen from noble families before they reached the age of 10, the six Vestal Virgins served a 30-year term. Honored and revered by the Romans, the Vestals even had their own box opposite the emperor in the Colosseum.

As the name implies, a Vestal took a vow of chastity. If she served her term faithfully—abstaining for 30 years—she was given a huge dowry, honored with a statue (like the ones at left), and allowed to marry (life begins at 40?). But if they found any Virgin who

wasn't, she was strapped to a funeral car, paraded through the streets of the Forum, taken to a crypt, given a loaf of bread and a lamp...and buried alive. Many women suffered the latter fate.

• *Head to the Forum's west end (opposite the Colosseum). You'll pass by a space that was left open by design—kind of a "proto-piazza." Consider how the piazza is still a standard part of any Italian town—reflecting and accommodating the gregarious and outgoing nature of the Italian people since Roman times. Stop at the big, well-preserved brick building (on right) with the triangular roof and look in.*

⑩ The Curia (Senate House)

The Curia was the most important political building in the Forum. While the present building dates from A.D. 283, this was the site of Rome's official center of government since the birth of the republic. Three hundred senators, elected by the citizens of Rome, met here to debate and create the laws of the land. Their wooden seats once circled the building in three tiers; the Senate president's podium sat at the far end. The marble floor is from ancient times. Listen to the echoes in this vast room—the acoustics are great.

Rome prided itself on being a republic. Early in the city's history, its people threw out the king and established rule by elected representatives. Each Roman citizen was free to speak his mind and have a say in public policy. Even when emperors  became the supreme authority, the Senate was a power to be reckoned with. (Note: Although Julius Caesar was assassinated in "the Senate," it wasn't here—the Senate was temporarily meeting across town.) The Curia building (A.D. 280) is well preserved, having been used as a church since early Christian times. In the 1930s, it was restored and opened to the public as an historic site.

A statue and two reliefs inside the Curia help build our mental image of the Forum. The statue, made of porphyry marble in about A.D. 100, with its head, arms, and feet missing, was a tribute to an emperor, probably Hadrian or Trajan. The two relief panels may have decorated the Rostrum. Those on the left show people (with big stone tablets) standing in line to burn their debt records following a government amnesty. The other shows the distribution of grain (Rome's welfare system), intact architecture, and the latest fashion in togas.

• *Go back down the Senate steps to the metal guardrail and find a 10-foot-high wall at the base of Capitol Hill marked...*

⑪ Rostrum (Rostri)

Nowhere was Roman freedom more apparent than at this "Speaker's Corner." The Rostrum was a raised platform, 10 feet high and 80 feet long, decorated with statues, columns, and the prows of ships *(rostra)*.

On this stage, Rome's orators, great and small, tried to draw a crowd and sway public opinion. Mark Antony rose to offer Caesar the laurel-leaf crown of kingship, which Caesar publicly (and hypocritically) refused while privately becoming a dictator. Men such as Cicero railed against the corruption and decadence that came with the city's newfound wealth. In later years, daring citizens even spoke out against the emperors, reminding them that Rome was once free. Picture the backdrop these speakers would have had—a mountain of marble buildings piling up on Capitol Hill.

In front of the Rostrum are trees bearing fruits that were sacred to the ancient Romans: olives (provided food, light, and preservatives), figs (tasty), and wine grapes (made a popular export product).

• *The big arch to the right of the Rostrum is the...*

⑫ Arch of Septimius Severus

In imperial times, the Rostrum's voices of democracy would have been dwarfed by images of empire such as the huge, six-story-high Arch of Septimius Severus (A.D.

203). The reliefs commemorate the African-born emperor's battles in Mesopotamia. Near ground level, see soldiers marching captured barbarians back to Rome for the victory parade. Despite Severus' efficient rule, Rome's empire was crumbling under the weight of its own corruption, disease, decaying infrastructure, and the constant attacks by foreign "barbarians."

• *Pass underneath the Arch of Septimius Severus and turn left. On the slope of Capitol Hill are the eight remaining columns of the...*

⑬ Temple of Saturn

These columns framed the entrance to the Forum's oldest temple (497 B.C.). Inside was a humble, very old wooden statue of the god Saturn. But the statue's pedestal held the gold bars, coins, and jewels of Rome's state treasury, the booty collected by conquering generals.

• *Standing here, at one of the Forum's first buildings, look east at the lone, tall...*

⑭ Column of Phocas

This is the Forum's last monument (A.D. 608), a gift from the powerful Byzantine Empire to a fallen empire—Rome. Given to commemorate the pagan Pantheon's becoming a Christian church, it's like a symbolic last nail in ancient Rome's coffin. After Rome's 1,000-year reign, the city was looted by Vandals, the population of a million-plus shrank to 10,000, and the once-grand city center—the Forum—was abandoned, slowly covered up by centuries of silt and dirt. In the 1700s, an English historian named Edward Gibbon overlooked this spot from Capitol Hill. Hearing Christian monks

Rome Falls

Again, Rome lasted 1,000 years—500 years of growth, 200 years of peak power, and 300 years of gradual decay. The fall had many causes, among them the barbarians who pecked away at Rome's borders. Christians blamed the fall on moral decay. Pagans blamed it on Christians. Socialists blamed it on a shallow economy based on the spoils of war. (George W. Bush blamed it on Democrats.) Whatever the reasons, the far-flung empire could no longer keep its grip on conquered lands, and it pulled back. Barbarian tribes from Germany and Asia attacked the Italian peninsula and even looted Rome itself in A.D. 410, leveling many of the buildings in the Forum. In 476, when the last emperor checked out and switched off the lights, Europe plunged into centuries of ignorance, poverty, and weak government—the Dark Ages.

But Rome lived on in the Catholic Church. Christianity was the state religion of Rome's last generations. Emperors became popes (both called themselves "Pontifex Maximus"), senators became bishops, orators became priests, and basilicas became churches. The glory of Rome remains eternal.

singing at these pagan ruins, he looked out at the few columns poking up from the ground, pondered the "Decline and Fall of the Roman Empire," and thought, "Hmm, that's a catchy title...."

• *There are several ways to exit the Forum:*

East—Return to the Colosseum. Or visit Palatine Hill (the entrance is near the Arch of Titus); see next chapter.

West—Climb Capitol Hill. The stairs near the Arch of Septimius Severus are the most direct way, or take the pathway that winds past the Temple of Saturn and Mamertine Prison. (Both lead to the Capitol Hill Museum; see page 157.)

North—The ramp near Basilica Aemilia spills you out on Via dei Fori Imperiali (near Trajan's Forum; see page 123).

South—Passing by the Temple of Castor and Pollux, you climb to a small exit leading to the Theater of Marcellus and the Tiber River.

PALATINE HILL TOUR

(Monte Palatino)

While many tourists consider the Palatine Hill just extra credit after the Forum, it offers an insight into the greatness of Rome that's well worth the effort. (And, if you're visiting the Colosseum, you've got a ticket whether you like it or not.) While Palatine Hill is jam-packed with history—"the huts of Romulus and Remus," the huge Imperial Palace, a view of the Circus Maximus—there's only the barest skeleton of rubble left to tell the story. This tour will enable the thoughtful sightseer to bring the remains to life. Palatine Hill is ideal for those who want to get away from the crowds and discover the romantic, melancholy essence of ruins. Become a 19th-century poet or a painter on the Grand Tour meditating on the destiny of once-great civilizations, and wander through the remains of the palaces that Nature seems to have reclaimed for herself.

ORIENTATION

Cost: €10, includes Colosseum; also covered by €20 Archeologia Card.

Hours: Daily 9:00–19:00 or until an hour before sunset.

Getting There: Enter the Palatine Hill from within the Forum (the entrance closest to the Colosseum; Metro: Colosseo). Buy your ticket past the Arch of Titus.

Tour: Audioguides cost €4. Guided tours in English are offered once daily (€3.50); ask for information at the ticket booth.

Length of This Tour: Allow 90 minutes.

Services: You'll find some WCs at the ground level of the museum in the center of the site, and others are hiding among the orange trees in the Renaissance Gardens.

Palatine Hill

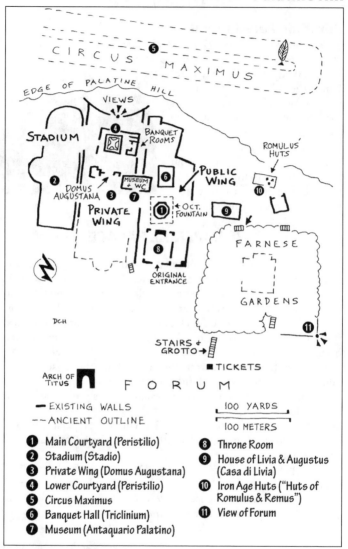

- ━ EXISTING WALLS
- ┅ ANCIENT OUTLINE

100 YARDS
100 METERS

1. Main Courtyard (Peristilio)
2. Stadium (Stadio)
3. Private Wing (Domus Augustana)
4. Lower Courtyard (Peristilio)
5. Circus Maximus
6. Banquet Hall (Triclinium)
7. Museum (Antaquario Palatino)
8. Throne Room
9. House of Livia & Augustus (Casa di Livia)
10. Iron Age Huts ("Huts of Romulus & Remus")
11. View of Forum

THE TOUR BEGINS

Climbing Palatine Hill

• *We'll start our tour on top of the hill at the Palatine Museum (Antiquario Palatino, see photo; the museum is #7 on the map).*

Getting to the museum: Climb the Palatine Hill to the one modern building at its crest. It's the big gray, 1930s-style building that houses the museum. We'll visit the museum later. For now, grab a stone and sit with your back to the museum and orient yourself, facing in the direction of the Forum (roughly north).

THE IMPERIAL PALACE

You're sitting at the center of what was once a huge palace, the residence of emperors for three centuries. Orgies, royal weddings, assassinations, concerts, intrigues, births, funerals, banquets, and the occasional Tupperware party took place within these walls. What walls? The row of umbrella pines about 200 yards to the east (to your right) now marks one edge of the palace. The reconstructed brick tower (at about 11 o'clock) was the northwest corner. The palace also stretched behind you (the area behind the museum) and beneath you, since some of the palace had a lower floor. (Right now, you're standing not on the original palace's ground level, but several floors up.)

The area in front was the official wing of the palace; behind were the private quarters. All in all, it made a cozy little 150,000-square-foot pad.

The palace was built by Emperor Domitian in about A.D. 81. A poet of the day described it as so grand that it "made Jupiter jealous."

• *Now proceed, following the map for this 11-stop tour. To your left (with your back to the museum) is a big rectangular field with an octagonal brick design in the center—the main courtyard of the palace.*

❶ Main Courtyard (Peristilio)

The brick octagon was a sunken fountain in the middle of an open-air courtyard. Like even the humblest Roman homes, this palace was built around an oasis of peace where you could enjoy the sun, catch the precious rain, and listen to the babble of moving water. The courtyard was lined with columns (notice the fragments) supporting an arcade for shade. Originally, the floor and walls of the courtyard were faced with shiny white marble.

• *The palace's stadium is 100 yards behind you (to the east), near the long row of pine trees. Belly up to the railing and look down on the elliptical track.*

❷ Stadium (Stadio)

This cigar-shaped, sunken stadium (500 feet long) was the palace's rec room. It looks like a racetrack and may have been used for foot and horse races, but it also held gardens with strolling paths. The oval running track at the south end was added later. The emperor had a raised box on the 50-yard line, in the curved apse across

from you. At the north end were changing rooms, and the marble fragments that litter the ground once held up an arcade.

❸ Private Wing of the Palace (Domus Augustana)

The area between the stadium and the museum held the private rooms of the emperor and his extended family. Today, a lone umbrella pine on a mound marks the courtyard of this wing. Wander through the maze of brick rooms (many of them reconstructed), noticing:

• The typical Roman building method: Build a rectangular shell of brick, fill it with concrete, then finish it with either plaster (you'll see an occasional faded fresco) or slabs of marble. The small, round pockmarks on many walls show where the marble was fastened.

• The square holes in the walls held wooden beams, used for scaffolding during construction and maintenance, for shelves, and for wooden floors.

• Over the doorways, the bricks in the walls form the pattern of an arch. These "blind arches" were structural elements that allowed the walls to be built higher. The iron bar clamps are recent additions and hold the crumbling walls together.

• Niches and apses once held statues. Every family had their own household gods and displayed small images of these guardian spirits, as well as busts of honored ancestors.

• The fragments of columns, reliefs, and sculpture scattered about suggest the wealth of this great palace.

- Finally, notice the floor plan—a complex, fantasyland maze of small, private, sometimes even curved rooms.

• *Walk through the private wing, behind the museum. In the south part of the Domus Augustana, you can look down on the ruins of the lower story.*

❹ Lower Courtyard (Peristilio)

This open-air courtyard has the concave-convex remains of a large

fountain that must have been a marvel. Try to mentally reconstruct the palace that surrounded this fountain. The emperors could look down on it from the upper story (where you're standing) or view it from the rooms around it on the lower story, where the emperor and his family ate their meals in private.

The lower story was built into the slope of the hill. The southern part of the palace was an extension of the hillside, supported beneath your feet by big arches.

• *Continuing to the southern edge of the hill (directly behind the museum), overlooking a long, wide, grassy field—what once was the Circus Maximus. Lean over the railing and you might be able to make out the concave shape of the palace's southern facade.*

❺ Circus Maximus

If the gladiator show at the Colosseum was sold out, you could always get a seat at the Circus Max. In an early version of today's demolition derby, Ben-Hur and his fellow charioteers once raced recklessly around this oblong course.

The chariots circled around the cigar-shaped mound in the center (notice the lone cypress tree that now marks one end of the mound). Bleachers (now grassy banks) originally surrounded the track (see artist's reconstruction, below).

The track was 1,300 feet long, while the whole stadium mea-

sured 2,130 feet by 720 feet and seated—get this—250,000 people. The wooden bleachers once collapsed during a race, killing thousands.

The horses began at a starting gate at the west end (to your right), while the public entered at the other end. Races consisted of seven laps (about 3.5 miles total). In such a small space, collisions and overturned chariots were common. The charioteers were usually poor lowborn people who used this dangerous sport to get rich and famous. Some succeeded. Most died.

The public was crazy about the races. There were 12 per day, 240 days a year. Four teams dominated the competition—Reds, Whites, Blues, and Greens—and every citizen was fanatically devoted to one of them. Obviously, the emperors had the best seats in the house; built into the palace's curved facade was a box overlooking the track. For their pleasure, emperors occasionally had the circus floor carpeted with designs in colored powders.

Picture the scene: intact palace; emperor watching; a quarter of a million Romans cheering, jeering, and furiously betting. Horses raced here for more than a thousand years. The track dates from 300 B.C., and the spectacles continued into the Christian era, until A.D. 549, despite Church disapproval.

From this viewpoint, looking to the left, you can see the ruins of the Baths of Caracalla (not worth touring if you've seen the Palatine) rising above the trees a half mile away. About a mile beyond that, the Appian Way led from a grand gate in the ancient wall, past the catacombs, to Brindisi.

• *Just to the left of the museum, check out the...*

❻ Banquet Hall (Triclinium)

The floor of the banquet room had a hollow space beneath it (you can see the 2-foot gap between the 2 original floors). Slaves stoked fires from underground stoves to heat the floor with forced air. At the far end of the room, the platform and curved apse mark the spot where the

emperor ate while looking down on his subjects.

Here, the wealthiest Romans enjoyed the spoils that poured into Rome from its vast empire. Reclining on a couch, waited on by

slaves, you'd order bowls of larks' tongues or a roast pig stuffed with live birds, then wash it down with wine. If you were full but tempted by yet another delicacy, you could call for a feather, vomit, and start all over. Dancing, dark-skinned slave girls from Egypt or flute players from Greece entertained.

If you fancied one, he or she was yours—the bedrooms were just down the hall.

Or so went the stories. In fact, many emperors were just and simple men, continuing the old Roman traditions of hard work and moderate tastes. But just as many were power-mad scoundrels who used their authority to indulge their every desire.

❼ Museum (Antiquario Palatino)

The museum contains statues and frescoes that help you imagine the luxury of the imperial Palatine. Upstairs (and to the left), pause at the statue of "Magna Mater" on her throne. This Great Mother brought life and fertility to the Roman people, who worshiped her at the nearby Temple of Cybele. Her arms and foot were destroyed by time, but there was always a cavity where her head should be—this was a standard Roman device in which interchangeable heads could be inserted. In this case, the Magna Mater's "head" was actually a sacred, black, cone-shaped meteorite that caused astonishment when it fell from the sky.

Also upstairs, Room V holds frescoes and statues from the time of Augustus and fine decorative terra-cotta panels. Room VII has busts of the notorious Emperor Nero *(Nerone)* and exquisite marble inlay work. In Room VIII is a statue fragment of a river god's stomach. And finally, back near the entrance is a large statue of a Muse that once decorated the Hippodrome.

Downstairs, there's a (well-described in English) model of the eighth-century B.C. Iron Age huts of Romulus (and a 20th-century WC).

You'll see marble scraps just outside the museum entrance and also strewn across Palatine Hill. Marble was used to boast of the power and vastness of the empire. Citizens would understand that the Numidian yellow was from Tunisia, the pink granite was from Aswan in Egypt, and the veined Cipollino (with swirling designs like an onion) was from the island of Euboea in Greece. This was all sliced and laid out in fine pavement and wall designs, enjoyed by those who could only be thankful they were on the winning team. In later centuries, the Christian Church used marble as well—to symbolize its conquest over the pagan world.

• *From the museum, head straight and a little left, about 300 feet to the Throne Room.*

❽ Throne Room

The nerve center of an empire that controlled some 50 million people from Scotland to Africa, this was the official center of power. The curved apse of the largest brick stump (there's now a plaque on it) marks the spot where the emperor sat on his throne for official business.

Imagine being a Roman citizen summoned by the emperor. You'd enter the palace through the main doorway (now a gap) at the far (Forum) end of the room, having climbed up three flights of a monumental staircase. The floor and walls dazzled with green, purple, red, white, and yellow marble. Along the walls were 12 colossal statues of Roman gods. The ceiling tow-

ered seven stories overhead. On either side were doorways leading to a basilica and the emperor's private temple.

You'd approach the emperor, who sat on a raised throne in the apse, dressed in royal purple, with a crown of laurel leaves on his head and a scepter cradled in his arm. Big braziers burned on either side, throwing off a flickering light. As you approached, you'd raise your arm to greet him, saying, *"Ave, Cesare!"* The words would echo through the great hall.

Now imagine yourself as emperor. Stand on the small white stone marking the location of the throne (a few feet in front of the plaque) and look out over your palace. (The ceiling was a barrel vault sitting upon towers as high as the brick tower in the distance to the left.)

• *From your throne, head left, climb the stairs to the black railing overlooking a low-laying modern building that protects the most ancient part of Palatine Hill.*

❾ House of Livia and Augustus (Casa di Livia)

Augustus, the first emperor, lived in this house (and the neighboring house to the left) with his wife, Livia. Peer down the hallways at the small rooms with honeycomb brick walls that surrounded a small courtyard. This relatively humble dwelling is a far cry from the later Imperial Palace. There are some fine frescoes inside (usu-

ally closed for restoration), but Casa di Livia had little of the lavish marble found in most homes of the wealthy.

Augustus was a modest man who believed in traditional Roman values. His wife and daughter wove the clothes he wore. He slept in the same small bedroom for 40 years. He

burned the midnight oil in his study, where he read and wrote his memoirs. Augustus set a standard for emperors' conduct that would last...until his death.

Augustus wanted to be the new Romulus, so he lived adjacent to the home of the mythological founder of Rome.

⑩ Iron Age Huts
("The Huts of Romulus and Remus")

Looking down into the pit from the railing (stand at the far right), you can make out some elliptical and rectangular shapes carved into the stony ground (under the metal roof) —the partial outlines of huts from about 850 B.C. Some have holes that once held the wooden posts of round, thatched huts.

Romulus and Remus were children of the first Vestal Virgin.

For complicated family reasons, she was executed and the babies were set adrift on the flooding Tiber, eventually to be washed ashore at the foot of Palatine Hill. In a cave just downhill from here, a shepherd discovered them being suckled by a mother wolf. He took them home—maybe right here—and raised them as his own. When Romulus grew up, he killed his brother and built a square wall (Roma Quadrata) on the hilltop, thus founding the city of Rome.

For centuries, the Romans believed this legend. They honored the wolf's cave (called the "Lupercal," where every February 15th, men dressed up in animal skins and whipped women), as well as the spot where Romulus lived. Lo and behold, in the 1940s, these huts were unearthed, and the legend became history. And the more they dig, the more they find that fact confirms the legends.

Here at Rome's birthplace, reflect on the rise of this great culture—from thatched hut to the modest house of Augustus to the massive Imperial Palace of Domitian, with its stadium and view over the Circus Maximus. It's no wonder that the hill's name gave us our English word "palace."

⑪ View of Forum Fit for an Emperor

Finish your tour with a stroll through the Renaissance gardens of the Farnese family. Admire the exotic plants, fountains, underground grotto, and pavilions. When you see the incredible view of the Forum from the end of the gardens, you'll know why the Palatine was Rome's best address.

TRAJAN'S COLUMN, FORUM, AND MARKET TOUR

(Colonna, Foro, e Mercati de Traiano)

Rome peaked under Emperor Trajan (ruled A.D. 98–117)—the empire stretched from Scotland to the Sahara, from Spain to the Fertile Crescent. A triumphant Trajan returned to Rome with his booty and shook it all over the city. He extended the Forum by building his own commercial, political, and religious center nearby, complete with temples, law courts, squares lined with shops, and a monumental column.

ORIENTATION

Cost and Hours: Trajan's Column and Forum are free and always viewable; Trajan's Market, including access to part of the Forum, costs €6.20 (summer Tue–Sun 9:00–18:30, winter Tue–Sun 9:00–16:30, always closed Mon, tel. 06-679-0048).

Getting There: Trajan's Column is just a few steps off Piazza Venezia, on Via dei Fori Imperiali, across the street from the Victor Emmanuel Monument. Trajan's Forum stretches southeast of the column toward the Colosseum. The entrance to Trajan's (dull) Market is uphill from the column on Via IV Novembre.

Length of This Tour: Allow 30 minutes, or an hour if you also enter Trajan's Market.

THE TOUR BEGINS

Trajan's Column

Rising 140 feet and decorated with a spiral relief of 2,500 figures trumpeting Trajan's exploits, this is the world's grandest column from antiquity. The ashes of Trajan and his wife were once held in the base, and the sun once glinted off a polished bronze statue of

Trajan's Forum

Trajan at the top. (Today, St. Peter is on top.) Built as a stack of 17 marble doughnuts, the column is hollow (note the small window slots) with a spiral staircase inside, leading up to the balcony.

The relief unfolds like a scroll, telling the story of Trajan's conquest of Dacia (modern-day Romania). It starts at the bottom with a trickle of water that becomes a river and soon picks up boats full of supplies. Then come the soldiers themselves, who spill out from the gates of the city. A river god (bottom band, south side) surfaces to bless the journey. Along the way (second band), they build roads and forts to sustain the vast enterprise, including (third band, south side) Trajan's half-mile-long bridge over the Danube, the longest for a

thousand years. (Find the 3 tiny, crisscross rectangles representing the wooden span.) Trajan himself (fourth band, in military skirt with toga over his arm) mounts a podium to fire up the troops. They hop into a Roman galley ship (5th band) and head off to fight the valiant Dacians in the middle of a forest (8th band). Finally, at the very top, the Romans hold a sacrifice to give thanks for the victory, while the captured armor is displayed on the pedestal.

Originally, the entire story was painted in bright colors. If you unwound the scroll, it would stretch over two football fields—it's far longer than the frieze around the Greek Parthenon. (An unscrolled copy is in E.U.R.'s Museum of Roman Civilization; see page 67.)

• *The best place to view the ruins of Trajan's Forum is on the pedestrian walkway (70 yards southeast of the column) that cuts right across the heart of the forum.*

Trajan's Forum (Foro di Traiano)

Trajan's Forum starts at Trajan's Column and runs about 120 yards southeast toward the Colosseum. It's mostly rubble today. The highlight of the forum, then and now, is Trajan's Market— the big, crescent-shaped brick structure that rises up the flank of Quirinal Hill.

In Roman times, you would have entered at the Colosseum end through a triumphal arch and been greeted in the main square by a large statue of the soldier-king on a horse. Continuing on, you'd enter the Basilica Ulpia (the gray granite columns near Trajan's Column), the largest law court of its day. Finally, at the far end, you would have found Trajan's Column, flanked by two libraries that contained the world's knowledge in Greek and Latin. Balconies on the libraries gave close-up looks at the upper reliefs of the column, in case anyone doubted the outcome of Trajan's war.

Trajan's Forum was a crucial expansion of the old Roman Forum, which was too small and ceremonial to fill the commercial needs of a booming city of more than a million people. Built with the staggering haul of gold plundered from Dacia (Romania), this was the largest forum ever—its opulence astounded even the jaded Romans.

To build his forum, Trajan literally moved mountains. He cut away a ridge that once connected the Quirinal and Capitol Hills, creating this artificial valley. Trajan's Column marks the hill's original height—140 feet.

Trajan's Market

Nestled into the cutaway curve of the hill is the semicircular brick complex of Trajan's Market. Part shopping mall, part warehouse, part administration office, it was a place that Romans gravitated to and a popular spot to bring out-of-town guests.

At ground level, the 13 tall arches housed (shallow) shops selling fresh fruit, vegetables, and flowers to shoppers who passed by on the street. The 26 arched windows (above) lighted a covered walkway lined with shops that sold wine and olive oil. On the roof (now lined with a metal railing) runs a street that held still more shops, making about 150 in all. Shoppers could browse through goods from every corner of Rome's vast empire—exotic fruits from Africa, spices from Asia, fish and chips from Londinium.

Above the semicircle, the upper floors of the complex housed bureaucrats in charge of a crucial element of city life—doling out free grain to unemployed citizens, who lived off the wealth plundered from distant lands. Better to pacify them than risk a riot. Above the offices, at the very top, rises a tower added in the Middle Ages.

Going inside the market (which costs €6.20) is worth it only for those with a good imagination, stamina for stairs, or a Masters in Food Distribution. As you walk by the shops in the welcome shade of the arcade, you'll get a better sense of how inviting the market must have been in its heyday. Today, only one shop is "furnished"—crammed with the clay jugs used to store olive oil (upstairs from ticket booth). Throughout the market, you'll get expansive views of the ancient Trajan's Forum and modern Victor Emmanuel Monument.

The market was beautiful and functional, filling the space of the curved hill perfectly and echoing the curved side of the forum's main courtyard. (The wall of rough tufa stones on the ground once extended into a semicircle.) Unlike most Roman buildings, the brick facade was never covered with plaster or marble. The architect liked the simple contrast between warm brick and the white stone lining the arches and windows.

Trajan's conquest of the Dacians was Rome's last and greatest foreign conquest. It produced this forum, which stood for centuries as a symbol of a truly cosmopolitan civilization.

PANTHEON TOUR

*The Roman Temple
and Nearby Churches*

If your imagination is fried from trying to reconstruct ancient buildings out of today's rubble, visit the Pantheon, Rome's best-preserved monument. Engineers still admire how the Romans built such a mathematically precise structure without computers, fossil-fuel machinery, or electricity. (Having unlimited slave power didn't hurt.) Stand under the Pantheon's solemn dome to gain a new appreciation for the enlightenment of these ancient people.

Several interesting churches are clustered nearby, easy to visit after you tour the Pantheon.

ORIENTATION

Cost: Free.

Hours: Mon–Sat 8:30–19:30, Sun 9:00–18:00, holidays 9:00–13:00.

Getting There: You can walk (it's a 15-min walk from the Forum), take a taxi, or catch a bus. Bus #64 carries tourists and pickpockets daily and frequently between the train station and Vatican City, stopping at Largo Argentina, a few blocks south of the Pantheon. The *elettrico* minibus #116 runs between Campo de' Fiori and Piazza Barberini via the Pantheon (daily, fewer on Sun).

Information: Tel. 06-6830-0230.

Length of This Tour: Allow 45 minutes.

Services: The nearest WCs are at bars and McDonald's on the square.

Cuisine Art: You'll find perhaps Rome's most exuberant gelato at Gelateria della Palma, two blocks in front of the Pantheon (Via della Maddalena 20). For lunch or dinner ideas, see page 268.

THE TOUR BEGINS

Overview

The Pantheon is the centerpiece of this tour, but we'll also see a chapel decorated by Caravaggio, the altar Galileo prayed at before facing the Inquisition, one church named for St. Ignatius, and another where he's buried.

• *Start the tour standing in front of...*

THE PANTHEON

Exterior

The Pantheon was a Roman temple dedicated to all *(pan)* of the gods *(theos)*. First built in 27 B.C. by Augustus' son-in-law (find "M. Agrippa" on the facade), it was completely rebuilt in about A.D. 120 by the emperor Hadrian. Some say that Hadrian, an amateur architect, helped design it.

The Pantheon looks like a pretty typical temple from the outside, but this is perhaps the most influential building in art history. Its dome was the model for the Florence cathedral dome, which launched the Renaissance, and for Michelangelo's dome of St. Peter's, which capped it all off. Even Washington, D.C.'s Capitol Building was inspired by this dome.

Back up or step to one side to look above the triangular pediment to the building itself. You'll see the beginnings of a roofline that was abandoned in mid-construction. The pediment was originally intended to be higher, but when the support columns arrived, they were shorter than ordered. Even the most enlightened can forget to "measure twice, cut once."

• *Pass between the enormous, one-piece (too-short) granite columns (most are original) and through the enormous, 2,000-year-old bronze door. Take a seat and take it all in.*

Interior

The dome, which was the largest made until the Renaissance, is set on a circular base. The mathematical perfection of this dome-on-a-base design is a testament to Roman engineering. The dome is as high as it is wide—142 feet from floor to rooftop and from side to side. To picture it, imagine a basketball set inside a wastebasket so that it just touches bottom.

The dome—newly cleaned and feeling loftier than ever—is made from concrete that gets lighter and thinner as it reaches the

top. The walls at the base are 23 feet thick and made from heavy travertine concrete, while near the top they're less than five feet thick and made with a lighter volcanic rock (pumice) mixed in. Both Brunelleschi and Michelangelo studied this dome before building their own (in Florence and in the Vatican, respectively). Remember, St. Peter's Cathedral is really only the dome of the Pantheon atop the Basilica of Constantine.

At the top, the oculus, or eye-in-the-sky, is the building's only light source and is almost 30 feet across. The 1,800-year-old floor has holes in it and slants toward the edges to let the rainwater drain. The marble floor is largely original. For a sense of how the walls once looked, check out the small section that has been restored in the original style (just to the right of the altar, about 20 feet up). Imagine that section extended all around.

In ancient times, this was a one-stop-shopping temple where you could worship any of the gods whose statues decorated the niches. Early in the Middle Ages, the Pantheon became a Christian church (from "all the gods" to "all the martyrs"), which saved it from architectural cannibalism and ensured its upkeep through the Dark Ages. The only major destruction came in the 17th century, when the pope took the bronze plating from the ceiling of the entry porch and melted it down—some was used to build the huge bronze canopy over the altar at St. Peter's.

About the only new things in the interior are the decorative statues and the tombs of famous people. The artist Raphael lies to the left of the main altar (in the glass case). The Latin inscription on his tomb reads: "In life, Nature feared to be outdone by him. In death, she feared she too would die." You'll also see the tombs of modern Italy's first two kings: Victor Emmanuel II (to the right) and Umberto I (to the left). These are a hit with royalists. In fact, there is often a blue-coated guard standing by a guestbook, where visitors can register their support for the Savoia family (which recently—with some controversy—returned from exile to the country they once ruled). And finally, under Umberto, lies his queen, Margherita...for whom pizza Margherita is named.

The Italian Royal Family...in Switzerland

From Italy's unification in 1870 to the end of World War II, the country had four kings, all members of the Savoy family. One of Europe's oldest royal families (from the 10th century), the Savoia had long ruled the kingdom of Piedmont (in present-day northern Italy).

In 1946, the Italians voted for a republic and sent the Savoia into exile. Until 2002, a law proclaimed that no male Savoia could set foot on Italian soil. That's why only the first two kings are buried in the Pantheon (the last two died in exile).

The Savoia lost favor with their Italian subjects for several good reasons: When Mussolini marched on Rome in 1922, King Victor Emmanuel III actually asked him to form a government. When the Mussolini government issued anti-Semitic laws, the king signed them. And in 1943, instead of standing by his people, the king abandoned Rome to the Germans and fled south to Allied protection.

Even today, the Savoia heir to Italy's throne is considered a jerk with a knack for saying stupid things. When asked to comment on the racist laws signed by his grandfather, he candidly answered that he was too young at the time so he did not need to apologize, and, he said, the laws were not really all that bad. When the Savoia were allowed back into Italy in 2003, their first mistake was to visit the pope rather than the president of the Republic. And while they live in stunning wealth in Switzerland, they still complain that Italy owes them more of the family riches.

The Pantheon is the only ancient building in Rome continuously used since its construction. When you leave, you'll notice how the rest of the city has risen on 20 centuries of rubble.

The Pantheon also contains the world's greatest Roman column. There it is, spanning the entire 142 feet from heaven to earth—the pillar of light from the oculus.

CHURCHES NEAR THE PANTHEON

• *These four churches are all less than 10 minutes' walk from the Pantheon.*

Church of San Luigi dei Francesi

The one truly *magnifique* sight in the French national church is the chapel in the far left corner, which was decorated by Caravaggio (free, but bring coins to buy light, Fri–Wed 7:30–12:30 & 15:30–19:00, Thu 7:30–12:30, sightseers should avoid Mass at 7:30 and 19:00, modest dress recommended).

Churches near the Pantheon

The Calling of St. Matthew (left wall of chapel)

Matthew (old man with beard) and his well-dressed, tax-collecting cronies sit in a dingy bar and count the money they've extorted. Suddenly, two men in robes and bare feet enter from the right—Jesus and Peter. Jesus' "Creation-of-Adam" hand emerges from the darkness to point at Matthew. A shaft of light extends the gesture, lighting up the face of Matthew, who points to himself *Last Supper*-style to ask, "You talkin' to me?" Jesus came to convince Matthew to leave his sleazy job and preach Love. Matthew did.

In this, his first large-scale work, 29-year-old Caravaggio (1571–1610) shocked critics and clerics by showing a holy scene in a down-to-earth location. Lower-class people in everyday clothes were his models; his setting was a dive bar (which he knew well). Christ's teeny gold halo is the only hint of the supernatural, as Caravaggio makes a bold proclamation—that miracles are natural events experienced in a profound way.

St. Matthew and the Angel (center wall)

Matthew followed Christ's call, traveled with him, and (supposedly) wrote His life's story (the Gospel according to Matthew). Here, Matthew is hard at work when he's interrupted by an angel with a few suggestions. Matthew's bald head, wrinkled face, and grizzled beard make him an all-too-human saint. Even the teen angel lacks a holy glow—he just hangs there. Caravaggio paints a dark background, then shines a dramatic spotlight on the few things that tell the story.

The Martyrdom of St. Matthew (right wall)

Matthew lies prone, while a truly scary man straddles him and brandishes a sword. The bystanders shrink away from this angry executioner. Caravaggio shines his harsh third-degree spotlight on Matthew and the killer, who are the focus of the painting. The other figures swirl around them in a circle (with the executioner's arm as the radius). Matthew, who thought he had given up everything to follow Christ, now gives up his life as well.

When the chapel was unveiled in 1600, Caravaggio's ultra-realism shocked Rome. (Find his bearded self-portrait in the background.) Although he died only 10 years later, his uncompromising details, emotional subjects, odd compositions, and dramatic lighting set the tone for later Baroque painters.

Gesù Church

The center of the Jesuit order and the best symbol of the Catholic Counter-Reformation, the Gesù Church is packed with overblown art and underappreciated history (free, daily 7:00–12:30 & 16:00–19:15, modest dress recommended).

Exterior

The facade looks ho-hum, like a thousand no-name Catholic churches scattered from Europe to Southern California...until you realize that this was the first, the model for the others. Its scroll-like shoulders were revolu-

tionary, breaking up the rigid rectangles of Renaissance architecture and signaling the coming of Baroque.

The building to the right of the church is where Ignatius of Loyola, the founder of the Jesuits, lived, worked, and died.

• *Step inside the church, grab a seat and look up at the huge painting on the ceiling.*

① Ceiling Fresco and Stucco—
*The Triumph of the Name
of Jesus* **(by Il Baciccio)**

The church's sunroof opens,
and we can see right up to
heaven. A glowing cross, with
the "I.H.S." of the Society
of Jesus, astounds the faithful and sends the infidels
plunging downward. The
twisted tangle of bodies—the
Damned—spills over the edge
of the painting's frame on
their way to Hell. The painted
bodies mingle with 3-D stucco
bodies and a riot of decoration
in a classic example of Baroque
multimedia.

During the Counter-
Reformation, when Catholics
fought Protestants for the
hearts and minds of the
world's Christians, art became
propaganda. The moral here
is clear—this is the fate of
Protestant heretics who dared
to pervert the true teachings of
Jesus.

② The Nave

When the church was originally built (1568), the walls
were white and the decor was
simple. It was designed for

Gesù

A P S E

T R A N S E P T

N A V E

ENTER

10 YARDS
10 METERS

PIAZZA DEL GESÙ

① Ceiling Fresco & Stucco
② Nave
③ Tomb & Altarpiece of St. Ignatius
④ "Religion Vanquishing Untruth"
⑤ Tomb & Altarpiece of
St. Francis Xavier
⑥ Bust of Cardinal Bellarmine
⑦ Manger Scene

what the Jesuits did best—teaching. The Jesuits wanted to educate
Catholics to prepare them for the onslaught of probing Protestant
questions. The church's nave is like one big lecture hall, with no
traditional side aisles.

In the 1500s, the best way to keep Protestants from stealing
your church members was to reason with them. By the 1600s, it
was easier to kill them, and so the Thirty Years' War raged across
Europe. The church became crusted over with the colorful, bom-
bastic, jingoistic Baroque we see today.

③ Tomb and Altarpiece of St. Ignatius of Loyola (left transept)

The gleaming statue of Ignatius spreads his arms wide and gazes up, receiving a vision from on high. Ignatius (1491–1556) was a Spanish soldier during the era of conquistadors. Then, at age 30, he was struck down by a cannonball. While convalescing, he was seized by the burning desire to change his life. He wandered Europe and traveled to Jerusalem. He meditated with monks. He lived in a cave. At 33, he enrolled in a school for boys to pick up the knowledge he'd missed. He studied in Paris and in Rome. Finally, after almost two decades of learning and seeking, he found a way to combine his military training with his spiritual aspirations.

In 1540, the pope gave approval to Ignatius and his small band of followers—the Society of Jesus (Jesuits). These monks, organized like a military company, vowed complete obedience to their "General," and placed themselves at the service of the pope. Their mission? To be the intellectual warriors doing battle with heretics. They were in the right place at the right time—Ignatius and Martin Luther were almost exact contemporaries.

Ignatius' body lies in the small coffin beneath the statue (near ground level). This simple, intense man might have been embarrassed by the lavish memorial to him, with its silver, gold, green marble, and lapis lazuli columns. Above Ignatius, a statue of God stands near a lapis lazuli globe (the biggest in the world) and gestures as though to say, "Go and spread the Word to every land"... which the Jesuits tried to do.

• *Look at the marble statue group to the right of Ignatius...*

❹ *Religion Vanquishing Untruth*

This statue (and a similar one to the left of Ignatius) shows the Church as an angry nun hauling back with a whip and just spanking a bunch of miserable Protestants. The serpent (Luther) is being stepped upon while the angry cherub rips pages out of a heretical book. Not too subtle.

Yes, the Jesuits got a reputation for unfeeling dedication to truth above all else, but their weapons were words, ideas, and critical reasoning. They taught and defended the recently revamped doctrines of the Council of Trent (1545–1563).

❺ **Tomb and Altarpiece of St. Francis Xavier (right transept)**

This was also the Age of Discovery, when Spain and Portugal were colonizing and Christianizing the world, using force if necessary. Francis Xavier joined a Portuguese expedition and headed out to convert the heathens. He touched down in Africa, India, Indonesia, China, and Japan. Along the way, he learned new languages and customs, trying to communicate a strange, monotheistic religion to puzzled polytheists.

He had been on the road for more than a decade (1552) when he died on an island off China (see the painting over the altar).

Thanks largely to zealous Jesuits such as Francis, Catholicism became a truly worldwide religion.

❻ Bust of Cardinal Robert Bellarmine (by Gian Lorenzo Bernini)
The great sculptor Bernini attended this church and honored Bellarmine with a bust. Robert Bellarmine (1542–1621), a theologian at the height of Catholic–Protestant differences, was a voice of reason in the often bitter controversy. He's best known as the man who ordered Galileo to stop teaching the Copernican theory, though he was actually a moderating influence in the debate.

The Jesuits produced some great, open-minded thinkers like Bellarmine, from the poet Gerard Manley Hopkins to modern mystic Pierre Teilhard de Chardin. But they also caught flak for being closed-minded to new ideas. In the 1700s, several countries expelled them, and finally the pope even banned the Society (1773). Chastened, they were brought back (1814), and today they fill the staff of many a Catholic college.

❼ Manger Scene
Don't leave before pressing the button to see water run, comets shoot, and angels fly. It's cheesy, but it carries on the Baroque tradition of using whiz-bang effects to make the supernatural seem tangible to the masses.

Church of Santa Maria sopra Minerva

Exterior
From the outside, survey the many layers of Rome: An Egyptian obelisk sits on a Baroque elephant in front of a Gothic church built over *(sopra)* a pre-Christian, pagan Temple of Minerva (free, daily 7:00–12:00 & 15:30–19:00, modest dress recommended).

Before stepping in, notice the high-water-mark plaques *(alluvione)* on the wall to the right of the door. Inside, you'll see that the lower parts of some frescoes were lost to floods. (After the last great flood, in 1870, Rome built the present embankments, finally breaking the spirit of the Tiber River.)

Nave
This is the only Gothic church you'll see in Rome. The ceiling has pointed, crisscross arches in a starry blue sky. When this Dominican church was built, Gothic was the rage in northern Europe, but Rome was almost a ghost

town. Little was built during this time. Much of what was built was later redone in the Baroque style. This church is a refreshing exception.

Main Altar

The body of St. Catherine of Siena lies under the altar (her head is in Siena). In the 1300s, this Italian nun was renowned for her righteousness and her visions of a mystical marriage with Jesus. Her impassioned letters convinced the pope to return from France to Rome, thus saving Italy from untold chaos.

In 1634, a frail, 70-year-old Galileo knelt at this altar on the way to his trial before the Inquisition in the Sopra Minerva monastery. Facing the fierce Dominican lawyers, he renounced his heretical belief that the earth moved around the sun. (Legend has it that as he walked out, he whispered, "But it *does* move.")

Left of the altar stands a little-known Michelangelo statue, *Christ Bearing the Cross*. Michelangelo gave Jesus an athlete's body (a striking contrast to the docile Christ of medieval art), but he left the face to one of his pupils. Originally, Christ was buck naked, but was later given a golden girdle by Counter-Reformation prudes.

The tomb of the great early Renaissance painter (and Dominican brother) Fra Angelico ("Beato Angelico 1387–1455") is farther to the left, just up the three stairs.

Over in the right (south) transept, pop in a coin for light, and enjoy a Filippino Lippi fresco showing scenes of the life of the great Dominican scholar St. Thomas Aquinas (big man in blue and white).

• *Exit the church via its rear door (behind the Michelangelo statue), walk down Fra Angelico lane (spying any artisans at work), turn left, and walk to the next square. On your right, you'll find the...*

Church of St. Ignazio

This church is a riot of Baroque illusions (free, daily 7:00–12:30 & 16:00–19:00, modest dress recommended).

In the nave, look up at the large, colorful ceiling fresco. St. Ignatius (in the center) is having a vision of Christ with the Cross. Heavenly light from the vision bounces off his chest, and the rays beam to the four corners of the earth (including America, to the left, depicted as a bare-breasted Indian maiden spearing naked men). Now fix your eyes on the arch at the far end of the painting. Walk up the nave, and watch the arch grow and tower over you.

Before you reach the center of the church, stop at the small yellow disk on the floor and look up into the central (black) dome. Watching the dome, walk under and past it. Building project runs out of money? Hire a painter to paint a fake, flat dome.

Back outside, the church faces the yellow headquarters of the Carabinieri police force, forming a square with several converging streets that has been compared to a stage set. Sit on the church steps, admire the theatrical yellow backdrop, and watch the "actors" enter one way and exit another, in the human opera that is modern Rome.

BATHS OF DIOCLETIAN TOUR

(Terme di Diocleziano)

Of all the marvelous structures built by the Romans, their public baths were arguably the grandest, and the Baths of Diocletian were the granddaddy of them all. These baths sprawled over 10 acres—roughly twice the area of the entire Forum—and could cleanse 3,000 Romans at once. Today, there are several sections you can visit:

The **Church of Santa Maria degli Angeli,** housed in the former main hall of the baths, is the single most impressive place. The entrance is on Piazza Repubblica (free, Mon–Sat 7:00–18:30, Sun 8:00–19:30, closed to sightseers during Mass).

The **Octagonal Hall** (Aula Ottagona), also facing Piazza Repubblica, is a well-preserved rotunda that displays sculpture from the baths. As you face the church entrance, the Octagonal Hall is 100 yards to your left (free, open sporadically, generally Tue–Sat 9:00–14:00, Sun 9:00–13:00, closed Mon, borrow the English-description booklet, handy WC hiding in the back corner through an unmarked door).

The **Museum of the Bath** (Museo Nazionale Romano Terme di Diocleziano), which contains tons of Roman tombstones and inscriptions, is least interesting—not worth the time or energy for most visitors, and therefore not described here. The entrance faces the Termini train station (€5, covered by €20 Archeologia Card, audioguide-€4, Tue–Sun 9:00–19:45, closed Mon, last entry 45 min before closing, Viale E. de Nicola 79, tel. 06-4782-6152).

Energetic architecture wonks can even walk the perimeter of the baths: from Via Torino to Piazza dei Cinquecento to Via Volturno to Via XX Settembre.

Baths of Diocletian

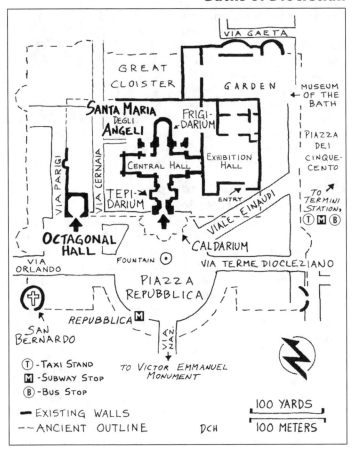

GREAT CLOISTER

GARDEN

MUSEUM OF THE BATH

SANTA MARIA DEGLI ANGELI

FRIGIDARIUM

PIAZZA DEI CINQUECENTO

VIA PARIGI

VIA CERNAIA

Central Hall

EXHIBITION HALL

TEPIDARIUM

ENTRY

VIALE EINAUDI

TO TERMINI STATION

OCTAGONAL HALL

FOUNTAIN

CALDARIUM

VIA ORLANDO

VIA TERME DIOCLEZIANO

PIAZZA REPUBBLICA

REPUBBLICA

SAN BERNARDO

TO VICTOR EMMANUEL MONUMENT

Ⓣ - TAXI STAND
Ⓜ - SUBWAY STOP
Ⓑ - BUS STOP

━ EXISTING WALLS
--- ANCIENT OUTLINE

DCH

|100 YARDS|
|100 METERS|

THE TOUR BEGINS

• *Start just outside the church of...*

SANTA MARIA DEGLI ANGELI

From noisy Piazza Repubblica, step through the curved brick wall of the ancient baths and into the cool church.

The Church's Entry Hall—The Baths' Tepidarium

This round-domed room with an oculus (open skylight, now with modern stained glass) was once the cooling-off room of the baths where medium, "tepid" temperatures were maintained. Romans loved to sweat out last night's indulgences at the baths. After stripping in the locker rooms, they'd enter the steam baths of the *caldarium*, located where Piazza Repubblica is today. The *caldarium* had wood furnaces—stoked by slaves—under the raised floors to heat the floors and hot tubs. The ceiling was low to keep the room steamy.

Next, you'd pass into this *tepidarium*, where masseuses would rub you down and scrape you off with a stick (Romans didn't use soap). Finally, you'd continue on to the central area of the baths...

The Church's Large Transept— The Baths' Central Hall

This hall retains the grandeur of the ancient baths. It's the size of a football field and seven stories high—originally higher, since the old floor was about 15 feet below its present level. The ceiling's crisscross arches were an architectural feat unmatched for a thousand years. The eight red granite columns are original, from ancient Rome—stand next to one and feel its five-foot girth. (Only the 8 in the transept proper are original. The others are made of plastered-over brick.) In Roman times, this hall was covered with mosaics, marble, and gold, and lined with statues.

From here, Romans could continue (through what is now the apse, near the altar) into a large, open-air courtyard to take a dip in the large 32,000-square-foot swimming pool (in the *frigidarium*) that paralleled this huge hall. Many other rooms, gardens, and courtyards extended beyond what we see here. The huge complex was built in only 10 years (around A.D. 300)—amazing when you think of the centuries it took builders of puny medieval cathedrals, such as Paris' Notre-Dame.

Mentally undress your fellow tourists and churchgoers, and imagine hundreds of naked or toga-clad Romans wrestling, doing jumping jacks, singing in the baths, networking, or just milling about.

The baths were more than washrooms. They were health clubs with exercising areas, equipment, and swimming pools. They had gardens for socializing. Libraries, shops, bars, fast-food vendors, pedicurists, depilatories, and brothels catered to every Roman need. Most important, perhaps, the baths offered a spacious, cool-in-summer/warm-in-winter place for Romans to get out of their stuffy apartments, schmooze, or simply hang out.

Admission was virtually free, requiring only the smallest coin. Baths were open to men and women—and during Nero's reign, coed bathing was popular—but generally there were either separate rooms or separate entry times. Most Romans went daily.

The church we see today was (at least partly) designed by Michelangelo (1561), who used the baths' main hall as the nave. Later, when Piazza Repubblica became an important Roman intersection, another architect renovated the church. To allow people to enter from the grand new piazza, he spun it 90 degrees, turning Michelangelo's nave into a long transept.

La Meridiana (1702)

On the floor of the right transept, the brass rod embedded in the floor is a meridian, pointing due north. It acts as a sundial. As the sun arcs across the southern sky, a ray of light beams into the church through a tiny hole high in the wall and a cut in the cornice of the right transept. (To find the hole, follow the rod south to the wall and look up 65 feet.) The sunbeam sweeps across the church floor, crossing the meridian rod at exactly noon. (Allow for variances due to daylight saving time and the approximate time zones of Greenwich Mean Time.)

This celestial clock is also a calendar. In summer, when the sun is high overhead, the sunbeam strikes the southern end of the rod. With each passing day, the sun travels up the rod (toward the apse), passing through the signs of the zodiac (the 28-day months of the moon's phases) marked alongside the rod. Many of the meridian's markings were intended for its other use, charting the movement of the stars. However, the tiny window that once let in light from the North Star (originally above the archway of the entrance to the apse) has been filled in.

Find some key dates in the Christian calendar, particularly the spring equinox and Easter (near Aries the Ram). Most Christians agree that Easter is the first Sunday after the first full moon after the vernal equinox (established with the Nicene Creed, A.D. 325). But it took large meridians like this to measure the sun's movements accurately enough to predict Easter and other holidays years in advance.

La Meridiana was the city of Rome's official timekeeper until 1846, when it was replaced by the cannon atop Gianicolo Hill that is (still) fired every day at exactly noon.

Sacristy

Step into the sacristy (free, left of main altar) for an English explanation of the church's architectural history and copies of Michelangelo's drawings. Notice the immensity and height of the ancient Roman brickwork in this room (just outside in the courtyard is a towering ancient brick wall and a WC). Large building projects like this were political security: They provided employment and fed the masses.

Diocletian (ruled A.D. 285–305) struggled with a system to rule his unwieldy empire. He broke it into zones ruled by four "tetrarchs." During Diocletian's "tetrarchs" period, architecture and art were grandiose, but almost a caricature of greatness—meant to proclaim to Romans that their city was still the power it had once been.

The baths were one of the last great structures built before Rome's 200-year fall. They functioned until A.D. 537, when barbarians cut the city's aqueducts, plunging Rome into a thousand years of poverty, darkness, and B.O.

• *Exit where you entered, turn right, and walk 100 yards to the entrance of the...*

OCTAGONAL HALL (AULA OTTAGONA)

This octagonal building, capped by a dome with a hole in the top, may have served as a cool room *(frigidarium)*, with small pools of cold water for plunging into. Or, because of its many doors, it may simply have been a large intersection, connecting other parts of the baths. Either way, it's one of Rome's best-preserved ancient rooms. Originally, the floor was 25 feet lower—as you can see through the glass-covered hole in the floor. The graceful iron grid overhead supported the canopy of a 1928 planetarium. Today, the hall is a free gallery showing off fine bronze and marble statues, some of which once decorated the Baths of Caracalla. Of the statues (mostly Roman copies of Greek originals—athletes, gods, Hercules, satyrs, and portraits), one merits a close look:

The Boxer at Rest (Pugilatore, 1st century B.C.)

An exhausted boxer sits between rounds and gasps for air. See the brass-knuckle-type Roman boxing gloves. Textbook Hellenistic, this bronze statue is realistic and full of emotion. His face is scarred, his back muscles are knotted, and he's got cauliflower ears. He's losing.

Slumped over, he turns with a questioning look ("Why am I losing again?"), and eyes that once held glass now make him look empty indeed. I coulda been a contender.

PIAZZA DELLA REPUBBLICA

The piazza, shaped like an exedra (a semicircular recess in a wall or building), echoes the wall of a stadium adjoining the original baths. It was called Piazza Esedra until Italian unification (and is still called that by many Romans). The thundering Via Nazionale starts at what was an ancient door. Look down it (past the erotic nymphs of the Naiad fountain) to the Victor Emmanuel Monument. The Art Nouveau fountain of the four water nymphs created quite a stir when unveiled in 1911. The nymphs were modeled after a set of twins, who kept coming to visit as late as the 1960s to remind themselves of their nubile youth.

NATIONAL MUSEUM OF ROME TOUR

(Museo Nazionale Romano Palazzo Massimo alla Terme)

Rome lasted a thousand years...and so do most Roman history courses. But if you want a breezy overview of this fascinating society, there's no better place than the National Museum of Rome.

Rome took Greek culture and wrote it in capital letters. Thanks to this lack of originality, ancient Greek statues were preserved for our enjoyment today. But the Romans also pioneered a totally new form of art—sculpting painfully realistic portraits of emperors and important citizens.

Think of this museum as a walk back in time. As you gaze at the same statues that the Romans swooned over, Rome comes alive—from Romulus sucking a she-wolf's teat to Julius Caesar's murder to Caligula's incest to the coming of Christianity.

ORIENTATION

Cost: €7, covered by €20 Archeologia Card.

Hours: Tue–Sun 9:00–19:45, closed Mon, last entry 45 min before closing.

Getting There: The museum is about 100 yards from the Termini train station (Metro: Termini). As you leave the station, it's the sandstone-brick building ahead on your left. Enter at the far end, at Largo di Villa Peretti.

Information: Tel. 06-481-5576.

Tours: An audioguide costs €4 (buy ticket first, then get audioguide at bookshop).

Length of This Tour: Allow two hours.

Starring: Roman emperor busts, *The Discus Thrower*, original Greek statues, and fine Roman copies.

THE TOUR BEGINS

Overview

The Palazzo Massimo is now the permanent home of the major Greek and Roman statues that were formerly scattered in other national museums around town.

The museum is rectangular, with rooms and hallways built around a central courtyard. The ground-floor displays follow Rome's history as it changes from a democratic republic to a dictatorial empire. The first-floor exhibits take Rome from its peak through its slow decline. The second floor houses rare frescoes and fine mosaics, and the basement displays coins and everyday objects. As you tour this museum, note that in Italian, "room" is *sala* and "hall" is *galleria*.

GROUND FLOOR— FROM SENATORS TO CAESARS

• *Buy your ticket and pass through the turnstile, where you'll find...*

Minerva

It's big, it's gaudy, it's a weird goddess from a pagan cult. Welcome to the Roman world. The statue is also a good reminder that all the statues in this museum—now missing limbs, scarred by erosion, or weathered down to the bare stone—were once whole and painted to look as lifelike as possible.

• *Turning to the right, you'll find Gallery I, lined with portrait busts.*

Gallery I—Portrait Heads from the Republic (500–1 B.C.)

Stare into the eyes of these stern, hardy, no-nonsense, farmer-stock people who founded Rome. The wrinkles and crags of these original "ugly Republicans" tell the story of Rome's roots as a small agricultural tribe, fighting for survival with neighboring bands.

These faces are brutally realistic, unlike more idealized Greek statues. Romans honored their ancestors and worthy citizens in the "family" *(gens)* of Rome. They wanted lifelike statues to remember them by, and to instruct the young with their air of moral rectitude.

In its first 500 years, Rome was a republic ruled by a Senate of wealthy landowners. But as Rome expanded throughout Italy and the economy shifted from farming to booty, changes were needed.

• *Enter Room I (Sala I). Along the wall between the doorways, find the portrait bust that some scholars think may be Julius Caesar.*

National Museum—Ground Floor

● Minerva	● Tiberius
● Portrait heads	● Caligula
● Julius Caesar	● Alexander the Great
● Augustus	● Socrates
● Four frescoes	● Niobid
● Livia	● Greek Mania

Room I

Julius Caesar *(Rilievo con Ritratto dalla collezione Von Bergen)*

Julius Caesar (c. 100–44 B.C.)—with his prominent brow, high cheekbones, and male-pattern baldness with the forward comb-over—changed Rome forever.

When this charismatic general swept onto the scene, Rome was in chaos. Rich landowners were fighting middle-class plebs, who wanted their slice of the plunder. Slaves such as Spartacus were picking up hoes and hacking up masters. And renegade generals—the new providers of wealth and security in a booty economy—were becoming dictators. (Notice the **life-size statue** of an unknown but obviously once-renowned general.)

Caesar was a people's favorite. He conquered Gaul (France), then sacked Egypt, then impregnated Cleopatra. He defeated rivals and made them his allies. He gave great speeches. Chicks dug him.

With the army at his back and the people in awe, he took the reins of government, instituted sweeping changes, made himself the center of power...and antagonized the Senate.

A band of Republican assassins surrounded him in a Senate meeting. He called out for help as one by one they stepped up to take turns stabbing him. The senators sat and watched in silence. One of the killers was his adopted son, Brutus, and Caesar—astonished that even Brutus joined in—died saying, *"Et tu, Brute?"*
• *At the end of Gallery I, turn left, then left again, into the large glassed-in Room V, with a life-size statue of Augustus.*

Room V—Augustus and Rome's Legendary Birth

Statue of Augustus as Pontifex Maximus
(Ritratto di Augusto in Vesta di Offerente)

Julius Caesar died, but his family name, his politics, and his flamboyance lived on. Julius had adopted his grandnephew, Octavian, who united Rome's warring factions and became the first emperor, Augustus.

Here, Emperor Augustus has taken off his armor and laurel-leaf crown, donning the simple hooded robes of a priest.
He's retiring to a desk job after a lifetime of fighting to reunite Rome. He killed Brutus and eliminated his rivals, Mark Antony and Cleopatra. For the first time in almost a century of fighting, one general reigned supreme. Octavian took the title "Augustus" and became the first of the emperors who would rule Rome for the next 500 years.

In fact, Augustus was a down-to-earth man who lived simply, worked hard, read books, listened to underlings, and tried to restore traditional Roman values after the turbulence of Julius Caesar's time. He outwardly praised the Senate, while actually reducing it to a rubber-stamp body. Augustus' reign marked the start of 200 years of peace and prosperity, the "Pax Romana."

See if the statue matches a description of Augustus by a contemporary—the historian Suetonius: "He was unusually handsome. His expression was calm and mild. He had clear, bright eyes, in which was a kind of divine power. His hair was slightly curly and somewhat golden." Any variations were made by sculptors who idealized features to make him almost godlike.

Augustus proclaimed himself a god—not arrogantly or blasphemously, as Caligula later did, but as the honored "father" of the "family" of Rome. As the empire expanded, the vanquished had to worship statues like this one as a show of loyalty.

• At this crucial dividing point in Roman history—from republic to empire—let's refresh our memory of Rome's legendary origins. At the opposite end of Room V, find...

Four Frescoes of Rome's Mythical Origins (*Fregio Pittorico,* etc.)

These cartoon-strip frescoes (read right to left) tell the story of Augustus' legendary forebears.

1. Upper right fresco: Aeneas (red skin and sword) arrives in Italy from Troy and fights the locals for a place to live.

2. Upper left: His wife (far left, seated, in purple) and son build a city wall around Rome to protect the womenfolk from battles raging outside.

3. Lower right: Several generations later, the God of War (lounging in center, with red skin) lies in wait to rape and impregnate a Vestal Virgin.

4. Lower left: Her disgraced babies, Romulus and Remus, are placed in a basket (center) and set adrift on the Tiber River. They wash ashore, are suckled by a she-wolf, and finally (far left) taken in by a shepherd. These legendary babies, of course, grow up to found the city that makes real history. The chisel marks were a preparation designed to help a later fresco (which was never applied) stick.

• Cross the hallway into Room IV. Find the bust near the doorway of the empress Livia.

Room IV—The Julio-Claudian Family: Rome's First Emperors (c. 50 B.C. –A.D. 68)

Julius Caesar's descendants ruled Rome for a century after his death, turning the family surname "Caesar" into a title.

Livia

Augustus' wife, Livia, was a major power behind the throne. Her stern, thin-lipped gaze withered rivals at court. Her hairstyle—bunched up in a peak, braided down the center, and tied in back—became the rage throughout the empire, as her face appeared everywhere in statues and on coins. Notice that by the next generation (Antonia Minore, Livia's daughter-in-law, next to Livia), a simpler bun was chic. And by the following generation, it was tight curls. Empresses dictated fashion the way that emperors dictated policy.

Livia bore Augustus no sons. She lobbied hard for Tiberius, her own son by a first marriage, to succeed as emperor. Augustus didn't like him, but Livia was persuasive. He relented, ate some bad figs, and died—the gossip was that Livia poisoned him to seal the bargain. The pattern of succession was established—adopt a son from within the extended family—and Tiberius was proclaimed emperor.

• *Over your left shoulder, in the corner of the room, is a well-worn...*

Tiberius (*Tiberio,* ruled A.D. 14–37)

Scholars speculate that acne may have soured Tiberius to the world (but this statue is pocked by erosion). Shy and sullen but diligent, he worked hard to be the easygoing leader of men that Augustus had been. Early on, he was wise and patient, but he suffered personal setbacks. Politics forced him to divorce his only beloved and marry a slut. His favorite brother died, then his son. Embittered, he let subordinates run things and retired to Capri, where he built a villa with underground dungeons. There he hosted orgies of sex, drugs, torture, really loud music, and execution. At his side was his young grandnephew, who he adopted as next emperor.

• *To your right, in the glass case, is the small bust of...*

Caligula (*Caligola,* ruled A.D. 37–41)

This emperor had sex with his sisters, tortured his enemies, stole friends' wives during dinner, then returned to rate their performance in bed, crucified Christians, took cuts in line at the Vatican Museum, and had men kneel before him as a god. Caligula has become the archetype of a man with enough power to act out his basest fantasies.

Politically, he squandered Rome's money, then taxed and extorted from the citizens. Perhaps he was made mad by illness, perhaps he was the victim of vindictive historians, but still, no one mourned when assassins ambushed him and ran a sword through his privates. Rome was tiring of this family dynasty's dysfunction.

• *Continue down Gallery II and turn left. Busts line Gallery III. Find Alexander and Socrates flanking the entrance into Room VII.*

Gallery III—Rome's Greek Mentors

Rome's legions easily conquered the less-organized but more-cultured Greek civilization that had dominated the Mediterranean for centuries. Romans adopted Greek gods, art styles, and fashions, and sophisticated Romans sprinkled their conversation with Greek phrases.

Alexander the Great (*Alessandro Magno*)

Alexander the Great (356–323 B.C.) single-handedly created a Greek-speaking empire by conquering, in just a few short years, lands from Greece to Egypt to Persia. Later, when the Romans conquered Greece (c. 200 B.C.), they inherited this pre-existing collection of cultured, Greek cities ringing the Mediterranean.

Alexander's handsome statues set the standard for those of later Roman emperors. His features were chiseled and youthful, and this statue was adorned with pompous decorations, like a golden sunburst aura (fitted into the holes). The greatest man of his day, he ruled the known world by the age of 30.

Alexander's teacher was none other than the philosopher Aristotle. Aristotle's teacher was Plato, whose mentor was...

Socrates *(Socrate)*
This nonconformist critic of complacent thinking is the father of philosophy. The Greeks were an intellectual, introspective, sensitive, and artistic people. The Romans were practical, no-nonsense soldiers, salesmen, and bureaucrats. Many a Greek slave was more cultured than his master, reduced to the role of warning his boss not to wear a plaid toga with a polka-dot robe.

• *Enter room VII between Alexander and Socrates.*

Room VII—Greek Beauty in Originals and Copies

Niobid (*Niobide Ferita,* 440 B.C.)
The Romans were astonished by the beauty of Greek statues. Niobid's smooth skin contrasts with the rough folds of her clothing. She twists naturally around an axis running straight up and down. This woman looks like a classical goddess awakening from a beautiful dream, but...

Circle around back. The hole bored in her back, right in that itchy place you can't quite reach, once held a golden arrow. The woman has been shot by Artemis, goddess of hunting, because her mother dared to boast to the gods about her kids. The Niobid reaches back in vain, trying to remove the arrow before it drains her of life.

Romans ate this stuff up: the sensual beauty, the underplayed pathos, the very Greekness of it. They crated up centuries-old

statues like this and brought them home to their gardens and palaces. Soon there weren't enough old statues to meet the demand. Crafty Greeks began cranking out knock-offs of Greek originals for mass consumption. In Rooms VII and VIII are originals (like Niobid) and copies—some of extremely high quality, while others were more like cheesy fake *David*s in a garden store. Appreciate the beauty of the world's rare, surviving Greek originals.

Rome conquered Greece, but culturally the Greeks conquered the Romans.

• *We've covered Rome's first 500 years. At the end of the hall are the stairs up to the first floor.*

FIRST FLOOR—
ROME'S PEAK AND SLOW FALL

As we saw, Augustus' family did not always rule wisely. Under Nero (ruled A.D. 54-68), the debauchery, violence, and paranoia typical of the Julio-Claudians festered to a head. When the city burned in the great fire of 64, the Romans suspected Nero of torching it himself to clear land for his enormous luxury palace.

Enough. Facing a death sentence, Nero committed suicide with the help of a servant. An outsider was brought in to rule— Vespasian, from the Flavian family.

• *At the top of the stairs, enter Room I. To your right is Vespasian.*

Room I—The Flavian Family

Vespasian (*Vespasianus,* ruled A.D. 69–79)

Balding and wrinkled, with a big head, a double chin, and a shy smile, Vespasian was a common man. The son of a tax collector, he rose through the military ranks with a reputation as a competent drudge. As emperor, he restored integrity, raised taxes, started the Colosseum, and suppressed the Jewish rebellion in Palestine.

• *In the center of the room is...*

Domitian (*Domitianus,* ruled A.D. 81–96)
Vespasian's son, Domitian, used his father's tax revenues to construct the massive Imperial Palace on Palatine Hill, home to emperors for the next three centuries. Shown with his lips curled in a sneering smile, he was a moralistic prude who executed several Vestal ex-Virgins, while in private he took one mistress after another. Until...

• *Over your left shoulder, find...*

Domitia
...his stern wife found out and hired a servant to stab him in the groin. Domitia's hairstyle is a far cry from the "Livia" cut, with a high crown of tight curls.

• *In the corner opposite Domitia is...*

Nerva (ruled A.D. 96–98)
Nerva realized that the Flavian dynasty was no better than its

National Museum—First Floor

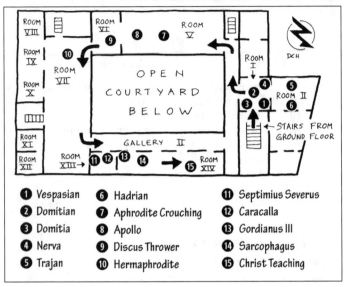

① Vespasian   **⑥** Hadrian   **⑪** Septimius Severus
② Domitian   **⑦** Aphrodite Crouching   **⑫** Caracalla
③ Domitia   **⑧** Apollo   **⑬** Gordianus III
④ Nerva   **⑨** Discus Thrower   **⑭** Sarcophagus
⑤ Trajan   **⑩** Hermaphrodite   **⑮** Christ Teaching

predecessors. Old and childless, he made a bold, far-sighted move—he adopted a son from outside of Rome's corrupting influence.
• *Entering Room II, Trajan is on the left wall.*

Room II—A Cosmopolitan Culture

Trajan (*Traianus-Hercules,* ruled A.D. 98–117)
Born in Spain, this conquering hero pushed Rome's borders to their greatest extent, creating a truly worldwide empire. The spoils of three continents funneled into a city of a million-plus people. Trajan could dress up in a lion's skin, presenting himself as a "new Hercules," and no one found it funny. Romans felt a spirit of Manifest Destiny: "The gods desire that the City of Rome shall be the capital of all the countries of the world." (Livy)
• *On the opposite wall...*

Hadrian (*Hadrianus,* ruled A.D. 117–138)
Hadrian was a fully cosmopolitan man. His beard—the first we've seen—shows his taste for foreign things; he poses like the Greek philosopher he imagined himself to be.

Hadrian was a voracious tourist, personally visiting almost every corner of the vast empire, from Britain (where he built Hadrian's Wall) to Egypt (where he sailed the Nile), from Jerusalem (where he suppressed another Jewish revolt) to Athens (where he soaked up classical culture). He scaled Sicily's Mount Etna just to see what made a volcano tick. Back home, he beautified Rome with the Pantheon and his Villa at Tivoli, a microcosm of places he'd visited.

Hadrian is flanked here by the two loves of his life. His wife, **Sabina** (left), with modest hairstyle and scarf, kept the home fires burning for her traveling husband. Hadrian was 50 years old when he became captivated by a teenage boy named **Antinous** (right), with his curly hair and full, sensual lips. Together they traveled the Nile, where Antinous drowned. Hadrian wept. Statues of Antinous subsequently went up through the Empire, much to the embarrassment of the stoic Romans.

Hadrian spent his last years at his lavish villa outside Rome, surrounded by buildings and souvenirs that reminded him of his traveling days.

• *Backtrack through Room I and turn right, down a hall that leads into the large Room V.*

Rooms V and VI—Rome's Grandeur

Pause at Rome's peak to admire the things the Romans found beautiful. Imagine these statues in their original locations, in the pleasure gardens of the Roman rich—surrounded by greenery, with the splashing sound of fountains, the statues all painted in bright, lifelike colors. Though executed by Romans, the themes are mostly Greek, with godlike humans and human-looking gods.

• *In the center of Room V is...*

Aphrodite Crouching (Afrodite Accovacciata)

The goddess of beauty crouches while bathing, then turns to admire herself. This sets her whole body in motion—one thigh goes down, one up; her head turns clockwise while her body goes reverse—yet she's perfectly still. The crouch creates a series of symmetrical love handles, molded by the sculptor into the marble like wax. Hadrian had good taste—he ordered a copy of this Greek classic for his bathroom.

• *Nearby, find the large statue of...*

Apollo

The god of light appears as a slender youth, not as some burly, powerful, autocratic god. He stands *contrapposto*— originally he was leaning against the tree—in a relaxed and very human way. His curled hair is tied with a headband, with strands that tumble down his neck. His muscles and skin are smooth. (The rusty stains come from the centuries

Apollo spent submerged in the Tiber.) Apollo is in a reflective mood, and the serenity and intelligence in his face show off classical Greece as a nation of thinkers.

• *At the end of the room is...*

The Discus Thrower (Discobolo)

An athlete winds up, about to unleash his pent-up energy and hurl the discus. The sculptor has frozen the moment for us, so that we can examine the inner workings of the wonder called Man. The perfect pecs and washboard abs make this human godlike. Geometrically,

you could draw a perfect circle around him, with his hipbone at the center. He's natural yet ideal, twisting yet balanced, moving while at rest. For the Greeks, the universe was a rational place, and the human body was the perfect em-bodi-ment of the order found in nature.

This statue is the best-preserved Roman copy (not one member is missing—I checked) of the original Greek work by Myron (450 B.C.). (The subtle nubs on his head were aids for a measuring device used when making copies.) Statues of athletes like this commonly stood in the baths, where Romans cultivated healthy bodies, minds, and social skills, hoping to live well-rounded lives. *The Discus Thrower*, with his geometrical perfection and godlike air, sums up all that is best in the classical world.

• *Continue into Room VII, where you'll run into a sleeping statue.*

Room VII

Hermaphrodite Sleeping (Ermafrodito Dormiente)

After leaving the baths, a well-rounded Roman may head posthaste to an orgy, where he might see a reclining nude like this, be titillated, circle around for a closer look, and say, "Hey! (Insert your own reaction here)!"

• *Exit Room VII at the far end and turn left. Then turn right into Room XIII, and look to the right to find the bust of Septimius Severus.*

Room XIII—Beginning of the End

Septimius Severus (ruled A.D. 193–211)

Rome's sprawling empire was starting to unravel, and it took a disciplined, emperor-warrior like this African to keep it together. Severus' victories on the frontier earned him a grand triumphal arch in the Forum, but here he seems to be rolling his eyes at the chaos growing around him.

• *Next to Severus is his son...*

Caracalla (ruled A.D. 211–217)

The stubbly beard, cruel frown, and glaring eyes tell us that Severus' son was bad news. He murdered his little brother to seize power, then proceeded to massacre thousands of loyal citizens on a whim. The army came to distrust rulers whose personal agenda got in their way, and Caracalla was stabbed in the back by a man whose brother had just been executed. Rome's long slide had begun.

Room XIV—The Fall

There are a lot of serious faces in this room. People who grew up in the lap of luxury and security were witnessing the unthinkable—the disintegration of a thousand years of tradition. Rome never recovered from the chaos of the third century. Disease, corruption, revolts from within, and "barbarians" pecking away at the borders were body blows that sapped Rome's strength.

• *At the near end of this long room, find...*

Gordianus III (ruled A.D. 238–244)

By the third century, the Roman army could virtually hand-pick an emperor to be their front man. At one point, the office of emperor was literally auctioned to the highest bidder.

Thirteen-year-old Gordianus, with barely a wisp of facial hair, was naive and pliable, the perfect choice—until he got old enough to question the generals. He was one of some 15 emperors in the space of 40 years who was saluted, then murdered, at the whim of soldiers of fortune. His assassins had no problem sneaking up on him because, as you can see, he had no ears.

Sarcophagus of a Procession (*Sarcofago con Corteo,* etc., A.D. 270)

A parade of dignitaries, accompanying a new Roman leader, marches up Capitol Hill. They huddle together, their backs to the wall, looking around suspiciously for assassins. Their faces reflect

the fear of the age. Rome would stagger on for another 200 years, but the glory of old Rome was gone. The city was becoming a den of thugs, thieves, prostitutes, barbarians...and Christians.

• *Farther along, on the right-hand wall, find the small...*

Seated Statuette of Christ Teaching (*Cristo Docente,* A.D. 350)

Christ sits like a Roman senator—in a toga, holding a scroll, dispensing wisdom like the law of the land. The statue comes from those delirious days when formerly persecuted Christians could now "come out" and worship in public. Emperor Constantine (ruled 306–337) legalized Christianity, and within two generations it was Rome's official religion.

Whether Christianity invigorated or ruined Rome is debated, but the fall was inevitable. Rome's once-great legions backpedaled, until even the city itself was raped and plundered by foreigners (410). In 476, the last emperor sold his title for a comfy pension plan, and "Rome" was just another dirty city with a big history. The barely flickering torch of ancient Rome was passed on to medieval Christians: Senators became bishops, basilicas became churches, the Pontifex Maximus (Emperor) became the Pontifex Maximus (Pope)...and the artistic masterpieces now in this museum became buried under rubble.

THE REST OF THE MUSEUM

The **second floor** contains frescoes and mosaics that once decorated the walls and floors of Roman villas. The frescoes—in black, red, yellow, and blue—show a few scenes of people and animals but are mostly architectural designs, with fake columns and "windows" that "look out" on landscape scenes.

The basement is worth a look. It houses a fascinating "Luxury in Rome" exhibit, featuring fine jewelry, common everyday objects, and a coin collection—a peek into the lives of Rome's well-to-do citizens. In A.D. 300, one denar bought one egg. Evaluate Roman life by studying Diocletian's wage and price controls (glass case 21).

Find your favorite emperor or empress on the **coins** by using remote-controlled magnifying glasses: Julius Caesar (case 8, #41–44), Augustus (case 8, #65–69, and case 9, #1–38), Augustus' system of denars (case 10), Tiberius (case 10, #1), Caligula (case 10, #17–28), and Nero (case 11, #2–33).

The displays trace Europe's money from denars to euros, including the monetary unit that is now history—*lire.*

CAPITOL HILL MUSEUM TOUR

(Musei Capitolini)

This enjoyable museum claims to be the world's oldest, founded in 1471 when a pope gave ancient statues to the citizens of Rome. Perched on the top of Capitol Hill Square, its two buildings (Palazzo dei Conservatori and Palazzo Nuovo) are connected by an underground passage that leads to the Tabularium and panoramic views of the Roman Forum.

ORIENTATION

Cost: €8; €9.90 combo-ticket includes Montemartini Museum (described on page 58).

Hours: Tue–Sun 9:00–20:00, closed Mon, last entry one hour before closing.

Getting There: From Piazza Venezia or the Forum, walk uphill to the top of Capitol Hill (Campidoglio in Italian). Tickets are sold only at the Palazzo dei Conservatori.

Information: You'll find some English descriptions within the museum. Free baggage check. Tel. 06-3996-7800, www.museicapitolini.org.

Tour: The €4 audioguide, available only at the Palazzo dei Conservatori entrance, is good.

Length of This Tour: Allow one hour.

Cuisine Art: There's a great view café, called Café Capitolino, upstairs in Palazzo dei Conservatori (enter from inside museum, also has exterior entrance for public—facing museum entrance, go to your right around building to Piazza Caffarelli and through door at #4, see page 158). The tent on the terrace outside offers full service; inside is self-service (pay first, then take receipt to bar; good salads and toasted sandwiches). Piazza Caffarelli is a fine place for a snooze or picnic.

Capitol Hill Overview

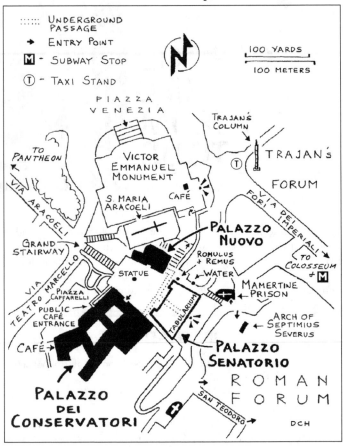

::::: UNDERGROUND
       PASSAGE
→   - ENTRY POINT
Ⓜ   - SUBWAY STOP
Ⓣ   - TAXI STAND

100 YARDS

100 METERS

PIAZZA
VENEZIA

TRAJAN'S
COLUMN

TO
PANTHEON

VICTOR
EMMANUEL
MONUMENT

TRAJAN'S

FORUM

VIA ARACOELI

S. MARIA
ARACOELI

CAFÉ

VIA DEI FORI IMPERIALI

PALAZZO
NUOVO

GRAND
STAIRWAY

ROMULUS
+ REMUS

TO
COLOSSEUM
& Ⓜ

STATUE

WATER

VIA TEATRO MARCELLO

PIAZZA
CAFFARELLI

MAMERTINE
PRISON

PUBLIC
CAFÉ
ENTRANCE

TABULARIUM

ARCH OF
SEPTIMIUS
SEVERUS

CAFÉ →

PALAZZO
SENATORIO

PALAZZO
DEI
CONSERVATORI

ROMAN
FORUM

SAN TEODORO

DCH

Starring: The original she-wolf statue, *Marcus Aurelius*, the *Dying Gaul*, the *Boy Extracting a Thorn*, and Forum views.

THE TOUR BEGINS

Overview

Capitol Hill Square, home to the museum, began in ancient Rome as a religious center, the site of temples to the gods Jupiter, Juno, and Minerva. In the 16th century, Michelangelo transformed the square from pagan to papal, while adding a harmonious and refined Renaissance touch. (For more on the square, see page 44.)

To identify the museum's two buildings, face the equestrian statue (with your back to the grand stairway). The Palazzo Nuovo (where you start this self-guided tour) is on your left, the Palazzo dei Conservatori (where you buy your ticket and finish) is on your right (closer to the river). Ahead is the Palazzo Senatorio (mayoral palace, not open to public—see photo at right); below it—and out of sight—are the Tabularium and underground passage connecting the two museum buildings.

With your ticket (valid for 3 hours), you can enter either museum (or connect the buildings underground).

Note that this museum is also referred to as the Capitoline Museums or Musei Capitolini.

• *Start at the...*

Palazzo Nuovo

• *After your ticket is checked, find the small courtyard. Behind glass is...*

Marcus Aurelius

This is the greatest surviving equestrian statue of antiquity. Marcus

Aurelius was a Roman philosopher-emperor (ruled A.D. 161–180), known more for his *Meditations* than his prowess on the battlefield. Notice that he doesn't use stirrups. An Asian invention, those new-fangled devices wouldn't arrive in Europe for another 500 years.

Christians in the Dark Ages thought that the statue's hand was raised in blessing, which probably led to their misidentifying him as Constantine, the first Christian emperor. While most pagan statues were destroyed by Christians, "Constantine" was spared. It has graced several prominent locations in medieval Rome, including the papal palace at San Giovanni in Laterano.

In 1538, Michelangelo placed this gilded bronze statue in the center of the square he designed, Capitol Hill Square, directly outside this museum. A few years ago, the statue was moved inside and restored, while a copy was placed on the square.

• *Go up the stairs and circle the building clockwise. The first room at the top contains one of the museum's most famous pieces.*

Dying Gaul

A first-century B.C. copy of a Greek original, this was sculpted to celebrate the Greeks' victory over the Galatians. This statue may have been part of a larger sculpture group (long since lost).

Wounded in battle, the dying Gaul holds himself upright, but barely. Minutes earlier, before he was stabbed in the chest, he'd been in his prime. Now he can only watch helplessly as his life ebbs away. His sword is useless against this last battle. With his messy hair, downcast eyes, and crumpled position, he poignantly reminds us that every victory means a defeat.

• *In the next few rooms, take a quick look at...*

Ancient Roman Statues and Busts

A reddish faun glories in grapes and life, oblivious to the loss of his penis (at least he still has his tail). The statue, found in a couple

dozen pieces in Hadrian's Villa, was skillfully restored. Check out the chandeliered ceilings in this room and elsewhere; this building is truly a *palazzo* (palace).

More sculpture from Hadrian's Villa (and elsewhere) fills the next room, the large hall. Notice the *Wounded Amazon* (near the window) undoing her delicate dress. This is a Roman copy of a fifth-century Greek original by Polycletus.

Roll through two rooms lined with busts—the Room of Philosophers (Socrates, Homer, Euripides, Cicero, and many more) and the Hall of Emperors (Constantine's mom Helena sits center stage, resting after her journey to Jerusalem to find Christ's Cross). In this 3-D yearbook of ancient history, there are few labels. The room's only purple bust is Caracalla. Infamous for his fervent brutality, he instructed his portraitists to stress his meanness. Directly across on the lower shelf is one of the finest busts of late antiquity, Emperor Gordiano. The bust shows the concerns and consternation of a ruler whose empire is in decline. In this room you can find classic expressions of confidence, brutality, and anguish—human drama through the ages. Don't miss the delicate elegance of the first-century A.D. woman with the complex hairdo by the window.

• *Enter the hallway and start down the hall. The small octagonal room— off to your left—contains one of the museum's treasures.*

Capitoline *Venus*

This is a Roman copy of a Greek fourth-century B.C. original by the master Praxiteles. Venus, leaving the bath, is suddenly aware that

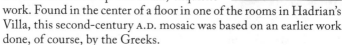

someone is watching her. As she turns to look, she reflexively covers up (nearly). Her blank eyes hold no personality or emotion. Her fancy hairstyle is the only complicated thing about her. She is simply beautiful—generically erotic.

• *Farther down the hallway, enter the small room to your left. Displayed on the wall is the...*

Mosaic of Doves

Four doves perch on the rim of a bronze bowl as one drinks water from the bowl. Minute bits make up this small, exquisite work. Found in the center of a floor in one of the rooms in Hadrian's Villa, this second-century A.D. mosaic was based on an earlier work done, of course, by the Greeks.

• *Head down the stairs to reach the underground passage (and WC). Follow signs back up one flight to the...*

Tabularium

Built in the first century B.C., these sturdy, vacant rooms once held the archives of ancient Rome. The word Tabularium comes from

"tablet," on which laws were written. Inside the Tabularium, you can look to your right to see the remains of an earlier temple, look up to see two huge white hunks of a temple overhang, and look down to see an underground passage, but the irresistible urge is to look out—at the Forum. This head-on view does justice to the Forum, giving you a more complete picture of the sprawl of ancient Rome.

The arcade of the Tabularium used to have more overlooks, but some of the arches were bricked up during the Middle Ages.

• *Leave the Tabularium by going back down the stairs, then take the underground passage and stairs up to the Palazzo dei Conservatori.*

Palazzo dei Conservatori

In the courtyard, enjoy the massive chunks of Constantine: his head, hand, and foot. When intact, this giant held the place of honor in the

Basilica of Constantine in the Forum. Also in the courtyard, as if still subservient to the emperor, are reliefs of conquered peoples—not in chains, but new members of an expansive empire.

• *Go up the staircase (the one in the corner of the courtyard) to the landing...*

Reliefs of Second-Century Imperial Grandeur

These four fine reliefs show great moments in an emperor's daily grind. Find Marcus Aurelius overseeing preparations to sacrifice a bull (with even the bull looking on curiously) on Capitol Hill. Also find Marcus Aurelius in an equestrian pose again (like the bronze statue), hand out, offering clemency to his vanquished foes. The detail, with expressive faces and banners blowing in the wind, is impressive. In the relief showing Marcus Aurelius in his chariot, someone's missing...it's Commodus, his wicked son (Russell Crowe's nemesis in *Gladiator*). After the assassination of Commodus, his memory was damned, so images of him were erased (or chiseled out, in this case).

• *Continue up the stairs to the first floor, where you'll find...*

Huge Statues, Huge Art—Roman Style

Here are more hunks of another statue of Constantine: head, finger, and a globe he held in his hand. The large wall paintings in this room commemorate the founding of Rome, from its wolfish origins (the twins Romulus and Remus nursed by a she-wolf) to the bloody battles fought with nearby tribes for supremacy. Everything in this room—the gargantuan *Constantine*, the gilded *Hercules*, and even the larger-than-life pope—is about power wielded by men.

• *For a contrast, power yourself straight ahead into the corner room to see one of the museum's highlights.*

Boy Extracting a Thorn (Spinario)

He's just a boy, intent only on picking a thorn out of his foot. As he

bends over to reach his foot, his body sticks out at all angles, like a bony chicken wing. He's even scuffed up, the way small boys get. At this moment, nothing matters to him but that splinter. Our lives are filled with these mundane moments (when we'd give anything for tweezers) rarely captured in art.

Art scholars speculate that the boy's head, tilted unnaturally down, and his body are from two separate statues spliced together.

• *In the next room...*

Capitoline *She-Wolf*

The original bronze *She-Wolf* suckles the twins Romulus and Remus. The wolf is Etruscan from the fifth century B.C., the boys an invention

of the Renaissance, and the result is the symbol of Rome. Look into the eyes of the wolf. An animal looks back, with ragged ears, sharp teeth, and staring eyes. This wild animal, teamed with the wildest creatures of all—hungry babies—makes a powerful symbol for the tenacious city/empire of Rome.

• *In the next room...*

From Michelangelo to Medusa

Along with a kindly bust of Michelangelo, this room contains Bernini's anguished bust of Medusa—with the writhing snakes on her head. This goes way beyond a bad hair day.

• *Walk between Michelangelo and Medusa to the next room to discover the remarkable bust of...*

Commodus as Hercules

This arrogant emperor brat used to run around the palace in animal skins. Here, he wears a lion's head over his own, and drapes the lion's paws over his chest. This lion king made a bad emperor (ruled A.D. 180–192).

• *Go upstairs to the...*

Painting Gallery

Wander among works by Van Dyck, Velázquez (self-portrait near entry), Titian, Tintoretto, and Giovanni Bellini. The highlights are two works by Caravaggio: *St. John the Baptist* and an earlier work, *The Fortune Teller* (both in the large Santa Petronilla room).

• *Head upstairs to the café.*

View Café

You've earned the café. Its huge outdoor view patio overlooks the domes of Rome. From the Tabularium, you saw the Forum, the heart of ancient Rome. From here, you see the churches, representing the religion that remained after Rome fell. Be here at sunset—it's divine.

BORGHESE GALLERY TOUR

(Galleria e Museo Borghese)

More than just a great museum, Galleria Borghese is a beautiful villa set in the greenery of surrounding gardens. You get to see art commissioned by the luxury-loving Borghese family displayed in the very rooms they were created for. Frescoes, marble, stucco, and interior design enhance the masterpieces. This is a place where—regardless of whether you learn a darn thing—you can sit back and enjoy the sheer beauty of the palace and its art.

ORIENTATION

Cost: €8.50, includes €2 reservation fee.

Hours: Tue–Sun 9:00–19:00, closed Mon.

Reservations: Reservations are mandatory and easy to get in English by booking online (www.ticketeria.it) or calling 06-328-101 (if you get an Italian recording, press 2 for English; office hours: Mon–Fri 9:00–18:00, Sat 9:00–13:00, office closed Sat in Aug and Sun year-round). Every two hours, 360 people are allowed to enter the museum. Entry times are 9:00, 11:00, 13:00, 15:00, and 17:00. Reserve a *minimum* of several days in advance for a weekday visit, at least a week ahead for weekends. Reservations are tightest at 11:00 and on weekends. When you reserve, request a day and time, and you'll get a claim number. While you'll be advised to come 30 minutes before your appointed time, I was told you can arrive 10 minutes beforehand. After that, you become a no-show, and your ticket is sold to stand-bys.

If you don't have a reservation, try calling to see if there are any openings, or just show up and hope for a cancellation. No-shows are released a few minutes after the top of the hour. Generally, out of 360 reservations, a few will fail to show (but more than a few may be waiting to grab them). You're most likely to land a stand-by ticket at 13:00.

Visits are strictly limited to two hours. Concentrate on the ground floor, but leave yourself 30 minutes—any time during your visit—for the paintings of the Pinacoteca upstairs (highlights are marked by the audioguide icons). The fine bookshop and cafeteria are best visited outside your two-hour entry window.

Getting There: The museum is in the Villa Borghese park. A taxi can get you within 100 yards of the museum (tell the cabbie your destination: gah-leh-REE-ah bor-GAY-zay). Getting to the museum by public transportation can be confusing, and requires a walk in the park. From the Spagna Metro stop, an escalator carries you up into the park, where you follow signs for 10 minutes. To avoid missing your appointment, allow yourself plenty of time to find the place.

Tours: Guided English tours are offered at 9:10 and 11:10 for €5; reserve with entry reservation (or consider the excellent audioguide tour for €4).

Length of This Tour: Allow two hours maximum.

Checkroom: Baggage check is free and mandatory.

Cuisine Art: A café is on-site.

Photography: No photos are allowed.

Starring: Sculptures by Bernini, Canova's *Venus*, and paintings by Caravaggio, Raphael, and Titian.

THE TOUR BEGINS

Portico
Ancient Roman reliefs (at either end), topped by Michelangelo-designed panels, capture the essence of the collection—a gathering of beautiful objects from every age and culture inside a lavish 17th-century villa. Cardinal Scipione Borghese built the villa, collected ancient works, and hired the best artists of his day. In pursuing the optimistic spirit of the Renaissance, they invented Baroque.

Main Entry Hall
Five Roman mosaics adorn the floor with colorful, festive scenes of slaughter. Gladiators fight animals and each other with swords, whips, and tridents. The Greek letter τ marks the dead. Notice some of the gladiators' pro-wrestler nicknames: "Cupid(-o)," "Serpent(-ius)," "Licentious(-us)."

Borghese Gallery—Ground Floor

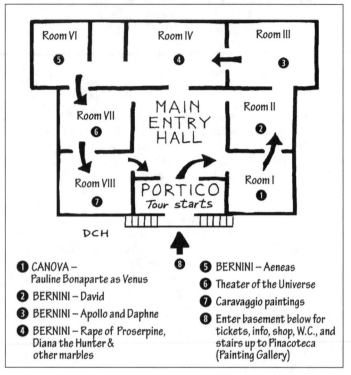

On the wall is a thrilling first-century Greek sculpture of a horse falling. The Renaissance-era rider was added by Pietro Bernini, father of the famous Gian Lorenzo Bernini.

Room I

Antonio Canova—*Pauline Bonaparte as Venus* (*Paolina Borghese Bonaparte*, 1808)

Napoleon's sister went the full monty for the sculptor Canova, scandalizing Europe. ("How could you have done such a thing?!" she

was asked. She replied, "The room wasn't cold.") With the famous nose of her conqueror brother, she strikes the pose of Venus as conqueror of men's hearts. Her relaxed afterglow and slight smirk say she's already had her man. The light dent she puts in the mattress makes this goddess human.

Notice the contrasting textures that Canova gets out of the pure-white marble: the rumpled sheet versus her smooth skin. The satiny-smooth pillows and mattress versus the creases in them. Her porcelain skin versus the hint of a love handle. Canova polished and waxed the marble until it looked as soft and pliable as cloth.

The mythological pose, the Roman couch, the ancient hairdo, and the calm harmony make Pauline the epitome of the neoclassical style.

Room II

Gian Lorenzo Bernini—*David* (1624)

Duck! David twists around to put a big rock in his sling. He purses his lips, knits his brow, and winds his body like a spring as his

eyes lock onto the target—Goliath, who's somewhere behind us, putting us right in the line of fire.

In this self-portrait, 25-year-old Bernini (1598–1680) is ready to take on the world. He's charged with the same fighting energy that fueled the missionaries and conquistadors of the Counter-Reformation.

Compared with Michelangelo's *David*, this is gritty realism—an unbalanced pose, bulging veins, unflattering face, and armpit hair. Bernini slays the pretty-boy *David*s of the Renaissance and prepares to invent Baroque.

To David's left, find the ancient sarcophagus on the wall with the ***Labors of Hercules*** (A.D. 160, at chest level). The twisting bodybuilders' poses were the Hellenistic inspiration for Bernini's Baroque. In the last scene, Hercules pauses while subduing a centaur to adjust himself.

Room III

Bernini—*Apollo and Daphne* (*Apollo e Dafne*, 1625)

Apollo—made stupid by Cupid's arrow of love—chases after Daphne, who has been turned off by the "arrow of disgust." Just as he's about to catch her, she calls to her father to save her. Magically, her fingers begin to sprout leaves, her toes become roots, her skin turns to bark, and she transforms into

Gian Lorenzo Bernini
(1598–1680)

A Renaissance man in Counter-Reformation times, Bernini almost personally invented the Baroque style, transforming the city of Rome. If you're visiting Rome, you will see Bernini's work, guaranteed.

Bernini was a child prodigy in his father's sculpting studio, growing up among Europe's rich and powerful. His flamboyant personality endeared him to his cultured employers—the popes in Rome, Louis XIV in France, and Charles I in England. He was extremely prolific, working fast and utilizing an army of assistants.

Despite the fleshiness and sensuality of his works, Bernini was a religious man, seeing his creativity as an extension of God's. In stark contrast to the Protestant world's sobriety, Bernini shamelessly embraced pagan myths and nude goddesses, declaring them all part of the "Catholic"—that is, universal—Church.

Bernini, a master of multimedia, was a...

- Sculptor (Borghese Gallery, *St. Teresa in Ecstasy*— page 49)
- Architect (elements of St. Peter's—see "Bernini Blitz," page 218, and the Church of Sant'Andrea al Quirinale)
- Painter (Borghese Gallery)
- Interior decorator (the *baldacchino* canopy and other stuff in St. Peter's, page 215)
- Civic engineer (he laid out St. Peter's Square—page 205, and he designed and renovated Rome's fountains in Piazza Navona—page 72, Piazza Barberini, Piazza di Spagna, and more).

Even works done by other artists a century later (such as the Trevi Fountain) can be traced indirectly to Bernini, the man who invented Baroque, the "look" of Rome for the next two centuries.

a tree. Frustrated Apollo will end up with a handful of leaves.

Stand behind the statue to experience it as Bernini originally intended. It's only when you circle around to the front that he reveals the story's surprise ending.

Walk slowly around the statue. Apollo's back leg defies gravity. Bernini has chipped away more than half of the block of marble, leaving airy, open spaces. The statue was two years in restoration (described to me as similar to dental work). The marble leaves at the top ring like crystal when struck. Notice the same scene, colorized, painted on the ceiling above.

Bernini carves out some of the chief features of Baroque art: He makes a supernatural event seem realistic. He freezes it at the most dramatic, emotional moment. The figures move and twist in unusual poses. He turns the wind machine on, sending Apollo's cape billowing behind him. It's a sculpture group of two, forming a scene, rather than a stand-alone portrait. And the subject is classical. Even in strict Counter-Reformation times, there was always a place for groping, if the subject matter had a moral—this one taught you not to pursue fleeting earthly pleasures. And, besides, Bernini tends to show a lot of skin, but no genitals.

Room IV

Bernini—*The Rape of Proserpine* (*Il Ratto di Proserpina*, 1622)

Pluto strides into the Underworld and shows off his catch—the beautiful daughter of the earth goddess. His three-headed guard dog, Cerberus, barks triumphantly. Pluto is squat, thick, and uncouth, with knotted muscles and untrimmed beard. He's trying not to hurt her, but she pushes her divine molester away and twists to call out for help. Tears roll down her cheeks. She wishes she could turn into a tree.

Bernini was the master of marble. Look how Pluto's fingers dig into her thigh like it was real flesh. Bernini picked out this Carrara marble, knowing that its relative suppleness and ivory hue would lend itself to a fleshy statue.

• *In a niche over Pluto's right shoulder, find...*

Artist Unknown—*Diana the Hunter (Artemide)*

The goddess has been running through the forest. Now she's spotted her prey, and slows down, preparing to string her (missing) bow with an arrow. Or is she smoking a (missing) cigarette? Scholars debate it.

The statues in the niches are classical originals. *Diana the Hunter* is a rare Greek original, with every limb and finger intact, from the second century B.C. The traditional *contrapposto* pose (weight on one leg) and idealized grace were an inspiration for artists such as Canova, who grew tired of Bernini's Baroque bombast.

The Marbles in Room IV

Appreciate the beauty of the different types of marble in the room: Bernini's ivory Carrara, *Diana*'s translucent white, purple porphyry emperors, granite-like columns that support them, wood-grained pilasters on the walls, and the different colors on the floor—green, red, gray, lavender, and yellow, some grainy, some "marbled" like a steak. Some of the world's most beautiful and durable things have been made from the shells of sea creatures layered in sediment, fossilized into limestone, then baked and crystallized by the pressure of the earth—marble.

Room VI

Bernini—*Aeneas (Enea che fugge, etc., 1620)*

Aeneas' home in Troy is in flames, and he escapes with the three most important things: his family (decrepit father on his shoulder, baby boy), his household gods (the statues in dad's hands), and the Eternal Flame (carried by son). They're all in shock, lost in thought, facing an uncertain future. Aeneas isn't even looking where he's going; he just puts one foot in front of the other. Little do they know that eventually they'll wind up in Italy, where—according to legend—Aeneas will found the city of Rome and house the flame in the Temple of Vesta.

Bernini was still a teenager when he started this, his first life-size work. He was probably helped by his dad, who nurtured the child prodigy much like Leopold mentored Mozart, but without the rivalry. Bernini's portrayal of human flesh—from baby fat to middle-aged muscle to sagging decrepitude—is astonishing. Still, the flat-footed statue just stands there—not nearly as interesting as the reliefs up at the ceiling, with their dancing, light-footed soldiers with do-si-do shields.

Room VII

The "Theater of the Universe"

The room's decor sums up the eclectic nature of the villa. There are Greek statues and Roman mosaics. There are fake "Egyptian" sphinxes and hieroglyphs (perfectly symmetrical in good neo-classical style). Look out the window past the sculpted gardens, at the mesh domes of the aviary once filled with exotic birds. Cardinal Borghese's vision was to make a place where art, history, music, nature, and science from every place and time would come together... "a theater of the universe."

Room VIII

Caravaggio

The paintings in this room change often, but you'll likely find at least one or two by the Baroque innova-tor Caravaggio (1571–1610). Caravaggio brought Christian saints and Greek gods down to earth with gritty realism. His saints are balding and wrinkled. His Bacchus (a self-portrait) is pale and puffy-faced. David sticks Goliath's sev-ered head (a self-portrait) right in your face. The Madonnas scarcely glow. The boy Jesus is buck naked. Ordinary people were his models. People emerge from a dark background, lit by a harsh, unflat-

tering light, which highlights part of the figure, leaving the rest in deep shadows. Caravaggio's straightforwardness can be a refreshing change in a museum full of (sometimes overly) refined beauty.

• *To reach the Pinacoteca, go outside and return to the basement where you got your ticket, follow signs to the Pinacoteca, show your ticket to the guard, and climb the long spiral stairway.*

Pinacoteca (Painting Gallery)

Remember, you're limited to only 30 minutes in the Pinacoteca, and you must visit it within the two-hour window of time printed on your ticket. Most visitors wait until the last half hour to see the Pinacoteca, so that's when it's most crowded (and the ground floor is less crowded). If you see the paintings first, remember that dur-ing a two-hour visit, the ground floor with the sculpture is worth most of that time.

• *Along the long wall of Room XIV, you'll find a number of statues and paintings, many of them by Bernini.*

Room XIV

Bernini—*Bust of Cardinal Borghese* (*Ritr. del Card. Scipione Borghese*, 1632)

Say *grazie* to the man who built this villa, assembled the collection, and hired Bernini to sculpt masterpieces. The cardinal is caught turning as though to greet someone at a party. There's a twinkle in his eye, and he opens his mouth to make a witty comment. This man of the cloth was, in fact, a sophisticated hedonist.

Notice that there are two identical versions of this bust. The first one started cracking along the forehead (visible) just as Bernini was finishing it. *No problema*, Bernini whipped out a replacement in three days.

• *On the wall above the table, find these paintings...*

Two Bernini Self-Portraits (*Autoritratto Giovanile,* 1623; and *Autoritratto in età Matura,* 1630/35)

Bernini was a master of many media, including painting. The younger Bernini looks out a bit hesitantly, as if he's still finding his way in high-class society. His jet-black eyes came from his Southern Italian mother who, it's said, also gave him his passionate personality.

In his next self-portrait, with a few masterpieces under his belt, Bernini shows himself with more confidence and facial hair—the dashing, flamboyant man who would rebuild Rome in Baroque style, from St. Peter's Square to the fountains that dot the piazzas.
• *On the table nearby, find the smaller...*

Bust of Pope Paul V

The cardinal's uncle was a more sober man, but he was also a patron of the arts with a good eye for talent who hired Bernini's father. When Pope Paul V saw sketches made by little Gian Lorenzo, he announced: "This boy will be the Michelangelo of his age."
• *Also nearby, find a small statue of...*

Two Babies Milking a Goat

Bernini may have been as young as 10 years old when he did this. That's about the age when I mastered how to make a Play-Doh snake.
• *Room IX is back near the top of the staircase you came up on.*

Room IX

Raphael (Raffaello Sanzio)—*Deposition* (*Deposizione di Cristo,* 1507)

Jesus is being taken from the cross. The men support him while the women support Mary (in purple), who has fainted. Mary Magdalene rushes up to take Christ's hand. The woman who com-

missioned the painting had recently lost her son. She wanted to show the death of a son and the grief of a mother. We see two different faces of grief—mother Mary faints at the horror, while Mary Magdalene still can't quite believe he's gone.

In true Renaissance style, Raphael (1483–1520) orders the scene with geometrical perfection. The curve of Jesus' body is echoed by the swirl of Mary Magdalene's hair, and then by the curve of Calvary Hill, where Christ met his fate.

Room X

Correggio—*Danaë* (c. 1531)

Cupid strips Danaë as she spreads her legs, most unladylike, to receive a trickle of gold from the smudgy cloud overhead—this

was Zeus' idea of intercourse with a human. The sheets are rumpled, and Danaë looks right where the action is with a smile on her face. It's hard to believe that a supposedly religious family would display such an erotic work. But the Borgheses felt that the Church was truly "catholic" (universal), and that all forms of human expression—including physical passion—glorified God.

• *Backtrack through the room of the two cardinal busts, then turn left and travel to the farthest room.*

Room XX

Titian (Tiziano Vecellio)—*Sacred and Profane Love* (*Amor Sacra e Amor Profane*, c. 1515)

The clothed woman at left was recently married, and she cradles a vase filled with jewels representing the riches of earthly love. Her naked twin on the right holds the burning flame of eternal, heavenly love. Baby Cupid, between them, playfully stirs the waters.

Symbolically, the steeple on the right points up to the love of heaven, while on the left, soldiers prepare to "storm the castle" of the new bride. Miss Heavenly Love looks jealous.

This exquisite painting expresses the spirit of the Renaissance—that earth and heaven are two sides of the same coin. And here in the Borghese Gallery, that love of earthly beauty can be spiritually uplifting—as long as you feel it within two hours.

VATICAN MUSEUM TOUR

(Musei Vaticani)

The glories of the ancient world displayed in a lavish papal palace, decorated by the likes of Michelangelo and Raphael...the Musei Vaticani. Unfortunately, many tourists see the Vatican Museum only as an obstacle between them and its grand finale, the Sistine Chapel. True, this huge, confusing, and crowded mega-museum can be a jungle—but with this book as your vine, you should swing through with ease, enjoying the highlights and getting to the Sistine just before you collapse. On the way, you'll enjoy some of the less appreciated but equally important sections of this ware-house of Western civilization.

ORIENTATION

Cost: €12, free (and packed) on last Sun of each month.

Dress Code: Modest dress (no short shorts or bare shoulders) is appropriate and often required.

Hours: March–Oct Mon–Fri 8:45–16:45, Sat 8:45–13:45; Nov–Feb Mon–Sat 8:45–13:45; closed Sun except last Sun of the month (when it's free, crowded, and open 8:45–13:45). Last entry is about 90 minutes before closing time.

   The museum is closed on many holidays (mainly religious ones) including, for 2006: Jan 1 (New Year's), Jan 6 (Epiphany), Feb 11 (Vatican City established), March 19 (Saint Joseph), April 16–17 (Easter Sunday and Monday), May 1 (Labor Day), May 25 (Ascension Thursday), June 15 (Corpus Christi Day), June 29 (Saints Peter and Paul), Aug 15 plus either Aug 14 or 16—it varies year to year (Assumption of the Virgin), Nov 1 (All Saints' Day), Dec 8 (Immaculate Conception), and Dec 25–26 (Christmas). Other holidays may pop up—search for "closed dates" at www.vatican.va.

The Sistine Chapel closes before the museum. Individual rooms may close at odd hours, especially after 13:00. TV screens inside the entrance list closures. The rooms described here are usually open. It's great to be in the Sistine Chapel at the quiet end of the day. Plan to finish here (the closing bell rings at 16:30 on days the museum closes at 16:45) in time to sneak directly into St. Peter's for a Mass or tour (see next chapter).

Avoiding Lines: The museum is generally hot and crowded. The most crowded days are Saturday, the last Sunday of the month, Monday, rainy days, and any day before or after a holiday closure. Afternoons are best. On days the museum closes at 16:45, arriving by 13:00 works well. Most mornings, there's a line to get in that stretches around the block. (Stuck in the line? Figure about a 10-minute wait for every 100 yards.)

Getting There: The nearest Metro stop, Cipro–Musei Vaticani, is a 10-minute walk from the entrance. From St. Peter's Square, it's about a 15-minute walk (follow the Vatican Wall). Taxis are reasonable (hop in and say, "moo-ZAY-ee vah-tee-KAH-nee").

Information: The info desk is under the electronic reader boards, immediately to your left as you enter. You'll find a bookstore kiosk in the lobby, another up the stairs, and others scattered throughout the museum. Some exhibits have English explanations. Tel. 06-6988-4947 or 06-6988-3333. For news about the pope, tours, and the museum, and to confirm hours, visit www.vatican.va. For more on Vatican City, see page 202.

Exchange windows with sinful rates are in the entry and exit. The post office is upstairs.

Tours: Tours in English are offered daily at 10:30, 12:00, and 14:00 (€10 plus admission, 2 hrs, fax 06-6988-5100 up to 30 days before your visit; with a confirmed booking you can skip queue and enter through exit—next to entry—to reach Guided Tours desk). If you rent a €6 audioguide, you lose the option of taking the shortcut from the Sistine Chapel to St. Peter's (because audioguide must be returned at museum entrance).

Length of This Tour: Until you expire or 2.5 hours, whichever comes first.

Cuisine Art: A cafeteria is upstairs, above the entrance. Cheaper choices: The great Via Andrea Doria produce market is three blocks north of the entrance (head across the street, down the stairs, and continue straight), and inexpensive Pizza Rustica shops (which sell pizza to go) line Viale Giulio Cesare. Good restaurants are nearby (see page 274).

Photography: No photos are allowed in the Sistine Chapel. Elsewhere in the museum, photos without a flash are permitted.

Vatican Museum Overview

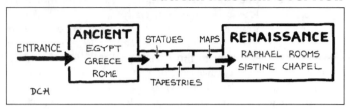

Starring: World history, Michelangelo, Raphael, *Laocoön*, the Greek masters, and their Roman copyists.

THE TOUR BEGINS

Overview

With the Fall of Rome, the Catholic (or "universal") Church became the great preserver of civilization, collecting artifacts from cultures dead and dying. Renaissance popes (15th and 16th centuries) collected most of what we'll see, using it as furniture to decorate their palace (today's museum). Combining the classical and Christian worlds, they found the divine in the creations of man.

We'll concentrate on classical sculpture and Renaissance painting. But along the way (and there's a lot of along-the-way here), we'll stop to leaf through a few yellowed pages from this 5,000-year-old scrapbook of humankind.

This heavyweight museum is shaped like a barbell—two buildings connected by a long hall. The entrance building covers the ancient world (Egypt, Greece, Rome). The one at the far end covers its "rebirth" in the Renaissance (including the Sistine Chapel). The halls there and back are a mix of old and new. Move quickly—don't burn out before the Sistine Chapel at the end—and see how each civilization borrows from and builds on the previous one.

• *Leave Italy by entering the doors. You may need to go through a security check (like at an airport). Go upstairs (or take the elevator) to buy your ticket, punch it in the turnstiles, then take the long escalator or spiral stairs up, up, up.*

At the top: To your right is the café and the Pinacoteca painting gallery (consider touring the Pinacoteca now if you want the option of taking the shortcut from the Sistine Chapel directly to St. Peter's; for information on the Pinacoteca, see the end of this chapter). To your left is the beginning of our tour. Go left, then take another left up a flight of stairs to reach the first-floor Egyptian Rooms (Museo Egizio). Don't stop until you find your mummy.

The Ancient World

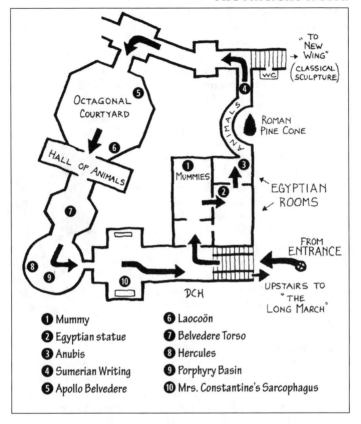

1 Mummy
2 Egyptian statue
3 Anubis
4 Sumerian Writing
5 Apollo Belvedere
6 Laocoön
7 Belvedere Torso
8 Hercules
9 Porphyry Basin
10 Mrs. Constantine's Sarcophagus

EGYPT (3000–1000 B.C.)

Egyptian art was for religion, not decoration. A statue or painting preserved the likeness of someone, giving him a form of eternal life. Most of the art was for tombs, where they put the mummies.

Mummies

This woman died three millennia ago. Her corpse was disemboweled, and her organs were placed in a jar like those you see nearby. Then the body was refilled with pitch, dried with natron (a natural sodium carbonate), wrapped in linen, and placed in a wood coffin, which

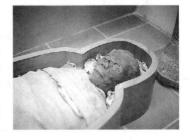

went inside a stone coffin, which was placed in a tomb. (Remember that the pyramids were just big tombs.) Notice the henna job on her hair—in the next life, the spirit was homeless without its body, and you wanted to look your best.

Painted inside the coffin lid is a list of what the deceased "packed" for the journey to eternity. The coffins were decorated with magical spells to protect the body from evil and to act as crib notes for the confused soul in the netherworld.

• *In the next room are...*

Egyptian Statues

Egyptian statues walk awkwardly, as if they're carrying heavy buckets, with arms straight down at their sides. Even these Roman reproductions (made for Hadrian's Villa) are stiff, two-dimensional, and schematic—the art is only realistic enough to get the job done. In Egyptian belief, a statue like this could be a stable refuge for the wandering soul of a dead man. Each was made according to an established set of proportions. Little changed over the centuries. These had a function, and they worked.

Various Egyptian Gods as Animals

Before technology made humans top dogs on earth, it was easier to appreciate our fellow creatures. Egyptians saw the superiority of animals and worshiped them as incarnations of the gods. Wander through a pet store of Egyptian animal gods. Find Anubis, a jackal in a toga. The lioness portrays the fierce goddess Sekhmet. The clever baboon is the god of wisdom, Thot. At the end of the hall is Bes, the patron of pregnant women (and beer-bellied men).

• *Continue through a curved corridor of animal gods, then through three more rooms, pausing at the glass case in the third room (Room VIII), which contains brown clay tablets.*

Sumerian Writing

Even before Egypt, civilizations flourished in the Middle East. The Sumerian culture in Mesopotamia (the ancestors of the ancient Babylonians and of Saddam Hussein) invented writing in about 3000 B.C. The clay tablets were written on by pressing into the wet clay with a wedge-shaped (cuneiform) pen. The Sumerians also rolled cylinder seals into soft clay to make an impression used to seal documents and mark property.

• *Go with the flow to a balcony that has a view of Rome out the window, then turn left into an octagonal courtyard.*

SCULPTURE—GREECE AND ROME
(500 B.C.–A.D. 500)

This palace wouldn't be here, this sculpture wouldn't be here, and our lives would likely be quite different if it weren't for a few thousand Greeks in a small city about 450 years before Christ. Athens set the tone for the rest of the West. Democracy, theater, economics, literature, and art all flourished in Athens during a 50-year "Golden Age." Greek culture was then appropriated by Rome and revived again 1,500 years later, during the Renaissance. The Renaissance popes built and decorated these palaces, re-creating the glory of the classical world.

Apollo Belvedere

Apollo, the god of the sun and of music, is hunting. He's been running through the woods, and now he spots his prey. Keeping his eye on the animal, he slows down and prepares to put a (missing) arrow into his (missing) bow. The optimistic Greeks conceived of their gods in human form... and buck naked.

The Greek sculptor Leochares, following the style of the greater Greek sculptor Praxiteles, has fully captured the beauty of the human form. The anatomy is perfect, his pose is natural. Instead of standing at attention, face forward with his arms at his sides (Egyptian style), Apollo is on the move, coming to rest, with his weight on one leg.

The Greeks loved balance. A well-rounded man was both a thinker and an athlete, a poet and a warrior. In art, the *Apollo Belvedere* balances several opposites. He's moving, but not out of control. Apollo eyes his target, but hasn't attacked yet. He's realistic but with idealized, godlike features. And the smoothness of his muscles is balanced by the rough folds of his cloak. The only sour note: his recently added left hand. Could we try a size smaller?

During the Renaissance, when this Roman copy of the original Greek work was discovered, it was considered the most perfect work of art in the world. The handsome face, eternal youth, and the body that seems to float just above the pedestal made *Apollo Belvedere* seem superhuman, divine, and godlike, even for devout Christians.

• *In the neighboring niche to the right, a bearded old Roman river god lounges in the shade. This pose inspired Michelangelo's Adam, in the Sistine Chapel (coming soon). While there are a few fancy bathtubs in this courtyard, most of the carved boxes you see are sarcophagi—Roman coffins and relic holders, carved with the deceased's epitaph in picture form.*

Laocoön

Laocoön (lay-AWK-oh-wahn), the high priest of Troy, warned his fellow Trojans: "Beware of Greeks bearing gifts." The attacking Greeks had brought the Trojan Horse to the gates as a ploy to get inside the city walls, and Laocoön tried to warn his people not to bring it inside. But the gods wanted the Greeks to win, so they sent huge snakes to crush him and his two sons to death. We see them at the height of their terror, when they realize that, no matter how hard they struggle, they—and their entire race—are doomed.

The figures (carved from 4 blocks of marble pieced together seamlessly) are powerful, not light and graceful. The poses are as twisted as possible, accentuating every rippling muscle and bulging vein. Follow the line of motion from *Laocoön*'s left foot, up his leg, through his body, and out his right arm (which some historians used to think extended straight out—until the elbow was dug up early in the 1900s). Goethe would stand here and blink his eyes rapidly, watching the statue flicker to life.

The *Laocoön* was sculpted four centuries after the Golden Age, after the scales of "balance" had been tipped. Whereas *Apollo* is a balance between stillness and motion, this is unbridled motion. *Apollo* is serene, graceful, and godlike, while *Laocoön* is powerful, emotional, and gritty.

Laocoön—the most famous Greek statue in ancient Rome and considered "superior to all other sculpture or painting"—was lost for more than a thousand years. Then, in 1506, it was unexpectedly unearthed in the ruins of Nero's Golden House near the Colosseum. The discovery caused a sensation. They cleaned it off and paraded it through the streets before an awestruck populace. No one had ever seen anything like its motion and emotion, having been raised on a white-bread diet of pretty-boy *Apollo*s. One of those who saw it was the young Michelangelo, and it was a revelation to him. Two years later, he started work on the Sistine Chapel, and the Renaissance was about to take another turn.

• *Leave the courtyard. Swing around the Hall of Animals, a jungle of beasts real and surreal, to the limbless Torso in the middle of the next large hall.*

Belvedere Torso

My experience with sculpting statues ends with snowmen. But standing face to face with this hunk of shaped rock makes you appreciate the sheer physical labor involved in chipping a figure out of solid rock. It takes great strength, but at the same time, great delicacy.

This is all that remains of an ancient statue of Hercules seated on a lion skin. Michelangelo loved this old rock. He knew that he was the best sculptor of his day. The ancients were his only peers—and his rivals. He'd caress this statue lovingly and tell people, "I am the pupil of the *Torso*." To him, it contained all the beauty of classical sculpture. But it's not beautiful. Compared with the pure grace of the *Apollo*, it's downright ugly.

But Michelangelo, an ugly man himself, was looking for a new kind of beauty—not the beauty of idealized gods, but the innate beauty of every person, even so-called ugly ones. With its knotty lumps of muscle, the *Torso* has a brute power and a distinct personality despite—or because of—its rough edges. Remember this *Torso*, because we'll see it again later on.

• *Enter the next, domed room.*

Round Room

This room, modeled on the Pantheon interior, gives some idea of

Roman grandeur. Romans took Greek ideas and made them bigger, like the big bronze statue of Hercules with his club, found near the Theater of Pompey (by modern-day Campo de' Fiori). The mosaic floor once decorated the bottom of a pool in an ancient Roman bath. The enormous Roman basin/hot tub/birdbath/vase decorated Nero's place. It was made of a single block of purple porphyry stone imported from the desert of Egypt. Purple was a rare, royal, expensive, and prestigious color in pre-Crayola days. This was the stone of emperors...and then of popes. Now it's all been quarried out, and the only porphyry available to anyone has been recycled.

• *Enter the next room.*

Sarcophagi

These two large porphyry marble coffins were made (though not used) for the Roman emperor Constantine's mother (Helena, on left) and daughter (Constanza, on right). Helena's coffin depicts a battle game showing dying victims in their barbarian dress.

Constanza's is decorated with a mix of Christian and pagan themes. Helena and Constanza were Christians—and therefore outlaws—until Constantine made Christianity legal in A.D. 312, and they became saints. Both sarcophagi were quarried and worked in Egypt. The technique for working this extremely hard stone (a special tempering of metal was required) was lost after this, and porphyry was not chiseled again until Renaissance times in Florence.

• *See how we've come full circle in this building—the Egyptian Rooms are ahead on your left. Go upstairs and prepare for the Long March down the hall lined with statues, toward the Sistine Chapel and Raphael Rooms.*

Overachievers may first choose to pop into the Etruscan wing—"Museo Etrusco"—located a few steps up from the Long March level. (Others have permission to save their aesthetic energy for the Sistine.)

THE ETRUSCANS (800–300 B.C.)

Room I

The chariot is from 550 B.C., when crude Romans were ruled by their more civilized neighbors to the north—the Etruscans. Imagine the chariot racing around the dirt track of the Circus Maximus, through the marshy valley of the newly drained Forum, or up Capitol Hill to the Temple of Jupiter—all originally built by Rome's Etruscan kings.

Room II

The golden breastplate (*Pectoral*, 650 B.C., immediately to the right), decorated with tiny winged angels and animals, shows off the sophis-

tication of the Etruscans. Though unwarlike and politically decentralized, these people were able to "conquer" all of central Italy around 650 B.C. through trade, offering tempting metalwork goods like this.

The Etruscan vases done in the Greek style remind us of the other great pre-Roman power—the Greek colonists who settled in southern Italy (Magna Graecia). The Etruscans traded with the Greeks, adopting their fashions. Rome, cradled between the two, grew up learning from both cultures.

A Greek-style bowl (far corner of the room) depicting a man

and woman in bed together would have scandalized early Roman farmers. He's peeing in a chamberpot, she's blowing a flute. Etruscan art often showed husbands and wives at ease together, giving them a reputation among the Romans as immoral, flute-playing degenerates.

Room III

This bronze warrior, whose head was sawed off by lightning, has a rare inscription that's readable (on armor below the navel). It probably refers to the statue's former owner: "Aha! Trutitis gave [this] as [a] gift." Archaeologists understand the Etruscans' Greek-style alphabet and some individual words, but they've yet to fully crack the code. As you look around at beautiful bronze pitchers, candlesticks, shields, and urns, ponder yet another of Etruria's unsolved mysteries—no one is sure where these sophisticated people came from.

Room IV

Most of our knowledge of the Etruscans is from sarcophagi and art in Etruscan tombs. Their funeral art is solemn, but hardly morbid—check out the sarcopha-guy with the bulging belly, enjoying a banquet for all eternity.

The Etruscans' origins are obscure, but their legacy is clear. In 509 B.C., the Etruscan king's son raped a Roman. The king was

thrown out, the republic was declared, Etruscan cities were conquered by Rome's legions, and their culture was swallowed up in Roman expansion. By Julius Caesar's time, the few remaining ethnic Etruscans were reduced to serving their masters as flute players, goldsmiths, surgeons, and street-corner preachers, like the one that Caesar brushed aside when he called out, "Beware the Ides of March..."

• *Backtrack, returning to the long hall (the Gallery of the Candelabras) leading to the Sistine Chapel and Raphael Rooms.*

THE LONG MARCH—SCULPTURE, TAPESTRIES, MAPS, AND VIEWS

This quarter-mile walk gives you a sense of the scale that Renaissance popes built on. Remember, this building was originally a series of papal palaces. The popes loved beautiful things—statues, urns, marble floors, friezes, stuccoed ceilings—and, as heirs of imperial Rome, they felt they deserved such luxury. The palaces and art represent both the peak and the decline of the Catholic Church in Europe. It was extravagant spending like this that inspired Martin Luther to rebel, starting the Protestant Reformation.

Gallery of the Candelabra: Classical Sculpture

In the second "room" of the long hall, stop at the statue *Diana the Huntress* on the left. Here, the virgin goddess goes hunting. Roman hunters would pray and give offerings to statues like this to get divine help in their search for food.

Farmers might pray to another version of the

same goddess, *Artemis,* on the opposite wall. This billion-breasted beauty stood for fertility. "Boobs or bulls' balls?" Some historians say that bulls were sacrificed and castrated, with the testicles draped over the statues as symbols of fertility.

• *Shuffle along to the next "room." On the left is* Bacchus, *with a baby on his shoulders.*

Fig Leaves

Why do the statues have fig leaves? Like *Bacchus,* many of these statues originally looked much different than they do now. First off, they were painted, often in gaudy colors. *Bacchus* may have had brown hair, rosy cheeks, purple grapes, and a leopard-skin sidekick at his feet. Even the *Apollo Belvedere,* whose cool gray tones we now admire as "classic Greek austerity," may have had a paisley pink cloak for all we know. Also, many statues had glass eyes like *Bacchus.*

And the fig leaves? Those came from the years 1550 to 1800, when the Church decided that certain parts of the human anatomy were obscene. (Why not the feet?)

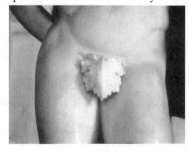

Perhaps Church leaders associated these full-frontal statues with the outbreak of Renaissance humanism that reduced their power in Europe. Whatever the cause, they reacted by covering classical crotches with plaster fig leaves, the same leaves Adam and Eve had used when the concept of "privates" was invented.

The Long March

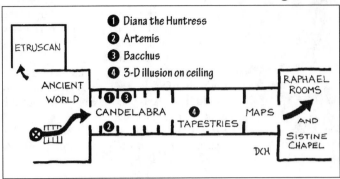

❶ Diana the Huntress
❷ Artemis
❸ Bacchus
❹ 3-D illusion on ceiling

ETRUSCAN

ANCIENT WORLD

CANDELABRA

TAPESTRIES

MAPS

RAPHAEL ROOMS

AND

SISTINE CHAPEL

DCH

Note: The leaves could be removed at any time if the museum officials were so motivated. There are suggestion boxes around the museum. Whenever I see a fig leaf, I get the urge to pick-it. We could start an organ-ized campaign...

• *Cover your eyes in case they forgot a fig leaf or two, and continue to the tapestries.*

Tapestries

Along the left wall are tapestries designed by Raphael's workshop and made in Brussels. They show scenes from the life of Christ, starting with the baby Jesus in the manger. The Resurrection tapestry is curiously interactive...as you walk, Jesus' eyes, feet, knee, and even the stone square follow you across the room.

Check out the beautiful sculpted reliefs on the ceiling, especially the lavender panel near the end of the first tapestry room showing a centurion ordering Eskimo Pies from a vendor. Admire the workmanship of this relief, then realize that it's not a relief at all—it's painted on a flat surface! Illusions like this were proof that painters had mastered the 3-D realism of ancient statues.

Map Gallery and View of Vatican City

This gallery still feels like a pope's palace. The crusted ceiling of colorful stucco and paint is pure papal splendor. The 16th-century maps on the walls show the regions of Italy. Popes could take visitors on a tour of Italy, from the toe (entrance end) to the Alps (far end), with east Italy on the right wall, west on the left. The scenes in the ceiling portray exciting moments in Church history in each of those regions. At the far end—where the pope would introduce you to the gallery's lay of the land—are Italy's four ports of entry (e.g., Venice) and the maps of Antique Italy (names in Latin, Roman political boundaries in gold) and New Italy.

The windows give you your best look at the tiny country of

Vatican City, formed in 1929. It has its own radio station (KPOP), as you see from the tower on the hill. What you see here is pretty much all there is—these gardens, the palaces you're in, and St. Peter's.

If you lean out and look left, you'll see the dome of St. Peter's the way Michelangelo would have liked you to see it—without the bulky Baroque facade.

• *Exit the map room, and take a breather in the next small tapestry hall before turning left into the crowded rooms leading to the Raphael Rooms.*

RENAISSANCE ART

Raphael Rooms: Papal Wallpaper

We've seen art from the ancient world; now we'll see its rebirth in the Renaissance. We're entering the living quarters of the great Renaissance popes—where they slept, worked, and worshiped. The rooms reflect the grandeur of their position. They hired the best artists—mostly from Florence—to paint the walls and ceilings, combining classical and Christian motifs.

• *Entering, you'll immediately see...*

The huge non-Raphael painting shows Sobieski liberating Vienna from the Muslim Turks in 1683, finally tipping the tide in favor of a Christian Europe. See the Muslim tents on the left and the spires of Christian Vienna on the right.

The second room's paintings celebrate the doctrine of the Immaculate Conception, establishing that Mary herself was conceived free from original sin. This medieval idea wasn't actually made dogma until a century ago. The largest fresco shows how the inspiration came straight from heaven (upper left) in a thin ray of light directly to the pope.

• *Next, you'll pass along an outside ramp that overlooks a courtyard (is that the pope's Fiat?), finally ending up in the first of the Raphael Rooms—the Constantine Room.*

Constantine Room

The frescoes (which after Raphael's death were finished by his assistants, notably Giulio Romano) celebrate the passing of the baton from one culture to the next. Remember, Rome was a pagan empire persecuting a new cult from the East—Christianity.

Then, on the night of October 27, A.D. 312 (left wall), as General Constantine (in gold, with crown) was preparing his troops for a coup d'état, he looked up and saw something strange. A cross appeared in the sky with the words, "You will conquer in this sign."

The next day (long wall), his troops raged victoriously into battle with the Christian cross atop their Roman eagle banners. There's Constantine in the center with a smile on his face, slashing through the enemy, while God's warrior angels ride shotgun overhead.

Constantine even stripped (right wall) and knelt before the pope to be baptized a Christian (some say). As emperor, he legalized Christianity and worked hand in hand with the pope (window wall). When Rome fell, its glory lived on through the Dark Ages in the pomp, pageantry, and learning of the Catholic Church.

Look at the ceiling painting. A classical statue is knocked backward, crumbling before the overpowering force of the cross. Whoa! Christianity triumphs over pagan Rome. (This was painted, I believe, by Raphael's surrealist colleague, Salvadorus Dalio.)

Raphael

Raphael was only 25 when Pope Julius II invited him to paint the walls of his personal living quarters. Julius was so impressed by Raphael's talent that he had the work of earlier masters scraped off and gave Raphael free rein to paint what he wanted.

Raphael lived a charmed life. He was handsome and sophisticated, and soon became Julius' favorite. He painted masterpieces effortlessly. In a different decade, he might have been thrown out of the Church as a great sinner, but his love affairs and devil-may-care personality seemed to epitomize the optimistic pagan spirit of the Renaissance. His works are graceful but never lightweight or frilly—they're strong, balanced, and harmonious in the best Renaissance tradition. When he died young in 1520, the High Renaissance died with him.

• *Continue through the next room and bookshop. In the following room, block the sunlight with your hand to see...*

The Liberation of St. Peter

Peter, Jesus' right-hand man, was thrown into prison in Jerusalem for his beliefs. In the middle of the night, an angel appeared and rescued him from the sleeping guards (Acts 12). The chains miraculously fell away (and were later brought to the St. Peter-in-Chains Church in Rome), and the

Raphael Rooms

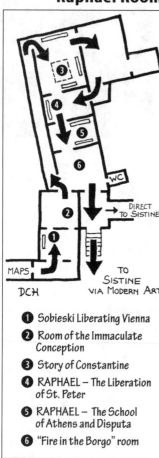

1. Sobieski Liberating Vienna
2. Room of the Immaculate Conception
3. Story of Constantine
4. RAPHAEL – The Liberation of St. Peter
5. RAPHAEL – The School of Athens and Disputa
6. "Fire in the Borgo" room

angel led him to safety (right), while the guards took hell from their captain (left). This little "play" is neatly divided into three separate acts that make a balanced composition.

Raphael makes the miraculous event even more dramatic with the use of four kinds of light illuminating the dark cell—half-moonlight, the captain's torch, the radiant angel, and the natural light spilling through the Museum's window. Raphael's mastery of realism, rich colors, and sense of drama made him understandably famous.

Find Pope Julius II (who also commissioned Michelangelo to do the Sistine ceiling) in the role of Peter in *The Liberation*, and as the kneeling pope in *The Mass of Bolsena* (opposite wall).

• *Enter the next room. Here in the pope's private study, Raphael painted...*

The School of Athens

In both style and subject matter, this fresco sums up the spirit of the Renaissance, which was not only the rebirth of classical art, but a rebirth of learning, discovery, and the optimistic spirit that man is a rational creature. Raphael pays respect to the great thinkers and scientists of ancient Greece, gathering them together at one time in a mythical school setting.

In the center are Plato and Aristotle, the two greatest. Plato points up, indicating his philosophy that mathematics and pure ideas are the source of truth, while Aristotle points down, showing his preference for hands-on study of the material world. There's their master,

Socrates (midway to the left, in green), ticking off arguments on his fingers. And in the foreground at right, bald Euclid bends over a slate to demonstrate a geometrical formula.

Raphael shows that Renaissance thinkers were as good as the ancients. There's Leonardo da Vinci, whom Raphael worshipped, in the role of Plato. Euclid is the architect Donato Bramante, who designed St. Peter's. Raphael himself (next to last on the far right, with the black beret) looks out at us. And the "school" building is actually an early version of St. Peter's Basilica (under construction at the time).

Raphael balances everything symmetrically—thinkers to the left, scientists to the right, with Plato and Aristotle dead center—showing the geometrical order found in the world. Look at the square floor tiles in the foreground. If you laid a ruler over them and extended the line upward, it would run right to the center of the picture. Similarly, the tops of the columns all point down to the middle. All the lines of sight draw our attention to Plato and Aristotle, and to the small arch over their heads—a halo over these two secular saints in the divine pursuit of knowledge.

While Raphael was painting this room, Michelangelo was at work down the hall in the Sistine Chapel. Raphael had just finished *The School of Athens* when he got a look at Michelangelo's powerful figures and dramatic scenes. He was astonished. From this point on, Raphael began to beef up his delicate, graceful style to a more heroic level. He returned to *The School of Athens* and added one more figure to the scene—Michelangelo, the brooding, melancholy figure in front, leaning on a block of marble.

• *On the opposite wall...*

The Disputa

As if to underline the new attitude that pre-Christian philosophy and Church thinking could coexist, Raphael painted *The Disputa* facing *The School of Athens*. Christ and the saints in heaven are overseeing a discussion of the Eucharist (the communion wafer) by mortals below. The classical-looking character in blue and gold looks out as if to say, "The pagans had their *School of Athens*, but we Christians (pointing up) have the School of Heaven." These rooms were the papal library, so themes featuring learning, knowledge, and debate were appropriate.

In Catholic terms, the communion wafer miraculously becomes the body of Christ when it's consecrated by a priest, bringing a little bit

of heaven into the material world. Raphael's painting also connects heaven and earth, with descending circles: Jesus in a halo, down to the dove of the Holy Spirit in a circle, which enters the communion wafer in its holder. Balance and symmetry reign, from the angel trios in the upper corners to the books littering the floor. Find Dante wearing his poet's laureate in the lower right. (Hint: He's the guy on your €2 coin. The coin was modeled after this detail of *The Disputa*.)

Moving along, the last Raphael Room (called the "Fire in the Borgo" Room) shows work done mostly by Raphael's students, who were influenced by the bulging muscles and bodybuilder poses of Michelangelo.

• *Get ready. It's decision time. From here, there are two ways to get to the Sistine Chapel. Leaving the final Raphael Room, you'll soon see two arrows—one pointing left to the Sistine (Cappella Sistina) and one pointing right to the Sistine. Left goes directly to the Sistine.*

But going right (5 min and a few staircases longer) leads to quiet rooms at the foot of the stairs, with benches where you can sit in peace and read ahead before entering the hectic Sistine Chapel. Also, you get to stroll through the impressive Modern Religious Art collection on the way (signs will direct you to the Sistine). Your call.

THE SISTINE CHAPEL

The Sistine Chapel contains Michelangelo's ceiling and his huge *Last Judgment*. The Sistine is the personal chapel of the pope and the place where new popes are elected. When Pope Julius II asked Michelangelo to take on this important project, he said, "No, *grazie*."

Michelangelo insisted he was a sculptor, not a painter. The Sistine ceiling was a vast undertaking, and he didn't want to do a half-vast job. But the pope pleaded, bribed, and threatened until Michelangelo finally consented, on the condition that he be able to do it all his own way.

Julius had asked for only 12 apostles along the sides of the ceiling, but Michelangelo had a grander vision—the entire history of the world until Jesus. He spent the next four years (1508–1512) craning his neck on scaffolding six stories up, covering the ceiling with frescoes of biblical scenes.

In sheer physical terms, it's an astonishing achievement: 5,900 square feet, with the vast majority done by his own hand. (Raphael only designed most of his rooms, letting assistants do the grunt work.)

First, he had to design and erect the scaffolding. Any materials had to be hauled up on pulleys. Then, a section of ceiling would be plastered. With fresco—painting on wet plaster—if you don't get it right the first time, you have to scrape the whole thing off and start over. And if you've ever struggled with a ceiling light fixture or worked underneath a car for even five minutes, you know how heavy your arms get. The physical effort, the paint dripping in his eyes, the creative drain, and the mental stress from a pushy pope combined to almost kill Michelangelo.

But when the ceiling was finished and revealed to the public, it simply blew 'em away. Like the *Laocoön* statue discovered six years earlier, it was unlike anything seen before. It both caps the Renaissance and turns it in a new direction. In perfect Renaissance spirit, it mixes Old Testament prophets with classical figures. But the style is more dramatic, shocking, and emotional than the balanced Renaissance works before it. This is a very personal work— the Gospel according to Michelangelo—but its themes and subject matter are universal. Many art scholars contend that the Sistine ceiling is the single greatest work of art by any one human being.

The Sistine Ceiling:
Understanding What You're Standing Under

The ceiling shows the history of the world before the birth of Jesus. We see God creating the world, creating man and woman, destroying the earth by flood, and so on. God himself, in his purple robe, actually appears in the first five scenes. Along the sides (where the ceiling starts to curve), we see the Old Testament prophets and pagan Greek prophetesses who foretold the coming of Christ. Dividing these scenes and figures are fake niches (a painted 3-D illusion) decorated with nude, statue-like figures with symbolic meaning.

The key is to see three simple divisions in the tangle of bodies:
1. The central spine of nine rectangular biblical scenes
2. The line of prophets on either side
3. The triangles between the prophets showing the ancestors of Christ

• *Ready? Within the chapel, grab a seat along the side (if there's room). Face the altar with the big* Last Judgment *on the wall (more on that later). Now look up to the ceiling and find the central panel of...*

The Creation of Adam

God and man take center stage in this Renaissance version of creation. Adam, newly formed in the image of God, lounges dreamily in perfect naked innocence. God, with his entourage, swoops in with a swirl of activity (which—with a little imagination—looks like a cross-section of a human brain...quite a strong humanist

The Sistine Ceiling

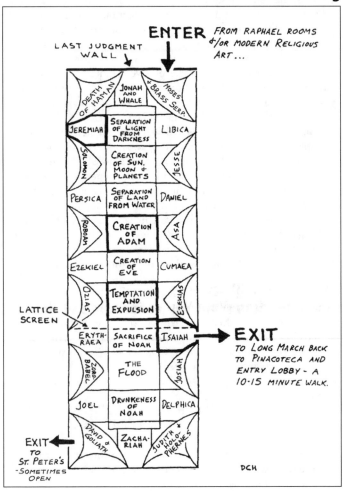

ENTER — FROM RAPHAEL ROOMS
&/OR MODERN RELIGIOUS
ART...

LAST JUDGMENT WALL

DEATH OF HAMAN
JONAH AND WHALE
MOSES & BRASS SERP.

JEREMIAH
SEPARATION OF LIGHT FROM DARKNESS
LIBICA

SOLOMON
CREATION OF SUN, MOON & PLANETS
JESSE

PERSICA
SEPARATION OF LAND FROM WATER
DANIEL

ROBOAM
CREATION OF ADAM
ASA

EZEKIEL
CREATION OF EVE
CUMAEA

OZIAS
TEMPTATION AND EXPULSION
EZEKIAS

LATTICE SCREEN

ERYTHRAEA
SACRIFICE OF NOAH
ISAIAH

EXIT — TO LONG MARCH BACK TO PINACOTECA AND ENTRY LOBBY – A 10·15 MINUTE WALK.

ZORO-BABEL
THE FLOOD
JOSIAH

JOEL
DRUNKENESS OF NOAH
DELPHICA

DAVID & GOLIATH
ZACHARIAH
JUDITH & HOLOPHERNES

EXIT — TO ST. PETER'S –SOMETIMES OPEN

DCH

statement). Their reaching hands are the center of this work. Adam's is limp and passive; God's is strong and forceful, His finger twitch-

ing upward with energy. Here is the very moment of creation, as God passes the spark of life to man, the crowning work of His creation.

This is the spirit of the Renaissance. God is not a ter-rifying giant reaching down to puny and helpless Man

The Sistine Schematic

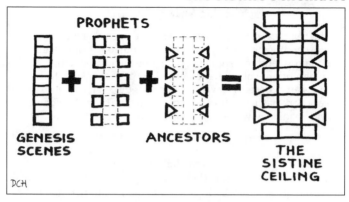

PROPHETS

+

GENESIS
SCENES

ANCESTORS

=

THE
SISTINE
CEILING

DCH

from way on high. Here they are on an equal plane, divided only by the diagonal patch of sky. God's billowing robe and the patch of green upon which Adam is laying balance each other. They are like two pieces of a jigsaw puzzle, or two long-separated continents, or like the yin and yang symbols finally coming together—uniting, complementing each other, creating wholeness. God and man work together in the divine process of creation.

• *This celebration of man permeates the ceiling. Notice the Adonises-come-to-life on the pedestals that divide the central panels. And then came woman.*

The Garden of Eden: Temptation and Expulsion

In one panel, we see two scenes from the Garden of Eden. On the left

is the leafy garden of paradise where Adam and Eve lie around blissfully. But the devil comes along—a serpent with a woman's torso—and winds around the forbidden Tree of Knowledge. The temptation to gain new knowledge is too great for these Renaissance people. They eat the forbidden fruit.

At right, the sword-wielding angel drives them from Paradise into the barren plains. They're grieving, but they're far from helpless. Adam's body is thick and sturdy, and we know they'll survive in the cruel world. Adam firmly gestures to the angel, like he's saying, "All right, already! We're going!"

The Nine Scenes from Genesis

Take some time with these central scenes to understand the story that the ceiling tells. They run in sequence, starting at the front:

The Cleaning Project

The ceiling and *The Last Judgment* have been cleaned, removing centuries of preservatives, dirt, and soot from candles, oil lamps, and the annual Papal Barbecue (just kidding). The bright, bright colors that emerged are a bit shocking, forcing many art experts to reevaluate Michelangelo's style. Notice the very dark patches left in the corner above *The Last Judgment*, and imagine how dreary and dark it was before the cleaning.

1. God, in purple, divides the light from darkness.
2. God creates the sun (burning orange) and the moon (pale white, to the right). Oops, I guess there's another moon.
3. God bursts toward us to separate the land and water.
4. *The Creation of Adam*
5. God creates Eve, who dives into existence out of Adam's side.
6. *The Garden of Eden: Temptation and Expulsion*
7. Noah kills a ram and stokes the altar fires to make a sacrifice to God.
8. The great Flood, sent by God, destroys the wicked, who desperately head for higher ground. In the distance, the Ark carries Noah's family to safety. (The blank spot dates to 1793, when a nearby gunpowder depot exploded, shaking the building.)
9. Noah's sons see their drunken father. (Perhaps Michelangelo chose to end it with this scene as a reminder that even the best of men are fallible.)

Prophets

You'll notice that the figures at the far end of the chapel are a bit smaller than those over the *Last Judgment*.

Michelangelo started at the far end, with the Noah scenes. By 1510, he'd finished the first half of the ceiling. When they took the scaffolding down and could finally see what he'd been working on for two years, everyone was awestruck—except Michelangelo. As powerful as his figures are, from the floor they didn't look dramatic enough for Michelangelo. For the other half, he pulled out all the stops.

Compare the Noah scenes (far end) with their many small figures to the huge images of God at the other end. Similarly, Isaiah (near the lattice screen, marked "Esaias") is stately and balanced, while Jeremiah ("Hieremias," in the corner by the *Last Judgment*) is a dark, brooding figure. This prophet who witnessed the destruction of Israel slumps his chin in his hand and ponders the fate of his people. Like the difference between the stately *Apollo Belvedere* and

The Last Judgment

HEAVEN

THE **GOOD,**

THE **BAD,**

& THE **UGLY**

DCH

❶ Christ with Mary at his side
❷ Trumpeting Angels
❸ The dead come out of their graves, the righteous ascend
❹ One of the damned
❺ Charon in his boat
❻ The demon/critic of nudity
❼ St. Bartholomew with flayed skin containing Michelangelo's self-portrait

the excited *Laocoön*, Michelangelo added a new emotional dimension to Renaissance painting.

The Last Judgment

When Michelangelo returned to paint the altar wall 23 years later (1535), the mood of Europe—and of Michelangelo—was completely different. The Protestant Reformation had forced the Catholic Church to clamp down on free thought, and religious wars raged. Rome had recently been pillaged by roving bands of mercenaries. The Renaissance spirit of optimism was fading. Michelangelo

himself had begun to question the innate goodness of mankind.

It's Judgment Day, and Christ—the powerful figure in the center, raising his arm to spank the wicked—has come to find out who's naughty and who's nice. Beneath him, a band of angels blows its trumpets Dizzy Gillespie–style, giving a wake-up call to the sleeping dead. The dead at lower left leave their graves and prepare to be judged. The righteous, on Christ's right hand (the left side of the picture), are carried up to the glories of Heaven. The wicked on the other side are hurled down to Hell, where demons wait to torture them. Charon, from the underworld of Greek mythology, waits below to ferry the souls of the damned to Hell.

It's a grim picture. No one, but no one, is smiling. Even many of the righteous being resurrected (lower left) are either skeletons or cadavers with ghastly skin. The angels have to play tug-of-war with subterranean monsters to drag them from their graves.

Over in Hell, the wicked are tortured by gleeful demons. One of the damned (to the right of the trumpeting angels) has an utterly lost expression, as if saying, "Why did I cheat on my wife?!" Two demons grab him around the ankles to pull him down to the bowels of Hell, condemned to an eternity of constipation.

But it's the terrifying figure of Christ that dominates this scene. He raises his arm to smite the wicked, sending a ripple of fear through everyone. Even the saints around him—even Mary beneath his arm (whose interceding days are clearly over)—shrink back in terror at loving Jesus' uncharacteristic outburst. His expression is completely closed, and he turns his head, refusing to even listen to the whining alibis of the damned. Look at Christ's bicep. If this muscular figure looks familiar to you, it's because you've seen it before—the *Belvedere Torso*.

When *The Last Judgment* was unveiled to the public in 1541, it caused a sensation. The pope is said to have dropped to his knees and cried, "Lord, charge me not with my sins when thou shalt come on the Day of Judgment."

And it changed the course of art. The complex composition, with more than 300 figures swirling around the figure of Christ, was far beyond traditional Renaissance balance. The twisted figures shown from every imaginable angle challenged other painters to try and top this master of 3-D illusion. And the sheer terror and drama of the scene was a striking contrast to the placid optimism of, say, Raphael's *School of Athens*. Michelangelo had Baroque-en all the rules of the Renaissance, signaling a new era of art.

With the Renaissance fading, the fleshy figures in *The Last Judgment* aroused murmurs of discontent from Church authorities. Michelangelo rebelled by painting his chief critic into the scene—in Hell. He's the jackassed demon in the bottom right corner, wrapped in a snake. Look at how Michelangelo covered his privates. Sweet revenge.

(After Michelangelo's death, prudish Church authorities painted the wisps of clothing that we see today.)

Now move up close. Study the details of the lower part of the painting from right to left. Charon, with Dr. Spock ears and a Dalí moustache, paddles the damned in a boat full of human turbulence. Look more closely at the J-Day band. Are they reading music, or is it the Judgment Day tally? Before the cleaning, these details were lost in murk.

The Last Judgment marks the end of Renaissance optimism epitomized in *The Creation of Adam*, with its innocence and exaltation of man. There, he was the wakening man-child of a fatherly God. Here, man cowers in fear and unworthiness before a terrifying, wrathful deity.

Michelangelo himself must have wondered how he would be judged—had he used his God-given talents wisely? Look at St. Bartholomew, the bald, bearded guy at Christ's left foot (our right). In the flayed skin he's holding is a barely recognizable face—the twisted self-portrait of a self-questioning Michelangelo.

• *There are two exits from the Sistine Chapel. If you exit through the side door next to the screen, you'll soon find yourself facing the Long March back to the museum's entrance (10–15 min away) and the Pinacoteca. You're one floor below the long corridor that you walked to get here.*

Or, if you're planning to visit St. Peter's Basilica next, exit out the back corner of the Sistine Chapel—on the right, with your back to the altar. (When the cardinals used this room to elect a new pope, this is where they put the small old-fashioned stove for ballot burning—its chimney snakes up and out this corner of the room. White smoke signals that a pope has been chosen.) This route shortcuts directly to St. Peter's Basilica, saving a 30-minute walk (10–15 min back to Vatican Museum entry/exit, then a 15-min walk to St. Peter's). Though this corner door is likely labeled "Exit for private tour groups only," you can often just slide through with the crowds. Note that if you take this shortcut, you'll miss the Pinacoteca art gallery (near the Vatican Museum entrance), unless you saw it at the beginning.

The Long March Back

Along this corridor, you'll see some of the wealth amassed by the popes, mostly gifts from royalty. Find your hometown on the 1529 map of the world—look in the land labeled "Terra Incognita." The elaborately decorated library that branches off to the right contains rare manuscripts.

• *The corridor eventually spills out back outside. Follow signs to the...*

PINACOTECA

Like Lou Gehrig batting behind Babe Ruth, the Pinacoteca (Painting Gallery) has to follow the mighty Sistine & Co. But after the Vatican's artistic feast, this little collection of paintings is a delicious, 15-minute after-dinner mint.

See this gallery of paintings as you'd view a time-lapse blossoming of a flower, walking through the evolution of painting from medieval to Baroque with just a few stops.

• *Enter, passing a model of Michelangelo's* Pietà *(offering a handy close-up look), and stroll up to Room IV.*

Melozzo da Forli—*Musician Angels*

Salvaged from a condemned church, this playful series of frescoes shows the delicate grace and nobility of Italy during the time known fondly as the Quattrocento (1400s). Notice the detail in the serene faces; the soothing primary colors; the bright and even light; and the classical purity given these religious figures. Rock on.

• *Walk on to the end room (Room VIII), where precious Raphael-designed tapestries that once hung in the Sistine Chapel now surround the highlight of this collection. They've turned on the dark to let Raphael's* Transfiguration *shine. Take a seat.*

Raphael—*The Transfiguration*

Christ floats above a stumpy mountaintop, visited in a vision by the prophets Moses and Elijah. Peter, James, and John, who wanted

visual proof that Jesus was Lord, cower in awe under their savior, "transfigured before them, his face shining as the sun, his raiment white as light" (as described by the evangelist Matthew—who can be seen taking notes in the painting's lower left).

Raphael composes the scene in three descending tiers: Christ, the holiest, is on top, then Peter–James–John, and finally, the nine remaining apostles surround a boy possessed by demons. They direct him and his mother to Jesus for healing.

Raphael died in 1520, leaving this final work to be finished by his pupils. The last thing Raphael painted was the beatific face of Jesus, perhaps the most beautiful Christ in existence. When Raphael was buried (in the Pantheon, at age 37), this work accompanied the funeral.

• *Heading back down the parallel corridor, stop in Room IX at the brown, unfinished work by Leonardo.*

Leonardo da Vinci—
St. Jerome (c. 1482)
Jerome squats in the rocky desert. He's spent too much time alone, fasting and meditating on his sins. His soulful face is echoed by his friend, the roaring lion.

Pinacoteca

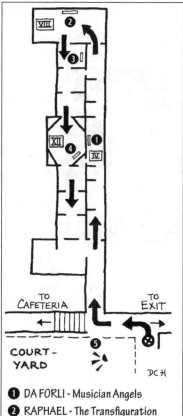

TO CAFETERIA

TO EXIT

COURT-YARD

DCH

❶ DA FORLI - Musician Angels
❷ RAPHAEL - The Transfiguration
❸ LEONARDO DA VINCI - St. Jerome
❹ CARAVAGGIO - Deposition
❺ View of the Dome

This unfinished work gives us a glimpse behind the scenes at Leonardo's technique. Even in the brown undercoating, we see the psychological power of Leonardo's genius. Jerome's emaciated body on the rocks expresses his intense penitence, while his pleading eyes hold a glimmer of hope for divine forgiveness. Leonardo wrote that a good painter must paint two things: "man and the movements of his spirit." (The patchwork effect is due to Jerome's head having been cut out and used as the seat of a stool in a shoemaker's shop.)

• Roll on through the sappy sweetness of the Mannerist rooms into the gritty realism of Caravaggio (Room XII).

Caravaggio—*Deposition* (1604)

Christ is being buried. In the dark tomb, the faces of his followers

emerge, lit by a harsh light. Christ's body has a death-like color. We see Christ's dirty toes and Nicodemus' wrinkled, sunburned face.

Caravaggio was the first painter to intentionally shock his viewers. By exaggerating the contrast between light and dark, shining a brutal third-degree-interrogation light on his subjects, and using everyday models in sacred scenes, he takes a huge leap away from the Raphael-pretty past and into the "expressive realism" of the modern world.

A tangle of grief looms out of the darkness as Christ's heavy, dead body nearly pulls the whole group with him from the cross into the tomb. After this museum, I know how he feels.

• Walk through the rest of the gallery's canvas history of art, enjoy one last view of the Vatican grounds and Michelangelo's dome, then follow the grand spiral staircase down. Go in peace.

ST. PETER'S BASILICA TOUR

(Basilica San Pietro)

St. Peter's is the greatest church in Christendom. It represents the power and splendor of Rome's 2,000-year domination of the Western world. Built on the memory and grave of the first pope, St. Peter, this is where the grandeur of ancient Rome became the grandeur of Christianity.

ORIENTATION

Cost: Free (€6 to climb dome).

Dress Code: The dress code is strictly enforced. No shorts or bare shoulders (applies to men, women, and children), and no miniskirts.

Hours of Church: Daily April–Sept 7:00–19:00, Oct–March 7:00–18:00. Mass is held daily (Mon–Sat at 8:30, 10:00, 11:00, 12:00, and 17:00; Sun and holidays at 9:00, 10:30, 11:30, 12:10, 13:00, 16:00, and 17:30; confirm schedule locally). The church often closes on Wednesday mornings during papal audiences. The best time to visit the church is early or late: I like to be here at 17:00, when the church is fairly empty, sunbeams can work their magic, and the late-afternoon Mass fills the place with spiritual music.

Hours of Dome: Daily April–Sept 8:00–17:45, Oct–March 8:00–16:45. Allow one hour for the full trip up and down, or a half hour to go only to the roof. Even after the elevator, it's a 323-step climb all the way to the top. The entry to the elevator is just outside the basilica on the north side of St. Peter's (near the secret Sistine exit—described on page 192). Look for signs to the cupola. For more on the dome, see the end of the chapter.

Vatican City

This tiny independent country of little more than 100 acres, contained entirely within Rome, has its own postal system, armed guards, helipad, mini-train station, and radio station (KPOP). Politically powerful, the Vatican is the religious capital of 1.1 billion Roman Catholics. If you're not a Catholic, become one for your visit.

The pope is both the religious and secular leader of Vatican City. For centuries, locals referred to him as "King Pope." Italy and the Vatican didn't always have good relations. In fact, after unification (in 1870), when Rome's modern grid plan was built around the miniscule Vatican, it seemed as if the new buildings were designed to be just high enough so no one could see the dome of St. Peter's from street level. Modern Italy was created in 1870, but the Holy See didn't recognize it as a country until 1929, when the pope and Mussolini signed the Lateran Pact, giving sovereignty to the Vatican and a few nearby churches.

Like every European country, Vatican City has its own versions of the euro coin. You're unlikely to find one in your pocket, though, as they are snatched up by collectors before falling into actual circulation. With John Paul II's passing, the coins will be redesigned to feature a portrait of the new pope, Benedict XVI.

Small as it is, Vatican City has two huge sights: St. Peter's Basilica (with Michelangelo's *Pietà*) and the Vatican Museum (with the Sistine Chapel). A helpful TI is just to the left of St. Peter's Basilica (Mon–Sat 8:30–19:00, closed Sun, tel. 06-6988-1662; Vatican switchboard tel. 06-6982, www.vatican.va). The thief-infested bus #64 and the safer #40 express stop near the basilica. The closest Metro stops are a 10-minute walk away from either sight: For St. Peter's, it's Ottaviano; for the Vatican Museum, it's Cipro–Musei Vaticani.

The Vatican **post office**, with offices on St. Peter's Square (next to TI) and in the Vatican Museum, is more reliable than Italy's mail service (Mon–Sat 8:30–19:00). The stamps are a collectible bonus. Vatican stamps are good throughout Rome, but to use the Vatican's mail service, you need to mail your cards from the Vatican; write your postcards ahead of time. (Note that the Vatican won't mail cards with Italian stamps.)

Seeing the Pope: Your best chances for a sighting are on Sunday and Wednesday. The pope usually gives a blessing at noon on Sunday from his apartment on St. Peter's Square (except summer, when he speaks at his summer residence at Castel Gandolfo, 25 miles from Rome; train leaves Rome's Termini station). St. Peter's is easiest (just show up) and, for most, enough of a "visit." Those interested in a more formal appearance (but not more intimate), can get a ticket for the Wednesday general audience (at 10:30) when the pope, arriving in his bulletproof Popemobile, greets

Vatican City Overview

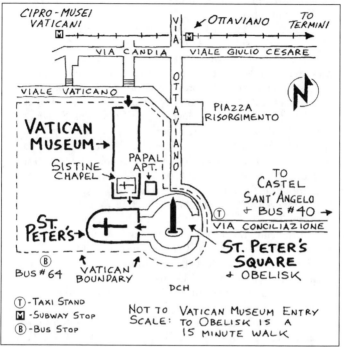

CIPRO - MUSEI VATICANI
M

TO OTTAVIANO
TERMINI
M

VIA CANDIA

VIALE GIULIO CESARE

VIA OTTAVIANO

VIALE VATICANO

N

VATICAN MUSEUM →

PIAZZA RISORGIMENTO

SISTINE CHAPEL →

PAPAL APT.

TO CASTEL SANT'ANGELO + BUS #40 →

ST. PETER'S

VIA CONCILIAZIONE

ST. PETER'S SQUARE + OBELISK

BUS #64

VATICAN BOUNDARY

DCH

(T) - TAXI STAND
(M) - SUBWAY STOP
(B) - BUS STOP

NOT TO SCALE: VATICAN MUSEUM ENTRY TO OBELISK IS A 15 MINUTE WALK

and blesses the crowds at St. Peter's from a balcony or canopied platform on the square (except in winter, when he speaks at 10:30 in the 7,000-seat Aula Paolo VI Auditorium, next to St. Peter's Basilica). While anyone can observe from a distance, you need a ticket to actually get close to the papal action. Tickets are free and easy to get, but must be picked up the day before—on Tuesday for the Wednesday service. Your hotelier may be able to arrange a ticket for you; or you can contact Santa Susanna Church (they get the ticket and you pick it up on Tue at their church between 17:00 and 18:45, Via XX Settembre 15, near recommended Via Firenze hotels, Metro: Repubblica, tel. 06-4201-4554, www.santasusanna .org) or you can go to St. Peter's Basilica on Tuesday and wait in a long line for a ticket (Swiss Guards hand out tickets from their station at the Bronze Doors, just to the right of the basilica, after 12:00 on Tue). To find out the pope's schedule or to book a free spot for the Wednesday general audience (either for a seat on the square or in the auditorium), call 06-6988-4631. If you only want to see the Vatican—but not the pope—minimize crowd problems by avoiding these times.

Warning: Within the church you'll see signs to the **Crypt** underneath the church. The Crypt, also referred to as the Grottoes, contains part of the foundations of the old St. Peter's, as well as the tombs of St. Peter and John Paul II. The Crypt is free, but beware—save it for the end of your visit, because the exit deposits you outside the church.

Getting There: Take the Metro to Ottaviano, then walk 10 minutes south on Via Ottaviano. Two city buses stop near St. Peter's Square. The #40 express drops off at Piazza Pio, next to Castel Sant'Angelo. The more crowded bus #64 is convenient for pickpockets and stops just outside St. Peter's Square to the south (after crossing the Tiber, take the first stop past the tunnel; backtrack toward the tunnel and turn left when you see the rows of columns). Taxis are reasonable (Termini train station to St. Peter's is about €10).

Information: The TI on the left (south) side of the square is excellent (Mon–Sat 8:30–19:00, closed Sun, free Vatican and church map, tel. 06-6988-1662). WCs are to the right and left (near TI) of the church and on the roof. Drinking fountains are at the obelisk and near WCs. The post office is next to the TI.

Tours: The Vatican TI conducts free 90-minute tours of St. Peter's (depart daily from TI at 14:15, many days also at 15:00, confirm schedule at TI, tel. 06-6988-1662). Audioguides can be rented near the checkroom.

Tours are the only way to see the Vatican Gardens; book at least a day in advance by calling 06-6988-4676 (€12, Tue, Thu, and Sat at 10:00, tours start at Vatican Museum tour desk and finish on St. Peter's Square).

To tour the Necropolis of St. Peter's and the saint's tomb, call the Excavations Office at 06-6988-5318 a minimum of a week before your visit (€10, 2 hrs, office open Mon–Sat 9:00–17:00). The Crypt is open for free to the public, but this tour gets you closer to St. Peter's tomb.

Length of This Tour: Allow one hour, plus another hour if you climb the dome (elevator plus 323 steps one-way).

Checkroom: The free, usually mandatory bag check is outside at the security check (to the right of the entrance).

Starring: Michelangelo, Bernini, St. Peter, a heavenly host...and, occasionally, the pope.

THE TOUR BEGINS

• *Find a shady spot where you like the view under the columns around St. Peter's oval-shaped "square." If the pigeons left a clean spot, sit on it.*

OLD ST. PETER'S

Nearly 2,000 years ago, this area was the site of Nero's Circus—a huge Roman chariot racecourse. The obelisk you see in the middle of the square stands where the chariots made their hairpin turns. The Romans had no marching bands, so for halftime entertainment they killed Christians. This persecuted minority was forced to fight wild animals and gladiators, or they were simply crucified. Some were tarred up, tied to posts, and burned—human torches to light up the evening races.

One of those killed here, in about A.D. 65, was Peter, Jesus' right-hand man, who had come to Rome to spread the message of love. At his own request, Peter was crucified on an upside-down cross, because he felt unworthy to die as his master had. His remains were buried in a nearby cemetery where, for 250 years, they were quietly and secretly revered.

When Christianity was finally legalized in 313, the Christian emperor Constantine built a church on the site of the martyrdom of this first "pope," or bishop of Rome, from whom all later popes claimed their authority as head of the Church. "Old St. Peter's" lasted 1,200 years (A.D. 329–1500).

By the time of the Renaissance, old St. Peter's was falling apart and was considered unfit to be the center of the Western Church. The new, larger church we see today was begun in 1506 and was actually built around the old one. As the project was completed 120 years later, after many changes of plans, old St. Peter's was dismantled and carried out of the new one. (A few bits survive from the first church: the central door, some columns in the atrium, eight spiral columns around the tomb from the Jerusalem Temple, the venerated statue of Peter, and Michelangelo's *Pietà*.)

• *Ideally, you should head out to the obelisk to view the square and read this. But let me guess—it's 95 degrees, right? OK, read on in the shade of these stone sequoias.*

ST. PETER'S SQUARE

St. Peter's Square, with its ring of columns, symbolizes the arms of the church welcoming everyone—believers and non-believers—with its motherly embrace. It was designed by the Baroque architect Giovanni Lorenzo Bernini, who also did much of the work that we'll see inside. Numbers first: 284 columns, 56 feet high, in stern Doric style. Topping them are Bernini's 140 favorite saints, each 10 feet tall. The "square" itself is elliptical, 660 by 500 feet.

The obelisk in the center is 90 feet of solid granite weighing more than 300 tons. Think for a second about how much history this monument has seen. Erected originally in Egypt more

St. Peter's Square

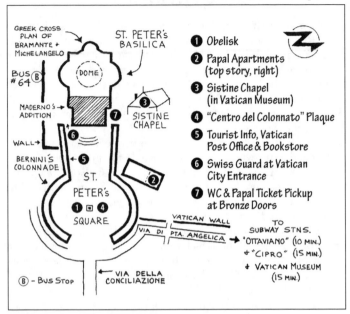

GREEK CROSS
PLAN OF
BRAMANTE +
MICHELANGELO

ST. PETER'S
BASILICA

BUS
#64 (B)

(DOME)

MADERNO'S →
ADDITION

SISTINE
CHAPEL

WALL →

BERNINI'S
COLONNADE

ST.
PETER'S
SQUARE

1 Obelisk

2 Papal Apartments
(top story, right)

3 Sistine Chapel
(in Vatican Museum)

4 "Centro del Colonnato" Plaque

5 Tourist Info, Vatican
Post Office & Bookstore

6 Swiss Guard at Vatican
City Entrance

7 WC & Papal Ticket Pickup
at Bronze Doors

VATICAN WALL

VIA DI PTA. ANGELICA →

TO
SUBWAY STNS.
"OTTAVIANO" (10 MIN.)
♦ "CIPRO" (15 MIN.)
♦ VATICAN MUSEUM
(15 MIN.)

(B) - BUS STOP

← VIA DELLA
CONCILIAZIONE

than 2,000 years ago, it witnessed the fall of the pharaohs to the Greeks and then to the Romans. It was then moved to imperial Rome by the emperor Caligula, where it stood impassively watching the slaughter of Christians at the racecourse and the torture of Protestants by the Inquisition (in the yellow-and-rust building just outside the square, to the left of the church). Today, it watches over the church, a reminder that each civilization builds on the previous ones. The puny cross on top reminds us that our Christian culture is but a thin veneer over our pagan origins.

• *Now venture out across the burning desert to the obelisk, which provides a narrow sliver of shade.*

Face the church, then turn about-face and say *"Grazie, Benito."* I don't make a habit of thanking fascist dictators, but in the 1930s, Benito Mussolini did open up this broad boulevard, finally letting people see the dome of St. Peter's, which had been hidden for centuries by the facade. From here at the obelisk, Michelangelo's magnificent dome can only peek its top over the bulky Baroque front entrance.

The gray building at two o'clock to the right (as you face the church), rising up behind Bernini's colonnade, is where the pope lives. The last window on the right of the top floor is his bedroom. To the left of that window is his study window, where he appears occasionally to greet the masses. If you come to the square at night

as a Poping Tom, you might see the light on—the pope burns much midnight oil.

On more formal occasions (which you may have seen on TV), the pope appears from the church itself, on the small balcony above the central door.

The Sistine Chapel is just to the right of the facade—the small gray-brown building with the triangular roof, topped by an antenna. The tiny chimney (the pimple along the roofline midway up the left side) is where the famous smoke signals announce the election of each new pope. If the smoke is black, a two-thirds majority hasn't been reached. White smoke means a new pope has been selected.

Walk to the right, five pavement plaques from the obelisk, to one marked "Centro del Colonnato." From here, all of Bernini's columns on the right side line up. The curved Baroque square still pays its respects to Renaissance mathematical symmetry.

• *Climb the gradually sloping pavement past crowd barriers and the huge statues of St. Paul (with his two-edged sword) and St. Peter (with his bushy hair and keys). Since 9/11, admission has been limited to the right side (where you'll go through an airport-type security check).*

On the square are two entrances to Vatican City—one to the left of the facade, one to the right in the crook of Bernini's "arm" (head for this one). Guarding this small but powerful country's

border crossing are the mercenary guards from Switzerland. You have to wonder if they really know how to use those pikes. Their colorful uniforms are said to have been designed by Michelangelo, though he was not known for his sense of humor.

• *Enter the atrium (entrance hall) of the church. You'll pass by the dress-code enforcers and a gaggle of ticked-off guys in shorts.*

THE BASILICA

The Atrium

The atrium is itself bigger than most churches. The huge white columns on the portico date from the first church (4th century). Five famous bronze doors lead into the church.

From Pope to Pope

On March 30, 2005, 84-year-old Pope John Paul II appeared at his apartment window overlooking St. Peter's Square, and—frail and unable to speak—he silently blessed the crowd. It was his final public appearance. Three days later, the Vatican Chamberlain approached his bedside, ritually called his name three times, and pronounced him dead.

John Paul II's body was carried by 12 pallbearers (flanked by the Swiss Guard) through the inner hallways of the Apostolic Palace, out the Vatican's Bronze Door entrance (on St. Peter's Square, under the colonnade to the right) and into the church. For four days, the body lay in state in front of St. Peter's main altar, beneath Michelangelo's dome and framed by Bernini's bronze canopy. Outside, hundreds of thousands of pilgrims lined up all the way down Via della Conciliazione, waiting up to 24 hours for one last look at their pope. Some five million people converged on Vatican City during the week.

The morning of April 8, 300,000 mourners, dignitaries, and security personnel gathered in wind-blown St. Peter's Square for the funeral. As they carried out John Paul II's coffin—decorated with an "M" for Mary—the crowd broke into applause, and many shouted *"Santo subito!"* insisting he be made a saint *(santo)* right now *(subito)*. During the eulogy, Cardinal Josef Ratzinger pointed to the pope's apartment window and told the crowd, "We can be sure that our beloved pope is standing today at the window of the Father's house."

Made from the melted-down bronze of the original door of old St. Peter's, the central door was the first Renaissance work in Rome (c. 1450). It's only opened on special occasions. The panels (from the top down) feature Jesus and Mary, Paul and Peter, and (at the bottom) how each was martyred: Paul decapitated, Peter crucified upside down.

The far-right entrance is the **Holy Door,** opened only during Holy Years. On Christmas Eve every 25 years, the pope knocks three times with a silver hammer and the door opens, welcoming pilgrims to pass through. After Pope John Paul II opened the door on Christmas Eve, 1999, he bricked it up again with a ceremonial trowel a year later to wait another 24 years. (A plaque above the door fudges a bit for effect: it says that Pope "IOANNES PAULUS II"

The next day, inside St. Peter's Basilica, the body—encased within three nested coffins—was carried from the altar, past Bernini's statue of St. Longinus and down the steps into St. Peter's Crypt where many popes have been laid to rest. He was buried near the tomb of St. Peter, next to the shrine of another popular 20th-century pope, John XXIII. The tomb has no monument, just a simple stone slab with the inscription: Joannes Paulus II (1920–2005).

Then came nine days of mourning—punctuated by a Mass each day in St. Peter's—as Cardinals representing the globe's 1.1 billion Catholics arrived to elect a new pope.

On April 18, 115 Cardinals dressed in crimson were stripped of their mobile phones, given a vow of secrecy, and locked inside the Sistine Chapel for the "conclave" (from Latin *cum clave*, with key). Two votes failed to reach a two-thirds majority, and they burned the ballots in a temporary furnace (at the altar end of the room), sending clouds of chemically-enhanced black smoke up and out over St. Peter's Square.

Finally, at 17:50 of April 19, an anxious crowd in St. Peter's Square looked up to see a puff of white smoke emerging from the Sistine Chapel's chimney. The bells in St. Peter's clock towers rang out gloriously (a new tradition) confirming that, indeed, a pope had been elected. The crowd erupted in cheers, and Romans watching on their TVs hailed taxis to hurry to the Square.

On the balcony of St. Peter's facade, a cardinal addressed the crowd below. "Brothers and sisters," he said in several languages, *"Habemus Papam."* We have a pope. As thousands chanted *"Viva il Papa,"* 78-year-old Josef Ratzinger of Germany stepped up, raised his hands, and was introduced as Pope Benedict XVI.

opened the door in the year "MM"—2000—and closed it in "MMI.") On the door itself, note Jesus' shiny knees, polished by pious pilgrims who touch them for a blessing.

The other doors are modern, reminding us that amid all this tradition, the Catholic Church has changed enormously even within our lifetimes. Door #2 (second from left) commemorates the kneeling pope, John (Giovanni) XXIII, who opened the landmark Vatican II Council in the early 1960s. This meeting of Church leaders brought the medieval Church into the modern age—they dropped outdated rituals, such as the use of Latin in the Mass—and made old doctrines "relevant" to modern times.

• *Now for one of Europe's great "wow" experiences. Enter the church. Gape for a while. But don't gape at Michelangelo's famous* Pietà *(on the right). That's this tour's finale. I'll wait for you at the round maroon pavement stone on the floor near the central doorway.*

The Church

This church is appropriately huge. Size before beauty: The golden window at the far end is two football fields away. The dove in the window has the wingspan of a 747 (OK, maybe not quite, but it *is* big). The church covers six acres. The babies at the base of the pillars along the main hall (the nave) are adult-size. The lettering in the gold band along the top of the pillars is seven feet high. Really. The church has a capacity of 60,000 standing worshipers (or 1,200 tour groups).

The church is huge and it feels huge, but everything is designed to make it seem smaller and more intimate than it really is. For example, the statue of St. Teresa near the bottom of the first pillar on the right is 15 feet tall. The statue above her near the top looks the same size, but is actually six feet taller, giving the impression that it's not so far away. Similarly, the fancy bronze canopy over the altar at the far end is as tall as a seven-story building. That makes the great height of the dome seem smaller.

Looking down the nave, we get a sense of the splendor of ancient Rome that was carried on by the Catholic Church. The floor plan is based on the ancient Roman basilica, or law-court building, with a central aisle (nave) flanked by two side aisles. In fact, many of the stones used to build St. Peter's were scavenged from the ruined law courts of ancient Rome.

On the floor near the central doorway is a round slab of porphyry stone in the maroon color of ancient Roman officials. This is the spot where, on Christmas night in A.D. 800, the French king Charlemagne was crowned "Holy Roman Emperor." Even in the Dark Ages, when Rome was virtually abandoned and visitors reported that the city had more thieves and wolves than decent people, its

imperial legacy made it a fitting place to symbolically establish a briefly united Europe.

St. Peter's was very expensive to build and decorate. The popes financed it by selling "indulgences," allowing the rich to buy

St. Peter's Basilica

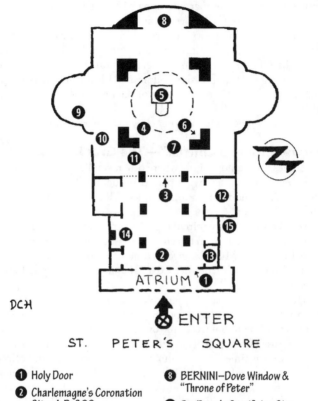

DCH

ENTER

ST. PETER'S SQUARE

1 Holy Door

2 Charlemagne's Coronation Site, A.D. 800

3 Extent of original "Greek Cross" Church Plan

4 St. Andrew Statue & View of Dome

5 Main Altar (Directly over Peter's Tomb)

6 Stairs Down to Crypt (Entrance May Move)

7 St. Peter Statue (With Kissable Toe)

8 BERNINI–Dove Window & "Throne of Peter"

9 St. Peter's Crucifixion Site

10 Museum Entrance

11 RAPHAEL–Transfiguration (Mosaic Copy)

12 Blessed Sacrament Chapel

13 MICHELANGELO–Pietà

14 Elevator to Roof and Dome-Climb (Possible Indoor Location)

15 Elevator to Roof and Dome-Climb (Possible Outdoor Location) forgiveness for their sins from the Church. This kind of corruption inspired an obscure German monk named Martin Luther to rebel and start the Protestant Reformation.

The ornate Baroque-style interior decoration—a riot of marble, gold, stucco, mosaics, columns of stone, and pillars of light—was part of the Church's "Counter-" Reformation. Baroque served as cheery propaganda, impressing followers with the authority of the Church, and giving them a glimpse of the heaven that awaited the faithful.

• *Now, walk straight up the center of the nave toward the altar.*

"Michelangelo's Church"—The Greek Cross

The plaques on the floor show where other, smaller churches of the world would end if they were placed inside St. Peter's: St. Paul's Cathedral in London (Londinense), the Florence Cathedral, and so on.

You'll also walk over circular golden grates. Stop at the second one (at the third pillar from the entrance). Look back at the entrance and realize that if Michelangelo had had his way, this whole long section of the church wouldn't exist. The nave was extended after his death.

Michelangelo was 71 years old when the pope persuaded him to take over the church project and cap it with a dome. He agreed, intending to put the dome over Donato Bramante's original "Greek Cross" floor plan (+), with four equal arms. In optimistic Renaissance times, this symmetrical arrangement symbolized perfection—the orderliness of the created world and the goodness of man (who was created in God's image). But Michelangelo was a Renaissance man in Counter-Reformation times. The Church, struggling against Protestants and its own corruption, opted for a plan designed to impress the world with its grandeur—the Latin cross of the Crucifixion, with its nave extended to accommodate the grand religious spectacles of the Baroque period.

• *Continue toward the altar, entering "Michelangelo's Church." Park yourself in front of the statue of St. Andrew to the left of the altar, the guy holding an X-shaped cross. Like Andrew, gaze up into the dome, and also like him, gasp. (Never stifle a gasp.)*

The Dome

The dome soars higher than a football field on end, 430 feet from the floor of the cathedral to the top of the lantern. It glows with light from its windows, the blue and gold mosaics creating a cool, solemn atmosphere. In this majestic vision of heaven (not painted by Michelangelo), we see (above the windows) Jesus, Mary, and a ring of saints, more rings of angels above them, and, way up in the ozone, God the Father (a blur of blue and red, without binoculars).

When Michelangelo died (1564), he'd completed only the drum of the dome—the base up to the windows flanked by half-columns—but the next architects were guided by his designs.

Listen to the hum of visitors echoing through St. Peter's and reflect on our place in the cosmos: half animal, half angel, stretched between heaven and earth, born to live only a short while, a bubble of foam on a great cresting wave of humanity.

• *But I digress.*

Peter

The base of the dome is ringed with a gold banner telling us in massive blue letters why this church is so important. According to Catholics,

Peter was selected by Jesus to head the church. The banner in Latin quotes from the Bible where Jesus says to him, "You are Peter *(Tu es Petrus)* and upon this rock I will build my church, and to you I will give the keys of the kingdom of heaven" (Matthew 16:18). (Every quote from Jesus to Peter found in the Bible is written out in 7-foot-tall letters that continue around the entire church.)

Peter was the first bishop of Rome. His prestige and that of the city itself made this bishopric more illustrious than all others, and Peter's authority has supposedly passed in an unbroken chain to each succeeding bishop of Rome—that is, the 250-odd popes that followed.

Under the dome, under the bronze canopy, under the altar, some 23 feet under the marble floor, rest the bones of St. Peter, the "rock" upon which this particular church was built. You can't see the tomb, but go to the railing and look down into the small, lighted niche below the altar with a box containing bishops' shawls—a symbol of how Peter's authority spread to the other churches. Peter's tomb (not visible) is just below this box.

Are they really the bones of Jesus' apostle? According to a papal pronouncement: definitely maybe. The traditional site of his tomb was sealed up when Old St. Peter's was built on it in A.D. 326, and it remained sealed until 1940, when it was opened for archaeological study. Bones were found, dated from the first century, of a robust man who died in old age. His body was wrapped in expensive cloth. Various inscriptions and graffiti in the tomb indicate that second- and third-century visitors thought this was Peter's tomb. Does that mean it's really Peter? Who am I to disagree with the pope? Definitely maybe.

Benedict XVI

When Josef Ratzinger became the 265th pope, he introduced himself as "a simple, humble worker in the vineyard of the Lord." But the man has a complex history, a reputation for intellectual brilliance, a flair for the piano, and a penchant for controversy for his unbending devotion to traditional Catholic doctrine.

Born in small-town Bavaria in 1927, he lived life under Nazi rule as many Germans did—outwardly obeying leaders while inwardly conflicted. Like all 14-year-old boys, he joined the Hitler Youth and, like most German men, was drafted into the Army. During World War II, he sprayed flak from anti-aircraft guns, saw Jews transported to death camps, and, like many Germans in the final days of the war, he deserted his post.

After the war, he completed his studies in theology and became a rising voice of liberal Catholicism, serving as an advisor at the Second Vatican Council (1962–1965). But after the May 1968 student revolts rocked Europe's Establishment, he became increasingly convinced that Church tradition was needed to offset the growing chaos of the world.

Pope John Paul II appointed him to several positions, and Ratzinger became John Paul II's closest advisor and good friend. Every Friday afternoon for two decades, they met for lunch, intellectual sparring, and friendly conversation.

Under John Paul II, Ratzinger served as the Church's "enforcer"

If you line up the cross on the altar with the dove in the window, you'll notice that the niche below the cross is just off-center compared with the rest of the church. Why? Because Michelangelo built the church around the traditional location of the tomb, not the actual location—about two feet away—discovered by modern archaeology.

Back in the nave sits a bronze statue of Peter under a canopy. This is one of a handful of pieces of art that was in the earlier church. In one hand he holds the keys, the symbol of the authority given him by Christ, while with the other hand he blesses us. He's wearing the toga of a Roman senator. It may be that the original statue was of a senator and that the bushy head and keys were added later to make it Peter. His big right toe has been worn smooth by the lips of pilgrims and foot-fetishists. Stand in line and kiss it, or, to avoid foot-and-mouth disease, touch your hand to your lips, then rub the toe. This is simply an act of reverence with no

of doctrine, earning the nickname "God's Rottweiler." He spoke out against ordaining women, chastised Latin American priests for fomenting class warfare (Liberation theology), reassigned bishops who were soft on homosexuality, reaffirmed opposition to birth control, and wrote thoughtful papers challenging the secular world's moral relativism. He also punished pedophile priests, though critics charged him with glossing over the issue to preserve the Church's image.

Ratzinger chose the name of "Benedict" to recall both Pope Benedict XV (who tried to bring Europeans together after World War I) and the original St. Benedict (c. 480–543), the monk who symbolizes Europe's Christian roots. A true pan-European who speaks many languages, Ratzinger heads a Church that thrives everywhere except Europe, which is becoming increasingly secular and Muslim. Vatican watchers expect Benedict XVI to continue John Paul II's two priorities: defending Catholic doctrine in a changing world and building bridges with fellow Christians.

legend attached, though you can make one up if you like.

Behind the statue of Peter is another popular stop among pilgrims: the tomb of Pope John XXIII (reigned 1958–1963), best known for spearheading the Vatican II reforms. Nicknamed "the good pope," this John brought the Church into the modern age. He allowed Mass to be conducted in the vernacular rather than in Latin. Women were allowed to wear pants and no longer had to wear hats. A populist, he referred to people as "brothers and sisters"...a phrase popular today among popes. In 2000, during the beatification process (a stop on the way to sainthood), Church authorities checked his body and it was surprisingly fresh. So they moved it upstairs, put it behind glass, and now old Catholics who remember him fondly enjoy another stop on their St. Peter's visit.

The Main Altar

The main altar beneath the dome and canopy (the white marble slab with cross and candlesticks) is used only when the pope himself says Mass. He sometimes conducts the Sunday morning service when he's in town, a sight worth seeing. I must admit, though, it's a little strange being frisked at the door for weapons at the holiest place in Christendom.

The tiny altar would be lost in this enormous church if it weren't for Gian Lorenzo Bernini's seven-story bronze canopy (God's "four-poster bed"), which "extends" the altar upward and reduces the perceived distance between floor and ceiling. The corkscrew columns echo the marble ones that surrounded the altar/tomb in Old St. Peter's. Some of the bronze used here was taken and melted down from the ancient Pantheon. On the marble base of the columns are three bees on a shield, the symbol of the Barberini family, who commissioned the work and ordered the raid on the Pantheon. As the saying went, "What the barbarians didn't do, the Barberini did."

Starting from the column to the left of the altar, walk clockwise

around the canopy. Notice the female faces on the marble bases, about eye level above the bees. Someone in the Barberini family was pregnant during the making of the canopy, so Bernini put the various stages of childbirth on the bases. Continue clockwise to the last base to see how it came out.

Bernini (1598–1680), the Michelangelo of the Baroque era, is the man most responsible for the interior decoration of the church. The altar area was his masterpiece, a "theater" for holy spectacles. Bernini did: 1) the bronze canopy; 2) the dove window in the apse, surrounded by bronze work and statues; 3) the statue of lance-bearing St. Longinus ("The hills are alive..."), which became the model for the other three statues; 4) much of the marble floor decoration; and 5) the balconies above the four statues, incorporating the actual corkscrew columns from Old St. Peter's, said to have been looted by the Romans from the Temple of Herod (called "Solomon's Temple") in Jerusalem. Bernini, the father of Baroque, gave an impressive unity to an amazing variety of pillars, windows, statues, chapels, and aisles.

• The apse is the front area with the golden dove window.

The Apse

Bernini's dove window shines above the smaller front altar used for everyday services. The Holy Spirit, in the form of a six-foot-high dove, pours sunlight onto the faithful through the alabaster windows, turning into artificial rays of gold and reflecting off swirling gold clouds, angels, and winged babies. This is the epitome

of Baroque—an ornate, mixed-media work designed to overwhelm the viewer.

Beneath the dove is the centerpiece of this structure, the so-called "Throne of Peter," an oak chair built in medieval times for a king. Subsequently, it was encrusted with tradition and encased in bronze by Bernini as a symbol of papal authority. Statues of four early Church Fathers support the chair, a symbol of how bishops should support the pope in troubled times—times like the Counter-Reformation.

Remember that St. Peter's is a church, not a museum. In the apse, Mass is said daily (Mon–Sat at 17:00, Sun at 17:30) for pilgrims, tourists, and Roman citizens alike. Wooden confessional booths are available for Catholics to tell their sins to a listening ear and receive forgiveness and peace of mind. The faithful renew their faith, and the faithless gain inspiration. Look at the light streaming through the windows, turn and gaze up into the dome, and quietly contemplate your deity (or lack thereof).

• *To the left of the main altar is the south transept. At the far end, left side, find the dark "painting" of St. Peter crucified upside down.*

South Transept—Peter's Crucifixion

This marks the exact spot (according to tradition) where Peter was killed 1,900 years ago. Peter had come to the world's greatest city to preach Jesus' message of love to the pagan, often hostile Romans. During the reign of Nero, he was arrested and brought to Nero's Circus so all Rome could witness his execution. When the authorities told Peter he was to be crucified just like his Lord, Peter said "I'm not worthy," and insisted they nail him on the cross upside-down. After he died on this spot, they buried him nearby (where the altar is today).

The Romans were actually quite tolerant of other religions, but they required their conquered peoples to worship the Roman emperor as a god. For most religions, this was no problem, but monotheistic Christians refused to worship the emperor even when burned alive, crucified, or thrown to the lions. Their bravery, optimism in suffering, and message of love struck a chord among slaves and members of the lower classes. The religion started by a poor carpenter grew, despite occasional pogroms (persecution of minorities) by fanatical emperors. In three short centuries, Christianity went from a small Jewish sect in Jerusalem to the official religion of the world's greatest empire.

This and all the other "paintings" in the church are actually mosaic copies made from thousands of colored chips the size of your little fingernail. Smoke and humidity would damage real

Bernini Blitz

Nowhere is there such a conglomeration of works by the flamboyant genius who remade the church—and the city—in the Baroque style. Here's your scavenger-hunt list. You have 20 minutes. Go.

1. St. Peter's Square: design and statues
2. Constantine equestrian relief (right end of atrium)
3. Decoration (stucco, gold leaf, marble, etc.) of side aisles (flanking the nave)
4. Tabernacle (the temple-like altarpiece) inside Blessed Sacrament Chapel
5. Much of the marble floor throughout church
6. Bronze canopy over the altar
7. St. Longinus statue (holding a lance) near altar
8. Balconies (above each of the four statues) with corkscrew, Solomonic columns
9. Dove window, bronze sunburst, angels, "Throne," and Church Fathers (in the apse)
10. Tomb of Pope Urban VIII (far end of the apse, right side)
11. Tomb of Pope Alexander VII (between the apse and the left transept, over a doorway, with the gold skeleton smothered in jasper poured like maple syrup).

Bizarre...Baroque...Bernini.

paintings. Around the corner on the right (heading back toward the central nave), pause at the copy of Raphael's huge "painting" (mosaic) of *The Transfiguration*, especially if you won't be seeing the original in the Vatican Museum.

• *Back near the entrance to the church, in the far corner, behind bulletproof glass is the...*

Pietà

Michelangelo was 24 years old when he completed this *Pietà* (pee-ay-TAH) of Mary with the dead body of Christ taken from the cross. It was Michelangelo's first major commission (by the French ambassador to the Vatican), done for Holy Year 1500.

Pietà means "pity." Michelangelo, with his total mastery of the real world, captures the sadness of the moment. Mary cradles her crucified son in her lap. Christ's lifeless right arm drooping down lets us know how heavy this corpse is. His smooth skin is accented by the rough folds of Mary's robe. Mary tilts her head down, looking at her dead son with sad tenderness. Her left hand turns upward, asking, "How could they do this to you?"

Michelangelo didn't think of sculpting as creating a figure, but as simply freeing the God-made figure from the prison of marble

around it. He'd attack a project like this with an inspired passion, chipping away to find what God put inside.

The bunched-up shoulder and rigor-mortis legs show that Michelangelo learned well from his studies of cadavers. But realistic as this work is, its true power lies in the subtle "unreal" features. Life-size Christ looks childlike compared with larger-than-life Mary. Unnoticed at first, this accentuates the subconscious impression of Mary enfolding Jesus in her maternal love. Mary—the mother of a 33-year-old man—looks like a teenager, emphasizing how Mary was the eternally youthful "handmaiden" of the Lord, always serving Him, even at this moment of supreme sacrifice. She accepts God's will, even if it means giving up her son.

The statue is a solid pyramid of maternal tenderness. Yet within this, Christ's body tilts diagonally down to the right and Mary's hem flows with it. Subconsciously, we feel the weight of this dead God sliding from her lap to the ground.

At 11:30 on May 23, 1972, a madman with a hammer entered St. Peter's and began hacking away at the *Pietà*. The damage was repaired, but that's why there's a shield of bulletproof glass today.

This is Michelangelo's only signed work. The story goes that he overheard some pilgrims praising his finished *Pietà*, but attributing it to a second-rate sculptor from a lesser city. He was so enraged he grabbed his chisel and chipped "Michelangelo Buonarroti of Florence did this" in the ribbon running down Mary's chest.

On your right (covered in gray concrete with a gold cross) is the inside of the Holy Door. It won't be opened until Christmas Eve, 2024, the dawn of the next Jubilee Year. If there's a prayer inside you, ask that St. Peter's will no longer need security checks or bulletproof glass when it's next opened.

Up to the Dome (Cupola)

A good way to finish a visit to St. Peter's is to go up to the dome for the best view of Rome anywhere (daily April–Sept 8:00–17:45, Oct–March 8:00–16:45).

There are two levels, the rooftop of the church and the very top of the dome. An elevator (€6) takes you to the first level, on the church roof just above the facade. Even from there, you have a commanding view of St. Peter's Square, the statues on the colonnade, Rome across the Tiber in front of you, and the dome itself—almost terrifying in its nearness—looming behind you.

From here, you can also go inside to the gallery ringing the interior of the dome, where you can look down inside the church. Notice the dusty top of Bernini's seven-story-tall canopy far below. Study the mosaics up close—and those huge letters! It's worth the elevator ride for this view alone.

From this level, if you're energetic, continue all the way up to the top of the dome. The staircase (free at this point) actually winds between the outer shell and the inner one. It's a sweaty, crowded, claustrophobic, 15-minute, 323-step climb, but worth it. The view from the summit is great, the fresh air even better. Admire the arms of Bernini's colonnade encircling St. Peter's Square. Find the big, white Victor Emmanuel Monument with the two statues on top and the Pantheon with its large, light, shallow dome. The large rectangular building to the left of the obelisk is the Vatican Museum, stuffed with art. Survey the Vatican grounds, with its mini-train system and lush gardens. Look down into the square on the tiny pilgrims buzzing like electrons around the nucleus of Catholicism.

THE REST OF THE CHURCH

The Crypt (a.k.a. Grottoes)

You can go down to the foundations of old St. Peter's, containing tombs of popes and memorial chapels. The staircase entrance is usually underneath the dome near St. Andrew. You'll descend to the floor level of the previous church, get a closer look at St. Peter's tomb, and walk by the simple tomb of Pope John Paul II. Out of 265 popes, two have been given the title "Great." That elite group may grow by 50 percent, as there's talk of calling the pope who died in 2005 "John Paul the Great." Seeing the Crypt is free, but the visit takes you back outside the church, a 15-minute detour. (Do it when you're ready to leave.)

The walk through the Crypt is free and easy—but you won't see St. Peter's tomb unless you take a tour. Formal tours with excellent Vatican guides take groups of 10 through the well-lit pagan Necropolis and give a close look at the actual tomb of St. Peter (€10, book a minimum of a week in advance by calling the Excavations Office at 06-6988-5318).

The Museum (Museo-Tesoro)

You must pay an admission fee to see an original corkscrew column from Old St. Peter's, the room-sized tomb of Sixtus IV by Antonio

Pollaiuolo, a big pair of Roman pincers used to torture Christians, and assorted jewels, papal robes, and golden reliquaries (a marked contrast to the poverty of early Christians). The museum is located on the left side of the nave, near the altar.

Blessed Sacrament Chapel

You're welcome to step through the metalwork gates into this oasis of peace reserved for prayer and meditation. It's located on the right-hand side of the church, about midway to the altar.

ST. PETER-IN-CHAINS TOUR

(San Pietro in Vincoli)

Michelangelo—Earth's greatest sculptor—died having failed to complete his greatest work, the tomb of Pope Julius II. Today, you can visit the powerful remains of that unfinished masterpiece, including the famous statue of Moses, housed in a historic church that also contains Peter's chains.

ORIENTATION

Cost: Free.
Dress Code: Modest dress is required.
Hours: Daily 7:00–12:30 & 15:30–18:00.
Getting There: The church is a 15-minute walk north of the Colosseum (Metro stop: Colosseo, exit Metro stop to the left and climb the staircase that's roughly 50 yards away, then work your way slowly uphill; or get off at Metro: Cavour, exit Metro and go up steep flight of steps, take a right at the top and walk a block).
Length of This Tour: Allow 30 minutes.
Cuisine Art: See the recommended eateries listed on page 274.

THE TOUR BEGINS

The Art

• In the far right corner of the church, you'll find a wall full of marble statues. In the center sits...

Michelangelo's *Moses* (1515)

Moses has just returned from meeting face-to-face with God. Now he senses trouble back home. Slowly he turns to see his followers worshiping a golden calf. As his anger builds, he glares at

them. His physical strength is symbolic of his moral and spiritual fortitude as a leader of his people. His powerful left leg tucks under and tenses, as he's just about to spring up out of his chair and punish the naughty Children of Israel with the Ten Commandments under his arm. Enjoy the cascading beard, one of the greatest in art history.

And if he did stand up, this statue would be 13 feet tall, nearly the height of Michelangelo's famous *David*. This Charlton Heston-with-horns is interesting in photographs...and awe-inspiring when confronted in person. His bare, muscular arms exude power. Michelangelo completed the statue after practicing for four years painting the seated prophets on the Sistine ceiling.

Like other Michelangelo statues, *Moses* is both at rest (seated) and in motion (his tensed leg, turning head, and nervous fingers). This restlessness may reflect Michelangelo's neo-Platonic belief that the soul is the claustrophobic prisoner of the body. Or it's the statue itself fighting to emerge from the stone around it. A frustrated Michelangelo, working to bring God's statue into existence, reportedly threw his chisel at the thing (some say causing a scar on *Moses*' right knee), yelling at it: "Speak, dammit, speak!"

The horns are the crowning touch. In medieval times, the Hebrew word for "rays of light" (halo) was mistranslated as "horns." Michelangelo knew better but wanted to give the statue an air of *"terribilità,"* a kind of scary charisma possessed by Moses, Pope Julius II...and Michelangelo. This Moses radiates the smoldering *terribilità* of a borderline-abusive father.

The Tomb Today

In 1542, some of the remnants of the tomb project were brought to St. Peter-in-Chains and pieced together by Michelangelo's assistants. What we see today is a far cry from the original design, which was to have been fully three-dimensional and five times as big. Some of the best statues ended up elsewhere, like the *Prisoners* in Florence, and the *Slaves* in the Louvre. Though the assistants had Michelangelo's original instruction manual, they were trying to assemble it with most of the parts missing.

Moses and the Louvre's *Slaves* are the only statues Michelangelo personally completed for the project. Flanking *Moses* are the Old Testament sister-wives of Jacob, Leah (to our left) and Rachel, both begun by Michelangelo but probably finished by pupils. On the second story, a Madonna and Child stand above a reclining, thoughtful-looking Pope Julius II on a coffin.

The Tomb of Pope Julius II

Moses sits on the bottom level of a three-story marble wall filled with statues. This is a puny, cobbled-together version of what was to have been a grand tomb for Pope Julius II.

In 1505, Pope Julius II hired young Michelangelo to build his tomb, a huge monument to be placed in St. Peter's Basilica. An excited Michelangelo sketched designs for a three-story, wedding-cake mountain of marble studded with 48 statues and bronze reliefs, and topped with a huge statue of the egomaniacal pope. *Moses* was to have been placed on an upper level on the right-hand corner, looking away from the monument.

Michelangelo traveled to Carrara, selected 100 tons of marble for the project, and started working. Then Julius changed his mind. He ordered Michelangelo to work on painting the Sistine Chapel instead. Michelangelo knocked it off in a mere four years so that he could return to his true masterwork. Michelangelo would spend 30 years of his life working in fits and starts on the tomb. But when Julius died (1513), the funding for the project petered out, and Michelangelo eventually moved on to other things. Julius was buried in a simple grave in St. Peter's at the Vatican.

The sheer variety of decoration we see here gives us a glimpse of the tomb's original scope—nearly 50 statues laced together with Pompeii-esque garlands and proto-Baroque scrolls.

Michelangelo went to his grave thinking that he'd wasted the best years of his life on the tomb. Today, we can only reconstruct it in our minds, imagining a monument intended to exceed (according to Giorgio Vasari) "every ancient or imperial tomb ever made."

The Church

Founded in 440, it's one of Rome's oldest, built to house Peter's chains. Though the church was greatly changed in 1475, the 20 Doric columns flanking the wide nave are from the original church. The central ceiling painting (c. 1700) shows the chains—with their miraculous curative powers in action—healing someone possessed by demons, on the steps of St. Peters Basilica in the Vatican.

• *On the altar is a gold-and-glass case, containing what tradition claims are...*

Peter's Chains

There are actually two different sets of chains, linked together. One set held Peter (it's said) when he and Paul were in the Mamertine Prison in Rome (near the Forum).

The other dates from when Herod jailed Peter in Jerusalem (Acts 12; see the scene frescoed on the left wall of the apse). During the night, "Peter was sleeping between two soldiers, bound with chains, while sentries were guarding the doors. And behold, an angel of the Lord appeared and a light shone in the cell. The angel struck Peter on the side and woke him, saying, 'Get up quickly.' And the chains fell off his hands." The angel led Peter, who thought he was dreaming, out of the prison to safety. (Raphael depicted this in the Vatican, page 187.)

In the waning days of ancient Rome, the Jerusalem chains ended up here as a gift from the Eastern empress to her son-in-law, the Western emperor. When they arrived and were paired with the Mamertine chains, the two sets—chink!—joined together miraculously.

PILGRIM'S ROME TOUR

Pilgrimage Churches

Rome is the "capital" of the world's 1.1 billion Catholics. In Rome, you'll rub elbows with religious pilgrims from around the world—Nigerian nuns, Bulgarian theology students, extended Mexican families, and everyday Catholics returning to their religious roots.

The pilgrim industry helped shape Rome after the fall of the empire. Ancient Rome's population peaked at about 1.2 million. When Rome fell in 476, barbarians cut off the water supply by breaking the aqueducts, Romans fled the city, and the Tiber flushed with silt. During the Dark Ages, mosquitoes ruled over a pathetic village of 50,000...bad news for pilgrims, bad news for the Vatican. Back then, the Catholic Church was the Christian Church. Because popes needed a place fit for pilgrimages, the Church revitalized the city. Owners of hotels and restaurants cheered.

In 1587, Pope Sixtus V reconnected aqueducts and built long, straight boulevards connecting the great churches and pilgrimage sites. Obelisks served as markers. As you explore the city, think like a pilgrim. Look down long roads and you'll see either a grand church or an obelisk (from which you'll see a grand church).

THE TOUR BEGINS

Overview

Pilgrims to Rome try to visit four great basilicas: St. Peter's, of course (page 201), Santa Maria Maggiore, San Giovanni in Laterano, and San Paolo Fuori le Mura (St. Paul's Outside the Walls, page 57). For your sightseeing pleasure, I've added a fifth—the fascinating and central San Clemente. And for the best Byzantine-style mosaics in Rome, pilgrims should visit the Church of Santa Prassede.

Pilgrim's Rome

SAN GIOVANNI IN LATERANO

Imagine the jubilation when this church—the first Christian church in the city of Rome—was opened in about A.D. 318. Christians could finally "come out" and worship openly without fear of reprisal. (Still, most Romans were pagan, so this first great church was tucked away from the center of things, near the wall.) After that glorious beginning, the church has served as the center of Catholicism and the home of the popes up until the Renaissance renovation of St. Peter's. Until 1870, all popes were "crowned" here. Even today, it's the home church of the Bishop of Rome—the pope.

The church is free and open daily 7:00–19:00 (tel. 06-0669-8643). It's located on Piazza San Giovanni in Laterano, Metro: San

Giovanni. From the Metro station, go through the old city walls and look left.

The **Via Sannio** market, selling clothing and some handicrafts every morning except Sunday, is a couple of blocks south of the church.

Exterior

The massive facade is 18th century, with Christ triumphant on the top. The blocky, peach-colored building adjacent on the right is the Lateran Palace, standing on the site of the old Papal Palace—residence of popes until about 1300. Across the street to your right are the pope's private chapel and the Holy Stairs (Scala Santa), popular with pilgrims (we'll see the stairs later). To the left is a well-preserved chunk of the ancient Roman wall.

• *Step inside the portico and look left.*

❶ Statue of Constantine (inside the portico, far left end)

It's October 28, A.D. 312, and Constantine—sword tucked under his arm and leaning confidently on a (missing) spear—has conquered Maxentius and liberated Rome. Constantine marched to this spot where his enemy's personal bodyguards lived, trashed their pagan idols, and dedicated the place to the god who gave him his victory—Christ. (In the relief above the statue, see one of Constantine's men straddling and decapitating an enemy.) The holes in Constantine's head once held a golden, halo-like crown for the emperor who legalized Christianity.

❷ Central Doorway (in the portico)

These tall green bronze doors, with their floral designs and acorn studs, are the original doors from ancient Rome's Senate House (Curia) in the Forum. The Church moved these here in the 1650s to remind people that from now on, the Church was Europe's lawmaker. The star borders were added to make these big doors bigger. Imagine, those cool little acorns date to the third century.

• *Now go inside the main part of the church. Stand in the back of the nave.*

❸ Baroque Nave

Very little survives from the original church—most of what you see was built after 1600. In preparation for the 1650 Jubilee, Pope Innocent X commissioned architect Francesco Borromini (rival to

San Giovanni in Laterano

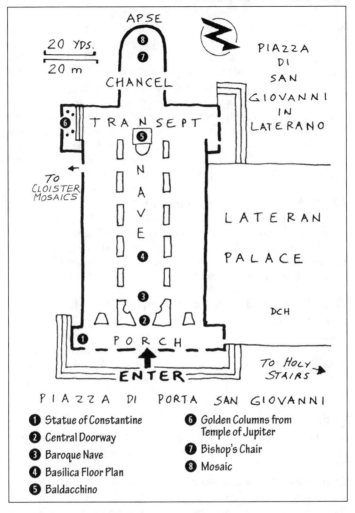

1. Statue of Constantine
2. Central Doorway
3. Baroque Nave
4. Basilica Floor Plan
5. Baldacchino
6. Golden Columns from Temple of Jupiter
7. Bishop's Chair
8. Mosaic

Bernini) to remake the interior. He redesigned the basilica in the Baroque style, reorganizing the nave, and adding the huge statues of the Apostles (they are stepping out of niches...symbolically bringing celestial Jerusalem to our world). The relief panels above the statues depict parallel events from the Old Testament (on the left) and New Testament (on the right). For instance, in the very back you'll see two resurrections: Jonah escaping the whale and Jesus escaping death. Only the ceiling (which should have been a white vault) breaks from the Baroque style—it's Renaissance and the pope wanted it to stay.

❹ Basilica Floor Plan

San Giovanni was the first public church in Rome and the model for all later churches, including St. Peter's. The floor plan—a large central hall (nave) flanked by two side aisles—was based on the ancient Roman basilica (law courts) floor plan. These buildings were big enough to accommodate the large Christian congregations. Note that Roman basilicas came with two apses. You came in through the main entrance, which was designed to stress the authority of the place by slightly overwhelming and intimidating those who entered. When the design was adapted for use as a church, a grand and welcoming entry (the west portal) replaced one of the apses. Upon entering, the worshipper could take in the entire space instantly, and the rows of columns welcomed him to proceed to the altar.

❺ Baldacchino (canopy over altar)

In the upper cage are two silver statues of saints Peter (with keys) and Paul (sword), which contain pieces of their...heads.

The gossip buzzing among Rome's amateur archaeologists is that the Vatican tested DNA from Peter's head (located here) and from his body (located at St. Peter's)...and they didn't match.

❻ Golden Columns from Temple of Jupiter (left transept)

Tradition says that these gilded bronze columns once stood in pagan Rome's holiest spot—the Temple of Jupiter, dedicated to the King of all Gods, on the summit of Capitol Hill (c. 50 B.C.). Now they support a triangular pediment inhabited by a bearded, Jupiter-like God the Father.

❼ Bishop's Chair (in apse)

The chair (or "cathedra") reminds visitors that this is the cathedral of Rome...and the pope himself is the bishop that sits here.

❽ Mosaic (in semicircular dome of apse)

The original design dates from about 450 (although it was made in the 13th century and heavily restored in the 19th century). Pop in a coin for light. You'll see a cross, animals, plants, and the River Jordan running along the base. Mosaic, of course, was an ancient Roman specialty adapted by medieval Christians. The head of Christ (above the cross) must have been a glorious sight to

early worshippers. It was one of the first legal images of Christ ever seen in formerly pagan Rome.

• *Fans of Cosmatesque marble inlay floor (c. 1100–1300) may want to visit the cloister (€2, entrance near left transept).*

The Holy Stairs are outside the church in a building across the street.

Holy Stairs (Scala Santa)

In 326, Emperor Constantine's mother (St. Helena) brought home the 28 marble steps of Pilate's residence. Jesus climbed these steps on the day he was sentenced to death. Each day, hundreds of faithful penitents climb these steps on their knees (reciting a litany of prayers, available at the desk to the right  of the entry). Covered with walnut wood with small glass-covered holes showing stains from Jesus' blood, the steps lead to the "Holy of Holies" (Sancta Sanctorum), the private chapel of the popes in the Middle Ages. With its world-class relics, this chapel was considered the holiest place on earth. While the relics are now in the Vatican and the chapel is locked up, you can climb the tourist staircases along the sides and look through the grated windows into the chapel.

On September 20, 1870, as nationalist forces unifying Italy took Rome and ended the pope's temporal power, Pope Pius IX left his Quirinal Palace home for the last time. He stopped here to climb the steps, pray in his chapel, and bless his supporters from the top of the steps. Then he fled to the Vatican, where he spent the rest of his days.

SANTA MARIA MAGGIORE

The basilica of Santa Maria celebrates Holy Mary, the mother of Jesus. One of Rome's oldest and best-preserved churches, it was built (A.D. 432) while Rome was falling around it. The city had been sacked by Visigoths (410), and the emperors were about to check out (476). Increasingly, popes stepped in to fill the vacuum of leadership. The fifth-century mosaics give the church the feel of the early Christian community. The general ambience of the church really takes you back to ancient times.

The church is free and open daily 7:00–19:00 (tel. 06-483-195). It's on Piazza Santa Maria Maggiore (Metro: Termini or Vittorio Emanuele).

Exterior

Mary's column originally stood in the Forum's Basilica of Constantine. The fifth-century church built in her honor proclaims she was indeed the Mother of God—a fact disputed by hair-splitting theologians of the day. When you step inside the church, you'll be exiting Italy and entering the Vatican—the *Maggiore* indicates that this church, a Vatican possession, was much more important than other churches dedicated to the Virgin Mary.

Interior

Despite the Renaissance ceiling and Baroque crusting, you still feel like you're walking into an early Christian church. The stately rows of columns, the simple basilica layout, the cheery colors, the spacious nave—it's easy to imagine worshipers finding an oasis of peace here as the Roman Empire crashed around them. (The 15th-century coffered ceiling is gilded with gold perhaps brought back from America by Columbus.)

• *In the center of the church is the main altar, under a purple and gold canopy. Underneath the altar, in a lighted niche, are...*

❶ Manger Fragments

A kneeling Pope Pius IX (who established the dogma of the Immaculate Conception in the 19th century) prays before a glass case with an urn that contains several pieces of wood, bound by iron—these pieces are said to be from Jesus' crib. The church, dedicated to Mary's motherhood, displays these relics as physical evidence that Mary was indeed the mother of Christ. (The church is also built on the site of a former pagan temple dedicated to Rome's mother goddess, Juno.) Is the manger the real thing? Look into the eyes of pilgrims who visit.

• *In the apse, topped with a semicircular dome, find...*

❷ Apse Mosaic

This 13th-century mosaic shows Mary being crowned by Jesus, both on the same throne. They float in a bubble representing heaven, borne aloft by angels. By the Middle Ages, Mary's cult status was secure.

• *Up in the arch that frames the outside of the apse, you'll find some of the church's oldest mosaics.*

❸ Mosaics in Chancel Arch

Colorful panels tell Mary's story in fifth-century Roman terms. Haloed senator-saints in white togas (top panel on left-hand side) attend to Mary, who sits on a throne, dressed in gold and crowned like an empress. The angel Gabriel swoops down to announce to Mary that she'll conceive Jesus, and the Dove of the

Santa Maria Maggiore

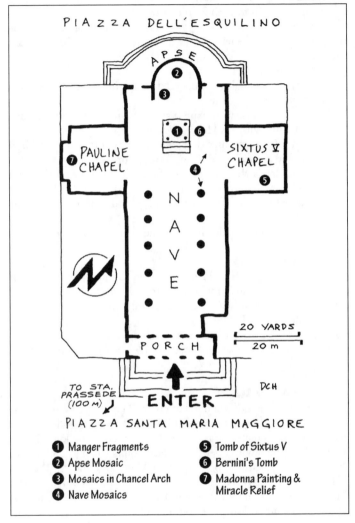

PIAZZA DELL'ESQUILINO

APSE

❷

❸

❶ ❻

PAULINE
❼ CHAPEL

SIXTUS Ⅴ
CHAPEL

❹

❺

N
A
V
E

20 YARDS
20 m

PORCH

TO STA.
PRASSEDE
(100 M)

DCH

ENTER

PIAZZA SANTA MARIA MAGGIORE

❶ Manger Fragments
❷ Apse Mosaic
❸ Mosaics in Chancel Arch
❹ Nave Mosaics

❺ Tomb of Sixtus V
❻ Bernini's Tomb
❼ Madonna Painting &
   Miracle Relief

Holy Spirit follows. Below (the panel in the bottom left corner) are sheep representing the apostles, entering the city of Jerusalem ("Hiervsalem").

❹ Nave Mosaics (right side of nave, starting near altar)

The church contains some of the world's oldest and best-preserved mosaics from Christian Rome. If the floodlights are on (it doesn't hurt to ask someone), those with good eyesight or binoculars will enjoy watching the story of Moses unfold in a series of surprisingly colorful and realistic scenes—more sophisticated than anything that would be seen for a thousand years.

The small, square mosaic panels are above the columns, on the right-hand side of the nave. Start at the altar and work back toward the entry.

1. It's a later painting—skip it.
2. Pharaoh's daughter (upper left) and her maids take baby Moses from the Nile.
3. Moses (lower half of panel) sees a burning bush that reconnects him with his Hebrew origins.
4. A parade of Israelites (left side) flee Egypt through a path in the Red Sea, while Pharaoh's troops drown.
5. Moses leads them across the Sinai desert (upper half), and God provides for them with a flock of quail (lower half).
6. Moses (upper half) sticks his magic rod in a river to desalinate it.
7. The Israelites battle their enemies while Moses commands from a hillside.
8. Skip it.
9. Moses (upper left) brings the Ten Commandments, then goes with Joshua (upper right) to lie down and die.
10. Joshua crosses the (rather puny) Jordan River...
11. ...and attacks Jericho...
12. ...and then the walls come a-tumblin' down.

• *Enter the chapel in the right transept. On the right-hand wall is a statue of a praying pope, atop the...*

❺ Tomb of Sixtus V

The Rome we see today is due largely to Pope Sixtus V (or was it Fiftus VI)? This energetic pope (1585–1590) leveled shoddy medieval Rome and erected grand churches connected by long, broad boulevards spiked with obelisks as focal points (such as the obelisk in Piazza dell'Esquilino behind Santa Maria Maggiore). The city of Rome has 13 Egyptian obelisks—all of Egypt has only five. The relief panels (especially the one in the upper right) show some of the obelisks and buildings he commissioned.

• *Between the right transept and the main altar, you'll find on the floor a plaque marking...*

❻ Bernini's Tomb

The plaque reads, "Ioannes Laurentivs Bernini"—Gian Lorenzo Bernini (1598–1680) —"who brought honor to art and the city, here humbly rests." Next to it is another plaque to the "Familia Bernini." It's a simple memorial for the man who grew up in this neighborhood, then went on to remake Rome in the ornate Baroque style. (For more on Bernini, see page 168.)

• In the left transept, over the altar, you'll see a...

❼ Madonna Painting and Miracle Relief

The altar, a geologist's delight, is adorned with jasper, agate, amethyst, lapis lazuli, and gold angels. Amid it all is a simple, iconic version of the lady this church is dedicated to: Mary.

Above the painting is a bronze relief panel showing a pope, with amazed bystanders, shoveling snow. One hot August night in the year 432, Mary appeared to Pope Liberius in a dream, telling him: "Build me a church where the snow falls." The next morning, they discovered a small patch of snow here on the Esquiline Hill—on August 5—and this church, dedicated to Santa Maria, was begun.

• After looking around Santa Maria Maggiore, fans of mosaics, Byzantines, and the offbeat should consider a visit to the nearby church of Santa Prassede, about 100 yards away.

Exiting Santa Maria Maggiore, walk away from the church, past Mary on her column, and turn right down the small street Via S. Giovanni Gualberto.

CHURCH OF SANTA PRASSEDE

The mosaics, from A.D. 822, are the best Byzantine-style mosaics in Rome. The Byzantine Empire, with its capital in Constantinople (modern Istanbul), was the eastern half of the Roman Empire. Unlike the western half, it didn't "fall," and its inhabitants remained Christian, Greek-speaking, and cultured for a thousand years while their distant cousins in Italy were fumbling for the light switch in the Dark Ages. Byzantine craftsmen preserved the techniques of ancient Roman mosaicists (who decorated floors and walls of villas and public buildings), then reinfused this learning into Rome during the city's darkest era. Take the time to let your eyes adjust, and appreciate the Byzantine glory glowing out of the dark church.

The church is free and open daily 7:00–12:00 & 16:00–18:30. Bring €0.50 coins to buy floodlighting.

• The best mosaics are in the apse (behind the main altar) and in the small Chapel of St. Zeno along the right (north) side of the nave.

Apse Mosaics

On a blue background is Christ, standing in a rainbow-colored river, flanked by saints. Christ has commanded Peter (to our right of Christ, with white hair and beard) to spread the Good News to all the world. Beneath Christ, 12 symbolic sheep leave Jerusalem's city gates to preach to the world. Peter came here to the world's biggest city to preach love...and was met with a hostile environment. He turns his palm up in a plea for help. Persecuted Peter was taken in by a hospitable woman named Pudentia (next to him) and her sister, Praxedes (to the left of Christ, between two other saints), whose house was located on this spot. (The church is named for Praxedes.)

The saint on the far left (to left of Praxedes) is Pope Paschal I, who built the church in the 800s in memory of these early sisters, hiring the best craftsmen in the known world to do the mosaics.

Chapel of St. Zeno

The ceiling is gold, representing the Byzantine heaven. An icon-like Christ emerges from the background, supported by winged angels in white. On the walls are saints walking among patches of flowers. In the altar-niche, Mary and the child Jesus are flanked by the sisters Praxedes and Pudentia.  On the side wall, the woman with the square blue halo (indicating she was alive at the time this was made) is Theodora, the mom of the pope who built this.

The chapel, covered completely with mosaics, may be underwhelming to our modern eyes, but in the darkness of Rome's medieval era, it was known as the "Garden of Paradise."

SAN CLEMENTE

Here, like nowhere else, you'll enjoy the layers of Rome—a 12th-century basilica sits atop a fourth-century Christian basilica, which sits atop a second-century Mithraic Temple and some even earlier Roman buildings. Upper church is free, €3 for lower churches, open Mon–Sat 9:00–12:30 & 15:00–18:00, Sun 10:00–12:30 & 15:00–18:00, on Via di San Giovanni in Laterano, Metro: Colosseo. Tel. 06-7045-1018.

Upper Church—12th Century

The church (at today's ground level) is dedicated to the fourth pope, Clement, who shepherded the small Christian community when the religion was, at best, tolerated, and at worst, a capital offense. Clement himself was martyred by drowning in about A.D. 100—tied to an anchor by angry Romans and tossed overboard. You'll see his symbol, the anchor, around the church. The painting on the ceiling shows Clement being carried aloft to heaven.

While today's main entry is on the side, the original entry was through the courtyard in back, a kind of defensive atrium common in medieval times. To reach the original entry, enter the church

through today's main entrance, walk diagonally toward the right, and exit again into this courtyard. Turn around and face the original entry. As you enter the church from here, notice (on the left) the reproductions of some ancient frescoes. You'll see the faded originals in the lower church, but notice the splendid detail of these first. (Note particularly the middle fresco on the top row showing Clement and Sisinnius, discussed below.)

The carved marble choir enclosure in the middle of the church (Schola Cantorum) was where the cantors sat. About 1,200 years ago, it stood in the old church beneath us, before that church was looted and destroyed by invading Normans.

In the apse, study the fine 12th-century mosaics. The delicate Crucifixion—with Christ sharing the cross with a dozen apostles as doves—is engulfed by a Tree of Life richly inhabited by deer, birds, and saints. The message is clear: All life springs from God in Christ. Above it all, a triumphant Christ, one hand on the Bible, blesses the congregation.

St. Catherine Chapel

The chapel near the side (tourists') entrance—considered one of the first great Renaissance masterpieces—is dedicated to **St. Catherine of Alexandria**, a noblewoman martyred for her defense of persecuted Christians. The fresco on the left wall—which shows an early Renaissance three-dimensional representation of space—is by the Florentine master Masolino (1428), perhaps aided by his young assistant, Masaccio. Working from left to right (on the left wall), follow her story:

1. Catherine (lower left panel), in black, confronts an assembly of the pagan Emperor Maxentius and his counselors. She bravely ticks off arguments on her fingers why Christianity should be legalized. Her powerful delivery silences the crowd.

2. Under the rotunda of a pagan temple (upper left panel), Catherine, in blue, points up at a statue and tells a crowd of pagans, "Your gods are puny compared to mine."

3. Catherine, in blue (upper right panel, left side), is thrown in prison, where she's visited by the emperor's wife (in green). Catherine converts her.

4. Emperor Maxentius, enraged, orders his own wife killed. The executioner (upper panel, right side), standing next to the empress' decapitated corpse, impassively sheathes his sword.

5. In the most well-known scene (the middle panel on the bottom), Maxentius, in black, looks down from a balcony and condemns Catherine (in black) to be torn apart between two large, spiked wheels turned by executioners. But suddenly, an angel swoops in with a sword to cut her loose.

6. Catherine is eventually martyred (lower right panel). Now dressed in green, she kneels before the executioner, who raises his sword to finish the job.

7. Finally, on the top of holy Mount Sinai (lower right panel, upper right side), two angels bear Catherine's body to its final resting place.

Taking a few steps back, look up at the arch that frames the chapel, topped by the delightful Annunciation fresco (top of the arch) by Masolino. Also notice the big St. Christopher, patron saint of travelers (left pillar), with 500-year-old graffiti scratched in by pilgrims.

Lower Church—Fourth Century

Buy a €3 ticket in the bookshop, and descend 1700 years to the time when Christians were razzed on their way to church by pagan neighbors. The first room you enter was the original atrium (entry hall) —the nave extends to the right. (Everything you'll visit from here on was buried until the 19th century.)

Pagan Inscription (in atrium)

This two-sided, marble, recycled burial slab—one side (with leafy decorations) for a Christian, the other for a pagan (you can turn it)—shows how the two Romes lived side by side in the fourth century.

Fresco of St. Clement and Sisinnius (in nave near altar, on left wall)

Clement (center) holds a secret Mass for early Christians back when it was a capital crime. Theodora, a prominent Roman (in yellow, to the right), is one of the undercover faithful. Her pagan husband, Sisinnius, has come to retrieve and punish her when—zap!—he's struck blind and has to be led away (right side).

But Sisinnius is still unconvinced. When Clement cures his blindness, Sisinnius (very faded, lower panel, far right) orders two servants to drag Clement off to the authorities. But through a miraculous intervention, the servants mistake a column for Clement and drag that out of the house instead. The inscription (crossword-style on right, faded) is famous among Italians because it's one of the earliest examples of the transition from Latin to Italian. Sisinnius encourages his servants by yelling *"Fili dele pute, traite!"* ("You sons of bitches, pull!")

• *In the far left corner of the lower church, near the staircase leading down, is the...*

Presumed Burial Place of St. Cyril

Cyril, who died in A.D. 869 (see the modern icon-like mosaic of him), was an inveterate traveler who spread Christianity to the Slavic lands and Russia—today's Russian Orthodox faithful. Along the way, he introduced the Cyrillic alphabet still used by Russians and many other Slavs.

Temple of Mithras (Mithreum)—Second Century

Now descend farther to the dark, dank Mithraic Temple (Mithreum). Nowhere in Rome is there a better place to experience this weird cult.

Worship Hall (the barred room to the left)

Worshippers of Mithras—men only—reclined on the benches on either side of the room. At the far end is a small statue of the god Mithras, in a billowing cape. In the center sits an altar carved with a relief showing Mithras fighting with a bull that contains all life. A scorpion, a dog, and a snake try to stop Mithras, but he wins, running his sword through the bull. The blood spills out, bringing life to the world.

Mithras' fans gathered here, in this tiny microcosm of the universe (the ceiling was decorated with stars), to celebrate the victory with a ritual meal. Every spring, Mithras brought new life again, and so they ritually kept track of the seasons—the four square shafts in the corners of the ceiling represent the seasons,  the seven round ones were the great constellations. Initiates went through hazing rituals representing the darkness of this world, then emerged into the light-filled world brought by Mithras.

Rome's official pagan religion had no real spiritual content and did not offer any concept of salvation. As the empire slowly crumbled, people turned more and more to Eastern religions (including Christianity), in search of answers and comfort. The cult of Mithras, stressing loyalty and based on the tenuousness of life, was popular among soldiers. Part of its uniqueness and popularity (in this very class-conscious society) was due to its belief that all were equal before God. It dates back to the time of Alexander the Great, who brought it from Persia. In 67 B.C., soldiers who had survived the bloody conquest of Asia Minor returned to Rome swearing by Mithras. When Christians gained power, they banished the worship of Mithras.

Facing the barred room are two Corinthian columns supporting three arches of the temple's entryway, decorated with a fine stucco, coffered ceiling. At the far end of the hallway, another barred door marks the equivalent of a Mithraic Sunday School room. Peeking inside, see a faded fresco of bearded Mithras (right wall) and seven niches carved into the walls representing the seven stages a novice had to go through. Exit signs direct you down. You'll pass a very narrow ancient alleyway separating Roman walls barely three feet across. Step into this and imagine the first Western city to reach one million. Forget the two churches above you, and imagine standing on this exact spot and looking up at the sky 2,000 years ago. Now climb back through the centuries to today's street level.

SLEEPING

For hassle-free efficiency, I favor accommodations and restaurants handy to your sightseeing activities. Rather than listing hotels scattered throughout Rome, I describe my favorite neighborhoods and recommend the best-value accommodations in each, ranging from hotels to less expensive hostels and convents.

Hotels in Rome are generally pricey and the cheaper hotels can be depressing. Tourist-information services cannot give opinions on quality. A major feature of this book is its extensive listing of good-value rooms. I like places that are clean, small, central, quiet at night, traditional, inexpensive, and friendly, with firm beds—and those not listed in other guidebooks. In Rome, for me, a hotel with six out of these nine attributes means it's a keeper.

As you look over the listings, you'll notice that many hotels promise special prices to my readers who book directly (without using a room-finding service, which takes a commission). To get these rates, mention this book when you reserve, then show the book upon arrival. During slow times, rooms might be offered for even less than listed. To get the best price, first ask the price, then request the discount with the book. Many places prefer hard cash. "Rack rates" (the highest rates a hotel charges) are much higher.

TYPES OF ACCOMMODATIONS

Hotels
Double rooms listed in this book will range from about €50 (very simple, toilet and shower down the hall) to €450 (maximum plumbing and more), with most clustering around €130 (with private bathrooms). I've favored these pricier options, because intense and grinding Rome is easier to enjoy with air-conditioning and a welcoming oasis to call home.

Three or four people economize by sharing larger rooms. Solo travelers find that the cost of a *camera singola* is often only 25 percent less than a *camera doppia*. Most listed hotels have rooms for anywhere from one to five people. If there's room for an extra cot, they'll cram it in for you. English works in all but the cheapest places.

Prices are fairly standard. Shopping around earns you a better location and more character, but rarely a better price. However, prices at many hotels get soft if you do any of the following: arrive late in the day during slow season (especially July–Aug and Nov–mid-March) and haggle, offer to pay cash, mention this book, and/or stay at least three nights. Room rates are lowest in sweltering August. Unless otherwise indicated, breakfasts are included.

Traffic in Rome roars. With the recent arrival of double-paned windows and air-conditioning, night noise is not the problem it once was. Even so, light sleepers who ask for a *tranquillo* room will likely get a room on the back...and sleep better.

Nearly all places offer private bathrooms. Generally rooms with a bath or shower also have a toilet and a bidet (which Italians use for quick sponge baths). The cord that dangles over the tub or shower is not a clothesline. You pull it when you've fallen and can't get up.

Double beds are called *matrimoniale*, even though hotels aren't interested in your marital status. Twins are *due letti singoli.*

Many hotel rooms have a TV and phone. Rooms in fancier hotels usually come with a small safe, air-conditioning (sometimes you pay an extra per-day charge for this, and often the air-con is turned on only in summer), and a small fridge called a *frigo bar* (FREE-goh bar) stocked with drinks that aren't free.

When you check in, the receptionist will normally ask for your passport and keep it for a couple of hours. Hotels are legally required to register each guest with the local police. Relax. Americans are notorious for making this chore more difficult than it needs to be.

Rooms are safe. Still, zip cameras and keep money out of sight. More pillows and blankets are usually in the closet or available on request. In Italy, towels and linen aren't always replaced every day. Hang your towel up to dry.

Your hotel can point you to the nearest Internet café or launderette; also see page 25.

Most hotels are eager to connect you with a shuttle service to the airport. It's reasonable and easy for departure, but upon arrival, I just catch a cab or the train into the city.

Almost no hotels have parking, but nearly all have a line on spots in a nearby garage (about €24/day).

Convents

Although I list only four, Rome has many convents that rent out rooms. See the Church of Santa Susanna's Web site for a long list (www.santasusanna.org, select "Coming To Rome," then "Convents"). At convents, the beds are twins and English is often in short supply, but the price is right.

Consider these nun-run places: the expensive but divine **Suore di Santa Elisabetta** and the **Istituto "Il Rosario"** (both near Basilica Santa Maria Maggiore, see page 248), **Casa San Giuseppe** (secular but convent-run, in Trastevere, see page 252), and the most user-friendly of all, **Casa per Ferie Santa Maria alle Fornaci dei Padri Trinitari** (near the Vatican, see page 255).

Hostels and Dorms

For easy communication with young, friendly entrepreneurs, €20 dorm beds, and some inexpensive doubles—within a 10-minute hike of the Termini train station—consider the following places (see page 248 for descriptions): **The Beehive** (with the best €70 doubles in town, 2 blocks from train station), **Gulliver's House Rome** (off Via Nazionale), and **Casa Olmata** (near Basilica Santa Maria Maggiore).

PRACTICALITIES

Phoning

To phone Italy, you'll need to know its country code: 39. To call Italy from the United States or Canada, dial 011-39 and the entire local number (which appears in each accommodation listing below). If calling Italy from another European country, dial 00-39-local number.

Making Reservations

It's possible to visit Rome without booking ahead, but given the high stakes and the quality of the gems I've found for this city guide, I'd highly recommend making reservations. Easter, September, and Christmas are the most crowded and expensive (see list of holidays on page 5). On Easter (April 16 in 2006), the entire city gets booked up.

Reserve your room with an e-mail, fax, or phone call as soon as you can commit to a date. Most hotels listed are accustomed to English-only speakers. E-mail is a steal, fax costs are affordable, and simple English is usually fine. To fax, use the handy form in the appendix; for e-mailers, the form is online at www.ricksteves .com/reservation. If you don't get an answer to your fax request, consider that a "no." (Many smaller places get 20 faxes a day after they're booked up and can't afford to respond.)

A two-night stay in August would be "2 nights, 16/8/06 to 18/8/06" (Europeans write the date day/month/year, and hotel jargon uses your day of departure). You'll often receive a response back requesting one night's deposit.

Your credit-card number will usually be accepted as the deposit. Be sure to fax your card number (rather than e-mail it) to keep it private, safer, and out of cyberspace. You can pay with your card or cash when you arrive; if you don't show up, your card will be billed for one night.

Always reconfirm your reservations several days in advance by phone. On the small chance that a hotel loses track of your reservation, bring along their faxed confirmation or a hard copy of their e-mailed confirmation.

Honor your reservations, or cancel them by phone or e-mail. Long distance is cheap from public phone booths.

ACCOMMODATIONS IN ROME

Via Firenze

I generally stay on Via Firenze because it's safe, handy, central, and relatively quiet. It's a 10-minute walk from the Termini train station and the airport shuttle, and two blocks beyond Piazza della Repubblica and the TI. The Defense Ministry is nearby, so you've got heavily armed guards watching over you all night.

The neighborhood is well-connected by public transportation (with the Repubblica Metro stop nearby). Virtually all the city buses that rumble down Via Nazionale (#64, #70, #115, #640, and the #40 express) take you to Piazza Venezia (Forum) and Largo Argentina (Pantheon). From Largo Argentina, electric trolley #8 goes to Trastevere (get off at first stop after crossing the river) and the #64 bus (jammed with people and thieves) and the #40 express bus both continue to St. Peter's.

A 24-hour **pharmacy** near the recommended hotels is Farmacia Piram (Via Nazionale 228, tel. 06-488-4437).

$$ Hotel Oceania is a peaceful slice of air-conditioned heaven. This 15-room, manor house-type hotel is spacious and quiet, with spotless, tastefully decorated rooms, run by a pleasant father-and-son team. While Armando (the dad) serves world-famous coffee, Stefano (the son) works to give their hotel all the extra touches, including a plasma TV in the lounge for guests to watch classic movies set in Rome...and Italy episodes from my TV series (Sb-€118, Db-€148, Tb-€178, Qb-€198, prices good through 2006 with this book and cash, 25 percent less in Aug and winter, large roof terrace, family suite, Via Firenze 38, 3rd floor, tel. 06-482-4696, fax 06-488-5586, www.hoteloceania.it, info@hoteloceania.it; Anna, Radu, and Enrico round out the staff).

Sleep Code

(€1 = about $1.20)
To help you easily sort through these listings, I've divided the rooms into three categories based on the price for a standard double room with bath:

$$$ **Higher Priced**—Most rooms €180 or more.
$$ **Moderately Priced**—Most rooms between €120–180.
$ **Lower Priced**—Most rooms €120 or less.

To give maximum information in a minimum of space, I use the following code to describe accommodations. Prices listed are per room, not per person. Unless I note otherwise, the staff speaks English and breakfast is included. You can assume a hotel takes credit cards unless you see "cash only" in the listing.

S = Single room (or price for one person in a double).
D = Double or Twin room. "Double beds" are often two twins sheeted together and are usually big enough for nonromantic couples.
T = Triple (generally a double bed with a single).
Q = Quad (usually two double beds).
b = Private bathroom with toilet and shower or tub.
s = Private shower or tub only (toilet is down the hall).

According to this code, a couple staying at a "Db-€140" hotel would pay a total of €140 (about $170) for a double room with a private bathroom.

$$ Hotel Aberdeen, which perfectly combines high quality and friendliness, is warmly run by Annamaria, with support from cousins Sabrina and Cinzia and sister Laura. The 37 comfy, modern, air-conditioned, and smoke-free rooms are a terrific value. Enjoy the frescoed breakfast room (Sb-€87, Db-€135, Tb-€150, Qb-€165, these special prices promised through 2006 with this book, 30 percent less in Aug and winter, check Web site for deals, Via Firenze 48, tel. 06-482-3920, fax 06-482-1092, www  .travel.it/roma/aberdeen, hotel.aberdeen@travel.it).

$$ Residenza Cellini is a gorgeous six-room place that feels like the guest wing of a neoclassical palace. It offers "ortho/anti-allergy beds" and four-star comforts and service (Db-€165, larger Db-€185, extra bed-€25, €30 less in Aug and mid-Nov–mid-March, prices good through 2006 with this book and cash, family apartment, air-con, elevator, Via Modena 5, tel. 06-4782-5204, fax

Hotels in East Rome

Map legend:
- ⓣ - Taxi Stand
- Ⓜ - Subway Stop
- Ⓑ - Bus Stop

1. Residenza Cellini & Residence Adler
2. Hotels Oceania & Nardizzi
3. Hotel Aberdeen
4. Hotel Sonya
5. Hotel Pensione Italia
6. Hotel Montreal
7. Istituto Il Rosario
8. Suore di Santa Elisabetta
9. To Gulliver's Place Rooms
10. Albergo Sileo & Fawlty Towers Hostel
11. Hotel Paba
12. Hotel Lancelot
13. The Beehive Hostel
14. Gulliver's House Hostel
15. Casa Olmata Hostel

06-4788-1806, www.residenzacellini.it, residenzacellini@tin.it; Barbara, Gaetano, and Donato).

$ Residence Adler offers breakfast on a garden patio, wide halls, and eight quiet, simple, air-conditioned rooms in a good location. It's run the old-fashioned way by a charming family (Db-€120, Tb-€150, Qb-€180, Quint/b-€195, prices through 2006 with this book, additional 5 percent off if you pay with cash, 15 percent less in Aug and winter, elevator, Via Modena 5, 2nd floor, tel. 06-484-466, fax 06-488-0940, www.hoteladler-roma.com, info @hoteladler-roma.com, gracious Sr. Brando Massini doesn't speak English but tries).

$ Hotel Nardizzi Americana offers 33 simple, pleasant, air-conditioned rooms and a delightful rooftop terrace. Though loosely run, it's a fine value (Sb-€95, Db-€115, Tb-€145, Qb-€160, prices through 2006 with this book, 10 percent discounts for off-season and long stays, additional 10 percent off with cash, elevator, Via Firenze 38, 4th floor, tel. 06-488-0035, fax 06-488-0368, www .hotelnardizzi.it, info@hotelnardizzi.it).

Between Via Nazionale and Basilica Santa Maria Maggiore

$$ Hotel Sonya is small and family-run but impersonal, with 23 well-equipped rooms, a central location, and decent prices (Sb-€85, Db-€125, Tb-€140, Qb-€160, Quint/b-€180, prices through 2006 with this book, 5 percent less if you pay cash, big discounts off-season, air-con, elevator, free Internet, faces the opera at Via Viminale 58, Metro: Repubblica or Termini, tel. 06-481-9911, fax 06-488-5678, www.hotelsonya.it, hotelsonyaroma@katamail.com, Francesca).

$ Hotel Pensione Italia, in a busy, interesting, and handy locale, is placed safely on a quiet street next to the Ministry of the Interior. Thoughtfully run by Andrea, Nadine, and Gabriel, it has 31 comfortable, clean, bright, non-smoking rooms (Sb-€80, Db-€110, Tb-€145, Qb-€165, prices through 2006 with this book and cash, all rooms 30 percent off mid-July–Aug and Nov–mid-March, most rooms have fans, air-con-€8/day, elevator, Via Venezia 18, just off Via Nazionale, Metro: Repubblica or Termini, tel. 06-482-8355, fax 06-474-5550, www.hotelitaliaroma.com, info@hotelitaliaroma .com). They also have eight decent annex rooms across the street.

$ Hotel Montreal, run with care, is a bright, solid, business-class place on a big street a block southeast of Santa Maria Maggiore (rates are soft, but these prices are promised with this book in 2006: Db-€115, Tb-€140; in July–Aug rates drop to Db-€90, Tb-€120; air-con, elevator, good security, Via Carlo Alberto 4, 1 block from Metro: Vittorio Emanuele, 3 blocks west of Termini train station, tel. 06-445-7797, fax 06-446-5522, www.hotelmontrealroma.com, info@hotelmontrealroma.com).

$ Suore di Santa Elisabetta is a heavenly Polish-run convent with a peaceful garden and tidy rooms. Often booked long in advance, it's a super value (S-€36, Sb-€45, D-€58, Db-€76, Tb-€96, Qb-€116, Quint/b-€125, 23:00 curfew, elevator, fine view roof terrace, a block southwest of Basilica Santa Maria Maggiore at Via dell'Olmata 9, Metro: Termini or Vittorio Emanuele, tel. 06-488-8271, fax 06-488-4066, ist.it.s.elisabetta@libero.it).

$ Casa Olmata is a ramshackle, laid-back backpackers' place a block southwest of Basilica Santa Maria Maggiore, midway between the Termini train station and Colosseum (dorm beds-€20, S-€38, D-€57, laundry service, free Internet, video rentals, games, rooftop terrace with views and nearly free dinner parties, dinners twice weekly, communal kitchen, Via dell'Olmata 36, 3rd floor, Metro: Vittorio Emanuele, tel. 06-483-019, fax 06-486819, www.casaolmata.com, info@casaolmata.com, Mirella and Marco).

$ Gulliver's House Rome, run by helpful Simon and Sara, is a fun little hostel in a safe and handy location. Its 24 beds in cramped quarters work fine for backpackers. They host English-language movie evenings nightly in their lounge—you can start off the evening with my TV shows on Rome (€20 per bunk in 8-bed dorm, one D-€70, cash only, closed 12:00–16:00, 1:00 curfew, small kitchen, Via Palermo 36, tel. 06-481-7680, www.gullivershouse.com, stay@gullivershouse.com). They also offer five fun, funky double rooms at **Gulliver's Place**, in a large, secure building next to a university (D-€75, Db-€80, Tb-€100, air-con, elevator, east of the Termini train station at Viale Castro Pretorio 25, Metro: Castro Pretorio).

Sleeping Cheaply, Northeast of the Train Station

The cheapest beds in town are northeast of the Termini train station (Metro: Termini). Some travelers feel this area is weird and spooky after dark, but these hotels feel plenty safe. With your back to the train tracks, turn right and walk two blocks out of the station.

$ The Beehive gives vagabonds—old and young—a cheap, clean, and comfy home in Rome, thoughtfully and creatively run by a friendly young American couple, Steve and Linda. They offer seven great-value, artsy-mod double rooms (D-€70, this price promised through 2006 with this book) and an 8-bed dorm (€20 bunks; cash only, free Internet, private garden terrace, cheery café, 2 blocks north of Termini train station at Via Marghera 8, tel. 06-447-04553, www.the-beehive.com, info@the-beehive.com). Steve and Linda also run a B&B booking service (private rooms in the old center of Rome, Florence, and Venice; rates start at €30 per person, check out your options at www.cross-pollinate.com).

$ Albergo Sileo, with shiny chandeliers, has a contract to house train conductors who work the night shift—so its 10 simple, pleasant rooms are rented from 19:00 to 9:00 only. If you can handle this, it's a wonderful value. During the day, they store your luggage, and though you won't have access to a room, you're welcome to shower or hang out in the lobby or bar (D-€50, Db-€60, Tb-€65, Db for 24 hours-€62 when available, elevator, Via Magenta 39, 4th floor, tel. & fax 06-445-0246, www.hotelsileo .com, info@hotelsileo.com; friendly Alessandro and Maria Savioli don't speak English, but their daughter Anna does).

$ **Fawlty Towers Hostel** is well-run and ideal for backpackers arriving by train. It offers 50 beds and lots of fun, games, and extras (4-bed coed dorms-€22 per person, S-€47, D-€65, Db-€80, Q-€90, includes sheets, from station walk a block down Via Marghera and turn right to Via Magenta 39, tel. & fax 06-445-0374, www.fawltytowers.org, info@fawltytowers.org). Their nearby annex, Bubbles, offers similar beds and rates and shares the same reception desk.

Near the Colosseum

$$ **Hotel Paba** has six rooms, chocolate-box-tidy and lovingly cared for by Alberta Castelli. Though it overlooks busy Via Cavour just two blocks from the Colosseum, it's quiet enough (Db-€135, extra bed-€35, 5 percent discount for cash, huge beds, breakfast served in room, air-con, elevator, Via Cavour 266, Metro: Cavour, tel. 06-4782-4902, fax 06-4788-1225, www.hotelpaba.com, info @hotelpaba.com).

$$ **Hotel Lancelot**, a favorite among United Nations workers, is a homey refuge. It's quiet, safe, and big (60 rooms), with a shady courtyard, bar, and restaurant. Well-run by Faris and Lubna Khan, it's popular with returning guests (Sb-€105, Db-€165, Tb-€190, Qb-€220, €15 extra for balcony, air-con, elevator, parking-€11/day, behind Colosseum near San Clemente Church at Via Capo d'Africa 47, tel. 06-7045-0615, fax 06-7045-0640, www.lancelothotel.com, info@lancelothotel.com, Lubna speaks the Queen's English).

Near Campo de' Fiori

You'll pay a premium (and endure a little extra night noise) to stay in the old center. But each of these places is romantically set deep in the tangled back streets near the idyllic Campo de' Fiori and, for many, worth the extra money.

$$ **Casa di Santa Brigida** overlooks the elegant Piazza Farnese. With soft-spoken sisters gliding down polished hallways, and pearly gates instead of doors, this lavish 23-room convent makes exhaust-stained Roman tourists feel like they've died and gone to heaven. If you don't need a double bed, this is worth the splurge (Sb-€100, twin Db-€170, 3 percent extra if you pay with credit card, air-con, tasty €20 dinners, roof garden, plush library, Monserrato 54,

Hotels in the Heart of Rome

① Casa di Santa Brigida
② Hotel Smeraldo
③ Hotel in Parione
④ Hotel Nazionale
⑤ Albergo Santa Chiara
⑥ Hotel Due Torri
⑦ Hotel Giardino

tel. 06-6889-2596, fax 06-6889-1573, brigida@mclink.it, many of the sisters are from India and speak English). If you get no response to your fax or e-mail within three days, consider that a "no."

$$ Hotel Smeraldo, with 50 rooms, is well run, clean, and a great deal (Sb-€95, Db-€125, Tb-€145, prices promised through 2006 with this book, 20 percent less off-season, buffet breakfast-€7 extra, centrally controlled air-con, elevator, flowery roof terrace, Vicolo dei Chiodaroli 9, midway between Campo de' Fiori and Largo Argentina, tel. 06-687-5929, fax 06-6880-5495, www.smeraldoroma.com, albergosmeraldoroma@tin.it, Massimo).

$$ Hotel in Parione, also run by Hotel Smeraldo, crams 16 modern, high-ceilinged rooms into a tiny, adjacent building. It offers similar amenities and a fabulous location (Sb-€90, Db-€115, prices promised through 2006 with this book, €25 less off-season, breakfast-€7 extra, air-con, elevator, roof terrace, Via dei Chiavari 32, tel. 06-6880-2560, fax 06-683-4094, www.inparione.com, info@inparione.com).

In the Jewish Ghetto

To locate this hotel, see map on page 88.

$$ Hotel Arenula, with 50 decent rooms, is the only hotel in Rome's old Jewish ghetto. While it has the ambience of a gym and attracts lots of students, it's a fine value in the thick of old Rome (Sb-€92, Db-€125, Tb-€146, claim a 5 percent discount with this book in 2006, 20 percent less in July–Aug and winter, air-con, just off Via Arenula at Via Santa Maria de' Calderari 47, tel. 06-687-9454, fax 06-689-6188, www.hotelarenula.com, hotel .arenula@flashnet.it, Rosanna).

Near the Pantheon

These places are buried in the pedestrian-friendly heart of ancient Rome, each within a four-minute walk of the Pantheon. You'll pay more here—but you'll save time and money by being exactly where you want to be for your early and late wandering.

$$$ Hotel Nazionale, a four-star landmark, is a 16th-century palace that shares a well-policed square with the Parliament building. Its 92 rooms are served by lush public spaces, fancy bars, and a uniformed staff. It's a big, stuffy hotel with a revolving front door, but it's a worthy splurge if you want security, comfort, and ancient Rome at your doorstep (Sb-€210, Db-€325, giant deluxe Db-€450, 10 percent discount with this book in 2006, extra person-€65; less in Aug, winter, and when slow—check online for summer and weekend discounts; air-con, elevator, Piazza Montecitorio 131, tel. 06-695-001, fax 06-678-6677, www.nazionaleroma.it, hotel@nazionaleroma.it).

$$$ Albergo Santa Chiara is big, solid, and hotelesque, offering marbled elegance and all the hotel services in the old center. Its ample public lounges are dressy and professional, and its 100 rooms are quiet and spacious (Sb-€145, Db-€217, Tb-€250, ask for Rick Steves discount, check Web site for deals, elevator, behind Pantheon at Via di Santa Chiara 21, tel. 06-687-2979, fax 06-687-3144, www .albergosantachiara.com, info@albergosantachiara.com).

$$$ Hotel Due Torri, hiding out on a tiny, quiet street, is a little overpriced but beautifully located. It feels professional yet homey, with an accommodating staff, generous public spaces, and 26 comfortable-if-tight rooms (Sb-€118, Db-€190, family apartment-€250 for 3 and €275 for 4, air-con, Vicolo del Leonetto 23, a block off Via della Scrofa, tel. 06-6880-6956, fax 06-686-5442, www.hotelduetorriroma.com, hotelduetorri@interfree.it).

Near Piazza Venezia

$$ Hotel Giardino, thoughtfully run by Englishwoman Kate, offers 11 pleasant rooms in a central location three blocks northeast of Piazza Venezia (March–June and Sept–mid-Nov: Sb-€85, Db-€125; July–Aug and mid-Nov–Feb: Sb-€60, Db-€90; these prices promised through 2006 with this book and cash, check Web site for specials, air-con, double-paned windows, on a busy street off Piazza di Quirinale, Via XXIV Maggio 51, tel. 06-679-4584, fax 06-679-5155, www.hotel-giardino-roma.com, hotel_giardino@libero.it, Sergio also speaks English).

$ Istituto "Il Rosario" is a peaceful, well-run Dominican convent renting 40 rooms to both pilgrims and tourists in a good neighborhood (S-€38, Sb-€46, D-€72, Db-€80, Tb-€108, 23:00 curfew, roof terrace, midway between the Quirinale and Colosseum near bottom of Via Nazionale at Via Sant'Agata dei Goti 10, bus #40 or #64 from Termini, tel. 06-679-2346, fax 06-6994-1106, irodopre@tin.it).

Trastevere

Colorful and genuine in a gritty sort of way, Trastevere is a treat for travelers looking for a less touristy and more bohemian atmosphere. Choices are few here, but by trekking across the Tiber, you can have the experience of being comfortably immersed in old Rome. To locate the following two places, see the map on page 79.

$$ Hotel Santa Maria sits like a lazy hacienda in the midst of Trastevere. Surrounded by a medieval skyline, you'll feel as if you're on some romantic stage set. Its 19 small but well-equipped, air-conditioned rooms—former cells in a cloister—are all on the ground floor, circling a gravelly courtyard of orange trees and stay-awhile patio furniture (Db-€165, Tb-€210, Qb-€250; you must pay cash and stay at least 3 nights to get these 20–25 percent discounted rates, which are promised through 2006 with this book; you'll pay more for shorter stays and credit-card payment, smaller discounts off-season, suites available for 2–6 people, free loaner bikes and Internet access for guests, face church on Piazza Maria Trastevere and go right half a block to Vicolo del Piede 2, tel. 06-589-4626, fax 06-589-4815, www.htlsantamaria.com, hotelsantamaria@libero.it, Stefano).

$ Casa San Giuseppe is down a quiet, characteristic, laundry-strewn lane. While convent-run, it's a secular place renting 25 plain but peaceful, spacious, and spotless rooms (Sb-€75, Db-€105, Tb-€140, Qb-€160, air-con, elevator, just north of Piazza Trilussa, Vicolo Moroni 22, tel. 06-5833-3490, fax 06-5833-5754, casasangiuseppe@virgilio.it).

Near the Vatican Museum

Sleeping near the Vatican is expensive, but some enjoy calling this neighborhood home. Even though it's handy to the Vatican (when the rapture hits, you're right there), everything else is a long way away.

$$$ Hotel Sant'Anna is pricey, but located on a charming pedestrian street that fills up with restaurant tables at dinnertime. Its 20 comfy rooms, decorated with classical themes, are somewhere between tasteful and too much (Sb-€160, Db-€220; Db discounted to €150 in July–Aug, winter, and slow times; any time of year, ask for a Rick Steves discount; air-con, elevator, courtyard, Borgo Pio 133, near intersection with Mascherino, a couple blocks from entrance to St. Peter's, tel. 06-6880-1602, fax 06-6830-8717, www.hotelsantanna .com, santanna@travel.it, Viscardo).

$$$ Hotel Bramante sits like a grand medieval lodge in the shadow of the fortified escape wall that runs from the Vatican to Castel Sant'Angelo. The public spaces and 16 thoughtfully appointed rooms are generously sized, with rough wood beams and high ceilings (Sb-€140, Db-€195, Tb-€220, Qb-€230, these prices promised through 2006 with this book, air-con, no elevator, Vicolo delle Palline 24, tel. 06-6880-6426, fax 06-681-33339, www.hotelbramante.com, hotelbramante@libero.it, Maurizio and Loredana).

$$$ Hotel Alimandi Vaticano, facing the Vatican Museum, is beautifully designed. A new hotel run by the Alimandi family (see next listing), it features four stars, 24 spacious rooms, and all the modern comforts you can imagine (standard Db-€185, big Db with 2 double beds-€200, Tb-€210, Qb-€220, 5 percent discount with cash, air-con, elevator, Viale Vaticano 99, Metro: Cipro-Musei Vaticani, tel. 06-397-45562, fax 06-397-30132, www.alimandi.com, hotelali@hotelalimandie.191.it).

$$ Hotel Alimandi is a good value, run by the friendly and entrepreneurial Alimandi brothers—Paolo, Enrico, and Luigi—and the next generation, Marta, Irene, Barbara, and Germano. Their 35 rooms are air-conditioned, modern, and marbled in white (Sb-€90, Db-€160, Tb-€180, 5 percent discount for cash, closed Jan–mid-Feb, elevator, grand buffet breakfast served in great roof garden, small gym, pool table, piano lounge, down the stairs directly in front of Vatican Museum, Via Tunisi 8, Metro: Cipro–Musei Vaticani, reserve by phone, tel. 06-3972-6300, toll-free in Italy tel. 800-122-121, fax 06-3972-3943, www.alimandi .com, alimandi@tin.it). They offer free airport pick-up and drop-off for guests staying at either of their hotels, though you must reserve when you book your room and wait for a scheduled shuttle (every 2 hrs, see their Web site or lobby schedule).

Hotels and Restaurants in the Vatican Area

B – Bus Stop **M** – Subway Stop **T** – Taxi Stand

❶ Hotel Sant'Anna	❼ To Casa per Ferie Rooms
❷ Hotel Bramante	❽ Hostaria dei Bastioni Rest.
❸ Hotel Alimandi	❾ La Rustichella & Gelateria Millennium
❹ Hotel Alimandi Vaticano	❿ To Tre Pupazzi Rest.
❺ Hotel Spring House	⓫ Perilli in Prati Rest.
❻ To Hotel Gerber	

$$ Hotel Spring House, part of the Best Western chain, has a hotelesque feel and 51 attractive rooms—some with balconies or terraces (standard Db-€160, superior Db-€190, Tb-€195, Qb-€210, 15 percent discount July–Aug and Jan–Feb through 2006 with this book, air-con, elevator, free loaner bikes, Via Mocenigo 7, 2 blocks from Vatican Museum, Metro: Cipro–Musei Vaticani, tel. 06-3972-0948, fax 06-3972-1047, www.hotelspringhouse.com, info@hotelspringhouse.com, Stefania).

$$ Hotel Gerber, set in a quiet residential area, is modern and air-conditioned, with 27 well-polished, businesslike rooms (two S without air-con-€60, Sb-€105, Db-€140, Tb-€160, Qb-€180; discounts with this book through 2006: 10 percent discount beyond their best price in high season, 15 percent in low season; Via degli Scipioni 241, at intersection with Ezio, a block from Metro: Lepanto, tel. 06-321-6485, fax 06-321-7048, www.hotelgerber .it, info@hotelgerber.it, Peter and Simonetta speak English, but friendly dog Kira doesn't).

$ Casa per Ferie Santa Maria alle Fornaci dei Padri Trinitari houses pilgrims and secular tourists with simple class just a short walk south of the Vatican in 54 stark, identical, utilitarian, mostly twin-bedded rooms. This is the most user-friendly convent-type place I found (Sb-€65, Db-€85, Tb-€120, groups welcome, air-con, elevator; bus #64 from train station to St. Peter's Station, then walk 100 yards to Piazza S. Maria alle Fornaci 27; tel. 06-393-67632, fax 06-393-66795, www.trinitaridematha.it, cffornaci@tin.it).

EATING

The Italians are masters of the art of fine living. That means eating...long and well. Lengthy, multicourse lunches and dinners and endless hours sitting in outdoor cafés are the norm. Americans eat on their way to an evening event and complain if the check is slow in coming. For Italians, the meal is an end in itself, and only rude waiters rush you. When you want the bill, mime-scribble on your raised palm or ask for it: *"Il conto?"*

Even those of us who liked dorm food will find that the local cafés, cuisine, and wines become a highlight of our Italian adventure. Trust me, this is sightseeing for your palate, and even if the rest of you is sleeping in cheap hotels, your taste buds will relish an occasional first-class splurge. You can eat well without going broke. But be careful: You're just as likely to blow a small fortune on a disappointing meal as you are to dine wonderfully for €20.

Restaurants

When restaurant-hunting, choose places filled with locals, not the place with the big neon signs boasting, "We speak English and accept credit cards." Restaurants parked on famous squares generally serve bad food at high prices to tourists. Locals eat better at lower-rent locales. Family-run places operate without hired help and can offer cheaper meals.

The word *osteria* (normally a simple, local-style restaurant) stokes my appetite. For unexciting but basic values, look for a *menù turistico*, a three- or four-course, set-price menu. Galloping gourmets order à la carte with the help of a menu translator. (The *Marling Italian Menu Master* is excellent. *Rick Steves' Italian Phrase Book & Dictionary* has enough phrases for intermediate eaters.)

A full meal consists of an appetizer (*antipasto*, €3–6), a first course (*primo piatto*, pasta or soup, €4–8), and a second course

Tipping

Tipping is an issue only at restaurants that have waiters and waitresses. If you order your food at a counter, don't tip. (Many Italians don't ever tip.)

If the menu states that service is included *(servizio incluso)*, there's no need to tip beyond that, but if you like to tip and you're pleased with the service, throw in €1 to €2 per person.

If service is not included, you could tip 5 to 10 percent by rounding up or leaving the change from your bill. Leave the tip on the table, or hand it to your server. It's best to tip in cash, even if you pay with your credit card; otherwise, the tip may never reach your server.

(secondo piatto, expensive meat and fish dishes, €6–12). Vegetables *(contorni, verdure)* may come with the *secondo* or cost extra (€3–4) as a side dish. The euros can add up in a hurry. Light and budget eaters get a *primo piatto* each and share an *antipasto*. Another good option is sharing an array of *antipasti*—either several specific dishes or a big plate of mixed delights assembled from a buffet. Italians admit that the *secondo* is the least-interesting aspect of the local cuisine.

Restaurants normally pad the bill with a cover charge *(pane e coperto*—"bread and cover charge," about €1) and a service charge *(servizio*, 15 percent, see "Tipping," above); these charges are listed on the menu.

Wine Bars

An *enoteca* (wine bar) is a popular, fast, and inexpensive option for lunch. Surrounded by the local office crowd, you can get a fancy salad, plate of meats and cheeses, and a glass of good wine (see blackboards for the day's selection and price per glass). The area around the Parliament (popular with that crowd) has plenty of *enoteche* handy for your sightseeing lunch break (see page 268).

Bars/Cafés

Italian "bars" are not taverns but cafés. These local hangouts serve coffee, mini-pizzas, sandwiches, and drinks from the cooler. Many dish up plates of fried cheese and vegetables from under the glass counter, ready to reheat. This budget choice is the Italian equivalent of English pub grub.

For quick meals, bars usually have trays of cheap, ready-made sandwiches *(panini* or *tramezzini)* —some kinds are delightful grilled. To save time for sightseeing and room for dinner, consider a ham-and-cheese *panino* at a bar (called *toast*, have it grilled twice if you want it really hot) for lunch. To get food "to go," say, *"Da portar via"* (for the road). All bars have a WC *(toilette, bagno)* in the back, and customers (and the discreet public) can use it.

Coffee: Coffee is as important as wine in Rome, and Italian coffee is some of the world's best. If you ask for *"un caffè,"* you'll get espresso. Cappuccino is served to locals before noon and to tourists any time of day. (To an Italian, cappuccino is a breakfast drink and a travesty after eating anything with tomatoes.) Italians like it only warm. To get it hot, request *"Molto caldo"* (very hot) or *"Più caldo, per favore"* (hotter, please; pew KAHL-doh, pehr fah-VOH-ray).

Romans like iced coffee in the summer. It's slightly diluted, sugared espresso, called *caffè freddo*; to get it with ice, say *con ghiaccio* (kohn ghee-AH-choh, with a hard g). *Cappuccino freddo* is cold cappuccino served in a tall glass.

Experiment with a few of the hot options:

- *cappuccino:* espresso with foamed milk on top
- *caffè latte:* tall glass with espresso and hot milk mixed
- *caffè hag:* instant decaf (you can order decaffeinated versions of any coffee drink—ask for it *decaffeinato*)
- *macchiato* (mah-kee-AH-toh): espresso with only a little milk
- *caffè americano:* espresso diluted with water
- *caffè corretto:* espresso with a shot of liqueur

Juice: *Spremuta* means freshly squeezed as far as *succa* (fruit juice) is concerned. (Note: *spumante* means champagne.)

Beer: Beer on tap is *alla spina*. Get it *piccola* (33 cl, 11 oz), *media* (50 cl, 17 oz), or *grande* (a liter, 34 oz).

Wine: To order a glass (*bicchiere*; bee-kee-AY-ree) of red *(rosso)* or white *(bianco)* wine, say, *"Un bicchiere di vino rosso/bianco."* *Corposo* means full-bodied. House wine *(vino della casa)* often comes in a quarter-liter carafe *(un quarto)*. For more on wine, see below.

Other Drinks: A common *digestivo* in Rome is an *amaro*, which means bitter. These alcoholic brews are often homemade by restaurants from a secret combination of herbs to aid digestion. Popular commercial brands are *Fernet Branca* and *Montenegro*. If your tastes run sweeter, try an anise-flavored liqueur called *Sambuca*, served *alla moscha* (with three "flies"—coffee beans).

Prices: You'll notice a two-tiered price system. Drinking a cup of coffee while standing at the bar is cheaper than drinking it at a table. If you're on a budget, don't sit without first checking out the financial consequences. Ask, "Same price if I sit or stand?" by saying, *"Costa uguale al tavolo o al banco?"* (KOH-stah oo-GWAH-lay ahl TAH-voh-loh oh ahl BAHN-koh).

If the bar isn't busy, you'll often just order and then pay when you leave. Otherwise: 1) Decide what you want; 2) find out the price by checking the price list on the wall, the prices posted near the food, or by asking the barman; 3) pay the cashier; and 4) give the receipt to the barman (whose clean fingers handle no dirty euros) and tell him what you want.

Delis, Cafeterias, Pizza Shops, and *Tavola Calda* (Hot Table) Bars

Rome offers many cheap alternatives to restaurants. Stop by a *rosticceria* for great cooked deli food; a self-service cafeteria (called "free flow" in Italian) that feeds you without the add-ons; a *tavola calda* bar for an assortment of veggies; or a Pizza Rustica shop for stand-up or take-out pizza by the slice.

Pizza is cheap and everywhere. Key pizza vocabulary: *capricciosa* (generally ham, mushrooms, olives, and artichokes), *funghi* (mushrooms), *marinara* (tomato sauce, oregano, garlic, no cheese), *quattro formaggi* (4 different cheeses), and *quattro stagioni* (different toppings on each of the 4 quarters, for those who can't choose just 1 menu item). If you ask for *peperoni* on your pizza, you'll get

Ordering Food at *Tavola Caldas*

plate of mixed veggies	*piatto misto di verdure*	pee-AH-toh MEES-toh dee vehr-DOO-ray
"Heated, please."	*"Scaldare, per favore."*	skahl-DAH-ray, pehr fah-VOH-ray
"A taste, please."	*"Un assaggio, per favore."*	oon ah-SAH-joh, pehr fah-VOH-ray
artichoke	*carciofi*	kar-CHOH-fee
asparagus	*asparagi*	ah-spah-RAH-jee
beans	*fagioli*	fah-JOH-lee
green beans	*fagiolini*	fah-joh-LEE-nee
broccoli	*broccoli*	BROK-oh-lee
cantaloupe	*melone*	May-LOH-nay
carrots	*carote*	kah-ROT-ay
ham	*prosciutto*	proh-SHOO-toh
mushrooms	*funghi*	FOONG-ghee
potatoes	*patate*	pah-TAH-tay
rice	*riso*	REE-zoh
spinach	*spinaci*	speen-AH-chee
tomatoes	*pomodori*	poh-moh-DOH-ree
zucchini	*zucchine*	zoo-KEE-nay
breadsticks	*grissini*	gree-SEE-nee

(Excerpted from *Rick Steves' Italian Phrase Book & Dictionary*)

green or red peppers, not sausage. Kids like the bland *margherita* (cheese with tomato sauce) or *diavola* (the closest thing in Italy to American pepperoni). At Pizza Rustica take-out shops, slices are sold by weight (100 grams, or *un etto*, is a hot and cheap snack; 200 grams, or *due etti*, makes a light meal).

For a fast, cheap, and healthy lunch, find a *tavola calda* bar with a buffet spread of meat and vegetables, and ask for a mixed plate of vegetables with a hunk of mozzarella *(piatto misto di verdure con mozzarella)*. Don't be limited by what you can see. If you'd like a salad with a slice of cantaloupe and a hunk of cheese, they'll whip that up for you in a snap. Belly up to the bar and, with a pointing finger and key words in the chart in this chapter, you can get a fine mixed plate of vegetables. If something's a mystery, ask for a small taste (*un assaggio*; oon ah-SAH-joh).

Many places sell roasted pork sandwiches with rustic bread (look for *porchetta*, por-KET-ah).

Beware of cheap eateries sporting big color photos of pizza and piles of different pastas. They have no kitchens and simply microwave disgusting prepackaged food. Unless you like lasagna with ice in the center, avoid these.

Picnics

In Rome, picnicking saves lots of euros and is a great way to sample local specialties. For a colorful experience, gather your ingredients in the morning at one of Rome's open-air produce markets (see page 281); you'll probably visit several small stores or market stalls to put together a complete meal. A local *alimentari* is your one-stop corner grocery store. A *supermercato* gives you more efficiency with less color for less cost. You'll find handy late-night supermarkets near the Pantheon (Via Giustiniani), Spanish Steps (Via della Vittoria), Trevi Fountain (Via del Bufalo), and Campo de' Fiori (Via di Monte della Farina). Many *alimentari* and even supermarkets will gladly make you a fresh sandwich, charging you only for the weight of what you take and the piece of bread.

Juice-lovers can get a liter (34 ounces) of O.J. for the price of a Coke or coffee. Look for "100% *succo*" (juice) on the label. Hang onto the half-liter mineral-water bottles (sold everywhere for about €1). Buy juice in cheap liter boxes, then drink some and store the extra in your water bottle. Tap water—*acqua del rubinetto*—is fine; I drink water from the public taps found all over the city.

Picnics can be an adventure in high cuisine. Be daring. Try the fresh mozzarella, *presto* pesto, shriveled olives, and any UFOs the locals are excited about. Shopkeepers are happy to sell small quantities of produce. It is customary to let the merchant choose the produce for you. Say *"Per oggi"* (pehr OH-jee), or "For today," and he'll grab you something ready to eat, weigh it, and make the sale. A typical picnic for two might be fresh rolls, 100 grams of cheese, 100 grams of meat (*un etto* = 100 grams = about a quarter pound), two tomatoes, three carrots, two apples, yogurt, and a liter box of juice. Total cost—about €10.

ROMAN CUISINE

In ancient times, the dinner party was the center of Roman social life. It was a luxurious affair, set in the *triclinium* (formal dining room). Guest lists were small (3–9 people), and the select few reclined on couches during the exotic multicourse meal. Today the couches are gone, and the fare may not include jellyfish, boiled tree fungi, and flamingo, but the *cucina Romana* influence remains.

Roman meals are still lengthy social occasions. Simple, fresh, seasonal ingredients dominate the dishes. The *cucina* is robust, strongly flavored, and unpretentious—much like the people who created it over the centuries. It is said that Roman cooking didn't come out of emperors' or popes' kitchens, but from the *cucina povera*—the home cooking of the common people. This may explain the fondness Romans have for meats known as the *quinto quarto* (fifth quarter), such as tripe, tail, brain, and pigs' feet, as well as their interest in natural preservatives like chili peppers and garlic. Rome belongs to the warm, southern region of Lazio, which produces a rich variety of flavorful vegetables and fruit that are the envy of American supermarkets. Rome's proximity to the Mediterranean also allows for a great variety of seafood (especially on Fridays) that can be pricey if you're dining out. Beware: On menus, seafood and steak are often priced by the *etto* (100 gram unit, about a quarter pound), rather than by the portion.

Today, eating like a Roman means stopping at the local bar each morning for a pastry and coffee (usually cappuccino or espresso). Lunch (between 13:00 and 15:00) is traditionally the largest meal of the day, eaten at home, although work habits have changed this for many people who don't want to spend time commuting. Instead, they grab a quick meal in a *tavola calda* (cafeteria) buffet, or a *panino* or *tramezzino* (sandwich). Dinnertime is generally 20:00 to 22:00, and in restaurants it is a multicourse affair.

When it's hot outside, a *granita* at a *grattachecce* (grah-tah-KAY-chay) cools you down fast. These little booths scrape shavings off ice blocks and then flavor them with syrups. Try the combo-flavors such as *limoncocco*—lemon and coconut syrups with fresh chunks of coconut.

Local specialties you may find on a menu include:

Antipasti (Appetizers)

Antipasto misto: A plate of marinated or grilled vegetables (eggplant, artichokes, peppers, mushrooms), cured meats, or seafood (anchovies, octopus).

Bruschetta: Toast brushed with olive oil and garlic or chopped tomatoes.

Prosciutto e melone: Thin slices of ham wrapped around pieces of cantaloupe.

Primi Piatti (First Courses)

Spaghetti alla carbonara: Any type of pasta with a sauce made from beaten eggs, fried *pancetta* (bacon) or *guanciale* (cured pork cheek), cheese (*pecorino romano* or *parmigiano reggiano*), and black pepper.

Bucatini all'amatriciana: Thin pasta tubes with a sauce of tomatoes, onion, pork, and pecorino cheese on top.

Gnocchi alla romana: Small dumpling-like disks made from semolina, instead of potato, and baked with butter and cheese.

Penne all'arrabbiata: Literally, "angry quills"—quill-shaped pasta topped with a spicy tomato sauce of chili peppers *(peperoncini),* garlic, and bacon or pork.

Rigatoni con la pajata: Medium-size wide pasta tubes topped with a stew of milk-fed calf intestines.

Sracciatella alla romana: Meat broth with eggs, semolina, and parmesan cheese.

Spaghetti alle vongole veraci: Small clams in the shell sautéed with white wine and herbs, served over pasta.

Secondi Piatti (Second Courses)

Saltimbocca alla romana: Literally "jump-in-the-mouth"—thinly sliced veal layered with prosciutto and sage, then lightly fried.

Abbacchio alla scottadito: Baby lamb chops grilled and eaten as finger food.

Trippa alla romana: Tripe braised with onions, carrots, and mint.

Coda alla vaccinara: Oxtail braised with garlic, wine, tomato, and celery.

Involtini al sugo: Veal cutlets rolled with prosciutto, celery, and cheese in a tomato sauce.

Anguillette in umido: Stewed baby eels from nearby Lake Bracciano.

Filetti di baccalà: Dried cod fried in a batter.

Contorni (Side Dishes)

Sometimes the second course is not served with a vegetable, and you may want to order a side dish separately. If you get a salad, note

---

Eating with the Seasons

Italian cooks love to serve you fresh produce and seafood at its tastiest. If you must have porcini mushrooms outside of October and November, they'll be frozen. To get the freshest veggies at a fine restaurant, request *"Un piatto di vedure della stagioni, per favore"* ("A plate of veggies in season, please").
Here are a few examples of what's fresh when:

April–May:	Calamari, squid, green beans, asparagus, artichokes, and zucchini flowers
April–May and Sept–Oct:	Black truffles
May–June:	Mussels, asparagus, zucchini, cantaloupe, and strawberries
May–Aug:	Eggplant
Oct–Nov:	Mushrooms and white truffles
Fresh year-round:	Clams, meats, and cheese

---

that olive oil and wine vinegar are the only dressings.

Carciofi alla giudia: Small artichokes flattened and fried.

Fiori di zucca fritti: Squash blossoms battered and fried.

Fave al guanciale: Fava beans simmered with *guanciale* (cured pork cheek) and onion.

Misticanza: Mixed green salad of arugula *(rucola)* and curly endive *(puntarelle)* with anchovies.

Dolci (Desserts)

Dessert can be a seasonal fruit such as *fragole* (strawberries) or *pesche* (peaches), or even cheese, such as *pecorino romano* (made from ewe's milk) or *caciotta romana* (made from a combination of ewe's and cow's milk).

Crostata di ricotta: A cheesecake-like dessert with ricotta, Marsala wine, cinnamon, and bits of chocolate.

Bignè: Profiterole-like pastries filled with *zabaglione* (egg yolks, sugar, and Marsala wine).

Tartufo: Rich dark-chocolate gelato. *Con panna* gets you whipped cream on top.

Gelato: Rather than order dessert in a restaurant, I like to stroll with a cup or cone of gelato picked up at one of Rome's popular *gelaterias*.

Vini (Wine)

No large meal in Italy is complete without wine. Although Lazio is not the most notable wine region in Italy, it produces several pleasant white wines and a few reds.

Frascati, probably the best-known wine of the region, is an inexpensive dry white made from Trebbiano and Malvasia grapes. **Castelli Romani**, from the hills just south of Rome, is also from the Trebbiano grape and is similar to **Marino**, **Colli Albani**, and **Velletri**, all light and fairly dry. **Torre Ercolana** is known as Lazio's finest red. This dense wine is made from the local Cesanese grape, as well as Cabernet and Merlot. Produced in small quantities, it must be aged for at least five years.

RESTAURANTS

Although I've listed a number of restaurants, I recommend that you just head for a scenic area and explore. Piazza Navona, the Pantheon area, Campo de' Fiori, and Trastevere are neighborhoods packed with characteristic eateries. Sitting with tourists on a famous square, enjoying the scene works fine. (As my Roman friend explained: "When you're in a bad restaurant, the best way to survive is bread, olive oil, and salt.") But for more of a local flavor, consider my recommendations. In general, I'm impressed by how small the price difference is from a mediocre restaurant to a fine one. You can pay about 20 percent more for double the quality.

Trastevere

Colorful Trastevere is now pretty touristy. Still, Romans join the tourists to eat on the rustic side of the Tiber River. Start at the central square (Piazza Santa Maria). Then choose: Eat with tourists enjoying the ambience of the famous square, or wander the back streets in search of a mom-and-pop place with barely a menu. My recommendations are within a few minutes' walk of each other (between Piazza Santa Maria Trastevere and Ponte Sisto; see map on page 79).

Trattoria de "Gli Amici" serves good food on a super square (reservations smart—popular with dressy locals) or fine interior for a fair price while employing locals with disabilities. At this "Inn of the Friends," waiters do their work with a unique passion. Each has mental problems and is paired with a volunteer aide from the Community of Sant'Egidio. Pictures on the walls show what can be accomplished by mentally disabled people who are successfully integrated into the community like this (€7 pastas, €9 *secondi*, Mon–Sat from 19:30, closed Sun, 2 blocks off main square at Piazza Sant'Egidio 6, tel. 06-580-6033).

Trattoria da Lucia lets you enjoy simple, traditional food at a good price in a great scene. It offers the quintessential, rustic, 100 percent Roman Trastevere dining experience and has been family-run since World War II. You'll meet Renato, his uncle Ennio, and Ennio's mom—pictured on the menu in the 1950s (cheap, Tue–Sun

12:30–15:30 & 19:30–24:00, closed Mon, homey indoor or evocative outdoor seating, Vicolo del Mattonato 2, tel. 06-580-3601, no English spoken).

Osteria Ponte Sisto, a rough-and-tumble little place, specializes in traditional Roman cuisine with a menu that changes often. Just outside the tourist zone, it caters mostly to Romans and offers a fine value (but be careful when ordering the unpriced fish dishes). It's also easy to find: Crossing Ponte Sisto (pedestrian bridge) toward Trastevere, continue across the little square (Piazza Trilussa) and you'll see it on the right (daily 12:30–15:00 & 19:30–24:00, Via Ponte Sisto 80, tel. 06-588-3411).

Ristorante Checco er Carettiere is a big, classic, family-run place that's been a Trastevere fixture for three generations. While a bit pricey, you'll eat well among lots of fun commotion (€13 pastas, €16 *secondi*, open daily, Via Benedetta 10/13, tel. 06-580-0985).

Gelateria alla Scala is a terrific little ice cream place that dishes up delightful cinnamon *(cannella)* and oh-wow pistachio (daily 12:00–24:00, Piazza della Scala 51, across from the church on Piazza della Scala). Seek this place out.

On and near Campo de' Fiori

While it is touristy, Campo de' Fiori offers a sublimely romantic setting. And, since it's so close to the collective heart of Rome, it remains popular with locals. For greater atmosphere than food value, circle the square, considering each place. Bars and pizzerias seem to overwhelm the square. The **Taverna** and **Vineria** (#16 and #15) offer good perches from which to people-watch and nurse a glass of wine.

Ristorante la Carbonara has the ultimate Campo de' Fiori setting, with dressy waiters and superb on-the-square seating. While the service gets mixed reviews, the food and Italian ambience are wonderful (€10 pastas, €15 *secondi*, Wed–Mon, closed Tue, Campo de' Fiori 23, tel. 06-686-4783). Meals on small surrounding streets may be a better value, but they lack that Campo de' Fiori magic.

Ostaria da Giovanni ar Galletto is nearby, on the more elegant and peaceful Piazza Farnese. It has an upscale local crowd, pleasant outdoor seating, and reasonable prices. Say hi to Angelo, who's committed to serving fine food. Regrettably, service can be horrible and single diners aren't treated very well. Still, if you're in no hurry and ready to just savor my favorite *al fresco* setting in Rome, this is a good bet (Mon–Sat 12:15–15:00 & 19:30–23:00, closed Sun, tucked in corner of Piazza Farnese at #102, tel. 06-686-1714).

Osteria Enoteca al Bric is a mod bistro-type place run by a man who loves to cook and serve good wine. Wine-case lids decorate the wall like happy memories. With candlelit grace and no

Restaurants in the Heart of Rome

1. Rest. la Carbonara, Taverna & Vineria
2. Ostaria da Giovanni ar Galletto
3. Osteria Enoteca al Bric
4. Filetti de Baccala
5. Trattoria der Pallaro
6. Rist. Grotte del Teatro di Pompeo
   & Hostaria Costanza
7. Cul de Sac Bar, L'Insalata Ricca Rest.
   & Ristorante Terra di Siena
8. Ristorante Pizzeria Sacro e Profano
9. Gelateria San Crispino
10. L'Antica Birreria Peroni

tourists, it's perfect for the wine snob in the mood for pasta and fine cheese. Aficionados choose their bottle from the huge selection that lines the walls near the entrance. Beginners order fine wine by the glass with help from the waiter when they order their meal (open from 19:30, closed Mon June–Sept, reserve after 20:30, 100 yards off Campo de' Fiori at Via del Pellegrino 51, tel. 06-687-9533). Al Bric offers my readers a special "Taste of Italy for Two" deal (fine plate of mixed cheese and meat with two glasses of full-bodied red wine and a pitcher of water) for €22 from 19:30, but you may need to finish by 20:30. This could be a light meal if you're kicking off an evening stroll, a substantial appetizer, or a way to check this place out for a serious meal later.

Filetti de Baccala, a tradition for many Romans, is basically a fish bar with paper tablecloths and cheap prices. Its grease-stained, hurried waiters serve old-time favorites—fried cod fillets, a strange bitter *puntarelle* salad, and their antipasto (delightful anchovies with butter)—to nostalgic locals (no credit cards, Mon–Sat 17:30–23:00, closed Sun, a block east of Campo de' Fiori tumbling onto long tables in a tiny and atmospheric square, Largo dei Librari 88, tel. 06-686-4018). Study what others are eating and order by pointing. Nothing is expensive (see the menu on wall). Urchins can get a cod stick to go and sit on the barnacle church doorsteps just outside. Say *ciao* to Marcello who runs the place like a swim coach.

Trattoria der Pallaro, which has no menu, has a slogan: "Here, you'll eat what we want to feed you." Paola Fazi—with a towel wrapped around her head turban-style—and her family serve up a five-course meal of typically Roman food for €21, including wine, coffee, and a tasty mandarin juice. Make like Oliver Twist asking for more soup and get seconds on the juice (Tue–Sun 12:00–15:00 & 19:00–24:00, closed Mon, indoor/outdoor seating on quiet square, a block south of Corso Vittorio Emanuele, down Largo del Chiavari to Largo del Pallaro 15, tel. 06-6880-1488).

Ristorante Grotte del Teatro di Pompeo, sitting atop an ancient theater, serves good food at great prices, perfect if you want to dine on a characteristic cobbled street, busy with strolling people and musicians. It's well-established, albeit a bit tired, but always popular (closed Mon and Aug, Via del Biscione 73, tel. 06-6880-3686). Their pasta radicchio (made with red endive) is good.

Hostaria Costanza has crisp-vested waiters, a local following, and lots of energy. You'll eat traditional Roman cuisine on a ramshackle patio or inside under arches from the ancient Pompeo Theater (closed Sun, Piazza Paradiso 63, tel. 06-686-1717).

Piazza Pasquino

Between Campo de' Fiori and Piazza Navona, these three bustling places have low prices and a happy clientele. As they are neighbors and each is completely different, check out all three before choosing:

Cul de Sac is packed with enthusiastic locals cobbling together fun meals from an Italian dim sum-type menu of traditional dishes (often crowded, daily 12:00–16:00 & 18:00–24:00, a block southwest of Piazza Navona on Piazza Pasquino). **L'Insalata Ricca**, next door, is a popular chain that specializes in hearty and healthy €7 salads and much less healthy pizzas (daily 12:00–15:45 & 18:45–24:00, Piazza Pasquino 72, tel. 06-6830-7881). **Ristorante Terra di Siena** is more traditional, with a Tuscan passion for meat (closed Sun, Piazza Pasquino 77, tel. 06-6830-7704).

Dining near the Pantheon

Ristorante da Fortunato is an Italian classic, with fresh flowers on the tables, and white-coated, black-tie waiters politely serving good meat and fish to local politicians, foreign dignitaries, and tourists with good taste. Don't leave without perusing the photos of their famous visitors—everyone from former Iraqi Foreign Minister Tariq Aziz to Bill Clinton seems to have eaten here. The outdoor seating is fine for watching the river of Roman street life flow by. For a dressy night out, this is a reliable choice. When it comes to cuisine, Fortunato is a master of simple elegance (surprisingly reasonable, plan to spend €30, Mon–Sat 12:30–15:00 & 19:30–23:30, closed Sun, a block in front of the Pantheon at Via del Pantheon 55, tel. 06-679-2788).

Eating Cheap and Colorful near the Pantheon

Eating on the square facing the Pantheon is a temptation (there's even a McDonald's that offers some of the best outdoor seating in town), and I'd consider it just to relax and enjoy the Roman scene. But if you walk a block or two away, you'll get less view and better food. Here are some suggestions:

Ristorante Enoteca Corsi is a wine shop that grew into a thriving lunch-only restaurant. The Paiella family serves straightforward, traditional cuisine at great prices to an appreciative crowd of office workers. Check the blackboard for daily specials (gnocchi on Thursday, fish on Friday, and so on). Friendly Ilaria and Manuela welcome diners to step into their wine shop and pick out a bottle. For the cheap take-away price, plus a euro or two, they'll uncork it at your table. With €5 pastas, €8.50 main dishes, and fine wine at a third the price you'd pay in normal restaurants, this is a superb value (Mon–Sat 12:00–15:00, closed Sun, a block toward the Pantheon from the Gesù church at Via del Gesù 87, tel. 06-679-0821).

Miscellanea is run by much-loved Mikki, who's on a mission to keep foreign students well-fed. You'll find cheap pasta, hearty and fresh €3 sandwiches, and a long list of €6 salads. Mikki often

Restaurants near the Pantheon

TO PIAZZA DEL POPOLO →
TO Ⓜ BARB. →
VIA TRITONE
TO TREVI
SABRINA
MURATTE
STELL.
UFF.
VICARIO
PARL.
P. MONTE.
P. COL.
VACC.
COPPELLE
POZZO CORN.
AQUIRO
P. PIETRA
PASTINI
ORT.
GIUST.
SALV.
CRESC.
SEMINARIO
CARA.
S. EUST.
P. COLL. ROM.
S. APOST.
TIME ELEVATOR ROMA
GALLERIA DORA PAMPHILJ
SAN LUIGI →
SAN IGNAZIO
TO PIAZZA NAVONA
PANTHEON
S. MARIA SOPRA MINERVA
VIA VITTORIO
ARGEN.
CESTARI
GESÙ
EMANUELE
ARACOELI
DCH
LARGO ARGENTINA RUINS →
FLOR.
BOTT. OSC.
TO CAPITOL HILL

100 YARDS
100 METERS

Ⓣ - TAXI STAND
Ⓜ - SUBWAY STOP
Ⓑ - BUS STOP

❶ Ristorante da Fortunato
❷ Ristorante Enoteca Corsi
❸ Miscellanea Restaurant
❹ Osteria da Mario & Restaurant Coco
❺ Taverna le Coppelle
❻ Cafeteria Brek
❼ Antica Salumeria
❽ Crèmeria Monteforte
❾ Gelateria Giolitti
❿ Gelateria della Palma

tosses in a fun little extra, including—if you have this book on the table—a free glass of Mikki's "sexy wine" (homemade from *fragolina*—strawberries). This place is popular with American students on foreign study programs (daily 11:00–24:00, indoor/outdoor seating, a block toward Via del Corso from the Pantheon at Via delle Paste 110).

Osteria da Mario, a homey little mom-and-pop joint with a no-stress menu, serves traditional favorites in a fun, homey little dining room or on tables spilling out onto a picturesque old

Roman square (Mon–Sat 13:00–15:30 & 19:00–23:00, closed Sun, from the Pantheon walk 2 blocks up Via Pantheon, go left on Via delle Coppelle, take first right to Piazza delle Coppelle 51, tel. 06-6880-6349).

Restaurant Coco is a perfect place for a quick and atmospheric lunch with friendly service. They put out a wonderful €10 lunch buffet on weekdays. After grazing through the great selection of tempting dishes, you'll sit on the square among a produce market, watching local politicians stroll in and out of their dining hall across the way (classy indoor and rustic outdoor seating; €10 gets you a big main plate, bread, dessert, water and coffee; Mon–Fri 12:30–15:30, Piazza delle Coppelle 54, tel. 06-6813-6545).

Taverna le Coppelle is good—especially for pizza—with a checkered-tablecloth ambience (daily, Via delle Coppelle 39, tel. 06-6880-6557).

Cafeteria Brek, on Largo Argentina just south of the Pantheon, is an appealing self-service restaurant with a modern, efficient atmosphere and cheap prices (daily 12:00–15:30 & 19:00–22:15, skip the sandwiches and pizza slices downstairs and go to the cafeteria upstairs, northwest corner of square, Largo Argentina 1, tel. 06-6821-0353).

Picnic on the Pantheon Porch: **Antica Salumeria** is an old-time *alimentari* (grocery store, daily 8:00–21:00) on the Pantheon square. Eduardo speaks English and will help you assemble your picnic: artichokes, mixed olives, bread, cheese, meat, and wine (with plastic glasses). While you can create your own (sold by the weight, more fun, and cheaper), they also sell quality ready-made sandwiches. Now take your peasant's feast over for a temple-porch picnic. Enjoy the shade at the base of a column and munch your meal. For dessert...

Gelato

Three fine gelaterias are within a two-minute walk of the Pantheon. Rome's most famous and venerable ice-cream joint is **Gelateria Caffè Pasticceria Giolitti** (with cheap take-away prices and elegant Old World seating, just off Piazza Colonna and Piazza Monte Citorio at Via Uffici del Vicario 40, tel. 06-699-1243). Another good option is **Gelateria della Palma** (2 blocks directly in front of the Pantheon at Via della Maddalena 20). Bright with neon and filled with every type of candy imaginable, kids of all ages will enjoy their huge selection of colorful, tasty gelati. However, taste purists look down on bright colors. For mellower hues and more traditional quality, try **Crèmeria Monteforte**, facing the right side of the Pantheon (Tue–Sun 11:00–24:00, closed Mon, Via della Rotonda 22).

Near the Spanish Steps

To locate these restaurants, see the "Dolce Vita Stroll" map on page 283.

Ristorante il Gabriello is inviting and small—modern under medieval arches—and offers a peaceful and local-feeling respite from all the top-end fashion shops in the area. Claudio serves with charisma, while his brother cooks creative Roman cuisine using fresh, organic products from his wife's farm. Simply close your eyes and point to anything on the menu (pastas-€9, *secondi*-€12; dinner only, Mon–Sat 19:00–24:00, closed Sun, air-con, dress respectfully—no shorts please, reservations smart, Via Vittoria 51, 3 blocks from Spanish Steps, tel. 06-6994-0810). Italians normally just trust the waiter and say "Bring it on." Tourists are understandably more cautious, but you can be trusting here. Invest €40 (not including wine) in "Claudio's Extravaganza," and he'll shower you with edible kindness.

These two neighboring places are nothing special, just lively and simple, offering €8 plates with good indoor and outdoor seating near the Spanish Steps. **Ristorante Difronte**, with a fresh, stylish ambience, serves big, fun €8 salads and pizzas (Tue–Sun 12:00–15:30 & 17:30–24:00, closed Mon, Via della Croce 38, tel. 06-678-0355). Stepping next door takes you back about 100 years to the bustling **Fiaschetteria**, serving traditional Italian cuisine (closed Sun, Via della Croce 39).

Ristorante alla Rampa, just around the corner from the touristy crush of the Spanish Steps, offers quality Roman cooking, appealing indoor/outdoor ambience at a moderate price, and impersonal service. They take no reservations, so arrive by 19:30, or be prepared to wait. For a simple meal, go with the €9 *piatto misto all'ortolana*—a self-service trip to their magnificent antipasto spread with meat, fish, and veggies. Even though you get just one trip to the buffet, this can be a meal in itself (closed Sun, 100 yards east of Spanish Steps at Piazza Mignanelli 18, tel. 06-678-2621).

Near the Trevi Fountain

L'Antica Birreria Peroni is Rome's answer to a German beerhall. Serving hearty mugs of the local Peroni beer and lots of just plain fun, beer-hall food, the place is a hit with locals for a cheap night out (Mon–Sat 12:00–24:00, closed Sun, midway between Trevi Fountain and Capitol Hill, a block off Via del Corso at Via di San Marcello 19, tel. 06-679-5310).

Ristorante Pizzeria Sacro e Profano fills an old church with spicy south Italian (Calabrian) cuisine and some pricey, exotic dishes. Run with enthusiasm and passion by Pasquale and friends, this is just far enough away from the Trevi mobs. Their hearty €13 antipasti plate offers a delightful montage of Calabrian taste treats—plenty of food for a light, memorable meal (Mon–Sat 12:00–15:00 & 18:00–22:00, closed Sun, a block off Via del Tritone at Via dei Maroniti 29, tel. 06-679-1836). For dessert...

Around the corner, **Gelateria San Crispino**, well-respected by locals, serves particularly tasty, gourmet gelato using creative ingredients such as balsamic vinegar, pear, and cinnamon (Wed–Mon 12:00–24:00, closed Tue, Via della Panetteria 42, tel. 06-679-3924).

Eating Cheaply between the Colosseum and St. Peter-in-Chains Church

You'll find good views but poor value in the restaurants directly behind the Colosseum. To get your money's worth, eat at least a block away. Here are two handy eateries at the top of Terme di Tito (a block uphill from Colosseum, near St. Peter-in-Chains church—of Michelangelo's *Moses* fame; se page 36).

Caffè dello Studente is a lively spot popular with local engineering students attending the nearby U. of Rome. Pina, Mauro, and their perky daughter Simona (speaks English, but you can teach her some more) give my readers a royal welcome and serve typical *bar gastronomia* fare: toasted sandwiches and simple pastas and pizzas. You can get your food to go *(da portar via)*; stand up and eat at the crowded bar; sit at an outdoor table and wait for a menu; or—if it's not busy—show this book when you order at the bar and sit without paying extra at a table (Mon–Sat 7:30–21:00, Sun 9:00–18:00, tel. 06-488-3240).

Ostaria da Nerone, next door, is more of a restaurant: less friendly and more aggressive. Their €7.50 antipasti plate is the best value; add €2 and you get meat and shellfish (Mon–Sat 12:00–15:00 & 19:00–23:00, closed Sun, indoor/outdoor seating, Via delle Terme di Tito 96, tel. 06-481-7952, run by Teo).

Near Via Firenze

You have plenty of eating options near my recommended hotels on Via Firenze.

Ristorante del Giglio is a circa-1900 place with a long family tradition of serving traditional Roman dishes. You'll eat in a big elegant hall of about 20 tables with dressy locals and tourists following the recommendation of the many nearby hotels (€8 pastas, €15 *secondi*, Mon–Sat 12:00–15:00 & 19:00–23:00, closed Sun, Via Torino 137, tel. 06-488-1606).

Ristorante da Giovanni is a reasonable, budget option that has fed locals and hungry travelers now for 50 years (tired but filling €14 *menu*, Mon–Sat 12:00–15:00 & 19:00–22:30, closed Sun and in Aug, just off Via XX Settembre at Via Antonio Salandra 1, tel. 06-485-950).

Restaurants in East Rome

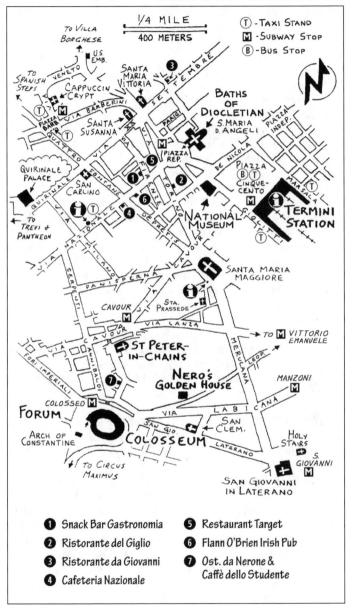

1/4 MILE
400 METERS

(T) - TAXI STAND
(M) - SUBWAY STOP
(B) - BUS STOP

TO VILLA BORGHESE

TO SPANISH STEPS

US. EMB.

VENETO

CAPPUCCIN CRYPT

SANTA MARIA VITTORIA

BATHS OF DIOCLETIAN

S. MARIA D. ANGELI

PIAZZA INDEP.

VIA BARBERINI

PIAZZA BARB.

SANTA SUSANNA

QUIR.

QUATTRO

PIAZZA REP.

DE NICOLA

PIAZZA CINQUE-CENTO

QUIRINALE PALACE

FONTANE

SAN CARLINO

TERMINI STATION

MARSALA

TO TREVI & PANTHEON

NATIONAL MUSEUM

VIA NAZIONALE

PANISPERNA

SANTA MARIA MAGGIORE

VIA SERPENTI

CAVOUR

STA. PRASSEDE

VIA CANZA

TO VITTORIO EMANUELE

FORI IMPERIALI

ST PETER-IN-CHAINS

NERO'S GOLDEN HOUSE

MERCANA

LEOP.

MANZONI

COLOSSEO

FORUM

ARCH OF CONSTANTINE

COLOSSEUM

SAN GIO

VIA

LABICANA

SAN CLEM.

LATERANO

HOLY STAIRS

S. GIOVANNI

TO CIRCUS MAXIMUS

SAN GIOVANNI IN LATERANO

---

1. Snack Bar Gastronomia
2. Ristorante del Giglio
3. Ristorante da Giovanni
4. Cafeteria Nazionale

5. Restaurant Target
6. Flann O'Brien Irish Pub
7. Ost. da Nerone & Caffè dello Studente

Cafeteria Nazionale, with woody elegance, offers light lunches—including salads—at fair prices. It's noisy with local office workers being served by frantic red-vested wait staff (Mon–Sat 7:00–20:00, closed Sun, Via Nazionale 26–27, at intersection with Via Agostino de Pretis, tel. 06-4899-1716). Their lunch buffet is a delight but gets picked over early (small dish €7.50, Mon–Sat 12:00–15:00).

Restaurant Target is a modern, handy place serving decent pizza and pasta near recommended hotels (Mon–Sat 12:00–15:30 & 19:00–24:00, Sun 19:00–24:00, indoor/outdoor seating, don't expect great service, Via Torino 33, tel. 06-474-0066).

The **McDonald's** restaurants on Piazza della Repubblica (free piazza seating outside), Piazza Barberini, and Via Firenze offer air-conditioned interiors and salad bars.

Flann O'Brien Irish Pub is an entertaining place for a light meal (of pasta or something *other* than pasta, such as grilled beef, served early and late, when other places are closed), fine Irish beer, live sporting events on TV, and perhaps the most Italian crowd of all. Walk way back before choosing a table (daily 7:30–24:00, Via Nazionale 17, at intersection with Via Napoli, tel. 06-488-0418).

Snack Bar Gastronomia is a local joint with one table and a booming take-out business—especially popular for its Greek-style yogurt with fruit and honey (€3–5, confirm price before ordering as there are several versions; fresh meat or veggie sandwiches, salads, freshly squeezed juices, daily 7:00–24:00, Via Firenze 34). An old-fashioned *alimentari* (grocery), with everything you'd need for a picnic, is across the street (7:00–19:30), just uphill from the McDonald's.

Near the Vatican Museum and St. Peter's

Avoid the restaurant pushers handing out fliers near the Vatican: bad food and expensive menu tricks. Try any of these instead (see map on page 254).

Perilli in Prati is bright, modern, and just far enough away from the tourist hordes. While friendly Lucia and Massimo specialize in pizza and grilled meats, the highlight is their excellent lunch buffet on weekdays (€5.50 small plate or €7.50 for large, Mon–Fri 12:00–15:00, also open Mon–Sat for dinner, 1 block from Ottaviano Metro stop, Via Otranto 9, tel. 06-370-0156).

Hostaria dei Bastioni, run by Antonio and his family, has tasty food and friendly service. It's conveniently located midway on your hike from St. Peters' to the Vatican Museum, with noisy street-side seating and a quiet interior. The house fettuccine and the risotto with seafood are good (pastas-€6, *secondi*-€8-12, no cover charge, Mon–Sat 12:00–15:00 & 19:00–23:30, closed Sun, at corner of Vatican wall, Via Leone IV 29, tel. 06-3972-3034).

La Rustichella serves a sprawling *antipasti* buffet (€7 for a single meal-sized plate). Arrive when they open at 19:30 to avoid a line and have the pristine buffet to yourself (Tue–Sun 12:30–15:00 & 19:30–23:00, closed Mon, near Metro: Cipro–Musei Vaticani, opposite church at end of Via Candia, Via Angelo Emo 1, tel. 06-3972-0649). Consider the fun and fruity **Gelateria Millennium** next door.

Viale Giulio Cesare is lined with cheap **Pizza Rustica** shops, self-serve places, and inviting eateries. Restaurants such as **Tre Pupazzi** (closed Sun, tel. 06-686-8371), which line the pedestrian-only Borgo Pio—a block from Piazza San Pietro—are worth a look.

Turn your nose loose in the wonderful **Via Andrea Doria** open-air market, three blocks north of the Vatican Museum (Mon–Sat roughly 7:00–13:30, until 16:30 Tue and Fri except summer, corner of Via Tunisi and Via Andrea Doria). If the market is closed, try the nearby **IN's supermarket** (Mon–Sat 8:30–13:30 & 16:00–20:00, closed Thu eve and Sun, a half block straight out from Via Tunisi entrance of open-air market, Via Francesco Caracciolo 18).

In the Testaccio Neighborhood

For restaurant location, see the map on page 61.

Trattoria "Da Oio" A Casa Mia serves good quality, inexpensive, traditional cuisine to a local crowd. It's a upbeat little eatery where you understand the Testaccio passion for the "fifth quarter." (Testaccio, dominated for centuries by its slaughterhouses, is noted for restaurants expert at preparing undesirable meat parts.) The menu is a minefield of soft meats (closed Sun, Via Galvani 43, tel. 06-578-2680).

ROME WITH CHILDREN

Sorry, but Rome is not a great place for little kids. Parks are rare. Kid-friendly parks are more rare. Most of the museums are low-tech and lack hands-on fun.

The good news for kids? Pizza and gelato. Any person under 39 inches tall travels free on public transit. And Italians are openly fond of kids, so you'll probably get lots of friendly attention from locals.

Here are some tips:

- Take advantage of local information. *Roma c'è*, the periodical entertainment guide (€1.20, sold at newsstands), has a children's section in English. Ask at Rome's TIs about kid-friendly activities. TIs often have a helpful "kid's pack."
- Don't overdo it. Tackle only one or two key sights a day (Vatican Museum, or Colosseum and Forum) and mix with a healthy dose of fun activities, like exploring Rome's great public sites (Piazza Navona, Trevi Fountain, and Villa Borghese).
- Rome's hotels often give price breaks for kids. (Air-conditioning can be worth the splurge.)
- Eat dinner early (around 19:00) and you'll miss the romantic crowd. Skip the popular restaurants. Look instead for self-serve cafeterias, bars (kids are welcome), or even fast-food places where kids can move around without bothering others. Picnic lunches and dinners work well. For ready-made picnics that can please adults and kids, try the *rosticcerie* (delis). Pizza Rustica shops sell cheap take-out pizza; kids like *margherita* (tomato and cheese) and *diavola* (similar to pepperoni).
- Public WCs are hard to find: Try museums, bars, gelato shops, and fast-food restaurants.
- Follow this book's crowd-beating tips. Kids don't like standing in a long line for a museum (which they might not even want to see).

SIGHTS AND ACTIVITIES

Rome's many squares are traffic-free, with plenty of space to run and pigeons to feed while Mom and Dad enjoy a coffee at an outdoor table.

When visiting the ancient sites, have some fun with *Rome: Past and Present*, a book with plastic overlays showing how the ruins used to look. It's available at stalls near the entrance of ancient sites.

Explora, the children's museum in Rome, is a hands-on wonderland for kids 12 and under. The exhibits are in Italian, but kids probably won't care (kids under 3-free, kids 3–12-€7, adults-€6, parents must accompany children; 4 sessions/day: Tue–Fri 9:30, 11:30, 15:00, and 17:00; Sat–Sun 10:00, 12:00, 15:00, and 17:00; closed Mon, Via Flaminia 80, Metro: Flaminio, 10-min walk from Piazza del Popolo, tel. 06-361-3776, www.mdbr.it, helpful English-speaking staff).

The **Vatican Museum** comes with mummies and cool statues of animals. (There's an entire hall of statues with their penises broken off that my kids found entertaining.) Nearby, **Castel Sant'Angelo**—with Vatican views and weapon displays—appeals to young knights.

Villa Borghese is Rome's sprawling central park. The best kids' zones are near Porta Pinciana, where you'll find rental bikes, pony rides, and other amusements (Metro: Spagna). Rome's **zoo**, Bioparco, in the northeast section of the park, houses about 900 animals—including the endangered black lemur, pygmy hippopotamus, Gila monster, and painted hunting dog (kids under 3-free, kids 3–12-€6.50, adults-€8.50, daily Nov–March 9:30–17:00, April–Oct 9:30–18:00, last entry 1 hour before closing, café and picnic areas, Piazzale del Giardino Zoologico 1, Metro: Flaminio, tel. 06-360-8211, www.bioparco.it).

The spooky tunnels of the **Catacombs** and the ghoulish **Cappuccin Crypt** are goblin pleasers. (For Catacombs, see pages 52 and 64; for Crypt, page 51.) The **Church of St. Ignazio**, with its false dome, fascinates kids and adults (see page 46).

Your children can visit Egypt—without the diarrhea—by visiting Rome's funky little **pyramid** (free and always viewable, Metro: Piramide, page 60).

Bocca della Verità, the legendary Mouth of Truth, draws a young crowd and parents with cameras. Stick your hand in the mouth of the gaping stone face on the wall. As the legend goes, if you're a liar, your hand will be gobbled up. (The mouth is free and always open, in the porch of the Church of Santa Maria in Cosmedin, on Piazza Bocca della Verità, near the north end of Circus Maximus.)

Budding **soccer** stars could enjoy a local match at either of the stadiums: Flaminio (Metro to Flaminio) or Olympic (Metro to Flaminio, then tram #225 to Piazza Mancini).

Rome feels safe at night, and you can easily take your kids on the **walks** suggested in this book, such as the "Dolce Vita Stroll" on page 284. On the Night Walk Across Rome (page 69), children like slurping up chocolaty *tartufo* at the Tre Scalini café on Piazza Navona and tossing coins in the Trevi Fountain.

Rome has a big water park called **Hydromania** (€13.50 Mon–Fri, €15 Sat–Sun, cheaper if you arrive after 14:00, open Mon–Fri 9:30–18:30, Sat–Sun 9:30–19:00, Vicolo Casal Lumbroso 200, exit 33 off ring freeway west of the city, tel. 06-6618-3183, www.hydromania.it). **Acquapiper**, another water park, is near Tivoli (Via Maremmana Inferiore, in Guidonia, 15-min drive east of Rome, tel. 0774-326-536); ask about their free shuttle bus from the center of Rome. **LunEUR** at E.U.R. is a tired old amusement park (Mon and Wed–Fri 15:00–19:00, Sat 15:00–2:00 in the morning, Sun 10:00–13:00 & 15:00–22:00, closed Tue, Metro to Magliana, then bus to Via delle Tre Fontana, tel. 06-592-5933, www.luneur.it).

Older children might like exploring **Pompeii** (see page 318). For a long day trip, consider a train ride to **Pisa** (3 hours one-way) to visit its famous tipsy tower. It's open for climbing, but you need to reserve a time slot when you buy your ticket—and you might have to wait a few hours. It's best to book online at www.opapisa.it/boxoffice for a €2 charge (tower climb-€15, daily 8:30–20:30, off-season 9:00–17:00).

SHOPPING

Shops are open from 9:00 to 13:00 and from 16:00 to 19:00. They're often closed on summer Saturday afternoons and winter Monday mornings.

If all you need are souvenirs, a surgical strike at any souvenir shop will do. Otherwise, try...

Department Stores

Large department stores offer relatively painless one-stop shopping. A good upscale department store is **La Rinascente** (like Nordstrom or Macy's). Its main branch is on Piazza Fiume, and there's a smaller store on Via del Corso. **COIN**, near Piazza Fiume, is also fashionable. **UPIM** is the Roman JC Penney (many branches, including inside Termini station, Via Nazionale 111, Piazza Santa Maria Maggiore, and Via del Tritone 172). **Oviesse**, a cheap clothing outlet, is near the Vatican Museum (on the corner of Via Candia and Via Mocenigo, Metro: Cipro–Musei Vaticani). **Cinecittà Due** is the nearest shopping mall (Via P. Togliatti 2, Metro: Subaugusta, tel. 06-722-0902).

Shopping Neighborhoods

A good, mid-range shopping area is all along **Via del Corso**, with prices increasing as you head toward Piazza di Spagna. **Via Nazionale** also features a range of affordable shops, especially for clothes. Cheapskates scrounge through the junky but dirt-cheap shops in the gritty area around **Piazza Vittorio.**

Boutiques

For top fashion, stroll the streets around the Spanish Steps, including **Via Condotti**, **Via Borgognona** (for the big-name shops), and **Via del Babuino** (trendy design shops and galleries). For antiques,

Getting a VAT Refund

Wrapped into the purchase price of your Roman souvenirs is a Value Added Tax (VAT) of about 20 percent. If you purchase more than €155 worth of goods at a store that participates in the VAT refund scheme, you're entitled to get most of that tax back. Personally, I've never felt that VAT refunds are worth the hassle, but if you do, here's the scoop.

If you're lucky, the merchant will subtract the tax when you make your purchase. (This is more likely to occur if the store ships the goods to your home.) Otherwise, you'll need to:

Get the paperwork. Have the merchant completely fill out the necessary refund document, called a "cheque." You'll have to present your passport.

Get your stamp at the border. Process your cheque(s) at your last stop in the EU with the customs agent who deals with VAT refunds. It's best to keep your purchases in your carry-on for viewing, but if they're too large or dangerous (such as knives) to carry on, track down the proper customs agent to inspect them before you check your bag. You're not supposed to use your purchased goods before you leave. If you show up at customs wearing your new leather shoes, officials might look the other way—or deny you a refund.

Collect your refund. You'll need to return your stamped document to the retailer or its representative. Many merchants work with a service, such as Global Refund (www.globalrefund.com) or Premier Tax Free (www.premiertaxfree.com), which have offices at major airports, ports, or border crossings. These services, which extract a 4 percent fee, can refund your money immediately in your currency of choice or credit your card (within two billing cycles). If you have to deal directly with the retailer, mail the store your stamped documents and then wait. It could take months.

stroll **Via de Coronari** (between Piazza Navona and the bend in the river), **Via Giulia** (between Campo de' Fiori and the river), and **Via Margutta** (classier, with art galleries too, from Spanish Steps to Piazza del Popolo). For funkier, unique items, try **Via Giubbonari**—packed with artsy little boutiques—and other streets near Campo de' Fiori.

Flea Markets

For antiques and fleas, the granddaddy of markets is the **Porta Portese** *mercato delle pulci* (flea market). This Sunday-morning market is long and spindly, running between the actual Porta Portese (a gate in the old town wall) and the Trastevere train station. Starting at Porta Portese, walk through the long, tacky parade of stalls selling cheap bras and shoes. Along the way, check out the con artists with the shell games. Each has shills in the crowd "winning big money" to get suckers involved. Hang on to your wallet—literally, in your front pocket. This is a den of thieves. The heart of the market for real flea-market junk (hiding a few little antique treasures) is the area from Piazza Ippolito Nievo to the Trastevere station (6:30–13:00 Sun only, on Via Portuense and Via Ippolito Nievo; to get to the market, catch bus #75 from Termini station or tram #3 from Largo Argentina; get off the bus or tram on Viale Trastevere and walk toward the river—and the noise).

At the **Via Sannio** market, you'll find clothing and some handicrafts (Mon–Sat 8:00–13:00, closed Sun, a couple of blocks south of San Giovanni in Laterano, Metro: San Giovanni).

Open-Air Produce Markets

Rome's outdoor markets provide a fun and colorful dimension of the city that even the most avid museum-goer should not miss. Wander through the easygoing neighborhood produce markets, which clog certain streets and squares every morning (7:00–13:00) except Sunday. Consider the huge **Mercato Andrea Doria** (3 blocks in front of Vatican Museum at Via Andrea Doria). Smaller but equally charming slices of everyday Roman life are at markets on these streets and squares: **Piazza delle Coppelle** (near Pantheon), **Via Balbo** (near Termini station and recommended hotels off Via Nazionale), and **Via della Pace** (near Piazza Navona). The covered **Mercato di Testaccio** sells mostly produce and is a hit with photographers and people-watchers (Piazza Testaccio, near Metro: Piramide). And **Campo de' Fiori**, while renovated to fit European Union standards, is still a fun scene.

Airport Souvenirs

Fiumicino (a.k.a. Leonardo da Vinci) airport sells Italian specialty foods vacuum-packed to clear U.S. customs. Most shops are near the departure gates (after you check your bags and pass through security). Try *parmigiano reggiano* cheese, dried porcini mushrooms or peppers, and better olive oil than you can buy at home. Don't bother buying any salami or prosciutto unless it's canned; you're not allowed to bring fresh meat into the United States.

Customs

You can take home $800 in souvenirs per person duty-free. The next $1,000 is taxed at a flat 3 percent. After that, you pay the individual item's duty rate. You can also bring in duty-free a liter of alcohol (slightly more than a standard-sized bottle of wine), a carton of cigarettes, and up to 100 cigars. As for food, anything in cans or sealed jars is acceptable. Skip dried meat, cheeses, and fresh fruits and veggies. To check customs rules and duty rates, visit www.customs.gov.

NIGHTLIFE

Romans get dressed up and eat out in casual surroundings for their evening entertainment. For most visitors, the best after-dark activity is simply to stroll the medieval lanes that connect the romantic, floodlit squares and fountains. Head for Piazza Navona, the Pantheon, Campo de' Fiori, Trevi Fountain, Spanish Steps, Via del Corso, Trastevere (around the Santa Maria in Trastevere Church), or Monte Testaccio. ✪ See Night Walk Across Rome, page 69, and "Dolce Vita Stroll," page 284.

Get a copy of one of the entertainment guides, *Roma c'è* (€1.20, sold at newsstands) or *Passepartout* (free at TIs). Look at the current listings of concerts, operas (the opera house is at Via Firenze 72, near recommended Via Nazionale hotels; tel. 06-481-601), dance, and films. Classical music-lovers will seek out the Rome Auditorium (Parco della Musica), a mega-music complex with three concert halls (Via Vittorio Veneto 96, bus #53, #217, #231, or #910, or take Metro to Flaminio and then catch tram #2, www.musicaperroma.it). Posters around town also advertise upcoming events.

At **Pasquino**, Rome's English-language movie theater, you'll find movies daily in English (3 screens, in Trastevere at Piazza S. Egidio 9, catch tram #8 from Largo Argentina, tel. 06-580-3622). **Warner Village Moderno** shows some films in English (Piazza Repubblica, near train station and recommended hotels, tel. 06-477-791). Some theaters around town run movies in their original language (look for "V.O."—*versione originale*).

An interesting place for club-hopping is **Monte Testaccio.** After 21:00, ride the Metro to Piramide and follow the noise. Monte Testaccio, once an ancient trash heap, is now a small hill whose cool caves house funky restaurants and trendy clubs. (It stands amid a pretty rough neighborhood, though.)

Pub Crawls, offered year-round by several companies, attract a boisterous crowd. I tried one, and had never seen 50 young, drunk people having so much fun. Look for fliers locally.

Some **museums** have later opening hours (especially on Sat in summer), offering a good chance to see art in a cooler, less crowded environment. Ask the TI if any museums are currently open late. The Capitol Hill Museum and Castel Sant'Angelo stay open until 20:00 daily except Monday.

Dolce Vita Stroll

This is the city's chic stroll, from Piazza del Popolo (Metro: Flaminio) down a wonderfully traffic-free section of Via del Corso, and up Via Condotti to the Spanish Steps each evening around 18:00 (Sat and Sun are best). Shoppers, people-watchers, and flirts on the prowl fill this neighborhood of Rome's most fashionable stores (open after siesta 16:30–19:30).

Throughout Italy, early evening is time to stroll. While elsewhere in Italy this is called the *passeggiata*, in Rome it's a cruder, big-city version called the *struscio*. (*Struscio* means "to rub.") Unemployment among Italy's youth is very high; many stay with their parents even into their thirties. They spend a lot of time being trendy and hanging out. Hard-core cruisers from the suburbs, which lack pleasant public spaces, congregate on Via del Corso to make the scene. The hot *vroom-vroom* motorscooter is their symbol; haircuts and fashion are follow-the-leader. They are called the *coatto*. In a more genteel small town, the *passeggiata* comes with sweet whispers of *"bella"* and *"bello"* ("pretty" and "handsome"). In Rome, the admiration is stronger, oriented toward consumption—they say *"buona"* and *"buono"*—meaning "good" (terms used to describe food). But despite how lusty this all sounds, you'll see as many chunky, middle-aged Italians on this walk as hormone-charged youth. If you get hungry during your stroll, see page 271 for descriptions of nearby restaurants.

Start on **Piazza del Popolo.** The delightfully car-free square is marked by an obelisk that was brought to Rome by Augustus after he conquered Egypt. (It used to stand in the Circus Maximus.) In medieval times, this area was just inside Rome's main entry.

The Baroque church of **Santa Maria del Popolo,** on the square, contains Raphael's Chigi Chapel (KEE-gee, third chapel on left) and two paintings by Caravaggio (the side paintings in chapel left of altar). The church is open daily (Mon–Sat 7:00–12:00 & 16:00–19:00, Sun 8:00–13:30 & 16:30–19:30, next to gate in the old wall, on far side of Piazza del Popolo, to the right as you face gate).

From Piazza del Popolo, shop your way down **Via del Corso.** If you need a rest or a viewpoint, join the locals sitting on the steps of various churches along the street.

Dolce Vita Stroll

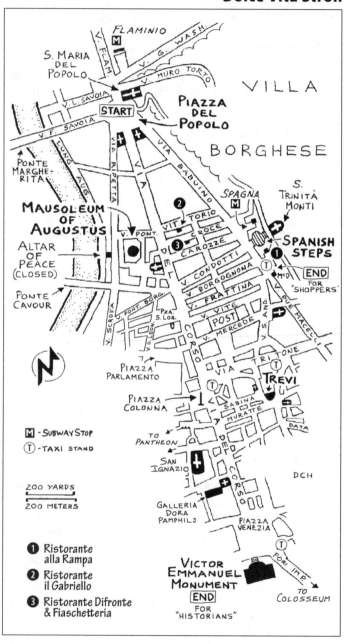

FLAMINIO

S. MARIA DEL POPOLO

V. G. WASH.

V. MURO TORTO

VILLA

PIAZZA DEL POPOLO

BORGHESE

START

V. L. SAVOIA

V. F. SAVOIA

PONTE MARGHE-RITA

LUNG. AUG.

VIA BABUINO

VIA DI RIPETTA

SPAGNA

S. TRINITÀ MONTI

MAUSOLEUM OF AUGUSTUS

V. PONT.

VITTORIO

❷

SPANISH STEPS

❶

ALTAR OF PEACE (CLOSED)

CROCE

CARROZZE

❸

V. CONDOTTI

END FOR "SHOPPERS"

McD

PONTE CAVOUR

V. BORGOGNONA

V. FRATTINA

V. SCROFA

V. FONT. BORG.

PZA. S. LOR.

V. LEON.

POST

VITE

MERCEDE

DUE MACELLI

CORSO

PIAZZA PARLAMENTO

VIA

TRITONE

TREVI

PIAZZA COLONNA

SABINA

MURATTE

DATA

Ⓜ – SUBWAY STOP

Ⓣ – TAXI STAND

TO PANTHEON

SAN IGNAZIO

DCH

200 YARDS
200 METERS

CORSO

GALLERIA DORA PAMPHILJ

PIAZZA VENEZIA

❶ Ristorante alla Rampa

❷ Ristorante il Gabriello

❸ Ristorante Difronte & Fiaschetteria

VICTOR EMMANUEL MONUMENT

END FOR "HISTORIANS"

FORI IMP.

TO COLOSSEUM

At Via Pontefici, historians turn right and walk a block to see the massive, rotting, round-brick **Mausoleum of Augustus**, topped with overgrown cypress trees. Beyond it, next to the river, is Augustus' Ara Pacis, or Altar of Peace (likely open again in 2006 after renovation).

From the mausoleum, return to Via del Corso and the 21st century, continuing straight until **Via Condotti.** Shoppers should take a left to join the parade to the **Spanish Steps.** The streets that parallel Via Condotti to the south (Borgognona and Frattini) are just as popular. You can catch a taxi home at the taxi stand a block south of the Spanish Steps (at Piazza Mignonelli, near American Express and McDonald's).

Historians: Ignore Via Condotti and forget the Spanish Steps. Stay on Via del Corso, which has been straight since Roman times, a half mile down to the Victor Emmanuel Monument. Climb Michelangelo's stairway to his glorious (especially when floodlit) square atop Capitol Hill. From the balconies at either side of the mayor's palace, catch the lovely views of the Forum as the horizon reddens and cats prowl the unclaimed rubble of ancient Rome.

TRANSPORTATION CONNECTIONS

Train Stations

Rome's main train station, **Termini**, is a minefield of tourist services: a TI (daily 8:00–21:00), train info office (daily 7:00–21:00), ATMs, late-hours banks, 24-hour thievery, and the handy, cheery Food Village Chef Express Self-Service Ristorante (daily 11:00–22:30, WC at entrance, near east end of station). In the modern mall downstairs (under the station), you'll find a grocery (oddly named "Drug Store," daily 7:00–24:00) and pharmacy (daily 7:30–22:00). Luggage deposit is along track 24, downstairs (€4 for up to 5 hrs, €0.60/hr thereafter). The train to Leonardo da Vinci/Fiumicino Airport runs from tracks 25 and 26 (see "Airports," below).

Termini is also a local transportation hub. The city's two Metro lines intersect at the Termini Metro station (downstairs). Buses (including the city orientation tour—see page 34) leave from the square directly in front of the main station hall. Taxis queue in front, along the right side of the square; avoid con men hawking "express taxi" services in unmarked cars (only use ones marked with the word *taxi* and a phone number). To avoid the long taxi line, simply hike out past the buses to the main street and hail one. The station has some sleazy sharks with official-looking business cards; avoid anybody selling anything at the station.

From the train station, most of my accommodation listings are easily accessible by foot (for hotels near the Termini train station) or by Metro (for hotels in the Colosseum and Vatican neighborhoods).

Types of Trains

You'll encounter several types of trains in Italy. Along with the various pokey, milk-run trains, there are the slow IR (Interregional) and *diretto* trains, the medium *espresso*, the fast IC (Intercity), and the bullet-train T.A.V. (Treno Alta Velocità; supplement costs €16

Italy's Public Transportation

KEY:
— RAIL
⊥ PRIVATE RAIL
···· SHIP
--- BUS

NOT TO SCALE

even if you have a railpass). Fast trains, even with supplements, are affordable (e.g., a second-class ticket on a Rome–Venice express train costs about €50 total). Purchasing supplements on the train comes with a nasty penalty. Buying them at the station can be a time-waster unless you use the big gray-and-yellow automatic ticket dispensers, which work well and also provide schedule information. Generally, it's easiest to buy tickets and supplements at travel agencies in towns (Quo Vadis or American Express—see page 25). The cost is the same, the lines and language barrier are smaller, and you'll save time.

Schedules

Newsstands sell up-to-date regional and all-Italy timetables (€5, ask for the *orario ferroviario*). On the Web, check http://bahn.hafas .de/bin/query.exe/en or www.trenitalia.it.

When using the schedules posted at the station, note that the town you're going to may be listed in fine print as an intermediate destination. For example, if you're going from Rome to Orvieto, scan the schedule and you'll notice that trains that go to Florence usually stop in Orvieto en route. Travelers who read the fine print end up with a greater choice of trains.

Strikes are common. They generally last a day, and train employees will simply say *"sciopero"* (strike). Still, sporadic trains—following no particular schedule—lumber down the tracks during most strikes.

By Train from Rome to: Venice (6/day, 5–8 hrs, overnight possible), **Florence** (12/day, 2 hrs, most stop at Orvieto en route), **Assisi** (every 2 hrs, 2.5 hrs, many direct), **Pisa** (8/day, 3–4 hrs), **Genoa** (7/day, 6 hrs, overnight option), **Milan** (12/day, 5 hrs, overnight possible), **Naples** (6/day, 2 hrs), **Brindisi** (2/day, 9 hrs, overnight available), **Amsterdam** (2/day, 20 hrs, overnight unavoidable), **Bern** (5/day, 10 hrs, overnight possible), **Frankfurt** (4/day, 14 hrs, overnight available), **Munich** (5/day, 12 hrs, overnight option), **Nice** (2/day, 10 hrs, overnight possible), **Paris** (5/day, 16 hrs, overnight available), **Vienna** (3/day, 13–15 hrs, overnight option).

Bus Station

Long-distance buses (e.g., from Siena and Assisi) arrive at Rome's small **Tiburtina** station, which is on Metro line B, with easy connections to the Termini train station (a straight shot 4 stops away) and the entire Metro system.

Airports

Rome's two airports—Fiumicino (a.k.a. Leonardo da Vinci) and the small Ciampino—share the same Web site (www.adr.it).

Fiumicino Airport: Rome's major airport has a TI (daily

8:00–19:00, tel. 06-6595-6074), ATMs, banks, luggage storage, shops, and bars.

A slick, direct **train** connects the airport and Rome's central Termini train station in 30 minutes. Trains run twice hourly in both directions from roughly 6:00 to 23:00. From the airport, trains depart at :07 and :37 past the hour. From the airport's arrival gate, follow signs to Stazione/Railway Station. Buy your ticket from a machine or the Biglietteria office (€9.50). Make sure the train you board is going to the central "Roma Termini" station, not "Roma Orte" or others.

Going from the Termini train station to the airport, trains depart at :20 and :50 past the hour, usually from track 25 or 26; to reach these tracks, take a long 10-minute walk along track 24 to the end of the station (near the corner of Giovanni Giolitti and Via Lamarmora, moving walkways are inside the building to the right on the lower level). Check the departure boards for "Fiumicino Aeroporto"—the local name for the airport—and confirm with an official or a local on the platform that the train is indeed going to the airport (€9.50, buy ticket from computerized yellow ticket machines, any tabacchi shop in station, or at the desk near entrance to track 26). Read your ticket: If it requires validation, stamp it in the yellow machine near the platform before boarding. Know whether your plane departs from terminal A, B, or C.

Shuttle van services run to and from the airport. Consider **Rome Airport Shuttle** (€23/person, 30 percent more late night or early morning, tel. 06-4201-4507 or 06-420-13469, www.airportshuttle.it).

Your hotel can arrange a **taxi** to the airport at any hour for about €40. To get from the airport into town cheaply by taxi, try teaming up with any tourist also just arriving (most are heading for hotels near yours in the center). Be sure to wait at the taxi stand. Avoid unmarked, unmetered taxis; these guys will try to tempt you away from the taxi stand line-up by offering an immediate (rip-off) ride.

For **airport information**, call 06-65951. To inquire about flights, call 06-6595-3640 (Alitalia: tel. 06-2222, British Airways and SAS: tel. 06-6501-0771, Delta: toll-free tel. 800-477-999, KLM/Northwest: tel. 06-6501-1441, Lufthansa: tel. 06-6568-4004, Swiss International: tel. 848-868-120, United: tel. 848-800-692, Air Europa: tel. 06-6595-5695).

Ciampino Airport: Rome's smaller airport (tel. 06-794-941) handles budget airlines, such as easyJet or Ryanair, and charter flights. To get to downtown Rome from the airport, you can take the LILA/Cotral bus (2/hr, 40 min) to the Anagnina Metro stop, where you can connect by Metro to the stop nearest your hotel. Rome Airport Shuttle (listed above) also offers service to and from Ciampino.

Driving in Italy

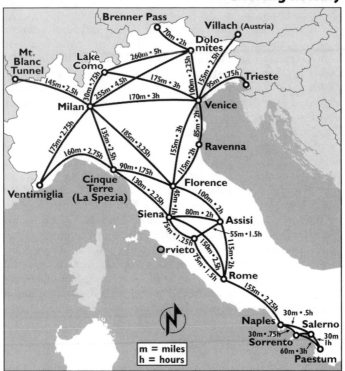

Tips for Drivers

The Grande Raccordo Anulare circles greater Rome. This ring road has spokes that lead you into the center. Entering from the north, leave the autostrada at the Settebagni exit. Following the ancient Via Salaria (and the black-and-white *Centro* signs), work your way doggedly into the Roman thick of things. This will take you along the Villa Borghese park and dump you right on Via Veneto in downtown Rome. Avoid rush hour and drive defensively: Roman cars stay in their lanes like rocks in an avalanche. Parking in Rome is dangerous. Park near a police station or get advice at your hotel. The Villa Borghese underground garage is handy (Metro: Spagna). Garages charge about €24 per day.

Consider this: Your car is a worthless headache in Rome. Avoid a pile of stress and save money by parking at the huge, easy, and relatively safe lot behind the train station in the hill town of Orvieto (follow *P* signs from autostrada) and catching the train to Rome (every 2 hrs, 75 min).

DAY TRIPS
FROM ROME

There's so much to see and do in Rome that you could easily fill a vacation without ever leaving the city limits. But here are several nearby sights that might match your particular interest. Ostia Antica is similar to Pompeii but without the crowds. This excavated ancient city is located an easy hour by Metro and train from Rome. Tivoli is less accessible (consider seeing via private tour) but you're rewarded with the ruins of Hadrian's Villa and with the lush gardens and recently-restored fountains of Villa d'Este.

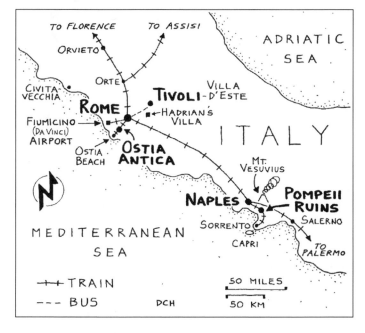

Thanks to Italy's excellent train system, Naples is a direct 2-hour train ride away, landing you right in the middle of town. Visit the wonderful Archaeological Museum, stroll Spaccanapoli street, and have lunch in the city where pizza was born, sampling the exotic chaos of southern Italy. History hounds can venture an hour farther south of Naples to see the ultimate in ruined Roman cities—Pompeii—frozen in time by the eruption of Mt. Vesuvius.

Arrive back in Rome for a late dinner at a sidewalk café to recount your busy day over a glass of wine.

OSTIA
ANTICA
DAY TRIP

For an exciting day trip, pop down to the Roman port of Ostia, which is similar to Pompeii but a lot closer and, in some ways, more interesting. Because Ostia was a working port town, it shows a more complete and gritty look at Roman life than wealthy Pompeii. Wandering around today, you'll see the remains of the docks, warehouses, apartment flats, mansions, shopping arcades, and baths that served a once-thriving port of 60,000 people.

ORIENTATION

Cost: €4 for site and museum.

Hours: Summer Tue–Sun 8:30–18:30 (you can linger on the grounds until 19:00), winter Tue–Sun 8:30–17:00, always closed Mon.

Getting There: To get to Ostia Antica from downtown Rome, you'll take a 45-minute combination Metro/train ride. It'll cost you just one Metro ticket each way (€2 total round-trip). From Rome, take the Metro (line B) to the Piramide stop (which really *is* next to a pyramid—see page 60). Exit and walk to the left, following overhead signs for the *Ferrovia Roma–Lido* train, which you'll ride to Ostia Antica (4/hr, keep your Metro ticket handy, get off at the stop before Lido Nord). At the train station at Ostia Antica, cross the road via the blue sky-bridge and walk straight down Via della Stazione di Ostia Antica, continuing straight until you reach the parking lot. The entrance is on the left.

Tip: To maximize sightseeing efficiency on your Ostia day trip, consider visiting the sights in south Rome—such as St. Paul's Outside the Walls, Montemartini Museum, and the Testaccio neighborhood—on your return (see page 60).

Information: Tel. 06-5635-8099.
Tour: The well-done audioguide (not always available) costs €5.
Length of This Tour: Allow two hours.
Cuisine Art: A cafeteria is in Ostia's museum.

History

Located at (and named for) the mouth *(ostium)* of the Tiber, Ostia was founded in about 620 B.C. Its main attraction was the salt gleaned from nearby salt flats, which was a precious preserver of meat in ancient times. Later, as Rome began expanding (around 400 B.C.), Ostia was conquered, and a fort, or *castrum*, was built here. Ostia—often called Rome's first colony—served as a naval base, protecting Rome from any invasion by river. By A.D. 150, when Rome controlled the Mediterranean, Ostia's importance became commercial rather than military. Rome eventually outgrew the port of Ostia, and a vast new port was dug nearby (where Rome's airport now stands). But Ostia remained a key administrative and warehousing center, busy with the big business of keeping more than a million Romans fed and in sandals. With the fall of Rome, the port was abandoned. Over time, the harbor silted up, and the Tiber retreated about one mile away. The mud that eventually buried Ostia actually protected it from the ravages of time—and stone-scavenging medieval peasants.

THE TOUR BEGINS

Overview

Consider your visit a three-part affair: 1) Follow this tour, which leads you straight down Decumanus Maximus (the town's main drag), with a couple of slight detours, finishing at the forum (the main square). 2) Pop into the museum and consider a bite to eat at the cafeteria. 3) Explore the back lanes—going on a visual scavenger hunt—as you wander your way back to the entry point.

• *Find the map (30 yards inside the gate, on the right) for an orientation. Notice how the core of Ostia is a rectangular Roman military camp, with two major roads crossing at the forum. One of four city gates lies ahead, and on your left is the...*

❶ Cemetery (Necropolis)

Ancient Romans buried their dead outside the city walls. Detour to find family sepulchres—private open-air rooms lined with niches for ash-filled urns. Until the first century A.D., cremation was common. In the second and third centuries A.D., the Romans here buried their dead in marble and terra-cotta sarcophagi in tombs.

• *Ahead (where the road narrows) you enter the ancient city of Ostia through the scant remains of the gate called...*

Ostia Antica

- ❶ Necropolis
- ❷ Porta Romana
- ❸ Republican Warehouses
- ❹ Baths of Neptune
- ❺ Theater
- ❻ Square of the Guilds
- ❼ Mill
- ❽ Via Casa Diana
- ❾ Forum
- ❿ Forum Baths
- ⓫ Museum

❷ Porta Romana

Just as Rome's Porta Ostiense faced Ostia, Ostia's Porta Romana faced Rome. Just inside to the left (under the big tree), you can see on the gate the bits of the Latin inscription that greeted all who entered. It reads: "The Senate and the people of the colony of Ostia constructed the walls." The "colony" reference is a reminder that Ostia was the first bit of the Roman Empire.

From the gate, Ostia's main street (named Decumanus

Maximus) leads straight to the forum, where this walk ends. Note that this road was elevated above some buildings' foundations. Over the centuries, Ostia's ground level rose. You can actually identify buildings from the republic (centuries before Christ) and the empire (centuries after Christ) by their level. Anything you walk down into is from the earlier period.

• Just inside the gate and to the right are the...

❸ Republican Warehouses (Magazzini Repubblicani)

The first century B.C. was busy with activities relating to the river port. Walking along the main street, you pass vast warehouses on the right. The goods of the port—such as grain from Sicily, Egypt, and all of North Africa—were processed and stored in warehouses here before being consumed by Rome.

• At the little well in the road, you'll see a viewpoint (with railings, above on right). Climb up for a view of the...

❹ Baths of Neptune (Terme di Nettuno)

Examine the fine mosaic with Neptune riding four horses through the sea. Apart from the cupid riding the dolphin, the sea looks pretty frightening—which it was. The large square to the left of the mosaic would have been busy with people wrestling, stretching, doing jumping jacks, and getting rubdowns. The niches that ring the square housed small businesses.

• As you walk into the square, you'll see a path to your left. Follow this path (paralleling the main street), which crosses a typical street lined with apartments (insulae), *to get to the...*

❺ Theater (Teatro)

Up to 4,000 residents could gather here for entertainment. The three rows of marble steps near the orchestra were for big shots. While this theater seems big, it was twice as high in ancient times. (The upper two-thirds of what you see today is reconstructed.) In its day, a wall rose behind the stage, enclosing the theater. Even today, this place—one of the oldest brick theaters anywhere—is used for concerts. Climb to the top of the theater for a fine view.

• In front of the theater is the...

❻ Square of the Guilds (Piazzale delle Corporazioni)

This grand square evolved from a simple place where businessmen would stroll and powwow together to become a monumental square lined with more than 60 offices of ship owners and traders. This was the bustling center of Rome's import/export industry. Along the sidewalk, second-century A.D. mosaics advertise the services offered by the various shops. Walking counterclockwise, circle the square to "read" the mosaics that advertised in Latin and in a sign language for illiterate or non-Latin-reading sailors. The most common symbol—the lighthouse—was the sign of the port of Ostia. Grain containers are reminders that grain was the major import of Ostia. The elephant marking the office of the Sabratans (a place in present-day Libya) symbolized the sale of ivory or perhaps of exotic animals (great for parties and private spectacles). One shipper advertised dealings with Narbon (Narbonne in present-day France). In the far corner, you'll see a mosaic that shows porters loading containers from a seagoing ship to a river-going ship and the three-mouthed delta of a river (probably the Nile). Statues of notable local guild members and business leaders decorated the courtyard. The temple in the center was likely related to Ceres, the goddess of harvest and abundance (prosperity from good business). As you leave, notice the small white altar on the right. This would have been used to sacrifice animals—such as the rams carved into the corners—to ask for favor from the gods. The entrails would be read to divine the future, and to determine whether the gods were for or against a particular business venture.

• *Continue straight ahead, then go to the right on the main street. About two blocks down (look for* Tempio Repubblicano *on the corner to the right), Via dei Molini marks the wall of the original military* castrum *(rectangular camp). Before continuing into that oldest part of Ostia, turn right down Via dei Molini, then turn left into the...*

❼ Mill (Molino)

This mill building *(panificio)* dates from A.D. 120. Before you are several lava millstones that were used to grind grain. Study the workings: A bowl-like lower structure carefully cupped a moving upper section. Grain would be sprinkled in from a sack hanging from the ceiling. Mules or workers would power the grinding by walking in circles, pushing inserted wood poles. Powdery flour (with not much grit) would eventually tumble out of the bottom of the mill, ready to be made into bread. A nearby room contains two ovens.

• *Now, backtrack down Via dei Molini and take the first right onto...*

❽ Via Casa di Diana

There are three places of interest along this street: the House of Diana, a tavern, and stairs leading to the second floor of an apartment flat for a commanding view.

The **House of Diana** is a great example of an *insula* (a multistoried tenement complex where the lower-middle class lived). The House of Diana originally had three or four floors (reaching the 66-foot maximum height allowed by Ostia's building codes).

Across the street is an inn called the **Insula of the Thermopolium**. Belly up to this tavern's bar. You'll see display shelves for food and drinks for sale, a small sink, and scant remains of wall paintings.

Across the street, stairs lead to the top floor of the **Insula of** the **Paintings**. Climb these for a good view and a chance to imagine life as an apartment dweller in ancient Rome.

• *Now, walk straight ahead toward the high brick temple that marks Ostia's...*

❾ Forum

Whenever possible, Rome imposed a grid road plan on its conquered cities. After Rome conquered Ostia in about 400 B.C., it built a military camp, or *castrum*—a rectangular fort with east, west, north, and south gates and two main roads converging on the forum. Throughout the empire, Romans found comfort in this familiar city plan.

Ostia's main square became a monumental forum in the imperial period. And dominating this square, like most Roman towns, was the **grand temple** (from A.D. 120). The marble veneer was scavenged in the Middle Ages, leaving only the core brickwork. Note the reinforcement arches in the brick. The temple, called the Capitolium (after the original atop Capitol Hill in Rome), was dedicated to the pagan trinity of Jupiter, Juno, and Minerva. A forum dominated by a Capitolium temple was a standard feature of colonies throughout the empire. The purpose: to transport the Roman cult of Jupiter, Juno, and Minerva to the newly conquered population.

Opposite the Capitolium is the **Temple of Roma and Augustus.** Its position is powerfully symbolic. The power of the emperor stands equal, facing the power of the Capitolium Triad.

The **basilica** (from about A.D. 100) lines the side of the forum. This is where legal activities and commercial business took place. Its central nave and two side aisles lead to the "high altar" where the judge sat.

Behind the Capitolium temple, the pink, modern building houses the fine little **Ostia Museum**. Behind that is a shop and a modern cafeteria (with a tiny Tiber view). And Decumanus Maximus continues through the forum into a vast urban expanse, great for simply wandering (see "Archaeological Scavenger Hunt," below).

• *But first, make one more stop. From the forum, a street marked by a grand arch (as you're facing the Temple of Roma and Augustus, it's on your left) leads to Ostia's best and largest baths (entrance on right).*

❿ Forum Baths (Terme del Foro)

As you wander around this huge complex, try to imagine it peopled, steaming, and busy. Government-subsidized baths were a popular social and business meeting place in any Roman city. Roman engineers were experts at radiant heat. A huge furnace heated both the water and air that flowed through pipes under the floors and in

Housing in Ancient Rome

In ancient times, the lower classes lived in miserable, cramped apartment buildings, an average of five floors high (the highest was 10 floors). People living on the higher floors climbed treehouse-type stairs to get to their rooms.

Made cheaply of wood and with weak foundations, many buildings burned or collapsed. The apartments had no heat, no kitchen (food was cooked or purchased elsewhere), and no plumbing. Garbage was tossed out the windows. Chariot and cart traffic were allowed only at night, with the noise (increased by the absence of glass in windows) making sleeping a challenge.

The wealthier classes, on the other hand, lived in sprawling and luxurious homes. These were generally built on one floor, with a series of rooms facing a central open courtyard. Decorative pools collected rainwater. Statues, mosaics, and frescoes were everywhere. Rome's wealthy were as comfortable as the poor were wretched.

the walls. Notice the fine marble steps—great for lounging—that led to the pools. People used olive oil rather than soap to wash, so the water needed to be periodically skimmed by servants. The octagonal room (for sunbathing) leads to the elliptical *laconicum* (sweating room), two *tepidaria* (where Romans were rubbed down by masseuses), and the once-steamy *caldarium* with three pools.

From the baths, you can look across the street to the 20-hole **latrine** (across from the entry to the baths). You can still see the pivot hole in the floor that once supported its revolving door. The cutout below the seat was to accommodate the washable sponge on a stick, which was used rather than toilet paper. Rushing water below each seat (brought in by aqueduct) did the flushing.

OSTIA MUSEUM

This small museum (**⓫**) offers a delightful look at some of Ostia's finest statuary. Without worrying too much about exactly what's what, just wander and imagine these fine statues—tangled wrestlers, kissing cupids, playful gods—adorning the courtyards of wealthy Ostia families. Most of the statues are second- and third-century A.D. Roman pieces inspired by rare and famous Greek originals. The portrait busts are of real people—the kind you'd sit next to in the baths (or toilets).

A forte of Roman sculptors was realistic busts. Roman religion revered the man of the house (and his father and grandfather). A statue of daddy and grandpa was common in the corner of any proper house. Also, with the emperor considered a god, you'd find his bust in classrooms, at the post office, and so on.

The sarcophagi (marble coffins) generally show mythological scenes of Dionysus, the Greek god who relates to the afterlife and immortality. A few humble frescoes give a feeling for how living quarters may have been "wallpapered."

Perhaps the most interesting room (to the left as you enter) features statuary from religions of foreign lands. Being a port town, Ostia accommodated people (and their worship needs) from all over the known world. The large statue of a man sacrificing a bull is a Mithraic altarpiece.

The **cafeteria** and **shop** are in a modern building just behind the museum.

ARCHAEOLOGICAL SCAVENGER HUNT

As you return to the entry gate, get off the main drag and explore Ostia's back streets. Wandering beyond the forum and then taking the back lanes as you return to the entry, see if you can find:
- Tarp- and sand-protected mosaic flooring.
- White cornerstones put into buildings to fend off wild carts and reflect corners in the dark.
- Fast-food fish joint (on Decumanus Maximus, just beyond the forum).
- Hidden bits of fresco (clue: under hot tin roofs).
- Republican buildings and buildings dating from the empire.
- Stucco roughed up for fresco work (before applying the wet plaster of a fresco, the surface needs to be systematically gouged so the plaster can grip the wall).
- Mill stones for grinding grain (Ostia's big industry).
- Floor patterns made colorful with sliced columns.
- A *domus* (single-family dwellings always faced a fancy, central open-air courtyard).

TIVOLI DAY TRIP

At the edge of the Sabine Hills, 18 miles east of Rome, sits the medieval hill town of Tivoli, a popular retreat since ancient times. Today, it's famous for two very different villas: Hadrian's Villa (the emperor's Versailles-like place of government, which enabled him to rule from outside but still near the capital city), and recently restored Villa d'Este (the lush and watery residence of a cardinal in exile).

The town of Tivoli, with Villa d'Este in its center, is about 2.5 miles from Hadrian's Villa (Villa Adriana in Italian). The **TI** is on Largo Garibaldi near the bus stop (closed Mon, tel. 0774-311-249).

Note that Hadrian's Villa is open daily and Villa d'Este is closed on Monday.

Getting to Tivoli

Tivoli is famous, but a pain to reach. (See map on page 291.) From Rome, take a Metro/bus combination. Ride Metro line B to Ponte Mammolo, then take the local blue LILA/Cotral bus (every 10 min, direction: Tivoli). For Hadrian's Villa, take the bus labeled *autostrada* (2/hr, confirm destination with driver), which will drop you 300 yards from the gate; the other, non-autostrada bus leaves you a half-mile hike from the villa. Both buses continue to Tivoli.

Context Rome, Rome Walks, and Through Eternity each offer private tours of the villas (see their respective Web sites for specifics, listed on page 33).

Hadrian's Villa

Built at the peak of the empire by Hadrian (ruled A.D. 117–138), this was the emperor's retreat from the political complexity of court life in Rome. The Spanish-born Hadrian—an architect, lover of Greek

culture (nicknamed "The Little Greek"), and great traveler—created a microcosm of the cosmopolitan Roman Empire, which at that point stretched from Scotland to the Euphrates and encompassed countless diverse cultures. In the spirit of Legoland, Epcot Center, and Las Vegas, he re-created famous structures from around the world, creating a kind of diorama of his empire in the form of the largest and richest Roman villa anywhere. Just as Louis XIV ruled France from Versailles rather than Paris, Hadrian ruled Rome from this villa of more than 300 evocative acres. He basically spent his last decade here.

Start your visit at the plastic model of the villa. Find the Egyptian Canopus (sanctuary of the god Serapis, a canal lined with statues), the Greek Pecile (from Athens), and the Teatro Marittimo (a circular palace, Hadrian's favorite retreat on an island where he did his serious thinking). Regrettably, this "Versailles of Ancient Rome" was plundered by barbarians. The marble was burned to make lime for cement. The art was scavenged and wound up in the Vatican Museum, the Louvre, and other museums throughout Europe.

While getting to Hadrian's Villa is complicated and time-consuming, many find it well worth the trouble.

Cost and Hours: €8.50, audioguide-€4, daily from 9:00 until 1 hour before sunset, last entry 1 hour before closing, tel. 0774-382-733.

Villa d'Este

Ippolito d'Este's grandfather, Alexander VI, was the pope...probably the only reason Ippolito became a cardinal. Ippolito's claim to fame: his pleasure palace at Tivoli. In the 1550s, Ippolito destroyed a Benedictine monastery to build this fanciful, late-Renaissance palace. Like Hadrian's Villa, it's a large residential estate. But this one features hundreds of Baroque fountains, all gravity-powered. The Aniene River, frazzled into countless threads, weaves its way entertainingly through the villa. At the bottom of the garden, the exhausted little streams once again team up to make a sizable river.

The cardinal had a political falling-out with Rome and was exiled. With this watery wonderland on a cool hill with fine views, he made sure Romans would come to visit. It's symbolic of the luxury and secular interests of the cardinal.

After years of disuse, the villa has been completely restored. All the most eye-popping fountains have been put back in operation, and—with the exception of the two highest jets of the central fountain, which are electric-powered—everything still operates on natural hydraulics. A new terrace restaurant has been installed on the highest level of the garden, opportunely placed to catch cool afternoon sea breezes coming in across the plain of Rome.

Ironically, senior travelers—the least able to handle its many stairs—like this villa best.

Cost and Hours: €6.50, audioguide-€4, Tue–Sun 8:30–18:45, closed Mon, closes earlier off-season, last entry 1 hour before closing (tel. 0774-312-070).

NAPLES AND POMPEII DAY TRIP

While the Eternal City can keep you busy for ages, here are two excuses to leave Rome for a day. The trip south to Naples and Pompeii is demanding (6 hours of train travel round-trip), but also rewarding, giving you the chance to wander ancient Rome's most evocative ruins and go on an urban safari in what is perhaps Europe's most intense city.

If you have a week in Rome and are interested in maximum travel thrills, take a day trip to Naples and Pompeii. (See map on page 291.) Note that Naples' Archaeological Museum is closed on Tuesday. Pompeii is open daily.

Naples
(Napoli)

If you like Italy as far south as Rome, go farther south. It gets better. If Italy is getting on your nerves, don't go farther. Italy intensifies as you plunge deeper. Naples is Italy in the extreme—its best (birthplace of pizza and Sophia Loren) and its worst (home of the Camorra, Naples' "family" of organized crime).

Naples—Italy's third-largest city, with more than two million people—has almost no open spaces or parks, which makes its position as Europe's most densely populated city plenty evident. Watching the police try to enforce traffic sanity is almost comical in Italy's grittiest, most polluted, and most crime-ridden city. But Naples surprises the observant traveler with its impressive knack for living, eating, and raising children in the streets with good humor and decency. Overcome your fear of being run down or ripped off long enough to talk with people—enjoy a few smiles and jokes with the man running the neighborhood tripe shop or the woman taking her day-care class on a walk through the traffic. (For a conversation starter, ask a local about the New Year's Eve tradition of tossing chipped dinner plates off of balconies into the streets.)

Twenty-five hundred years ago, Neapolis ("new city") was a thriving Greek commercial center. It remains southern Italy's leading city, offering a fascinating collection of museums, churches, and eclectic architecture.

The pulse of Italy throbs in Naples. Like Cairo or Bombay, it's appalling and captivating at the same time, the closest thing to "reality travel" that you'll find in western Europe. But this tangled mess still somehow manages to breathe, laugh, and sing—with a captivating Italian accent.

Planning Your Time

Breakfast on the early Rome–Naples express (about 7:00–9:00). From Naples, go directly to Pompeii, either by taxi or by Circumvesuviana (commuter train that leaves from the basement of the central train station). Tour the excavation (11:00–14:00), then take a taxi or the same train back to Naples. Visit the Archaeological Museum, do the Naples urban-jungle walk, have pizza in its birthplace, and ride the late evening train (2 hrs) back to Rome. In the afternoon, Naples' street life slows and many sights close as the temperature soars. The city comes back to life in the early evening.

Arrival in Naples

There are several Naples stations. You want Napoli Centrale (facing Piazza Garibaldi), which has a Circumvesuviana stop for commuter trains to Pompeii, baggage check, and a TI (Mon–Sat 8:30–20:00, maybe also Sun 9:00–13:00, with your back to the tracks, TI is in the lobby to your left, look for *Ente Provinciale Turismo* sign, for info call 081-402-394).

While on the train to Naples, ask the conductor which Naples stations your train stops at. Centrale is ideal (but it's a dead-end station, so many through trains stop at Piazza Garibaldi, which is actually a subway station just downstairs from Centrale). If your train does not stop at Centrale or Garibaldi, get off at the Mergellina station (has a TI) or Campi Flegrei station. Campi Flegrei and Mergellina are connected to Centrale by a direct subway route; a railpass or train ticket to Napoli Centrale covers the ride (subway trains depart about every 10 min). Be on the lookout for thievery (see "Theft Alert," below).

Continuing to Pompeii: For about €70–80, you can take a **taxi** from Naples to Pompeii; agree on a fixed price without the meter and pay upon arrival.

Naples and Pompeii are connected by a **commuter train**—the Ferrovia Circumvesuviana—handy for tourists, commuters, and

Naples

pickpockets. Catch it in the basement of Naples' central train station; look for the ticket windows marked *Circumvesuviana*. Schedules are posted on the wall. When you buy your ticket, ask which track your train will depart from (*"Che binario?"*—kay bee-NAH-ree-oh). Don't go through the turnstiles (for the Metro) opposite the ticket windows. Instead, continue down the corridor and jog right when it does, down another long corridor that has turnstiles at the end (insert your ticket). The platforms are just beyond. Two trains per hour, marked "Sorrento," get you to Pompeii in 40 minutes (€2.20 one-way, not covered by railpasses; check schedule carefully or confirm with a local before boarding to make sure the train is going to Pompeii). The faster express trains are marked "DD" on the schedule (12/day). When returning to Naples Centrale station on the Circumvesuviana, get off at the second-to-last station, the Collegamento FS or Garibaldi stop (Centrale station is just up the escalator).

Theft Alert: Err on the side of caution. Don't venture into neighborhoods that make you uncomfortable. Walk with confidence, as if you know where you're going and what you're doing. Assume able-bodied beggars are thieves. Tighten your money belt and keep it completely hidden. Stick to busy streets and beware of gangs of hoodlums. A third of the city is unemployed, and past local governments set an example that the Mafia would be proud of. Assume con artists are cleverer than you. Any jostle or commotion is probably a thief-team smokescreen. Any bags are probably kept safest when checked at the central train station (daily 7:00–23:00, *deposito bagagli* near track #24).

Perhaps your biggest risk of theft is while catching or riding the Circumvesuviana commuter train. Remember, if you're connecting from a major train, you'll be stepping from a relatively secure compartment into a crowded Naples subway filled with thieves hunting disoriented American tourists with luggage. While I ride the Circumvesuviana comfortably and safely, each year I hear of many who get ripped off on this ride. You won't be mugged—just conned or pickpocketed. Con artists may say you need to "transfer" by taxi to catch the Circumvesuviana; you don't. Anyone offering to help you with your bags is likely a thief, despite displayed credentials. There are no porters at the Centrale station or in the basement where the Circumvesuviana station is located. Wear your money belt, hang on to your bag, and don't display any valuables.

Getting Around Naples

Naples' subway, the Servizio Metropolitano, runs from the Centrale station through the center of town (direction: Pozzuoli), stopping at Piazza Cavour (Archaeological Museum), Piazza Dante, and Montesanto (top of Spanish Quarter and Spaccanapoli). Tickets are €1 and good for 90 minutes. All-day tickets cost €3. If you can afford a taxi, don't mess with the buses. A short taxi ride costs about €5 (insist on the meter; €2 supplement after 22:00, €1.50 supplement charged on Sun).

Getting to the Museum: From the Centrale train station, follow signs to *Metropolitano* (downstairs, buy tickets from yellow kiosk opposite Circumvesuviana ticket windows, ask which track—*"Binario?"*—to Piazza Cavour, it's usually track 4, *quattro*, direction Pozzuoli; go through a *solo metropolitano* turnstile and ride the subway one stop). As you leave the Metro, follow signs to *linea 1* through the underpass to the yellow Metro line. Take the elevator or escalators up. At the top, head left around the corner and follow signs to *Museo*. Go right at the top of the stairs and either surface to street level or continue to the museum down the corridor (to your left at 11 o'clock).

SIGHTS

▲▲▲**Museo Archeologico**—For lovers of antiquity, this museum alone makes Naples a worthwhile stop. It offers the best possible peek into the artistic jewelry boxes of Pompeii and Herculaneum. The actual sights are impressive but barren; the finest art and all the artifacts ended up here.

Cost, Hours, and Information: €6.50, extra for special exhibits, Wed–Mon 8:30–19:00, closed Tue. For a guided visit, try to find Pina—look for her licensed guide nametag. She pulls together small groups for €10 tours (at least 1.5 hrs). To visit the **Secret Room**—which contains lascivious art from Pompeii—you may have to make an appointment as you enter (depends on crowds, ask when you buy your ticket; see below for description). Audioguides cost €4 (at ticket desk, rentable for 3 hrs). Photos are allowed without a flash. The shop sells a worthwhile green guidebook, titled *National Archeological Museum of Naples* (€7.50). Bag check is obligatory and free.

Orientation: Be warned that the entire museum is in flux—everything is being moved around and renovated. Try to get an up-to-date floor plan as you enter. The huge first floor (top of the grand staircase) contains bronze statues from Herculaneum (a nearby town destroyed in the same eruption that devastated Pompeii), frescoes from Pompeii, and vases from Paestum (a temple complex south of Naples, part of a once-thriving region known as Greater Greece). The Pompeii mosaics and the Secret Room (Gabinetto Segreto), are on the small mezzanine level (up the grand staircase and to the left). The Farnese Collection of marble statues is on the ground floor (turn right past the staircase). Stairs behind the grand staircase lead to the basement WCs. If you can't find a particular work, ask a museum custodian, *"Dov'è?"* ("Where?"), followed by the item's name.

Statues, Frescoes, and Artifacts (top floor): Climb the stairs to the top floor. Before you enter the great hall (left), head to the right to visit the collection of bronze statues. These 50 statues (79 B.C. copies of fourth-century B.C. originals) decorated the holiday home (Villa dei Papyri in Herculaneum) of Julius Caesar's father-in-law. Look into the lifelike blue eyes of the two intense *atleta* (athletes) —bent on doing their best. *Resting Hermes* (with his tired little heel wings) is taking a break. The *Drunken Faun* (singing and snapping his fingers to the beat, with a wineskin at his side) is clearly living for today—true to the *carpe diem* preaching of the Epicurean philosophy. Caesar's father-in-law was an Epicurean philosopher, and his library—with 2,000 papyrus scrolls—supported his outlook.

Next, step into the huge hall. This was the great hall of the university (17th and 18th centuries) until the building became the royal museum in 1777. The sundial (from 1791) still works. At noon, a sunray strikes the spot indicating today's date…if you know your zodiac. With your back to the entrance, the rooms on your left feature the Pompeii frescoes, paintings, and artifacts (including interesting ancient glass). Just beyond the glass objects, a model shows the Pompeii archaeological site circa 1879 *(plastico di Pompeii)*. The wall model shows the site in 2004, after more excavations. The rooms on your right from the great hall feature ancient Greek art: a model of Paestum and ancient vases discovered on-site. If you contrast all of this ancient art with the darkness of medieval Europe, it's easy to see how the classical era inspired and enlightened the Renaissance greats.

House of the Faun Mosaics: On the mezzanine floor below (directly under the bronze statues from Herculaneum), you'll find a small, exquisite collection of Pompeian mosaics. Most of these mosaics were taken from Pompeii's House of the Faun. The house's delightful centerpiece is a 20-inch-high statue of the *Dancing Faun*. This rare surviving Greek bronze statue (from the 4th century B.C.) is surrounded by some of the best mosaics from the age. A highlight is the grand *Battle of Alexander* (a 2nd-century B.C. copy of a 3rd-century B.C. Greek original). It decorated a floor in the House of the Faun. It was found intact; the damage you see occurred as this treasure was moved from Pompeii to the king's collection here. The painting (on left, made before it was moved) shows how it once looked. Notice the dynamism, shading, perspective—everything the Renaissance artists worked so hard to accomplish.

The **Secret Room (Gabinetto Segreto)**, on the other side of the partition from the *Battle of Alexander* mosaic, contains a sizable assortment of erotic frescoes, well-spun pottery, and perky statues that once decorated bedrooms, meeting rooms, brothels, and even shops at Pompeii and Herculaneum. Sometimes you'll have to make an appointment to view the room (see "Orientation," above), and at those times, you might also be escorted by local guide (offering a 20-minute tour primarily in Italian but, if you ask nicely, likely in English). Even without a guide, the art speaks for itself (and comes with good printed descriptions in English).

These bawdy statues and frescoes—often found in Pompeii's grandest houses—were entertainment for guests. (By the time they made it to this museum, in 1819, the frescoes could only be viewed with permission from the king.) The Roman nobles commissioned the wildest scenes imaginable. Think of them as ancient dirty jokes: a faun playfully pulling the sheet off a beautiful woman, only to be grossed out by the plumbing of a hermaphrodite. (Perhaps the original *"Mamma mia!"*) Find the homosexual pygmies from Africa in action. Venus, the patron goddess of Pompeii, was a favorite pin-up girl. In a particularly high-quality statue, a goat and a satyr illustrate the sin of sodomy.

The room full of phallic talismans make the point that a massive penis was not necessarily a sexual symbol, but a magical amulet used against the evil eye. The phallus symbolized fertility, happiness, good luck, riches, straight A's, and general well-being. Across from the talismans, a room is furnished and decorated as an ancient brothel might have been (c. A.D. 79).

So, now that your travel buddy is finally showing a little interest in art...the best stuff awaits downstairs.

Farnese Collection (ground floor): The museum's ground floor alone has enough Greek and Roman art to put any museum on the map. Its highlight is the Farnese

Collection, a grand hall of huge, bright, and wonderfully restored statues excavated from Rome's Baths of Caracalla. The *Toro Farnese*—a tangled group with a woman being tied to a bull—is the largest intact statue from antiquity and (at 13 feet) the tallest ancient marble group ever found. Actually a third-century A.D. copy of a lost bronze Hellenistic original, it was carved out of one piece of marble. It was "restored" by Michelangelo and others at the pope's request—meaning that they integrated surviving bits into a new work. Panels on the wall show which pieces are actually by Michelangelo (in blue on the chart: the head of the boy in front, the upper part of the aunt, and the dog).

Here's the story: Once upon an ancient Greek time, King Lykos was bewitched by Dirce and abandoned his pregnant wife (standing regally in the background). The single mom gave birth to twin boys (shown here), who grew up to kill their deadbeat dad and tie Dirce to the horns of a bull to be bashed against a mountain. You can almost hear the bull snorting.

At the far end of the hall (opposite the *Toro*, behind Hercules), a small room contains the sumptuous Farnese Cup, a large ancient cameo made of agates (2nd century B.C., from Egypt). Its decorations are both Egyptian (the Nile toting a lush cornucopia) and Greek (Medusa's head).

Don't leave without visiting *Doriforo*. (Ask a guard, *"Dov'è il Doriforo?"*) This seven-foot-tall "spear-thrower" (the literal translation of *doriforo*) is a marble copy of a fifth-century B.C. bronze original by Polycletus. Found in a Pompeii gym, it inspired athletes with the ideal proportions of Greek beauty. This most-copied Greek statue—so full of motion, and so realistic in its *contrapposto* pose (weight on one foot) —inspired Donatello and Michelangelo.

▲▲▲**The Slice-of-Neapolitan-Life Walk**—Walk from the museum through the heart of town and back to the station (allow at least 2 hours, plus a pizza and sightseeing stops). Sights are listed in the order you'll see them on this walk.

Naples, a living medieval city, is its own best sight. Couples artfully make love on Vespas surrounded by more fights and smiles per cobblestone than anywhere else in Italy. Rather than seeing Naples as a list of sights, see the one great museum and then capture its essence by taking this walk through the core of the city. Should you become overwhelmed or lost, step into a store and ask for directions: "Where is the train station?" in Italian is *"Dov'è la stazione centrale?"* (DOH-vay lah staht-zee-OH-nay chen-TRAH-lay?). Or point to the next sight in this book.

Via Toledo and the Spanish Quarter (city walk, first half): Leaving the Archaeological Museum at the top of Piazza Cavour (Metro: Piazza Cavour), cross the street and walk through the ornate galleria (the grand, arched gallery) on your way to Via Pessina to your right. The first part of this walk is a straight one-mile ramble down this boulevard to Galleria Umberto I near the Royal Palace.

Busy Via Pessina leads downhill to Piazza Dante—marked by a statue of **Dante.** Originally, a statue of a Spanish Bourbon king stood here. The grand red-and-gray building is typical of the Bourbon buildings from that period. In 1861, with the unification of Italy, the king (symbolic of Italy's colonial subjugation) was replaced by Dante—considered the father of the Italian language and a strong symbol of Italian nationalism.

Poor old Dante looks out over the urban chaos with a hopeless gesture. The **Alba Gate,** part of Naples' old wall and the entrance to a small street often lined with street-side book vendors, is to Dante's left. Via Pessina, the long, straight road that we're walking, originated as a military road built by Spain around 1600. It skirted the old town wall to connect the Spanish military headquarters (now the museum) with the Royal Palace (down by the bay).

A new subway station has recently been built here on Piazza Dante. Construction was slowed by the city's rich underground history: 15 feet down—Roman ruins, 25 feet down—Greek ruins.

Continue walking downhill, remembering that here in Naples red traffic lights are considered "decorations." Try to cross with a local. The people here are survivors; a long history of corrupt and greedy colonial overlords has taught Neapolitans to deal with authority creatively. Many credit this aspect of Naples' past for the advent of organized crime here.

The Slice-of-Neapolitan-Life Walk

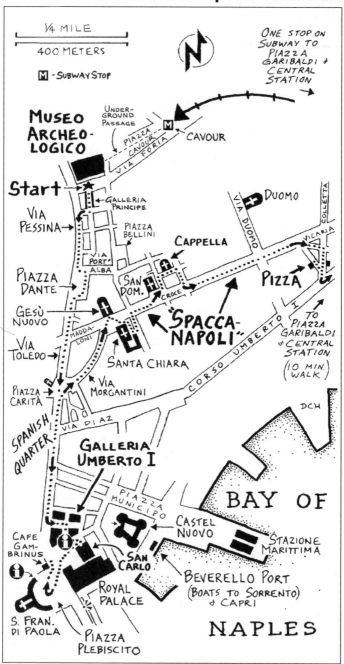

Via Pessina becomes Via Toledo, Naples' principal shopping street. In 1860, from the white marble balcony (on the neoclassical building) overlooking Piazza Sette Settembre, the famous revolutionary Garibaldi declared Italy united and Victor Emmanuel its first king. A year later, the dream of Italian unity was actually realized.

Continue straight on Via Toledo (even though the arterial jogs left). At the next left (Via Maddaloni), about three blocks below Piazza Dante, you cross the long, straight street called **Spaccanapoli** (literally, "split Naples"). Look left. Look right. Since ancient times, this thin street (which changes names several times) has bisected the city. (We'll be returning to this street later. If you want to abbreviate this walk, turn left here and skip down to the Spaccanapoli section.)

Via Toledo runs through Piazza Carità (also known by its new name, Piazza Salvo d'Acquisto), with fascist architecture (from 1938, sternly straight and obedient lines) overlooking the square. Wander down Via Toledo a few blocks, past more fascist architecture—the two banks on the left. Try robbing the second one (Banco di Napoli, Via Toledo 178).

Up the hill to your right is the **Spanish Quarter,** Naples at its rawest, poorest, and most historic. Thrill-seekers (or someone in need of a prostitute) can take a stroll up one of these streets and loop back to Via Toledo.

The only thing predictable about this Neapolitan tide pool is the ancient grid plan of its streets (which survives from Greek times), the friendliness of its shopkeepers, and the boldness of its mopeds. Concerned locals will tug on their lower eyelids, warning you to be wary. Pop into a grocery shop and ask the man to make you his best ham-and-mozzarella sandwich. Trust him on the price—it should be around €3.

Continue down Via Toledo (with more people than cars) to the immense Piazza Plebiscito, which celebrates the 1861 vote when Naples chose to join Italy. From here, you'll see the Church of San Francesco di Paola with its Pantheon-inspired dome and broad, arcing colonnades. Opposite is the **Royal Palace,** which has housed Spanish, French, and even Italian royalty. Each of the eight kings in the niches is from a different dynasty (left to right: Norman, German, French, Spanish, Spanish, Spanish, French—the brother-in-law of Napoleon—and, finally, Italian: Victor Emmanuel II, King of Savoy). The statues were done at the request of V.E. II's son, so his dad is the most dashing of the group.

The huge and lavish palace welcomes the public (€4, Thu–Tue 9:00–19:00, closed Wed, shorter hours off-season, last entry 1 hr before closing, audioguide-€4/1 person, €5/2 people). Next door, peek inside the neoclassical Teatro San Carlo, Italy's second-most-respected opera house—after Milan's La Scala (guided visit-€5, English tours  about every 20 min, Mon–Sat 9:00–18:00, closed Sun, tel. 081-664-545). The huge castle on the harborfront just beyond the palace houses government bureaucrats and the Civic Museum, featuring 14th- to 16th-century art (€5, Mon–Sat 9:00–19:00, closed Sun).

Under the Victorian iron and glass of the 100-year-old **Galleria Umberto I**, enjoy a coffee break or sample a unique Neapolitan pastry called *sfogliatella* (crispy scallop shell-shaped pastry filled with sweet ricotta cheese). Go through the tall yellow arch at the end of Via Toledo or across from the opera house. Gawk up.

Once inside, **Gambrinus Café**—taking you back to the elegance of 1860—is the classic place for a *sfogliatella*. Or you might prefer the mushroom-shaped, rum-soaked doughnuts called *baba* (huge variety). Pay double to sit, or stand at the bar.

Spaccanapoli back to the station (city walk, second half): To continue your walk, double back up Via Toledo to Piazza Carità, veering right on Via Morgantini to Via Maddaloni. You're back at the straight-as-a-Greek-arrow street, Spaccanapoli—formerly the main thoroughfare of the Greek city of Neapolis.

The rest of this walk is basically a straight line down the series of streets locals have nicknamed Spaccanapoli. Stop at Piazza Gesù Nuovo to visit the two bulky old churches. The square is marked by a towering monument to the Counter-Reformation (Baroque, early 18th century). With Naples' Spanish heritage, Jesuits were powerful here. But locals never attacked Protestants with the full fury of the Spanish Inquisition.

Check out the austere, fortress-like church of **Gesù Nuovo**. The unique pyramid grill facade was from a fortress (1470), which predated the church (1600s). Step inside for a brilliant Baroque interior. The second chapel on the right features a much-kissed statue of Giuseppe Moscati, a Christian doctor famous for helping the poor. Moscati was made a saint in 1987. Continue on to the third chapel and enter the Sala Moscati for a huge room filled with *Ex Voto*—tiny red-and-silver plaques of thanksgiving for miracles attributed to Saint Moscati. Each has a relief symbolic of the ailment cured. Naples' practice of *Ex Voto*, while incorporated into its Catholic rituals, goes back to its pagan Greek roots. A glass case displays possessions and photos of the great doctor. As you leave, notice the big bomb casing hanging in the corner. It fell through the church's dome in 1943 but never exploded...yet another miracle.

Across the street, the simpler Gothic church of **Santa Chiara** dates from a period of French Angevin rule (14th century). Notice the stark Gothic/Baroque contrast between this church and the Gesù Nuovo. The faded Trinity (from the school of Giotto, left of entry) is an example of the fine frescoes that once covered the walls (most removed during Baroque times). The altar is adorned with the finely carved Gothic tomb of an Angevin king. The Bourbon chapel, stacked with Bourbon royalty, is just to the right (both churches free, Mon–Sat 6:30–13:30 & 16:00–18:30, Sun 6:30–16:00).

Continue straight down traffic-free Via B. Croce. Since this is a university district, you'll see lots of students and bookstores. This neighborhood is also extremely superstitious. You may see incense-burning women with carts of good-luck charms for sale. At Via Santa Chiara, a detour left leads to shops of antique musical instruments.

The next square is Piazza S. Domenico Maggiore—marked by an ornate 17th-century plague monument. The venerable **Scaturchio Pasticceria** is another good place to try Naples' *sfogliatella* pastry (€1.30 to go, costs double at a table on the square, daily 7:20–20:40).

From this square, detour left along the right side of the castle-like church, then follow yellow signs and take first right for one block to **Cappella Sansevero** (€5, Mon & Wed–Sat 10:00–18:00, Sun 10:00–13:30, closed Tue, Via de Sanctis 19). No photos are allowed in the chapel (postcards available in gift shop).

This small chapel is a Baroque explosion mourning the body of Christ, who lies on a soft pillow under an incredibly realistic veil. It's also the personal chapel of Raimondo de Sangro, an eccentric Freemason. The monuments to his relatives have a second purpose: to share the Freemason philosophy of freedom through enlightenment. For example, the statue of *Despair* struggling with a marble rope net (carved out of a single piece of marble) shows how knowledge—in the guise of an angel—frees the human mind.

Study the incredible *Veiled Christ* in the center. It's all carved out of marble and is like no other statue I've seen (by Giuseppe "howdeedoodat" Sammartino, 1753). The Christian message (Jesus died for our salvation) is accompanied by a Freemason message. (The veil represents how the body and ego are an obstacle to real spiritual freedom.) As you walk from Christ's feet to his head, notice how the expression of Jesus' face goes from suffering to peace. When you stand directly behind Him, the veil over the face and knees disappears.

Pizza in Naples

Naples, baking just the right combination of fresh dough, mozzarella, and tomatoes in traditional wood-burning ovens, is the birthplace of pizza. Drop by one of the two most traditional pizzerias. **Antica Pizzeria da Michele**, a few blocks from the train station, is for purists (Mon–Sat 10:00–24:00, closed Sun, filled with locals; from the station, head to the left off Piazza Garibaldi, turn left onto Corso Umberto—juts off Piazza Garibaldi at 11 o'clock with the station to your back—then turn right on Via Pietro Colletta, look

for the vertical, red *Antica Pizzeria* sign, tel. 081-553-9204). It serves two kinds: *margherita* (tomato sauce and mozzarella) or *marinara* (tomato sauce, oregano, and garlic, no cheese). A pizza with beer costs €5. Some locals prefer **Pizzeria Trianon** across the street. Da Michele's archrival offers more choices, higher prices (€3.50–7), air-conditioning, and a cozier atmosphere. In their entryway pizza kitchen, you can survey the evolution of a humble wad of dough into a smoldering, bubbly feast (daily 10:00–15:30 & 18:30–23:00, Via Pietro Colletta 42, tel. 081-553-9426).

Raimondo de Sangro, an inventor, created the deep green pigment used on the ceiling fresco. To the right of *Despair* and the net, an inlaid M.C. Escher-esque maze on the floor leads to de Sangro's tomb. The maze is another Freemason reminder of the importance of how the quest for knowledge gets you out of the maze of life. Your Sansevero finale is downstairs: two mysterious...skeletons. Perhaps another of the mad inventor's fancies: injecting a corpse with a fluid to fossilize the veins so that they'll survive the body's decomposition.

Return to Via B. Croce, turn left, and continue your Spaccanapoli cultural scavenger hunt. At the intersection of Via Nilo, find the statue of *The Body of Naples* on your left, with the abundant cornucopia symbolizing the abundance of Naples. (I asked a Neapolitan man to describe the local women, who are famous for their beauty. He replied simply, "Abundant.") This intersection is considered the center of old Naples.

Five yards farther down (on the right) is the tiny **"Chapel of Maradona"**—a niche on the wall dedicated to Diego Maradona, a soccer star who played for Naples in the 1980s. Locals consider soccer almost a religion...and this guy was practically worshipped. You can even see a "hair of Diego" and a teardrop from the city when he went to another team for more money. In later years he was sullied with organized crime, drugs, and police problems.

A few blocks farther, at the little square, Via San Gregorio Armeno leads left into a very colorful district (kitschy Baroque church on left with a Vesuvius lava shrine in its portico, lots of shops selling tiny components of fantastic manger scenes).

As Via B. Croce becomes Via S. Biagio dei Librai, notice the gold and silver shops. Some say stolen jewelry ends up here, is melted down immediately, and appears in a salable form as soon as it cools. The wonderful Sr. Grassi runs the Ospedale delle Bambole (doll hospital) at #81.

Cross busy Via Duomo. The street and side-street scenes along Via Vicaria intensify. This is known as a center of the Camorra (organized crime). Paint a picture with these thoughts: Naples has the most intact street plan of any ancient Roman city. Imagine this city then (retain these images as you visit Pompeii), with street-side shop-fronts that close up after dark to form private homes. Today, it's just one more page in a 2,000-year-old story of a city: all kinds of meetings, beatings, and cheatings; kisses, near misses, and little-boy pisses.

You name it, it occurs right on the streets today, as it has since ancient times. People ooze from crusty corners. Black-and-white death announcements add to the clutter on the walls. Widows sell

cigarettes from buckets. For a peek behind the scenes in the shade of wet laundry, venture down a few side streets. Buy two carrots as a gift for the woman on the fifth floor if she'll lower her bucket to pick them up. The neighborhood action seems best at about 18:00.

At the tiny fenced-in triangular park, veer right onto Via Forcella. Turning right on busy Via Pietro Colletta, walk 50 yards and step into the North Pole. Reward yourself for surviving this safari with a stop at the oldest *gelateria* in Naples (since 1931), **Polo Nord Gelateria** (Mon–Sat 10:00–24:00, Sun 10:00–14:00 & 17:00–24:00, sample their *bacio* or "kiss" flavor before ordering, Via Pietro Colletta 41). Via Pietro Colletta leads past Napoli's two most competitive **pizzerias** (see "Pizza in Naples" sidebar) to Corso Umberto.

Turn left on the grand-boulevardian Corso Umberto. From here to the station, it's a 10-minute walk (if you're tired, hop on a bus; they all go to the station). To finish the walk, continue on Corso Umberto—past a gauntlet of purse/CD/sunglasses salesmen and shady characters hawking stolen camcorders—to the vast, ugly Piazza Garibaldi. On the far side is the Centrale station.

Markets—Naples' **fish market** is fun for photos, with sawed-off swordfish, wriggly eels in pans, and mussels taking a shower. It's at Piazza Nolana, a few blocks southwest of the train station (at the piazza, follow your nose and go through the old gate; market spills down small street, Vico Sopramuro). A bigger **general market** starts at the far corner of Piazza Capuana (several blocks northwest of the train station), filling the street Via Sant'Antonio Abate with a mix of clothes, olives, bags of gnocchi, hanging hams, shoes, produce, umbrellas, and shoppers on foot or on Vespas (both markets open Mon–Sat 7:00–18:00, Sun 8:00–13:00).

Pompeii

Stopped in its tracks by the eruption of Mount Vesuvius in A.D. 79, Pompeii offers the best look anywhere at what life in Rome must have been like 2,000 years ago. An entire city of well-preserved ruins is yours to explore. A thriving commercial port of 20,000, Pompeii grew from Greek and Etruscan roots to become an important Roman city. Then it was buried under 30 feet of hot mud and volcanic ash. For archaeologists, this was a shake-and-bake windfall, teaching them almost all they know about daily Roman life. Pompeii was rediscovered in the 1600s; excavations began in 1748.

Getting to Pompeii: Pompeii is about 30 minutes from Naples by direct Circumvesuviana train (€2.20 one-way, not covered by railpasses, at least hourly). Make sure you're on the Naples–Sorrento train line. Get off at the "Pompei Scavi, Villa dei Misteri" stop. Check your bag at the train station (at the bar, €1.50, pick up by 19:00, 18:00 Oct–Feb), or, better yet, at the Pompeii site for free. From the train station, turn right and walk down the road about a block to the entrance (first left turn). The TI is farther down the street, but not a necessary stop for your visit.

Cost, Hours, Information: €10, or €18 combo-ticket includes Herculaneum and three lesser sites (valid 3 days), April–Oct daily 8:30–19:30, Nov–March daily 8:30–17:00. The ticket office closes 1.5 hours before closing time. A good map is included with admission (pick up at TI window left of WCs; for more information, check www.pompeiisites.org). A free baggage check is near the site entrance turnstiles (retrieve bags by 19:20).

Stop by the bookshop. A guidebook on Pompeii makes this site more meaningful. The small Pompeii and Herculaneum "Past and Present" book has a helpful text and allows you to re-create the ruins with plastic overlays—with the "present" actually being 1964 (available for €11 in bookstore unless they're "finished"; if you buy

Circumvesuviana Stops between Naples and Pompeii

I list these so that you can look at the scenery instead of your watch.

Napoli
Napoli Collegamento FS
    (a.k.a. Piazza Garibaldi;
    below Centrale station)
Gianturco
S. Giovanni
Barra
S. Maria d. Pozzo
S. Giorgio
Cavalli di Bronzo
Bellavista
V. Liberta

Ercolano Scavi
    (Herculaneum)
Ercolano Miglio d'Oro
Torre del Greco
V.S. Antonio
V. del Monte
V. Monaci
Villa della Ginestra
Leopardi
V. Viuli
Trecase
Torre Annunziata
Pompei Scavi (Pompeii site)

from a street vendor, pay no more than €11).

Good audioguides are available at the ticket booth for €6.50 (2 for €10, ID required). Live guides cluster near the ticket booth. If you gather 10 people, the price is reasonable when split (about €10 apiece, total cost about €115, 2 hrs). For a local guide, consider Gaetano Manfredi (tel. 081-863-9816, mobile 338-725-5620).

Background: Pompeii was a booming Roman trading city. Most streets would have been lined with stalls and jammed with customers from sunup to sundown. Chariots vied with shoppers for street space, and many streets were off-limits to chariots during shopping hours (you'll still see street signs with pictures of men carrying vases—this meant pedestrians only).

Fountains overflowed into the streets, flushing the gutters into the sea (thereby cleaning the streets). The stones you see at intersections allowed pedestrians to cross the constantly gushing streets. A single stone designated a one-way street (just enough room for one chariot, stone straddled by its two oxen), and two stones meant a two-way chariot street. There were no posh neighborhoods. Rich and poor mixed it up, as elegant homes existed side by side with simple homes throughout Pompeii. While nearby Herculaneum would have been a classier place to live (traffic-free streets, more elegant homes, far better drainage), Pompeii was the place for action and shopping. It served its estimated 20,000 residents with more than 40 bakeries, 30 brothels, and 130 bars, restaurants, and hotels. Rome controlled the entire Mediterranean 2,000 years ago—making it a kind of free-trade zone—and Pompeii was a central and booming port. With most buildings covered by brilliant, white ground-marble stucco, Pompeii in A.D. 79 was an impressive town. Remember, Pompeii's best art is in the Naples Archaeological Museum, described above.

Tour of Pompeii

Allow at least three hours to tour the site. Consider the following route, starting at the Porta Marina (town gate) after the ticket booth. Before Vesuvius blew, the sea came nearly to this gate. As you approach the Porta Marina, notice the two openings—big for chariots, small for pedestrians.

From the Porta Marina, Via Marina leads straight to Pompeii's main square, the forum.

The **forum** *(foro)*, Pompeii's commercial, religious, and political center, stands at the intersection of the city's two main streets. While the most ruined part of Pompeii, it's grand nonetheless—with temples, lots of pedestals that once sported statues (now in the museum in Naples), and the basilica (Pompeii's largest building, the ancient equivalent of law courts and stock market—on the right as you enter). The Curia (home of the government) stands at the end of the forum. It's built of brick and mortar, a Roman invention. While brick now, it was once faced with marble. Note that while Pompeii was destroyed by the eruption of A.D. 79, it was also devastated by an earthquake in A.D. 62. It's safe to assume that any brick you see dates from between A.D. 62 and A.D. 79—restoration work done by Pompeians after the quake.

Walk (away from the Curia) along the fenced, roofed area that runs alongside the forum. Behind the iron fence are piles of pottery and, at the end, some eerie casts of volcano victims. With the unification of Italy in the 1860s, national spirit fueled efforts to excavate Pompeii. During this period, archaeologists made these molds (during excavations, when they detected hollows underfoot—left by decomposed bodies—they'd pour liquid plaster into the cavities, let it dry, and dig up the casts).

Such a busy square needed a public toilet. Just past the warehouse, turn left into an ancient public WC. Notice the ditch that led to the sewer (marked by an arch in the corner). The stone supports once held wooden benches with the appropriate holes. Even back then, this area had pay toilets.

Continue on, leaving the forum through the gate at the end. Take an immediate right, then a left. You're on Via del Foro,

Pompeii

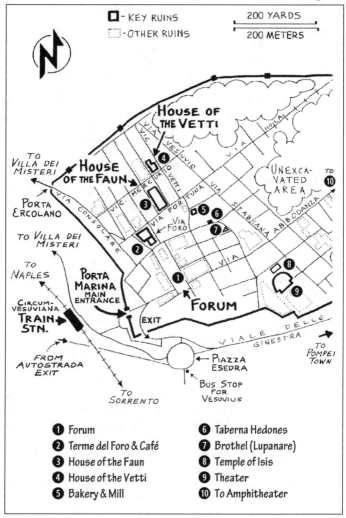

- □ – KEY RUINS
- ⬚ – OTHER RUINS
- 200 YARDS
- 200 METERS

N

TO
VILLA DEI
MISTERI

**HOUSE OF
THE VETTI**

VIA VESUVIO

VIC. DI VETTI

VIA DI MERCURIO

VIA
STABIANA

VIA NOLA

VIA
ABBODANZA

**HOUSE
OF THE FAUN**

PORTA
ERCOLANO

VIA CONSOLARE

VIC.

VIA FORTUNA

VIA
FORO

UNEXCA-
VATED
AREA

TO
⑩

TO VILLA DEI
MISTERI

TO
NAPLES

**PORTA
MARINA
MAIN
ENTRANCE**

VIA

FORUM

CIRCUM-
VESUVIANA
**TRAIN
STN.**

EXIT

FROM
AUTOSTRADA
EXIT

VIALE DELLE
GINESTRA

TO
POMPEI
TOWN

TO
SORRENTO

← PIAZZA
ESEDRA

BUS STOP
FOR
VESUVIUS

- ❶ Forum
- ❷ Terme del Foro & Café
- ❸ House of the Faun
- ❹ House of the Vetti
- ❺ Bakery & Mill
- ❻ Taberna Hedones
- ❼ Brothel (Lupanare)
- ❽ Temple of Isis
- ❾ Theater
- ❿ To Amphitheater

passing a convenient 21st-century cafeteria (decent value, gelato, books, WCs upstairs; a fancier restaurant in a more elegant ancient gymnasium setting is adjacent).

Head down Via del Foro and enter the impressive baths, **Terme del Foro** (on the left, past the cafeteria). You'll enter through the gymnasium. After working out, clients would find four rooms: a waiting room, warm bath *(tepidarium)*, hot bath *(caldarium)*, and cold-plunge bath *(frigidarium)*.

The Eruption of Vesuvius

At noon on August 24, A.D. 79, Mount Vesuvius blew, sending a mushroom cloud of ash, dust, cinders, and rocks 12 miles into the air. It spewed for 18 hours straight, with southerly winds blowing the cloud southward. The white-grey ash settled like snow on Pompeii, collapsing roofs and floors, but leaving the walls intact. Two thousand of the town's 20,000 residents were entombed under eight feet of fine powder.

The next morning, Vesuvius' column of ejected material collapsed, picking up speed as it fell to earth, creating a cloud of ash, pumice, and gas. The red-hot avalanche (a "pyroclastic flow") sped down the side of the mountain at nearly 100 mph. Four minutes later, it engulfed the city of Herculaneum four miles away, burying it in nearly 60 feet of hot mud. The mud cooled into stone, freezing the moment in time.

The *tepidarium* is ringed by mini-statues or *telamones* (male caryatids, figures used as supporting pillars), which divided clients' lockers. They'd undress and warm up here, perhaps stretching out on one of the benches near the bronze heater for a massage. Notice the ceiling: half crushed by the eruption and half surviving, with its fine blue-and-white stucco work.

Next, in the *caldarium*, you'd get hot. Notice the engineering. The double floor was heated from below—so nice with bare feet (look into the grate to see the brick support towers). The double walls with brown terra-cotta tiles held the heat. Romans soaked in the big tub, which was filled with hot water. To keep condensation from dripping annoyingly from the ceiling, the fluting (ribbing) was added to carry the drips down the walls.

Next came the cold plunge in the *frigidarium*—a circular marble basin with the spout spewing frigid water, opposite the entry.

Exit the baths. Notice the oxcart-wheel grooves and stepping stones in the street. In ancient times, rainstorms would turn the streets into filthy rivers. Do as the ancient Romans did. Keep your feet dry by using the stepping stones to cross the street. Directly in front of you is an ancient fast-food stand (notice the holes in the counters for pots). To your left, a few doors down, is the **House of the Tragic Poet** (Casa de Poeta Tragico), with its famous "Beware of Dog" *(Cave Canem)* mosaic in the entryway. On either side, grooves in the doorway indicate a shop with sliding doors.

Face the House of the Tragic Poet, then walk to your right two blocks to the House of the Faun (Casa del Fauno, Danzante). Notice the holes drilled into the curbs—to hitch your animal or perhaps to support an awning from your storefront.

Pompeii's largest home (with 40 rooms), the **House of the Faun**, provided Naples' Archaeological Museum with many of its top treasures, including the original dancing faun (you'll see a copy here) and the famous mosaic of the *Battle of Alexander*. Wander past the welcome mosaic (*HAVE* or "hail to you") and through its courtyards. The back courtyard leads to the exit. It's lined by pillars rebuilt after the A.D. 62 earthquake. Take a close look at the brick, mortar, and fake marble stucco veneer.

Back on the street, turn right and look for the exposed 2,000-year-old lead pipes in the wire cage (ahead and down on the ground to your right). The lead was imported from Roman Britannia. A huge water tank—fed by an aqueduct—stood at the high end of town. Three independent pipe systems supplied water to the city from here: one each for baths, private homes, and public water fountains. In the case of a water shortage, supply could be limited. Democratic priorities prevailed: first the baths were cut, then the private homes. The last water to be cut was that which fed the public fountains (where the people got their water for drinking and cooking).

Take your first left on Vicolo dei Vetti. Enter Pompeii's best-preserved home, the House of the Vetti (Casa dei Vetti).

The **House of the Vetti**, which has retained its mosaics and frescoes, was the bachelor pad of two wealthy merchant brothers. In the entryway, see if you can spot the erection. This is not pornography. There's a meaning here: The penis and the sack of money balance each other on the goldsmith scale above a fine bowl of fruit. The meaning: Only with a balance of fertility and money can you have abundance.

Step into the atrium, with its ceiling open to the sky to collect light and rainwater. The pool, while decorative, was a functional water-supply tank. It's flanked by large money boxes anchored to the floor. The brothers were certainly successful merchants, and possibly moneylenders, too.

Exit on the right, passing the tight servant quarters, and go into the kitchen, with its bronze cooking pots (and a touchable lead pipe on the back wall). The passage dead-ends in the little Venus Room, with its erotic frescoes behind glass.

Return to the atrium and pass into the big colonnaded garden. It was planted according to the plan indicated by traces of roots excavated in the volcanic ash. This courtyard is ringed by richly frescoed entertainment rooms. Circle counterclockwise. The dining room is finely decorated in "Pompeian red" (from iron rust) and black. Study the detail. Notice the lead humidity seal between the wall and the floor, designed to keep the moisture-sensitive frescoes dry. (Had Leonardo taken this clever step, his *Last Supper* in Milan might be in better shape today.) Continuing around, notice the square white stones inlaid in the floor. Imagine them reflecting like cat eyes as the brothers and their friends wandered around by oil lamp late at night. Frescoes in the Yellow Room (near the exit) show off the ancient mastery of perspective, which was not matched elsewhere in Europe for nearly 1,500 years.

Leaving the House of the Vetti, go left past the pipes again. Then turn right, following Vicolo dei Vetti to Via della Fortuna, where you'll see a public fountain. Intersections like this were busy neighborhood centers, where the rent was highest and people gathered.

Turn left on Via della Fortuna and take a quick right on Vicolo Storto, which leads down a curving street to the **bakery and mill** *(forno e mulini)*. The ovens look like a modern-day pizza oven. And the stubby stone towers are flour grinders: After grain was poured into the top, donkeys pushed wooden bars that turned the stones, and eventually powdered grain dropped out of the bottom as flour—flavored with tiny bits of rock.

Take the first left after the bakery onto Via degli Augustali, and check out the mosaics on the left at the Taberna Hedones. This must be the tavern of hedonism—see the cute welcome mosaic, like the one at the House of the Faun, reading *HAVE* ("hail to you"), with the bear licking his wounds.

Next, turn right, over the street dam, and follow the signs to the **brothel** *(lupanare)*, at #18. Prostitutes were nicknamed *lupe* (she-wolves). Wander into the brothel, a simple place with stone beds and pillows. The ancient graffiti includes stroke tallies and exotic names of the women, indicating they came from all corners of the Mediterranean. The faded frescoes above the cells may have served as a kind of menu for services offered. Note the idealized portrayal of women (white, considered beautiful) and men (dark, considered horny). Outside at #17 is a laundry—likely to boil the sheets (thought to guard against venereal disease).

Leaving the brothel, go down the hill to Pompeii's main drag, Via dell'Abbondanza. The forum (and exit) is to the right. (The huge amphitheater—which you can skip—is 10 min to your left.) Go straight down Via dei Teatri, then left before the columns, downhill to the **Temple of Isis** (on the right). This Egyptian temple served Pompeii's Egyptian community. The little shrine with the plastic roof housed holy water from the Nile. Pompeii must have had a synagogue, but it has yet to be excavated.

Exit the temple where you entered and take an immediate right down an alleyway to our last stop, the **theater.** Originally a Greek theater (Greeks built theirs with the help of a hillside), this marks the spot of the birthplace of the Greek port here in 470 B.C. During Roman times, the theater sat 5,000 in three price ranges: the five marble terraces up close (filled with romantic wooden seats for two), the main section, and the cheap nosebleed section (surviving only on the right). The square stones above the cheap seats used to support a canvas rooftop. Notice the high-profile boxes, flanking the stage, for guests of honor. From this perch, you can see the gladiator barracks—the colonnaded courtyard beyond the theater. They lived in tiny rooms, trained in the courtyard, and fought in the nearby amphitheater.

There's much more to see; 75 percent of Pompeii's 164 acres has been excavated. But this tour's over. When you're ready to leave, take the exit to the left of the steep hill at the entrance to the Foro. When it forks, head right to get back to the site entrance to pick up your baggage or revisit the bookshop. *Ciao!*

ROMAN HISTORY

THREE MILLENNIA IN SIX PAGES

History in a Hurry

Ancient Rome lasted a thousand years (500 B.C.–A.D. 500), half as an expanding republic, half as a dominating empire. When Rome

fell to invaders, all Europe suffered a thousand years of poverty and ignorance (A.D. 500–1500), though Rome's influence could still be felt in the Catholic Church. Popes rebuilt Rome for pilgrims—in Renaissance, then Baroque and neoclassical styles (1500–1800). As capital of a newly united Italy, Rome followed fascist Mussolini into World War II (and lost) but rebounded in Italy's postwar economic boom.

Want more?

Legendary Birth (1200–500 B.C.)

Aeneas flees burning Troy (1200 B.C.), wanders like Odysseus, and finally finds a home along the Tiber. His descendants, Romulus and Remus—orphaned at birth, suckled by a she-wolf, and raised by shepherds— grow up to steal wives and build a wall, thus founding Rome (753 B.C.).

Closer to fact, the local agrarian tribes were dominated by more sophisticated neighbors to the north (Etruscans) and south (Greek colonists). Their convenient location on the Tiber was perfect for a future power.

Sights

- Romulus' "hut" and wall (Palatine Hill)
- She-wolf statue (Capitol Hill Museum)
- Frescoes of Aeneas and Romulus (National Museum of Rome)
- Bernini's Aeneas statue (Borghese Gallery)
- Etruscan wing (Vatican Museum)
- Etruscan Museum (in Villa Borghese gardens)
- Etruscan legacy (the original Circus Maximus, the drained Forum)

The Republic (509-27 B.C.)

The city expands throughout the Italian peninsula (500–300 B.C.), then defeats Hannibal's North African Carthaginians (the Punic Wars, 264–146 B.C.) and Greece (168 B.C.). Rome is master of the Mediterranean, and booty and captured slaves pour in. Romans bicker among themselves over their slice of the pie, pitting the wealthy landowners (the ruling Senate) against the working class (plebs) and the rebellious slaves (Spartacus' revolt, 73 B.C.). In the chaos, charismatic generals like Julius Caesar, who can provide wealth and security, become dictators. Change is necessary...and coming.

Sights

- Forum's Curia, Temple of Saturn, Temple of Castor and Pollux, Rostrum, Basilica Aemilia, Temple of Julius Caesar, and Basilica Julia (all rebuilt later)
- Appian Way built, lined with tombs
- Aqueducts, which carry water to a growing city
- Portrait busts of citizens (National Museum of Rome)

- The republic's "S.P.Q.R." monogram and motto, seen today on statues, buildings, and even manhole covers: *Senatus Populusque Romanus*, or the "Senate and People of Rome." (Some northern Italians, who feel the South is dragging them down, translate S.P.Q.R. as *Sono Porci Questi Romani*—These Romans Are Pigs.)

The Empire—
The "Roman Peace," or Pax Romana (A.D. 1–200)

After Julius Caesar was killed by disgruntled Republicans, his adopted son Augustus took undisputed control, ended the civil wars, declared himself emperor, and adopted a family member to succeed him, setting the pattern of rule for the next 500 years.

Rome ruled an empire of 54 million people, stretching from Scotland to Africa, from Spain to Turkey. The city, with more than a million inhabitants, was decorated with Greek-style statues and monumental structures faced with marble...it was the marvel of the known world. The empire prospered on a (false) economy of booty, slaves, and trade, surviving the often turbulent and naughty behavior of emperors like Caligula and Nero.

Sights

- Colosseum
- Forum
- Palatine Hill palaces
- Poems by Virgil, Catullus, Horace, and Ovid (from time of Augustus)
- Augustus' house (Casa di Livia) on Palatine Hill
- Pantheon
- Trajan's Column and Forum
- Greek and Greek-style statues and emperor's busts (National Museum of Rome, Vatican Museum, Capitol Hill Museum)
- Piazza Navona (former stadium)
- Hadrian's Villa (Tivoli) and tomb (now Castel Sant'Angelo)

Rome Falls (200–476)

Corruption, disease, and the constant pressure of barbarians pecking away at the borders slowly drained the unwieldy empire. Despite Diocletian's division of the empire and Constantine's legalization of Christianity (313), the city was sacked (410), and the last emperor checked out (476). Rome fell like a huge column, kicking up dust that would plunge Europe into a thousand years of darkness.

Sights
- Arch of Constantine
- The Forum's Basilica of Constantine
- Baths of Diocletian
- Old Roman Wall (gates at Via Veneto or Piramide)

Medieval Rome (500–1500)
The once-great city of a million people dwindled to a rough village of 10,000, with a corrupt pope, forgotten ruins, and malaria-carrying mosquitoes. Cows grazed in the ruined Forum, and wolves prowled the Vatican at night. During the 1300s, even the popes left Rome to live in France. What little glory Rome retained was in the pomp, knowledge, and wealth of the Catholic Church.

Sights
- The damage done to ancient Roman monuments, caused by disuse, barbarian looting, and pillaging for pre-cut stones
- Early Christian churches built before Rome fell (Santa Maria Maggiore, San Giovanni in Laterano, and San Clemente)
- Churches of Santa Maria sopra Minerva and Santa Maria in Trastevere
- Castel Sant'Angelo

Renaissance and Baroque Rome (1500–1800)

As Europe's economy recovered, energetic popes rebuilt Rome to attract pilgrims. The best artists decorated palaces and churches, carved statues, and built fountains. The city was not a great political force, but as the center of Catholicism during the struggle against Protestants (c. 1520–1648), it was an influential religious and cultural capital.

Renaissance Sights
- Michelangelo's Sistine Chapel (Vatican Museum), dome of St. Peter's, *Pietà* (St. Peter's), *Moses* (St. Peter-in-Chains church), Christ statue (Santa Maria sopra Minerva), Capitol Hill Square, Santa Maria degli Angeli church (in former Baths of Diocletian)

- Raphael's *School of Athens* and *Transfiguration* (Vatican Museum)
- Paintings by Raphael, Titian, and others (Borghese Gallery)

Rome in World War II

By 1943, as bombs began falling just outside the walls of Rome, it was clear to all that Italy's alliance with Nazi Germany was a huge mistake, leading the country to ruin. The fascist Grand Council dismissed Mussolini, the king ordered his arrest, the ex-dictator fled north, and fascism collapsed without violence. Rome was declared an "open city" (meaning a city with no military bases). Italy surrendered to the Allies. The king fled to Allied-occupied southern Italy, abandoning Rome to Nazi forces, which occupied it for nine terrible months. The Romans and the Vatican joined forces to save many from the Nazis.

The Gestapo demanded 110 pounds of gold from the Roman Jews, who, with great difficulty and help from non-Jews, succeeded in providing it. Still, more than 2,000 Jews were deported to Germany. After Italian partisans planted a bomb near the Trevi Fountain that killed 32 Germans, more than 300 people randomly chosen from Rome's prison were killed in retaliation. As the Allies marched closer, they bombed Rome and its surroundings, but avoided striking the center.

Thankfully, Hitler granted the occupying Nazi troops permission to leave the city, which he declared a "place of culture" that should not be "the scene of combat operations." Pope Pius XII agreed, declaring, "Whoever raises a hand against Rome will be guilty of matricide to the whole civilized world and in the eternal judgment of God." Finally, the Germans marched out, the Americans marched in (through the gate of San Giovanni), and the exhausted city welcomed them with joy and relief.

Baroque Sights
- St. Peter's Square and interior (largely by Bernini)
- Bernini statues (at Borghese Gallery; also *St. Teresa in Ecstasy* at Santa Maria della Vittoria church) and fountains (Piazza Navona, Piazza Barberini)
- Ancient obelisks erected in squares (Piazza del Popolo, Piazza Navona)
- Trevi Fountain and Spanish Steps
- Gesù and St. Ignazio churches
- Caravaggio's *Calling of St. Matthew* (San Luigi dei Francesi Church) and other paintings (Borghese Gallery and Vatican Museum)
- Baroque paintings (Borghese Gallery)
- Borromini's facade of Santa Agnese Church (Piazza Navona)

Modern Rome (1800–present)

Rome becomes the capital of a newly reunited Italy (1870), is modernized by fascist Mussolini, and survives the destruction of World War II. Italy's postwar "economic miracle" makes Rome a world-class city of cinema, banking, and tourism.

Sights

- Victor Emmanuel II Monument, which honors modern Italy's first (democratic) king
- Mussolini: The balcony he spoke from (at Palazzo Venezia, on Piazza Venezia), his planned city (E.U.R.), grand boulevards (Via dei Fori Imperiali, Via della Conciliazione), and Olympic Stadium
- Cinecittà film studios and Via Veneto nightlife, which have faint echoes of Fellini's *La Dolce Vita* Rome
- Subway system, broad boulevards, smog

Rome Today

After surviving the government-a-year turbulence and Mafia-tainted corruption of the postwar years, Rome is stabilizing. Today, the average Roman makes more money than the average Englishman. The city is less polluted and more organized. Several years ago, in celebration of the millennium, the Eternal City gave its monuments a facelift. The world turned its attention on Rome once again in April of 2005, as the Vatican mourned the death of a pope...and elected a new one. Today's Rome is ready for pilgrims, travelers, and you to come and make more history.

APPENDIX

Let's Talk Telephones

Here's a primer on making phone calls . For information specific to Italy, see "Telephones" in the Introduction.

Making Calls within a European Country: About half of all European countries use area codes; the other half use a direct-dial system without area codes.

To make calls within a country that uses a direct-dial telephone system (Italy, Belgium, the Czech Republic, Denmark, France, Portugal, Norway, Spain, and Switzerland), you dial the same number whether you're calling across the country or across the street.

In countries that use area codes (such as Austria, Britain, Croatia, Finland, Germany, Hungary, Ireland, the Netherlands, Poland, Slovakia, Slovenia, and Sweden), you dial the local number when calling within a city, and you add the area code if calling long distance within the country.

Making International Calls: You always start with the international access code (011 if you're calling from the U.S. or Canada, or 00 from Europe), then dial the country code of the country that you're calling (see chart below).

What you dial next depends on the phone system of the country that you're calling. If the country uses area codes, drop the initial zero of the area code, then dial the rest of the number.

Countries that use direct-dial systems (no area codes) vary in how they're accessed internationally by phone. For instance, if you're making an international call to Italy, the Czech Republic, Denmark, Norway, Portugal, or Spain, simply dial the international access code, country code, and phone number. But if you're calling Belgium, France, or Switzerland, drop the initial zero of the phone number.

European Calling Chart

Just smile and dial, using this key:
AC = Area Code, LN = Local Number.

European Country	Calling long distance within ...	Calling from the U.S.A./ Canada to ...	Calling from a European country to ...
Austria	AC + LN	011 + 43 + AC (without the initial zero) + LN	00 + 43 + AC (without the initial zero) + LN
Belgium	LN	011 + 32 + LN (without initial zero)	00 + 32 + LN (without initial zero)
Britain	AC + LN	011 + 44 + AC (without initial zero) + LN	00 + 44 + AC (without initial zero) + LN
Croatia	AC + LN	011 + 385 + AC (without initial zero) + LN	00 + 385 + AC (without initial zero) + LN
Czech Republic	LN	011 + 420 + LN	00 + 420 + LN
Denmark	LN	011 + 45 + LN	00 + 45 + LN
Finland	AC + LN	011 + 358 + AC (without initial zero) + LN	00 + 358 + AC (without initial zero) + LN
France	LN	011 + 33 + LN (without initial zero)	00 + 33 + LN (without initial zero)
Germany	AC + LN	011 + 49 + AC (without initial zero) + LN	00 + 49 + AC (without initial zero) + LN
Greece	LN	011 + 30 + LN	00 + 30 + LN
Hungary	06 + AC + LN	011 + 36 + AC + LN	00 + 36 + AC + LN
Ireland	AC + LN	011 + 353 + AC (without initial zero) + LN	00 + 353 + AC (without initial zero) + LN
Italy	LN	011 + 39 + LN	00 + 39 + LN

European Country	Calling long distance within ...	Calling from the U.S.A./ Canada to ...	Calling from a European country to ...
Netherlands	AC + LN	011 + 31 + AC (without initial zero) + LN	00 + 31 + AC (without initial zero) + LN
Norway	LN	011 + 47 + LN	00 + 47 + LN
Poland	AC + LN	011 + 48 + AC (without initial zero) + LN	00 + 48 + AC (without initial zero) + LN
Portugal	LN	011 + 351 + LN	00 + 351 + LN
Slovakia	AC + LN	011 + 421 + AC (without initial zero) + LN	00 + 421 + AC (without initial zero) + LN
Slovenia	AC + LN	011 + 386 + AC (without initial zero) + LN	00 + 386 + AC (without initial zero) + LN
Spain	LN	011 + 34 + LN	00 + 34 + LN
Sweden	AC + LN	011 + 46 + AC (without initial zero) + LN	00 + 46 + AC (without initial zero) + LN
Switzerland	LN	011 + 41 + LN (without initial zero)	00 + 41 + LN (without initial zero)
Turkey	AC (if no initial zero is included, add one) + LN	011 + 90 + AC (without initial zero) + LN	00 + 90 + AC (without initial zero) + LN

- The instructions above apply whether you're calling a fixed phone or mobile phone.
- The international access codes (the first numbers you dial when making an international call) are 011 if you're calling from the U.S.A./Canada, or 00 if you're calling from anywhere in Europe.
- To call the U.S.A. or Canada from Europe, dial 00, then 1 (the country code for the U.S.A. and Canada), then the area code and number. In short, 00 + 1 + AC + LN = Hi, Mom!

Country Codes

After you've dialed the international access code (00 if calling from Europe, 011 if calling from the U.S. or Canada), dial the code of the country you're calling.

Austria—43	Italy—39
Belgium—32	Morocco—212
Britain—44	Netherlands—31
Canada—1	Norway—47
Croatia—385	Poland—48
Czech Rep.—420	Portugal—351
Denmark—45	Slovakia—421
Estonia—372	Slovenia—386
Finland—358	Spain—34
France—33	Sweden—46
Germany—49	Switzerland—41
Gibraltar—350	Turkey—90
Greece—30	U.S.A.—1
Ireland—353	

Useful Italian Phone Numbers

Emergency (English-speaking police help): 113
Emergency (military police): 112
Road Service: 116
Directory Assistance (for €0.50, an Italian-speaking robot gives the number twice, very clearly): 12
Telephone help (in English; free directory assistance): 170

Numbers and Stumblers

- Europeans write a few of their numbers differently than we do. 1 = 1 , 4 = 4, 7 = 7. Learn the difference or miss your train.
- In Europe, dates appear as day/month/year, so Christmas is 25/12/06.
- Commas are decimal points and decimals commas. A dollar and a half is 1,50, and there are 5.280 feet in a mile.
- When pointing, use your whole hand, palm down.
- When counting with fingers, start with your thumb. If you hold up your first finger to request one item, you'll probably get two.
- What Americans call the second floor of a building is the first floor in Europe.
- On escalators and moving sidewalks, Europeans keep the left "lane" open for passing. Keep to the right.

2006

JANUARY

S	M	T	W	T	F	S
1	2	3	4	5	6	7
8	9	10	11	12	13	14
15	16	17	18	19	20	21
22	23	24	25	26	27	28
29	30	31				

FEBRUARY

S	M	T	W	T	F	S
			1	2	3	4
5	6	7	8	9	10	11
12	13	14	15	16	17	18
19	20	21	22	23	24	25
26	27	28				

MARCH

S	M	T	W	T	F	S
			1	2	3	4
5	6	7	8	9	10	11
12	13	14	15	16	17	18
19	20	21	22	23	24	25
26	27	28	29	30	31	

APRIL

S	M	T	W	T	F	S
						1
2	3	4	5	6	7	8
9	10	11	12	13	14	15
16	17	18	19	20	21	22
23/30	24	25	26	27	28	29

MAY

S	M	T	W	T	F	S
	1	2	3	4	5	6
7	8	9	10	11	12	13
14	15	16	17	18	19	20
21	22	23	24	25	26	27
28	29	30	31			

JUNE

S	M	T	W	T	F	S
				1	2	3
4	5	6	7	8	9	10
11	12	13	14	15	16	17
18	19	20	21	22	23	24
25	26	27	28	29	30	

JULY

S	M	T	W	T	F	S
						1
2	3	4	5	6	7	8
9	10	11	12	13	14	15
16	17	18	19	20	21	22
23/30 24/31	25	26	27	28	29	

AUGUST

S	M	T	W	T	F	S
		1	2	3	4	5
6	7	8	9	10	11	12
13	14	15	16	17	18	19
20	21	22	23	24	25	26
27	28	29	30	31		

SEPTEMBER

S	M	T	W	T	F	S
					1	2
3	4	5	6	7	8	9
10	11	12	13	14	15	16
17	18	19	20	21	22	23
24	25	26	27	28	29	30

OCTOBER

S	M	T	W	T	F	S
1	2	3	4	5	6	7
8	9	10	11	12	13	14
15	16	17	18	19	20	21
22	23	24	25	26	27	28
29	30	31				

NOVEMBER

S	M	T	W	T	F	S
			1	2	3	4
5	6	7	8	9	10	11
12	13	14	15	16	17	18
19	20	21	22	23	24	25
26	27	28	29	30		

DECEMBER

S	M	T	W	T	F	S
					1	2
3	4	5	6	7	8	9
10	11	12	13	14	15	16
17	18	19	20	21	22	23
24/31	25	26	27	28	29	30

Public Holidays and Festivals

Italy has more than its share of holidays. Each town has a local festival honoring its patron saint. Italy (including most major sights) closes down on these national holidays: January 1, January 6 (Epiphany), Easter Sunday and Monday (April 16 and 17 in 2006), April 25 (Liberation Day), May 1 (Labor Day), Ascension Day (May 25 in 2006), June 2 (Anniversary of the Republic), August 15 (Assumption of Mary), November 1 (All Saints' Day), December 8 (Immaculate Conception of Mary), and December 25 and 26 (Christmas). In addition, June 29 (Saints Peter and Paul) is a major Roman holiday. This isn't a complete list. Holidays strike without warning.

Metric Conversions (approximate)

1 inch = 25 millimeters   32 degrees F = 0 degrees C
1 foot = 0.3 meter   82 degrees F = about 28 degrees C
1 yard = 0.9 meter   1 ounce = 28 grams
1 mile = 1.6 kilometers   1 kilogram = 2.2 pounds
1 centimeter = 0.4 inch   1 quart = 0.95 liter
1 meter = 39.4 inches   1 square yard = 0.8 square meter
1 kilometer = 0.62 mile   1 acre = 0.4 hectare

Rome's Climate

First line—average daily low; second line—average daily high;
third line—days of no rain.

J	F	M	A	M	J	J	A	S	O	N	D
40°	42°	45°	50°	56°	63°	67°	67°	62°	55°	49°	44°
52°	55°	59°	66°	74°	82°	87°	86°	79°	71°	61°	55°
13	19	23	24	26	26	30	29	25	23	19	21

Converting Temperatures: Fahrenheit and Celsius

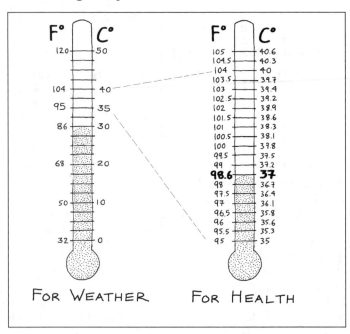

Italian Survival Phrases

Good day.	Buon giorno.	bwohn JOR-noh
Do you speak English?	Parla inglese?	PAR-lah een-GLAY-zay
Yes. / No.	Sì. / No.	see / noh
I (don't) understand.	(Non) capisco.	(nohn) kah-PEES-koh
Please.	Per favore.	pehr fah-VOH-ray
Thank you.	Grazie.	GRAHT-seeay
I'm sorry.	Mi dispiace.	mee dee-speeAH-chay
Excuse me.	Mi scusi.	mee SKOO-zee
(No) problem.	(Non) c'è un problema.	(nohn) cheh oon proh-BLAY-mah
Good.	Va bene.	vah BEHN-ay
Goodbye.	Arrivederci.	ah-ree-vay-DEHR-chee
one / two	uno / due	OO-noh / DOO-ay
three / four	tre / quattro	tray / KWAH-troh
five / six	cinque / sei	CHEENG-kway / SEHee
seven / eight	sette / otto	SEHT-tay / OT-toh
nine / ten	nove / dieci	NOV-ay / deeAY-chee
How much is it?	Quanto costa?	KWAHN-toh KOS-tah
Write it?	Me lo scrive?	may loh SKREE-vay
Is it free?	È gratis?	eh GRAH-tees
Is it included?	È incluso?	eh een-KLOO-zoh
Where can I buy / find...?	Dove posso comprare / trovare...?	DOH-vay POS-soh kohm-PRAH-ray / troh-VAH-ray
I'd like / We'd like...	Vorrei / Vorremmo...	vor-REHee / vor-RAY-moh
...a room.	...una camera.	OO-nah KAH-meh-rah
...a ticket to ___.	...un biglietto per ___.	oon beel-YEHT-toh pehr
Is it possible?	È possibile?	eh poh-SEE-bee-lay
Where is...?	Dov'è...?	DOH-veh
...the train station	...la stazione	lah staht-seeOH-nay
...the bus station	...la stazione degli autobus	lah staht-seeOH-nay DAYL-yee OW-toh-boos
...tourist information	...informazioni per turisti	een-for-maht-seeOH-nee pehr too-REE-stee
...the toilet	...la toilette	lah twah-LEHT-tay
men	uomini, signori	WOH-mee-nee, seen-YOH-ree
women	donne, signore	DON-nay, seen-YOH-ray
left / right	sinistra / destra	see-NEE-strah / DEHS-trah
straight	sempre diritto	SEHM-pray dee-REE-toh
When do you open / close?	A che ora aprite / chiudete?	ah kay OH-rah ah-PREE-tay / keeoo-DAY-tay
At what time?	A che ora?	ah kay OH-rah
Just a moment.	Un momento.	oon moh-MAYN-toh
now / soon / later	adesso / presto / tardi	ah-DEHS-soh / PREHS-toh / TAR-dee
today / tomorrow	oggi / domani	OH-jee / doh-MAH-nee

In the Restaurant

I'd like...	Vorrei...	vor-REHee
We'd like...	Vorremmo...	vor-RAY-moh
...to reserve...	...prenotare...	pray-noh-TAH-ray
...a table for one / two.	...un tavolo per uno / due.	oon TAH-voh-loh pehr OO-noh / DOO-ay
Non-smoking.	Non fumare.	nohn foo-MAH-ray
Is this seat free?	È libero questo posto?	eh LEE-bay-roh KWEHS-toh POH-stoh
The menu (in English), please.	Il menù (in inglese), per favore.	eel may-NOO (een een-GLAY-zay) pehr fah-VOH-ray
service (not) included	servizio (non) incluso	sehr-VEET-seeoh (nohn) een-KLOO-zoh
cover charge	pane e coperto	PAH-nay ay koh-PEHR-toh
to go	da portar via	dah POR-tar VEE-ah
with / without	con / senza	kohn / SEHN-sah
and / or	e / o	ay / oh
menu (of the day)	menù (del giorno)	may-NOO (dayl JOR-noh)
specialty of the house	specialità della casa	spay-chah-lee-TAH DEHL-lah KAH-zah
first course (pasta, soup)	primo piatto	PREE-moh peeAH-toh
main course (meat, fish)	secondo piatto	say-KOHN-doh peeAH-toh
side dishes	contorni	kohn-TOR-nee
bread	pane	PAH-nay
cheese	formaggio	for-MAH-joh
sandwich	panino	pah-NEE-noh
soup	minestra, zuppa	mee-NEHS-trah, TSOO-pah
salad	insalata	een-sah-LAH-tah
meat	carne	KAR-nay
chicken	pollo	POH-loh
fish	pesce	PEH-shay
seafood	frutti di mare	FROO-tee dee MAH-ray
fruit / vegetables	frutta / legumi	FROO-tah / lay-GOO-mee
dessert	dolci	DOHL-chee
tap water	acqua del rubinetto	AH-kwah dayl roo-bee-NAY-toh
mineral water	acqua minerale	AH-kwah mee-nay-RAH-lay
milk	latte	LAH-tay
(orange) juice	succo (d'arancia)	SOO-koh (dah-RAHN-chah)
coffee / tea	caffè / tè	kah-FEH / teh
wine	vino	VEE-noh
red / white	rosso / bianco	ROH-soh / beeAHN-koh
glass / bottle	bicchiere / bottiglia	bee-keeAY-ray / boh-TEEL-yah
beer	birra	BEE-rah
Cheers!	Cin cin!	cheen cheen
More. / Another.	Ancora un po.' / Un altro.	ahn-KOH-rah oon poh / oon AHL-troh
The same.	Lo stesso.	loh STEHS-soh
The bill, please.	Il conto, per favore.	eel KOHN-toh pehr fah-VOH-ray
tip	mancia	MAHN-chah
Delicious!	Delizioso!	day-leet-seeOH-zoh

For hundreds more pages of survival phrases for your trip to Italy, check out *Rick Steves' Italian Phrase Book & Dictionary* or *Rick Steves' French, Italian, and German Phrase Book.*

Making Your Hotel Reservation

Most hotel managers know basic "hotel English." Faxing or e-mailing are the preferred methods for reserving a room. They're more accurate than telephoning and much faster than writing a letter. Use this handy form for your fax or find it online at www.ricksteves.com/reservation. Photocopy and fax away.

One-Page Fax

To: _____ @ _____
hotel   *fax*

From: _____@ _____
name   *fax*

Today's date: _____/_____/_____
day   *month*   *year*

Dear Hotel _____ ,
Please make this reservation for me:

Name: _____

Total # of people:_____ # of rooms: _____ # of nights: _____

Arriving: _____/____/____   My time of arrival (24-hr clock): _____
day *month* *year*   (I will telephone if I will be late)

Departing: ____/____/____
day *month* *year*

Room(s): Single _____Double ____Twin _____Triple _____ Quad_____

With: Toilet _____ Shower_____Bath _____ Sink only _____

Special needs: View____ Quiet ____ Cheapest ____ Ground Floor ____

Please fax, mail, or e-mail confirmation of my reservation, along with the type of room reserved and the price. Please also inform me of your cancellation policy. After I hear from you, I will quickly send my credit-card information as a deposit to hold the room. Thank you.

_____
Signature

_____
Name

_____
Address

_____
City   *State*   *Zip Code*   *Country*

_____
E-mail Address

INDEX

RESEARCHERS

To annually update his four books on Italy, Rick relies on the help of these *fantastica* researchers:

AMANDA SCOTESE

AMANDA SCOTESE freelances as a journalist and editor in San Francisco. Her travels in Italy include a stint selling leather jackets in Florence's San Lorenzo Market, basking in the Sicilian sun, and of course, helping out with Rick Steves' guidebooks and tours.

`HEIDI SEWELL

HEIDI SEWELL lived in Italy for two years, learning to speak Italian and roll her own pasta. When she's not leading tours and scouring the Italian Peninsula for Back Doors worthy of Rick Steves' guidebooks, she resides in Seattle with her husband Ragen.

Start your trip at
www.ricksteves.com

Rick Steves' website is packed with over 3,000 pages of timely travel information. It's also your gateway to getting FREE monthly travel news from Rick— and more!

Free Monthly European Travel News

Fresh articles on Europe's most interesting destinations and happenings. Rick will even send you an e-mail every month (often direct from Europe) with his latest discoveries!

Timely Travel Tips

Rick Steves' best money-and-stress-saving tips on trip planning, packing, transportation, hotels, health, safety, finances, hurdling the language barrier…and more.

Travelers' Graffiti Wall

Candid advice and opinions from thousands of travelers on everything listed above, plus whatever topics are hot at the moment (discount flights, packing tips, scams…you name it).

Rick's Annual Guide to European Railpasses

The clearest, most comprehensive guide to the confusing array of railpass options out there, and how to choo-choose the railpass that best fits your itinerary and budget. Then you can order your railpass (and get a bunch of great freebies) online from us!

Great Gear at the Rick Steves Travel Store

Enjoy bargains on Rick's guidebooks, planning maps and TV series DVDs— and on his custom-designed carry-on bags, wheeled bags, day bags and light-packing accessories.

Rick Steves Tours

Every year more than 6,000 lucky travelers explore Europe on a Rick Steves tour. Learn more about our 30 different one-to-three-week itineraries, read uncensored feedback from our tour alums, and sign up for your dream trip online!

Rick on Radio and TV

Read the scripts and run clips from public television's "Rick Steves' Europe" and public radio's "Travel with Rick Steves."

Respect for Your Privacy

Ordering online from us is secure. When you buy something from us, join a tour, or subscribe to Rick's free monthly travel news e-mails, we promise to never share your name, information, or e-mail address with anyone else. You won't be spammed!

Have fun raising your Travel I.Q. at
www.ricksteves.com

Travel smart…carry on!

The latest generation of Rick Steves' carry-on travel bags is easily the best— benefiting from two decades of on-the-road attention to what really matters: maximum quality and strength; practical, flexible features; and no unnecessary frills. You won't find a better value anywhere!

Convertible, expandable, and carry-on-size:

Rick Steves' Back Door Bag $99

This is the same bag that Rick Steves lives out of for three months every summer. It's made of rugged water-resistant 1000 denier Cordura nylon, and best of all, it converts easily from a smart-looking suitcase to a handy backpack with comfortably-curved shoulder straps and a padded waistbelt.

This roomy, versatile 9" x 21" x 14" bag has a large 2600 cubic-inch main compartment, plus three outside pockets (small, medium and huge) that are perfect for often-used items. And the cinch-tight compression straps will keep your load compact and close to your back—not sagging like a sack of potatoes.

Wishing you had even more room to bring home souvenirs? Pull open the full-perimeter expando-zipper and its capacity jumps from 2600 to 3000 cubic inches. When you want to use it as a suitcase or check it as luggage (required when "expanded"), the straps and belt hide away in a zippered compartment in the back.

Attention travelers under 5'4" tall: This bag also comes in an inch-shorter version, for a compact-friendlier fit between the waistbelt and shoulder straps.

Convenient, expandable, and carry-on-size:

Rick Steves' Wheeled Bag $129

At 9" x 21" x 14" our sturdy Rick Steves' Wheeled Bag is rucksack-soft in front, but the rest is lined with a hard ABS-lexan shell to give maximum protection to your belongings. We've spared no expense on moving parts, splurging on an extra-long button-release handle and big, tough inline skate wheels for easy rolling on rough surfaces.

Wishing you had even more room to bring home souvenirs? Pull open the full-perimeter expando-zipper and its capacity jumps from 2600 to 3000 cubic inches.

Rick Steves' Wheeled Bag has exactly the same three-outside-pocket configuration as our Back Door Bag, plus a handy "add-a-bag" strap and full lining.

Our Back Door Bags and Wheeled Bags come in black, navy, blue spruce, evergreen and merlot.

For great deals on a wide selection of travel goodies, begin your next trip at the Rick Steves Travel Store!

Visit the Rick Steves Travel Store at
www.ricksteves.com

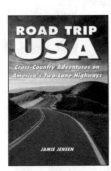

Rick Steves

More *Savvy*. More *Surprising*. More *Fun*.

COUNTRY GUIDES 2006

England
France
Germany & Austria
Great Britain
Ireland
Italy
Portugal
Scandinavia
Spain
Switzerland

CITY GUIDES 2006

Amsterdam, Bruges & Brussels
Florence & Tuscany
London
Paris
Prague & The Czech Republic
Provence & The French Riviera
Rome
Venice

BEST OF GUIDES

Best of Eastern Europe
Best of Europe

As the #1 authority on European travel, Rick gives you inside
information on what to visit, where to stay, and how to get
there—economically and hassle-free.

www.ricksteves.com

PHRASE BOOKS
& DICTIONARIES

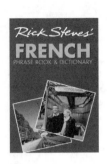

French
French, Italian & German
German
Italian
Portuguese
Spanish

MORE EUROPE FROM RICK STEVES

Easy Access Europe
Europe 101
Europe Through the Back Door
Postcards from Europe

RICK STEVES' EUROPE DVDs

All 43 Shows 2000-2005
Britain
Eastern Europe
France & Benelux
Germany, The Swiss Alps & Travel Skills
Ireland
Italy
Spain & Portugal

PLANNING MAPS

Britain & Ireland
Europe
France
Germany, Austria & Switzerland
Italy
Spain & Portugal

For a complete list of Rick Steves' guidebooks, see page 7.

Avalon Travel Publishing
An Imprint of Avalon Publishing Group, Inc.
1400 65th Street, Suite 250, Emeryville, CA 94608, U.S.A.

Printed in the U.S.A. by Worzalla
First printing August 2005

Portions of this book were originally published in *Rick Steves' Mona Winks* © 2001, 1998, 1996, 1993, 1988 by Rick Steves and Gene Openshaw, and in *Rick Steves' Italy* © 2005, 2004, 2003, 2002, 2001, 2000, 1999 by Rick Steves.

ISBN-10: 1-56691-732-8 • ISBN-13: 978-1-56691-732-2
ISSN 1527-4780

For the latest on Rick's lectures, guidebooks, tours, and public television series, contact Rick Steves' Europe Through the Back Door, Box 2009, Edmonds, WA 98020, 425/771-8303, fax 425/771-0833, www.ricksteves.com, rick@ricksteves.com.

Europe Through the Back Door Managing Editor: Risa Laib
ETBD Editors: Cameron Hewitt, Kevin Yip, Lauren Mills
Avalon Travel Publishing Series Manager & Editor: Patrick Collins
ATP Project Editor: Madhu Prasher
Copy Editor: Matthew Reed Baker
Research Assistance: Amanda Scotese (Naples and Pompeii)
Cover Design: Kari Gim, Laura Mazer
Interior Design: Jane Musser, Laura Mazer, Amber Pirker
Maps & Graphics: David C. Hoerlein, Lauren Mills, Laura VanDeventer, Mike Morgenfeld
Production & Typesetting: Patrick David Barber
Photography: Rick Steves, Gene Openshaw, Dominic Bonuccelli, Risa Laib, and others
Front matter color photos: p. i, the Pantheon, Rome © Phillis Greenberg/Unicorn Stock Photos, LLC; p. iv, Spanish Steps, Rome, Lazio, Italy at dusk © EJ Images/Alamy
Front cover photos: Front Image, Piazza Navona with Bernini's fountain © Jeff Cantarutti/ Lonely Planet Images; Back Image, Colosseum © Glenn Beanland / Lonely Planet Images